DATE DUE

DEMCO 38-296

R

Evaluating Social Programs
at the
State and Local Level

The JTPA Evaluation Design Project

Ann Bonar Blalock
Editor

Contributors
Ann Bonar Blalock, *Washington Employment Security Department*
Terry R. Johnson, *Battelle Human Affairs Research Center*
Ernst W. Stromsdorfer, *Washington State University*
Carl Simpson, *Western Washington University*
David Grembowski, *University of Washington*
Deborah Feldman, *Washington Employment Security Department*

1990

W. E. UPJOHN INSTITUTE for Employment Research
Kalamazoo, Michigan

Library of Congress Cataloging-in-Publication Data

Evaluating social programs at the state and local level : the JTPA
evaluation design project / Ann Bonar Blalock, editor :
contributors, Ann Bonar Blalock . . . [et al.].
    p.   cm.
Includes bibliographical references.
ISBN 0-88099-089-9. — ISBN 0-88099-090-2 (pbk.)
    1. Evaluation research (Social action programs)—United States.
I. Blalock, Ann B.
H62.5.U5E86 1990
361.6'072—dc20   ∞   89-21488
                                                       CIP

In this era of information technology, we have little trouble think-ing about the contribution sophisticated information systems make to the management of programs. But we know that computers do not replace good management practices or the development of policies responsive to the needs of the people social programs are designed to help. The technology we need to think more about in this respect is social science research. Although managers have always had responsibility for judging the adequacy of their pro-grams, they have not always had reliable, practical tools with which to evaluate them.

We now need evaluation tools not only for studying the return on the public's investment, but tools which help us manage our programs better. We need detailed analyses of each of the parts and processes within a program's system. We need to see where we are most effective and where we can make improvements.

When we think of evaluation technology as a management tool, we see it as something capable of helping us accomplish tasks that would be very difficult or impossible to achieve without that tool. It should be easier for the manager to make decisions. The infor-mation that comes out of an evaluation effort should provide direc-tion in setting policies and establishing procedures.

But we should understand that the use of evaluation may involve change. And change brings risk. As we consider the risks associated with conducting evaluations, we should also remember the risks we take in not using what applied social research can offer us in understanding our programs better. As Congress and the Presi-dent develop plans to balance the federal budget, the pressure will be on all domestic programs to prove their worth. If the technology of evaluation can be used to help us, we should seriously consider making the best use of it we can.

Isiah Turner, Commissioner
Washington State Employment Security Department

The JTPA Evaluation Design Project

Changes in the organization and operation of publicly supported social programs in the 1980s have vastly increased state and local responsibility for providing evidence of program accountability. The paucity of evidence required for federal reporting purposes, however, has often proved insufficient to establish the broader credibility of these programs or to guide decisions about how to adjust program policies or improve programs at those levels. Also, although evaluation research has been generally accepted since the late 1970s as the least biased means of establishing program accountability, most state and local service organizations have lacked the funds and specialized expertise to develop the ongoing evaluation capability now needed. Therefore, the new evaluation expectations and increased resource constraints of the last decade have created a novel dilemma.

This dilemma provided the context for a new national evaluation project, the *JTPA Evaluation Design Project*. Initiated, developed, and directed by the Washington State Employment Security Department, the project responded to new state and local oversight obligations authorized by the Job Training Partnership Act (JTPA). Ironically, although this legislation mandated program evaluation at the state level, it substantially reduced overall program funding compared with previous efforts targeted to the disadvantaged, unemployed, and poor and it placed tight restrictions on the use of this funding for administration, including program oversight. Although states could use a small set-aside for technical assistance, under which evaluation could be rationalized, this money was formally tied to the provision of fiscal incentives and technical assistance sanctions related to the level of state and local compliance with performance requirements.

Far removed from the affluent days of the 1960s and 1970s, when federal evaluation money flowed relatively freely to extensive national program evaluations, and still strongly affected by the legacy of state and local dependence on federal research efforts over that impressive period, the new mandate left most states struggling to define and meet the new obligations they had so precipitously inherited. Washington State was no exception.

An initial challenge was to develop new automated information systems for adequately monitoring decentralized programs against basic federal requirements. In the process of designing a new management information system (MIS) for the state of Washington, the commissioner of the Employment Security Department requested an issue paper anticipating information needs for evaluation activities. A monograph on the meaning and value of program evaluation, and the kinds of data and information system features it would be likely to involve, became the basis of a serious agency effort to search for outside funds to support oversight activities beyond the simple monitoring of programs to determine compliance with federal requirements.

The fund-search process increased agency awareness of the constraints felt by other states in developing an evaluation capability. The National Commission for Employment Policy expressed a similar concern that those directly responsible for the success of JTPA programs were inadequately equipped to evaluate their programs. The Commission was willing to consider an unsolicited proposal from the Employment Security Department to develop evaluation tools specifically oriented to the differing information needs of states and local areas. The Commission was particularly adamant that these technical assistance tools serve as *practical guides* for judging the value of JTPA in the context of a dramatically reduced federal evaluation presence. The result was the development of a project concept by Washington State, which was subsequently crafted into a proposal for possible joint funding.

This concept involved the design of two sets of complementary evaluation guides—one responsive primarily to state users, one to local. The guides were to be competent scientifically and useful pragmatically. Their application to ongoing JTPA programs was expected to produce objective information of direct and timely value to program decisionmakers at the least possible cost. The complementary nature of these tools and the commitment to competence suggested the preselection of an *interdisciplinary* group of evaluation *designers* whose range of training and expertise would provide the different perspectives needed in studying program implementation and impact.

The interest in pragmatism suggested that this team be selected within Washington, if possible, to demonstrate the general ability of state and local areas to acquire research advice within or near their own borders, from resources such as their own state university systems and private research firms. Viewing the designers as a *research partnership* was also consistent with the major feature of JTPA, namely the placement of ultimate control with public-private partnerships at the state and local level.

To enhance the utility of the guides, the Employment Security Department felt it was important to add a volume to the series that suggested ways in which states and local areas could develop a fiscal, organizational, and technical ability to engage in ongoing evaluation activities as an integral part of effective program management. Staff within the Employment Security Department who were experienced in fund search, organizational development, and evaluation research, and familiar with the innuendos of organizational politics, were added to the research partnership. In this way a design team was formed that strengthened both the quality and utility of the guides and provided a mutually beneficial learning experience for the team and the agency.

Again consistent with the JTPA partnership principle, a public-private *consortium of potential funders* was selected and became part of the project proposal. The National Commission for Employment Policy was recommended as the *JTPA Evaluation Design Project's* national sponsor.

The Commission has a respected research reputation, and its participation underlined the project's potential usefulness to state and local areas. Furthermore, the Commission viewed the project as a way to stimulate interest in state and local evaluation consistent with the Act, and to assist states and service delivery areas (SDAs) in developing the capability to produce information that was sufficiently comparable to make a contribution to national training policy.

To extend the partnership idea, private corporate funds were sought to match potential contributions from the Commission and the Employment Security Department. Since the priorities of IBM's Corporate Support Programs for 1986 included policy research, IBM was selected as the key private funding partner. Its stature as a major multinational corporation, and its interest in applying private sector quality control and research and development ideas to the public sector conveyed special credibility. Each of these three funders had something distinctive to contribute to the project. Therefore, each was requested to assist with a different component of an integrated project concept.

Submitting an unsolicited proposal to a national funder and preselecting research and funding partnerships constituted radical behavior on the part of a state agency and posed certain risks. However, in making the rationale for collaboration and a division of responsibility among funding partners explicit, potential funders knew precisely what product they would be subsidizing, and what their role was to be in the larger effort. Ultimately, the proposal was accepted, and all of the members of the funding and staffing partnerships participated in the project as proposed. In addition, important public-private in-kind contributions were obtained from the Safeco Insurance Companies of America; the Warwick International Hotels, Inc.; SPSS, Inc.; a national software corporation; and the Seattle-King County Private Industry Council.

The National Commission selected a *national advisory committee* for the project. The committee was composed of state and local representatives from six states, and supplemented by representatives of the major national public interest groups involved with employment and training and a number of nationally known evaluation researchers. This committee provided initial insights about evaluation issues of particular concern to the JTPA community across the country and reviewed successive drafts of the project's evaluation guides. The Employment Security Department organized an *in-house advisory group* to obtain input from Washington's state and local training councils and program directors. These advisory groups became an essential part of the process through which the series of guides was developed.

vii

In 1986, the project produced two sets of 10 volumes each, one for state and one for local users. These volumes covered evaluation planning; process, gross outcome, and net impact evaluations; cost-benefit analysis; quasi-experimental vs. experimental research designs; and MIS issues to be used in evaluating JTPA. The sets of volumes were distributed without cost to all state and local JTPA directors through joint funding from the Commission and the Employment Security Department, and are now available on microfiche in the ERIC system. The volumes and their authors are listed in Appendix C.

When the volumes were completed, an additional proposal was funded by the U.S. Department of Labor and the IBM Corporation to provide intensive regional evaluation workshops based on the evaluation guides for JTPA prac- titioners and to develop a new national evaluation journal, *Evaluation Forum,* which focused on state and local JTPA evaluation issues and activities. In- kind contributions to these additional project activities were made by regional offices of the Department of Labor, the National Alliance of Business, the National Governors' Association, and the National Association of Counties.

This book is an attempt to distill ideas from project materials produced by this unique undertaking that can be of general assistance in evaluating social programs, using JTPA as the case example. In this way the contributions of a diverse group have been refocused to benefit a larger audience.

Ann Bonar Blalock
Project Developer

Acknowledgements

Program evaluation has frequently lacked bureaucratic support. It has often been difficult to determine the ultimate tradeoff between its organizational and political risks and its information benefits. This is all the more reason to express our appreciation to the leadership of the Washington State Employment Security Department, which accepted certain risks to support better information production. Without the encouragement of Ernest La Palm, Deputy Commissioner of the Department, the *JTPA Evaluation Design Project* would neither have been conceived nor funded. He was a mentor throughout the project; we are in his debt for whatever contributions have been made to more effective training policies and program strategies through this emphasis on program evaluation. We also want to express our gratitude to the former commissioner of the agency, Norward Brooks, and to the current commissioner, Isiah Turner, who have made it possible for the project to obtain essential agency funds and supportive services, have afforded project staff the kind of professional autonomy needed, and have helped maintain the project's ties with other divisions of the agency important to its success.

In addition, we want to thank project funders, contributors, and the national advisory group. In particular, we appreciate the ideas and advice contributed by Patricia McNeil, a former director of the National Commission for Employment Policy and now Administrator of the Office of Strategic Planning and Policy Development, U.S. Department of Labor, and Kay Albright, formerly of the National Governors' Association and now Deputy Director of the Commission. We are similarly indebted to Jerrold Gross of the Wisconsin Department of Industry, Labor and Human Relations, and Greg Marutani of the San Francisco Private Industry Council.

We would like to express special gratitude to Gary Bodeutsch, who directed the project during the period when the evaluation guides were completed and was co-coordinator with Deborah Feldman of its workshop phase. Gary's calm, positive, and insightful approach and practical research experience were valuable sources of encouragement and assistance.

A number of staff in the word processing and public affairs divisions of the Employment Security Department provided essential help that was consistently timely and professional, and left us with a sense of optimism about finishing our task: Terry Ruiz, Kolleen Anderson, Gretchen Beerbower, Kathy Skye, Barbara Cameron, and Becky Clark.

It has been a distinct challenge to condense the materials produced by the project and then generalize the ideas to social programs other than those in the employment and training area. In this respect, we are indebted to Chris

King of the Center for the Study of Human Resources, University of Texas, for reviewing the first draft of the book and providing significant comments that enhanced its quality and usefulness. We are most grateful to Allan Hunt of the W. E. Upjohn Institute for Employment Research for his initial interest and ongoing support, his careful analysis of our plan for the book, his extensive review of our work, and his recommendations for improving the concept and the manuscript.

Finally, we must thank the many state and local employment and training professionals and evaluators across the country who offered practical suggestions about how we could make evaluation more relevant to the real world of social programs.

Project Team,
JTPA Evaluation Design Project

Contents

Part III
Organizational and Political Issues in Evaluating Programs

Part I

A
General Approach
to
Program Evaluation

This beginning section discusses the particular philosophy and approach to state and local program evaluation that serve as the framework for the book. The context and purpose of evaluation at these levels and the basic scientific principles and methods guiding evaluation activities are also explored.

A user-oriented, comprehensive concept of evaluation is described. Its purpose is to provide complementary information about program implementation and outcomes for improving ongoing social programs.

The organization of the book, and the use of a practical case example throughout, illustrate and apply this concept of evaluation.

1
Evaluating Programs

Ann Bonar Blalock
Washington Employment Security Department

*Decisionmakers, planners, project staff, and [program] partici-
pants are increasingly skeptical of common sense and conventional
wisdom as sufficient bases upon which to design social programs
that will achieve their intended goals.*

Peter Rossi and Howard Freeman
Evaluation: A Systematic Approach

Questions have always been raised about the value of tax-supported
program strategies for resolving major problems in society. Resistance
and inability to provide evidence of public value have, in the end, led to
social unrest and sometimes active protest. This is not likely to change.
Throughout history, those receiving and spending public money have had
to guarantee that a reasonable tradeoff would be honored between their
rights and *responsibilities*. Discretion and control have had to be balanced
by an accounting of the public good produced, of the kinds and in the ways
intended. Planned change has always required accountability.

There is a new element, however, in the historical exchange between
public privileges and obligations. It involves the *form* accountability
now takes. The scientific technology for developing evidence of value
and popular support for using scientific approaches and methods have
changed radically over the last three decades. Increased public education, breakthroughs in the automation of data processing and analysis,
and growing interest in the role of applied social science research in
weighing the risks and benefits of social initiatives have converged.

Evaluators can now perform statistical analyses of large amounts of
data rapidly and relatively inexpensively. Evaluation research has
become an established field within applied social research (Patton 1986),
and the public's sophistication about the contribution evaluation re-

3

search can make to more objective judgments of social programs has grown significantly. Most elected officials, government professionals and others responsible for social programs now accept science-based evaluation as an integral part of public policymaking.

Evaluation is less well-understood, however, as a *pragmatic management tool* for making general improvements in programs and testing new ways to organize and deliver services for particular client groups. At the state and local level, evaluation has not been fully utilized as an opportunity to infuse the policy and planning process with better information, but there are cogent reasons why this condition has prevailed, and why the situation is changing.

While the value and legitimacy of evaluation was reinforced, the conservative social policies of the 1980s substantially changed the *location of responsibility* for making judgments of the value of social programs. Control and responsibility were transferred downward, from federal to state government. The premise for this change involved a mix of new and older political philosophies: new fiscal conservatism emerging in response to economic, energy, and environmental problems and postindustrial changes in American society; older conservatism favoring states' rights and opposing "big government"; and the more idiosyncratic social welfare policies of the Reagan administration, designed primarily to shrink federal involvement in social programs altogether (Palmer 1986). However, this shift in the locus of accountability occurred in the context of little prior state training or experience in performing the tasks required by the new evaluative role.

Although the federal evaluation effort throughout the 1970s was extensive, it did little to enhance state-level evaluation capability.[1] Collecting the data essential in carrying out federal evaluations required the cooperation of state and local program professionals, but these professionals were rarely brought into the effort as partners, and the information coming back to them from federal studies offered few direct informational benefits in adjusting policies or improving programs.

Although states were required to develop automated reporting systems responsive to federal program goals, few incentives existed to incorporate an evaluation capability within their design, or to develop in-house evaluation expertise. When political changes required that states assume evaluation responsibilities, the infrastructure to support these activities was too often missing. Nevertheless, new provocative state and local oversight opportunities accompanied this unanticipated transfer of authority. Gradually recognizing these opportunities, states and local areas have begun to take a new interest in evaluation as an information tool.

The Purpose of the Book

This book is written for those at the state and local level who find themselves working within this new social welfare environment: those who develop program policies, oversee their translation into ongoing programs, and seek to judge their value.

Its purpose is to encourage them to view evaluation not simply as a new responsibility they now find themselves required to assume, but as a pragmatic policy and management tool that can directly inform their decisions and improve their programs. Its purpose is also to provide those given the responsibility for judging the value of state and local programs with practical guidance about how to develop or enhance their ability to evaluate, and offer them assistance in planning and carrying out program evaluations. Although these purposes are oriented primarily to the information needs and capabilities of those most involved with social programs at these levels, it is hoped that the book will be of interest and use to state and local elected officials, the evaluation research community, public interest and client advocacy groups, and ultimately the American taxpayer who makes social programs possible.

The new public-private decisionmaking partnerships, and the program administrators and staff who are now more responsible for seeing that programs meet their intent, have always wanted to be effective decisionmakers. Often they have not had sufficient in-depth information about their programs to feel comfortable about the decisions they must make. In an era that affords states and local areas vastly increased opportunities to think more imaginatively about defining accountability, evaluation is viewed in this book as a chance to obtain a better understanding of the much more complex and intriguing interplay of forces within programs, and between them and their environments. This understanding is necessary to the sound decisions practitioners want to make. Approaching evaluation as a new opportunity, states and local areas can use their increased autonomy to consider what information is essential to *them* in enhancing programs, particularly at the level where critical relationships between client and service provider occur.

Using Employment and Training Programs as a Case Example

Given the book's purpose, and its focus on the information needs of state and local program professionals, selecting an ongoing program as the key illustrative case throughout the book was considered a useful device for giving abstract concepts a richer and more practical meaning. Therefore, in each chapter the general ideas about evaluation, which are relevant to a range of social programs, are applied to a single case example.

The basic program for adults authorized in 1982 by the federal Job Training Partnership Act (JTPA) was selected as the illustration. JTPA exemplifies the contemporary trend in social programs, and its intricacies are well-known to the book's authors. The stimulus for writing the book was their development of a set of complementary evaluation guides for use by state and local JTPA council leaders and program practitioners.[2] Preparing the guides required a thorough knowledge of the legislative intent of JTPA and the actual operation of JTPA programs. This familiarity has permitted the authors to apply the concepts in the book to realistic program situations, drawing from actual employment and training program evaluations.

Frustrated by criticism of previous social program efforts to resolve unemployment and underemployment among the disadvantaged, and needing a bipartisan agreement on a new strategy, the architects of JTPA designed a program that made only incremental changes in the goals, services, and target groups of traditional employment and training programs, but substantially changed the philosophy and framework within which such programs were organized and implemented.

The proposed change agent in JTPA was the range of basic services common to previous approaches, with the major omission of public service employment and the restriction of training stipends to those most in need. The eligible client population remained the unemployed, the economically disadvantaged, the officially poor, and those with significant barriers to employment. The philosophy underlying JTPA was unique and anticipated future trends. This new initiative involved reduced funding and the decentralization of power and responsibility to public-private partnerships at the state and local level.

For the first time in the history of national public employment and training programs, and consistent with the strengthened role of the private sector, specific methods of quality control, i.e., federal *performance standards* that were to be met or exceeded by local service delivery areas (SDAs), were made an integral part of the legislation. State fiscal rewards and state sanctions in the form of mandatory technical assistance were incorporated into the legislation as reinforcements for local conformance with standards.

JTPA also required increased coordination with related programs, and encouraged new modes of organizing the provision of services, including performance-based subcontracting. Most relevant to this book, states and local areas were expected to move beyond *monitoring* program outcomes against a limited set of performance measures. The legislation mandated that states *evaluate* their programs as well. Seemingly novel at the time, many of JTPA's distinctive features became models for future publicly funded social programs. The reader will find it useful, in understanding the application of the book's central ideas to JTPA, to refer to the more detailed description of this program in the appendix.

The Framework of the Book

The *concept of evaluation* that provides the framework for this book is not an orthodox one. Despite the prolific literature that now characterizes the special field of evaluation research, most books and articles on program evaluation have been written primarily for researchers or oriented to those dealing with program issues at the national level. This literature has only rarely addressed state and local evaluation needs and interests, or been directed to those making decisions about social programs at levels closer to the client.

Consistent with its purpose, this book describes a somewhat novel concept of evaluation that is specifically responsive to the information needs of state and local program decisionmakers. This perspective on evaluation recognizes the expanded opportunities inherent in their new oversight responsibilities, and respects the singular constraints and supports for evaluation at the state and local level. It views program evaluation holistically as both an art and a science.

Studying programs in real-life environments does not take place in a social vacuum. It is impossible to isolate research activities from other important influences. The organizational, political, and technical activities involved in producing information to inform decisions are interdependent. Giving attention to the scientific principles and methods involved in studying programs is critical. Restricting the book to research issues would ignore the larger environment of evaluation that resists or supports the application of research. Therefore, the book seeks to integrate the technical aspects of evaluation with its organizational and political realities.

The content of the book focuses on the state and local users of evaluation information, the conditions under which they must make program decisions, and the kinds of decisions they are expected to make at key points in a program's planning and funding cycle. The assumption is that the timeliness and relevance of evaluation information, as well as its accuracy and reliability, predict its level of use. This does not presume that the mere presence of these qualities is sufficient to carve a predominant role for evaluation in shaping policies or directing the fate of programs. A strong visible role for information production of this kind is mitigated by many other compelling agendas.

Nevertheless, there are key points in the policy and planning cycle where personal, bureaucratic, and political influences compete with less subjective sources of information to produce decisions through negotiation, exchange, and compromise. The point in this decisionmaking process at which the *worth* of a program strategy must be judged is particularly vulnerable to the convergence of a variety of pressures, but it is precisely at this juncture where competent program evaluation can have its day in court.

Its case will not be heard, however, if evaluation information is not directly relevant to the content and context of the decisions being made, or if it reveals too little sensitivity to decisionmakers' information needs and technical sophistication. On the other hand, in the absence of empirically based usable information at this decision point, program adjustments will inevitably be based on more biased, and potentially misguided, considerations. To the extent that objective information can serve as one important influence among many other factors, state and local policies and the programs they generate will come closer to accurately defining and effectively resolving social problems.

In this context, the *comprehensive* concept of evaluation proposed in this book has a number of dimensions. Each is important, but the strength of the book is in its attempt to integrate these elements into an overall *evaluation strategy*. These dimensions can be expressed as interdependent sequential propositions.

1. Potential users of evaluations need to be identified and educated about the practical benefits of becoming *informed consumers of evaluation research* and *using it as a decisionmaking tool.*

2. State and local program councils and agencies need to develop an adequate *organizational capability to evaluate* their programs—to initiate, plan, and implement evaluations in-house or with the assistance of outside research consultants.

3. Evaluations should be planned with the *primary goal of improving programs.*

4. Evaluations will be of minimal utility in improving programs if evaluation sponsors fail to *seek answers to questions that are responsive to the interests and concerns of key decisionmakers.*

5. Relevant *insights from previous program evaluations* need to be considered in planning evaluations if the information from research studies is to contribute to program improvement and to the *accumulation of knowledge about social programs* from which decisionmakers can draw in the future.

6. The most useful knowledge base for decisionmaking is one that *integrates information obtained by using comparable evaluation approaches and methodologies* across different programs.
7. To be of maximum use in improving programs and contributing to general knowledge production, comparable evaluations should yield *complementary information about* (a) *program implementation, and* (b) *the relationship between services and outcomes.*
8. This complementary information will be more accurate and usable if studies of implementation and impact are based on the use of *common definitions and measures of the major variables,* involve the *same historical cohort of clients,* reflect the *same program context* and *environment,* and represent the *same time period.*
9. If this complementary information is to be fully used, it must be presented to decisionmakers in *user-oriented, nontechnical form at optimal points in the program planning cycle.*
10. Comprehensive evaluations providing complementary information to decisionmakers *make the best use of new state and local oversight opportunities.*

The Meaning of Evaluation

In promoting this concept of evaluation, it is important to define what we mean by program evaluation. Like any complex system, the organizations involved in implementing social programs are expected to perform certain essential functions that assure that programs are continued, can be fine-tuned to increase their effectiveness, and can be adapted to changing client needs and circumstances.

In exchange for funds, these organizations are typically required to *review* program plans, *monitor* the way those plans are carried out, and *evaluate* the extent to which programs meet their overall intent. These obligations, tied to fiscal support, are usually authorized by legislation or the formal policies of governing bodies. The contemporary form these expectations take is drawn from American industrial concepts. Although it is infinitely more difficult to define "production process," "consumer products," and functions such as "quality control" and "research and development" when dealing with human services, the same principles that have characterized the industrial process have been applied to social programs.

Certain consumers are selected as the key recipients of the goods produced, particular steps are taken in producing these goods, a certain level of consumption is maintained, and the consumer is affected by the product in some identifiable way. The characteristics of the process and products and the costs and benefits of the effort are observed and recorded. Marketing the product may be necessary, and research and development are accepted as a basis for change in the consumers targeted, the nature of the process, the product itself, the way it is introduced to the consumer, and the effect of the product on the recipient. Historically, these expectations have always attached to public expenditures in one form or another. We have simply made them more explicit and measurable and adapted them to the human service sector.

It is natural, then, that social programs meet such expectations and that certain oversight functions be established to assure quality and accountability. As the methods for carrying out these oversight functions have become more precise, automated, and reliant on scientific method, the distinctions among them have grown clearer and more consistent across different areas of social legislation. In this decade, review, monitoring, and evaluation are generally understood to be *distinct but related* accountability functions that have different purposes and require different expertise. Collectively, these assessments seek to *preserve the distinctive features of a program.*

The typical differences among these functions are suggested in chart 1.1. Based on these distinctions, evaluation is defined as the *systematic collection, analysis, and interpretation of information to answer questions about the efficiency and effectiveness of program implementation and impact, using the principles and methods of social science research* (Rossi and Freeman 1985).

When we study a program's efficiency, we want information on how well resources are used to achieve program goals; i.e., are we achieving maximum social benefits for a given outlay of resources? When we investigate program effectiveness, we want to know the tradeoff between

Chart 1.1
Program Accountability Functions

Oversight Responsibilities	Purpose	Definition	Information Produced	Expertise Required
Review	To determine the extent to which program *plans* are consistent with the legislative intent of the program.	One-time *planning* assessments of programs, special services, service delivery, and/or coordination *activities* judged against program *plans*.	Information about the extent to which *program activities* comply with those *planned*.	Professional *planning* expertise
Monitoring	To determine the level of compliance with *administrative policies and procedures* designed to interpret the legislative intent of the program.	Ongoing *managerial* assessments of selected aspects of the organizations operating programs, service delivery systems, target groups, and/or services and outcomes, judged against program *rules and regulations*.	Information about the extent to which programs comply with rules and regulations — in the way they are being *implemented* and the *outcomes* being experienced by those exposed to their services.	Professional *managerial* expertise
Evaluation	To determine to what extent a program is achieving its broader legislative intent in terms of producing the expected *effects* on the *individuals or other entities for whom the program was created*, using the *means* proposed.	One-time *scientific* assessments of the adequacy of program implementation and/or impact judged against the program's *broader intent*.	Information about *relationships among different aspects of programs*: • among different components of program *implementation* • among *client characteristics, service interventions, and outcomes.* • between *implementation and outcomes.*	Social science *research* expertise

nonmonetary costs and benefits as well as between monetary costs and benefits. Evaluation focuses not only on what is happening in a program, but also why and how. The emphasis is on studying *relationships* among different aspects of a program (Weiss 1972).

In gathering information on compliance for reporting purposes, monitoring provides information that is useful and sometimes essential to an evaluation effort. However, it is not the purpose of monitoring to collect the full range of data on the way programs are organized and carried out or on the relationship between their interventions and effects, which is required to answer critical relationship questions.

An interesting example of the differences between monitoring and evaluation is the mandating of official performance standards to monitor the outcomes of programs. The use of standards is an effort to formalize the provision of evidence that a certain level of goal achievement is being attained. The Department of Labor developed a set of standards, measures for each of the standards, and a monitoring process to compare JTPA employment, income, and welfare reduction outcomes and program costs against quantitative goals. Compliance with these standards is determined using a narrow set of easily accessible, low cost, quantitative measures, such as the number of clients placed in jobs and their hourly wages.

It would seem that using performance standards is a form of program evaluation, or at least illustrates a gray area between monitoring and evaluation. However, the performance standards strategy is limited to a set of proxies for a much broader array of evidence of program efficiency and effectiveness. Although we may be making an important assessment of a program's effects by monitoring selected outcomes against carefully selected but incomplete standards, we may also obtain a skewed view of a program's value.

Compliance with standards does not tell us anything about relationships among a more extensive set of potential outcomes, between outcomes and the organization of the program, or between outcomes and the way services are delivered to the client. Most significantly, the level of compliance does not inform us about the program's role *vis-a-vis* these outcomes; i.e., was compliance responsible for the outcomes, or were these outcomes due to chance or other influences?

Monitoring information is not intended to help us look in depth at what is going on and explain it (Blalock 1982). Unfortunately, however, monitoring requirements tend to preoccupy state and local administrators with a restricted view of outcomes, distracting them from considering the magnitude, quality, and durability of program effects, and dampening their natural curiosity about the "black box" that holds the secrets of how and why certain outcomes may have occurred. Consequently, decisions about adjusting programs are often made without sufficient information. It is helpful, then, to think about evaluation as distinct from monitoring regarding the questions each is expected to answer (see chart 1.2).

The Practical Benefits of State and Local Evaluation

Practitioners have little difficulty appreciating the need for planning, managing, and monitoring, or understanding the prerequisites and benefits of these activities. But they sometimes question what social science research can do for them that collective experience and conventional wisdom cannot. Classic stereotypes about evaluation persist: it is too costly, risky, esoteric, inconclusive, too easily underutilized or misused.

Evaluation *does* cost. However, the largest program outlay, other than personnel and services, has characteristically been the start-up costs for designing and placing in operation automated *management information systems (MISs)* for required monitoring purposes. As the reliability of the information in these systems has improved, and their technical sophistication for recording, storing, extracting, and analyzing data has grown, interrelated MISs now afford a basic information bank for evaluation, which can be easily and inexpensively supplemented with additional data. It is inefficient, in fact, *not* to use these systems as an evaluation opportunity. By making optimal use of the monitoring data already being routinely gathered, in terms of data analysis opportunities, evaluation can expand resources for improving state and local programs.

It is true that evaluations may sometimes produce results that policymakers and administrators would rather not know. Some evaluations may lead to the conclusion that a program has made little or no difference

Chart 1.2
Monitoring vs. Evaluation

Monitoring Questions	Evaluation Questions
Is the program complying with the way administrators interpret its intent through rules and regulations? That is, is the program consistent with its intent regarding:	Is the program meeting its broader legislative intent *efficiently in terms of cost, and effectively in terms of achieving program goals?*
<ul><li>How funds are to be spent</li><li>The selection of the target group</li><li>The way the program is to be organized</li><li>The services to be provided</li><li>The service delivery process to be used</li><li>The way outcomes are to be measured and reported</li></ul> Are the following in conformance with these rules and regulations: <ul><li>The target group served</li><li>The services provided</li><li>Client outcomes</li><li>Program organization</li><li>Costs</li></ul>	<ul><li>What is the scope and range of outcomes, positive and negative?</li><li>Were the outcomes those intended for the people expected to benefit?</li><li>Were the outcomes significantly different for participants than for similar individuals not receiving the program's services, and in what way?</li><li>Did the implementation features that distinguish the program from previous strategies work as intended?</li><li>What influence did these organizational and service delivery features seem to have in producing the outcomes?</li><li>What was the tradeoff between program costs and benefits?</li></ul>

for some of the people exposed to it. However, such results are useful in modifying unrealistic assumptions about the effect a program's implementation and service strategies should have, about the groups for whom such strategies are to work best, or about the kinds of changes needed to make programs more effective. Disappointing results can also alert practitioners to influences that should have been studied but were not, or to developing better definitions and measures of the factors that *were* studied. It may be problems such as these that explain nonsignificant or negative results rather than the characteristics of the program. Awareness of such issues can lead to a better understanding of programs and to more informed changes in the allocation and targeting of program resources.

It is well-known that evaluation findings and conclusions drawn from them are misused more often than we would prefer, but policy and management decisions clearly suffer more from an *absence* of scientific efforts to obtain objective information. More often than we think, evaluation offers new chances to demonstrate successful program aspects rarely revealed by monitoring information. Important outcomes that do not lend themselves to numerical measurement and are critical to a program's success are frequently missed in the monitoring process.

On the other hand, evaluation should not be oversold. Science cannot establish "the truth" beyond a doubt. Scientific method only brings us closer to the truth than more subjective and undisciplined methods. Nevertheless, myriad, rich, warm anecdotal reports no longer convince taxpayers, program managers, or legislators that a program is worth its cost, or even that it works. Accurate empirical evidence of the value of both *ends* and *means* is the contemporary measure of the worth of social initiatives.

Therefore, the challenge for states and local program areas at the beginning of a new decade is to develop the deeper and more expansive knowledge they must have in order to make important short- and long-term program decisions: how to determine needs appropriately, use resources wisely, target services so that those most in need or likely to benefit will have access to them, plan and manage programs effectively, coordinate with related programs in a meaningful way, and test new ideas as a basis for innovation.

An impressive benefit of evaluation in meeting this challenge is the *reduction of bias* in the information made available for decisionmaking. In the simplest terms, a scientific approach is *a guide map for obtaining the least-biased information available* about what is really happening in programs. Bias-free information must be an essential part of the range of influences to which decisionmakers expose themselves in making judgments of program value and recommending change.

Administrators often take the position that evaluation has little impact on the decisionmaking process, suggesting it is used mainly to support foregone decisions. This is often true, but this conclusion neglects the role evaluation plays in *narrowing the range of choices available to decisionmakers to those likely to be the best ones.* The development of performance standards in employment and training programs is again a good example. The measures selected to "stand for" employment, earnings, and welfare-reduction outcomes were based on a substantial number of previously undertaken national evaluations that tested the predictive ability of optional measures of these traditional program effects (Barnow 1987). Those with greatest predictive capability were suggested as a basis for federal decisions on performance standards indices. Administrative choices were thus directed to the most accurate, least-biased measures. The ultimate decision about standards favored these measures, benefiting from the framework for decisionmaking provided by insights from past evaluations.[3]

Changes made in programs are inevitable, but not always desirable. With increased state and local control, and the new flexibility to shape the purpose and content of change, administrators have the power to facilitate the kinds of change that will directly benefit their programs. Therefore, it is critical that state and local decisionmakers have a pool of unbiased information to balance other pressures for change.

Reducing Bias

Information about social programs is hardly lacking. The issues are the reliability and validity of that information. The practical benefits of program evaluation are tied to the need for *objective* information for decisionmaking. Important decisions about the future of programs are made on the basis of diverse information sources that vary in their approximation of the truth about a program's impact and the effectiveness of its implementation. Decisions are clearly more useful to society if they are informed by accurate information. Well-designed and competently conducted program evaluations that are responsive to state and local concerns are the most trustworthy source of information for making choices among alternative courses of action. An important purpose of evaluations is, therefore, to reduce *information bias*.

Biases can be viewed simply as factors other than those studied in an evaluation that may, or probably do, affect the answers we obtain to evaluation questions. The degree to which such answers may be biased is a function of the extent to which an evaluation plan can *control for* extraneous influences that may explain evaluation results as well as or better than those being studied. That is, ideally we want to eliminate competing explanations of our findings, so that we are assured that what we have learned applies specifically to the relationships we have selected for evaluation attention (Smith 1981).

Based on the principles and methods that characterize scientific method, the logical chronology of steps in the research process is designed to control for the effects of bias to the extent possible. This chronology describes methods that are within the control of the evaluator and methods that are fallback strategies to compensate for potential bias outside the evaluator's control. However, not even this systematic approach can eliminate *all* biases, since even in the most competent research many influences cannot be anticipated or measured. Knowledge about their potential effects may be lacking. It may be very difficult to quantify such influences for purposes of analysis. The cost of accessing such information may be prohibitive. Organizational or political constraints may exist. Nevertheless, conforming as much as possible to the classic steps in the research process brings us closer to the truth than any other method (Blalock 1982).

An overview of these steps is provided in chart 1.3, with the caveat that, in practice, the questions to be answered in this progression are highly interdependent and must often be dealt with simultaneously. To provide the reader with a clearer idea of the *kinds* of biases that may emerge at *each point* in the research process, a hypothetical work/welfare demonstration project is used as an illustration in chart 1.4.

The Range of Evaluation Options

As we try to conform to the research process, we should appreciate the alternatives available for evaluating state and local programs. A variety of distinctions can be made among these research options, but we will concentrate on two: (1) the *issues* given primary attention, and (2) the characteristics of the *research designs* used to study these issues.

Issues of Interest in Evaluating Social Programs: Studying Program Implementation vs. Program Outcomes

Most major national evaluations, such as studies of programs under the Comprehensive Employment and Training Act (CETA) and the more recent series of evaluations of state work/welfare programs, have focused singularly on a program's outcomes (Mirengoff 1982; Gueron 1986). Recognition of the significance of studying program implementation has evolved slowly, even though practitioners have always had an intuitive awareness of its importance. To select among various evaluation possibilities appropriately, in a way that is responsive to different information purposes and evaluation circumstances, we need to understand the difference between *outcome evaluations* and studies of program implementation, or *process evaluations*.

The major impetus for the development of social programs lies in the political arena as much as in the realities of life in societies. The definition of certain social phenomena as "problematic" is shaped strongly by the parameters of public debate, media attention, and the political process. Having been assigned problem status, pressures build to develop public policies to ameliorate or resolve these conditions. Some policies are subsequently translated into action programs through legislation. These programs are essentially strategies for change— change in individuals, organizations, institutions and their environments. Their purpose and content are progressively reinterpreted by a

Chart 1.3
The Evaluation Chronology

Steps in the Evaluation Process	Questions Answered
Conceptualization and Measurement	
Review of Past Evaluations Identification of insights from past research relevant to the subject of interest.	What reasonably reliable and vaild information does past research provide that can help direct this evaluation?
Identification of the assumptions underlying this research.	What assumptions did the evaluators make that can provide an effective rationale for selecting questions to be answered in this evaluation?
Conceptualization Identification of the important *issues* to study.	What program issues are most significant to study?
Identification of the major *variables* to investigate.	What influences have the greatest impact in shaping these issues?
Identification of the most important *relationships* on which to focus.	What relationships among the major influences should be the subject of the evaluation?
Formulation of a manageable set of top priority *research questions* to be answered.	What are the most important questions to be answered about these issues, influences, and relationships?
Identification of the *variables to be controlled* in answering the research questions.	What influences — *other than those selected for study* — may explain the answers yielded by the evaluation, and therefore must be given attention?
Specification of the assumptions made about what is most essential to study.	How can the focus of the evaluation be rationalized?
Measurement Definition of the *variables*, or influences to be studied.	How will the major influences be defined in order to study them?
Development of *indices* for each of the variables.	Consistent with the definition of these variables, what kinds of *measures* (data elements) will be used to *represent* each influence in the evaluation?
Definition and development of indices of the *variables to be controlled.*	How will influences other than what is being studied be defined and measured, in order to control for their potential effects?

Chart 1.3 *(Continued)*
The Evaluation Chronology

Steps in the Evaluation Process	Questions Answered
Methodology	
Research Design	
Development of a research approach, and a set of sampling, data collection and data analysis methods for answering the research questions, given the data available.	What kind of research *guide*, or *technical map*, will be used to direct the evaluation, so that it will yield the *least biased* information?
• Sampling Development of a sampling strategy for selecting the subjects of the evaluation: the sample of clients, and a comparison group (if used).	How should the individuals, groups or organizations to be studied be selected, in order to be able to generalize the results of the evaluation? How closely does the comparison group (if any) resemble the client group?
• Data Collection Development of a strategy for acquiring the information needed.	What is the most cost-effective way to collect a given quality and quantity of data? How should data on the measures selected be gathered, in order to obtain the most reliable information possible?
• Data Analysis The development of a strategy for analyzing the data collected, appropriate to the research design.	What statistical or other methods are most appropriate for analyzing the information obtained, in order to produce the most valid results possible?

Chart 1.3 *(Continued)*
The Evaluation Chronology

Steps in the Evaluation Process	Questions Answered
Use of Results	
Summarization of Findings The presentation of the most important evaluation results, given the research questions.	What was learned about the issues, influences, and relationships of interest? What are the answers to the research questions?
Interpretation of Findings The drawing of conclusions from the findings, given the qualifications to these results.	What conclusions can be drawn from the findings, considering the following: • What potential sources of bias were not measured, or were outside the evaluator's control, that may limit evaluation conclusions? • How do the nature of the research questions and the characteristics of those studied affect the usefulness of the conclusions? • To what extent can conclusions be generalized beyond the subjects of this evaluation, and the context and environment of the program evaluated?
Advice about Improving the Program Evaluated The development of recommendations about improving program policy and operation.	Based on the findings and conclusions, and considering the biases left unmeasured or uncontrolled, as well as the extent to which results can be generalized, what recommendations can be made from the evaluation that could improve program policies and operation?

Chart 1.4
Potential Sources of Bias in Evaluating a New Welfare Reform Project

Steps in Evaluation Process	Examples of Potential Sources of Bias
Review of Past Evaluations	If past evaluations of work/welfare programs are underutilized, or if the analysis of previous work/welfare studies does not give enough consideration to the methodology used or the qualifications that must be made to the findings, the evaluation questions that drive the evaluation of the demonstration project may be based on inadequate or faulty assumptions and conclusions; therefore, the answers may lack utility or be misleading. For example, some of the early evaluations of "workfare" programs have produced highly questionable results, whereas recent experimental studies of work/welfare programs have yielded much more trustworthy insights.
Conceptualization	If the least important, less relevant, or wrong variables and relationships are selected for study, the usefulness and cost-effectiveness of evaluation activities may not justify the effort. For example, the better studies of work/welfare programs suggest that the marital and family characteristics of the unit to be benefited by a program, and service interventions involving health services, day care, and supportive counseling, are key variables to measure in work/welfare programs. However, many studies have persisted in looking only at the standard demographic variables and the effects of standard employment and training services, probably missing the more important explanations for outcomes.
Measurement	If the essential service interventions, outcomes, and/or implementation features that characterize the new welfare reform program — and are the influences of greatest interest in evaluating it — are not defined precisely and accurately, the results will lack validity and lose their value in improving the new program. For example, in studying the effect of the mix and sequence of services provided to a given client, it is important to develop a precise, easily understandable definition of what each service in the mix is, and how sequence is to be defined. For example, the service intervention titled "classroom training" has many potential meanings. Precisely what activities it is to involve in the reform program must be established, and the meaning of "sequenced services" must be specified, if the effects of receiving this and other services, in particular sequences, are to be accurately determined.
Research Design	One set of biases that are difficult to control for, but must be dealt with in designing an evaluation, are *selection biases*. These can be biases due to clients' self-selection into a program, or biases due to the way program staff carry out intake, appraisal, service planning, service assignment and referral responsibilities. At each of the latter decision points, biases due to certain client and staff characteristics, and certain service delivery practices can interfere with obtaining valid results. For example, among those eligible only a subset apply for a program. With the reform, the applicant group may over-represent individuals of a certain age, with certain kinds of motivation and prior skills. The evaluator must somehow compensate for self-selection biases if the information desired from the evaluation is to apply to the entire group of eligibles.

Chart 1.4 *(Continued)*
Potential Sources of Bias in Evaluating a New Welfare Reform Project

Steps in Evaluation Process	Examples of Potential Sources of Bias
Research Design *(Continued)*	Staff frequently assign services on the basis of their own sense of who needs and will benefit from particular options, irrespective of formal policies and procedures — or formal policies themselves may require nonrandom assignment procedures. In evaluating the reform, the evaluator must determine what kinds of service assignment biases are likely to be introduced, so compensatory strategies can be used to reduce these biases.
Sampling	If the sample of individuals selected to be studied in evaluating the reform is not representative of those about whom information is desired, the results of the evaluation will lack generalizability: the results will only apply to a subset of those participating in the program, and it may even be difficult to identify precisely the kinds of individuals to whom the information does apply. For example, if we want to know the postprogram outcomes of all participants, but the sample we draw overselects participants with particular characteristics, we cannot then conclude that the outcomes hold for all participants — they may only hold true for the most disadvantaged or the most skilled program applicants.
	If the evaluator wants to compare individuals experiencing the reform with similar individuals who are experiencing the older program, and the comparison group is selected in such a manner that it does not adequately "match" the reform-treated individuals, then differences between these groups may simply reflect differences in prior individual characteristics rather than differences due to the program. For example, the comparison group may overrepresent men or minorities, skewing the outcome information.
Data Collection	If needed information is not collected consistent with the data gathering process that is part of the research design, the reliability of this information is in question. For example, if follow-up information is to describe the postprogram outcomes of all participants in the reform, but information is gathered only on those who found jobs following the program, or if follow-up information is collected only on those easiest to contact, it will be very difficult to compensate for the biases created.
Data Analysis	Methods of analysis must be appropriate to the purpose of the evaluation, the kind of information desired from it, and the nature of the data gathered. If the methods used are not appropriate vis-a-vis these criteria, or if appropriate methods are not applied correctly, the validity of the results will be jeopardized. For example, "content analysis" may be the most appropriate method for obtaining information about staff attitudes toward clients or new personnel responsibilities in the new reform, if questionnaires do not used scaled responses. If such responses are subsequently reclassified into scales after-the-fact, in order to use statistical analysis techniques, unknown biases may be introduced.

Chart 1.4 (Continued)
Potential Sources of Bias in Evaluating a New Welfare Reform Project

Steps in Evaluation Process	Examples of Potential Sources of Bias
Summary of Findings	The answers do not exist in a vacuum. Their context is the entire evaluation process. In reporting them, it is necessary to anticipate the conditions that must be imposed upon their interpretation.
Interpretation of Findings	In drawing conclusions from evaluation findings, the sources, nature, and extent of bias must be considered. Some of the biases introduced may have been eliminated or minimized by studying certain aspects of program implementation and compensating through the use of statistical techniques. However, no evaluation is perfect. Conclusions, therefore, need to be qualified so that the user can make a judgment about the reliability, validity, and generalizability of the information produced, and the replicability of the evaluation in another program setting. For example, if the sample sizes used to study client subpopulations in the reform turn out to be too small to yield trustworthy information — for critical groups such as single parents with preschool vs. school age children, for instance — then conclusions simply should not be drawn about these subgroups.
Advice about Improving the Evaluated Program	Researchers are not ordinarily expected to make policy or program recommendations based on their studies. However, social program evaluation is not solely a scientific effort. Its results are expected to lead to some kind of action. Just as the thrust of evaluation activities is to study the effects of planned change, evaluation information is to lead to positive action. Consequently the evaluation contract frequently requires that policy recommendations be made. The progression from evaluation findings to conclusions to recommendations for action is a sensitive one, potential biases presenting a challenge at each step. For example, the evaluation of the new welfare reform program may find that short-term welfare recipients benefited more from reform than chronic users. This does not necessarily justify leaping to the conclusion that the program does not work for long-term recipients of income subsidies, and the recommendation that services be targeted more exclusively to short-term welfare consumers. One would have to address issues such as the preprogram characteristics of these two groups and the differential effect of alternative service mixes and sequences on their outcomes.

succession of political and organizational actors with different perspectives and investments. Each program, however, can be understood in terms of a number of common attributes that reveal assumptions about (1) the nature of the problem the program is to address, (2) who and what should be changed, and (3) what types of changes are needed and how they are to be accomplished, i.e., the "theory of change" underlying the design of the program.

Each social program involves a variety of strategies for accomplishing change. The strategy that tends to receive the most public policy attention is the program's formal *service interventions* directed to participants. These involve particular mixes and sequences of services—and sometimes subsidies—that respond to a particular problem and distinguish a given program from others. Less visible to the public, but just as important to study, is the program's *implementation strategy,* or the organizational features of a program that are expected to provide an environment in which the service interventions can have maximum effect. This strategy represents an additional change agent, or set of *organizational interventions* that can influence the extent to which the desired changes are accomplished. These implementation characteristics are (1) the *structural* and *functional* aspects of the organizations responsible for a program, and (2) the nature of the *service delivery systems* operated by these organizations.

Service delivery systems expose the client to the program's service interventions, facilitating a satisfactory exchange between program effort and the social benefits associated with change. The way this exchange occurs is greatly influenced by the organizational context in which it takes place. In turn, this context has a significant impact on the program experiences of clients and client outcomes. Therefore, process evaluations that focus on how effectively and efficiently a program's organizational system works, and what influences it has on program outcomes, provide essential information. Studying implementation poses unique measurement dilemmas, however. Some aspects of organizational life cannot be defined in a form that lends itself to *statistical analysis*. Other methods can be used to summarize and draw inferences from such information, yielding useful insights about these lesser-known, but critical organizational interventions.

Outcome evaluations, on the other hand, focus more exclusively on relationships among the characteristics of clients entering a service delivery system that are thought to affect their outcomes, the program's service interventions targeted to these clients, and these clients' outcomes. Outcome evaluations typically seek information on the *net* effects of services on outcomes, requiring that the evaluator trade information scope for information accuracy.

Sometimes important measurement issues must be neglected in outcome studies, such as the precision of the definitions that distinguish one kind of service activity from another; the development of profiles that describe the most frequent configurations of services and sequences delivered; the capture of information on significant attributes of the service interventions, such as length, and the gathering of information on important characteristics of client outcomes, such as quality, magnitude, and duration. Furthermore, outcome evaluations have often been limited to the program's effects for participants at the point of program completion, neglecting longer-term impacts. And some outcome studies have ignored the program's impact on other key individuals and entities, such as employers, educators, or other social programs.

Nevertheless, studying outcomes is the major oversight responsibility in judging the value of social programs. If outcome evaluations are to provide information genuinely useful for policy, planning, and management purposes, the goal is to define and measure as inclusive a range of important interventions and outcomes as a feasible research plan permits. Process studies can then offer information regarding why and how the observed outcomes occur. *Comprehensive* program evaluations, therefore, will address both implementation and outcome issues, affording users *complementary* information about the different influences and effects that describe a particular program.

Again, using the work/welfare demonstration project as an example, chart 1.5 helps us sort out the different influences and effects studied in process vs. outcome evaluations.

Pressure to justify a program's costs by demonstrating its social utility has often encouraged resistance to conducting process and outcome evaluations simultaneously. Outcome evaluations represent an inefficient use of resources, however, if carried out in the absence of process evaluations that can help explain program effects. The goal of outcome evaluations—to estimate program impact—and the goal of process evaluations—to understand why such effects were produced and how service or implementation strategies can be modified to more fully and efficiently produce desired outcomes—are not in conflict. The achievement of both goals assures more comprehensive, complementary information for decisionmaking (Judd 1987).

The Characteristics of Evaluation Approaches and Methodologies

In seeking answers to complicated questions about program implementation and impact, the ultimate objective is to come as close as possible to establishing which influences are *causing* certain effects. Was it good case management or the formal service received that resulted in a better outcome? Untangling cause and effect is a difficult task. Science can give us accurate estimates but not certainty. And it can only offer greater precision if we follow scientific principles and methods very closely. Sometimes that is not possible. The questions lead us elsewhere, or there are organizational or political reasons why we cannot use a particular evaluation strategy. Not all of our evaluation options provide us with information on cause and effect. They may, however, offer extremely useful information of a different kind about the relationships in which we are interested.

One basis for differentiating among evaluation strategies is the extent to which different *research designs* produce information that explains *cause-effect* relationships, as compared with determining associations or *correlations* among influences (short of establishing cause and effect), or simply providing important clues or insights about the possible nature of such relationships. Following scientific principles and methods most closely, the *ideal experiment* gives us the most "unbiased" information about programs. In realistic social program settings, however, not even experimental designs can produce information miracles. Therefore, we need to appreciate the spectrum of design possibilities available to us. One way to describe this spectrum is found in chart 1.6.

Chart 1.5
Influences Studied in Process and Outcome Evaluations

Target Groups Expected to Receive Program Interventions

The Program's Participants: *Public Assistance Recipients*
Key Characteristics:

- Age
- Sex
- Education
- Marital status
- Number of children
- Work history
- Income history
- Frequency/duration of periods on public assistance

Other Entities Expected to Benefit from Program
Other Welfare Programs:

- Other training and employment programs
- Unemployment insurance program
- Other educational programs
- Health programs
- Economic development programs

Desired Outcomes of Program

For Program Participants

- Increased employability
- Increased occupational skills
- More durable employment
- Sufficient earnings to reduce or eliminate the need for a welfare grant
- Greater family stability/life quality

For Other Entities

- Reduced costs
- Reduced service demands
- Greater coordination and less duplication of effort
- Increased tax revenues
- Increased job creation

Potential Service Interventions Expected to Produce Desired Outcomes

Interventions Targeted to Participants			Interventions Targeted to Other Entities			
Employment/ Training Services	Services in Support of Employment/Training	Subsidies Associated with Employment/ Training	To Employers Services	Subsidies	Discounts	To Other Programs
• Educational/occupational skills testing • Basic education • Preparation for work • Skills training: work experience, classroom and on-the-job training • Job search assistance and placement • Follow-up	• Day care • Health care • Individual/family counseling • Financial counseling	• Basic income support • Training-related stipends	• Worker recruitment and screening • Special supportive services to workers through program's case management/ counseling effort	• Wage subsidies • Training subsidies	• Income tax credits	• Increased efforts to coordinate related services • Increased efforts to create new jobs

Chart 1.5 *(Continued)*
Influences Studied In Process And Outcome Evaluations

Program Implementation Features Expected to Foster Desired Outcomes

Characteristics of Welfare Reform Program As an Organizational System		Characteristics of the Welfare Reform Program's Service Delivery System
Structural Characteristics	Functional Characteristics	Policies and Practices
State Executive Committee	• Acquisition of funding • Needs assessment/resource allocation • Formulation of program policies • Coordination with related programs • Program accountability: plan review, program monitoring, program evaluation	• Outreach • Intake/eligibility determination • Appraisal/service planning • Service assignment • Case management • Supervision: in educational/training/employment sites • Referral to other programs/alternatives • Placement • Follow-up
State Advisory Committee	Provision of expert opinion to Executive Committee	
State Program Administration Structure	Central administration, planning, management, monitoring/reporting	
Local Program Management Structure	Local administration, planning, contracting, program operation, monitoring and reporting	
Public/Private Service Subcontractor Systems at the Community Level	Supervision of local service delivery systems and provision of services	
Community Councils	Provision of grassroots feedback from local clients and service providers to the local organizational	

Summary of Issues Investigated in Process vs. Outcome Evaluations

Studying Program Implementation	Studying Program Outcomes
The focus is on relationships among the organizational elements of a program and the potential influence of these organizational factors on program outcomes.	The focus is on relationships between the interventions targeted to program participants and the outcomes of the program for participants and other entities.

The characteristics of evaluation alternatives relevant to information about cause and effect are not the only attributes that distinguish one evaluation option from another. One must consider other characteristics, such as the *rigor* of the research design and the *realism* and *generalizability* of the information different kinds of evaluations provide.[4] Each alternative may vary in terms of these attributes, depending on the decisions made in developing the research design guiding an evaluation and the way this methodology is actually implemented. For example, for each type of design described in chart 1.6, there is a variety of methodological choices that differ in the extent to which they produce accurate information—information that realistically reflects a program's natural state and can be generalized beyond the individuals or other entities studied.

Even the ideal experimental design has its own set of tradeoffs in this respect. It is the most rigorous in the scientific sense, in that it provides maximum control over certain kinds of bias. However, control is achieved by randomly assigning eligible clients to served vs. nonserved groups. This essentially changes the program's expected implementation strategy, which calls for service assignment at the discretion of professional staff.

Even if staff do not subvert random assignment, and client advocacy groups do not demand that all eligibles be served, we still find ourselves asking, "How did random assignment *itself* affect program outcomes?" Or if, for a variety of reasons, the experimental sites for studying a program are not representative of the areas to which evaluation results are to be generalized, the information obtained will be of less value no matter how unbiased it is.

Experimental designs also place limits on the variables and relationships that can be studied, in order to institute control, which then leads us to wonder whether we have studied the most important influences and effects or missed something critical. In general, experimental designs are stronger with respect to rigor, or the ability to isolate certain of the effects of a program's interventions, but they tend to be weaker on realism, and often on generalizability (Blalock 1964).

Quasi-experimental designs interfere much less with a program's service delivery practices, but they produce information of varying

Chart 1.6
Research Designs

Type of Research Design	Primary Purpose	Examples
Nonexperimental Designs		
Exploratory	To *explore* relationships among implementation features, service interventions, outcomes, and/or the program's environment, in order to identify what factors operating in these relationships may be the most important ones to study, and to obtain insights about the nature of their influence for more systematic study.	*Participant-observation* and *case studies* ranging from informal to quite formalized studies.
Descriptive	To *describe* relationships among any or all of the above, focusing on influences and effects known or considered to be probable key factors, to determine the extent to which they are interrelated — i.e., associated statistically, or *correlated* — short of attempting to establish cause-effect.	Surveys or panel studies of program participants and other individuals to be changed by the program, ranging from relatively unstructured to highly sophisticated studies. An example is *descriptive gross outcome studies* that involve simple statistical analyses of program follow-up information.
Quasi-experimental	To *estimate cause-effect* relationships between a program's interventions and outcomes, comparing program participants' outcomes with a *statistically constructed comparison group* of individuals who have not received the programs' interventions.	*Differential gross outcome studies*, which compare the outcomes of particular subgroups of program participants who have been assigned different interventions, using one group as a *comparison group* for another, adjusting statistically for selection bias, and controlling for influences on the program's environment that could affect outcomes.
		Net impact studies, which compare the outcomes of program participants with those of a group of individuals as similar to these participants as possible and who have not received the interventions, statistically adjusting for selection bias, and controlling for the program's environment.
Experimental Designs	To *more precisely determine cause-effect* relationships between interventions and outcomes, comparing the outcomes of participants who received the program's interventions with those who have not received them, based on the *random assignment* of a pool of clients to a "treated" group and a "non-treated *control group*" prior to the introduction of the interventions.	*Field experiments*, which compare the outcomes of "treated" vs. "non-treated" groups that are *equivalent* in terms of preprogram charactistics that may affect outcomes, controlling statistically for influences in the program's environment.

accuracy depending on the methods used to control for bias. Again, the scope of an evaluation is necessarily limited, but there is greater flexibility in studying programs as they actually operate. If carefully developed, these designs can achieve the desired generalizability in terms of identifying program outcomes across diverse sites. Therefore, quasi-experimental designs are generally weaker in controlling bias than experimental designs, but frequently stronger with respect to realism and generalizability (Campbell 1963).

Exploratory and descriptive designs clearly do not offer as much control over biases as the two designs just discussed. Assuring that the information from surveys, panel studies, and case studies has been purged of subjective judgments is much more difficult. Within this constraint, however, the sampling, data collection, and data analysis methods incorporated within descriptive designs can vary from relatively unsophisticated to highly sophisticated.

Well-structured exploratory designs can also yield reliable information. Far more flexible in what can be studied, the more rigorous exploratory and descriptive designs can reflect the true complexities of programs in their natural settings better than other methodologies. If sampling strategies are adequate, information obtained using descriptive designs is very generalizable, competent survey research being a case in point. And these designs are appropriate for studying both implementation and outcomes (Davis 1967). However, they represent weaker methodologies in terms of rigor.

These tradeoffs among accuracy, realism, and generalizability need to be viewed positively, as providing a framework within which different compromises can be crafted in the context of other tradeoffs, particularly organizational and political ones. As we try to increase our proximity to the truth, we should appreciate the different tradeoffs and options available and make the best choice given the many demands and pressures surrounding that choice.

The Evaluation Approaches Emphasized in this Book

The three nonexperimental evaluation approaches selected for attention in this book represent only one set of choices. They were chosen because (1) they respond to the organizational and political realities of ongoing social programs; (2) they provide the least-biased information short of imposing random assignment procedures on service assignment policies; (3) they represent an integrated and comprehensive approach to studying programs over their planning cycles; and (4) they are oriented to the practical decisionmaking needs of those responsible for the success of such programs.

Net Impact Evaluation

The approach used in determining the net impact of programs, or their "return on the public investment," is based on the principle that this return cannot be estimated precisely without comparing the outcomes of participants with those of similar individuals who have not received the program's interventions. Therefore, the selection and measurement of an appropriate comparison group are key tasks. In this context, cause-effect relationships between interventions and outcomes for men vs. women are studied, using a rigorous quasi-experimental design. The influence of the length of time a client is exposed to a particular service intervention and the effects of local program environments are considered, focusing on the magnitude and duration of the outcomes achieved. A comparison group strategy utilizes regularly collected administrative data and adjusts for potential nonequivalence in the "treated" vs. "nontreated" groups through the application of statistical techniques.

Because of the rigorous research design required to estimate net program impact, such evaluations are necessarily more limited in the number and kinds of questions they can answer. However, they afford the best means of establishing what exclusive contribution the program is making to the short-term and longer-term fiscal and programmatic outcomes observed, as compared with other potential influences that could explain these outcomes.

Gross Outcome Evaluation

The approach used in studying a program's gross outcomes is a twofold strategy for gaining an understanding of a broader range of outcomes than those that can be studied in net impact evaluations and acquiring more in-depth information about the intensity, quality, and durability of such outcomes for client subgroups receiving different program interventions. This approach can make optimal use of and build upon a program's automated information system.

The first strategy utilizes a descriptive research design to study relationships between service interventions and gross client outcomes, as well as gross outcomes for others to be benefited by the program. The second strategy, referred to as a *differential gross outcome analysis*, uses a quasi-experimental design to analyze potential cause-effect relationships between program services and outcomes, sorted by types of interventions and kinds of clients. This approach does not involve the use of a comparison group of nontreated individuals. It relies, instead, on using one treated group as a comparison for another. This strategy also involves a study of service assignment practices and uses statistical techniques to compensate for selection biases. In this sense, the approach combines careful outcome evaluation with a complementary study of particular aspects of program implementation.

Process Evaluation

The approach taken in studying program implementation applies basic *systems analysis* concepts to social programs that are viewed as *organizational systems* (Mintzberg 1979). Emphasis is on how efficiently and effectively the parts of this system interrelate to achieve system goals, and on the influence the articulation among parts has on program outcomes. In evaluating implementation, the system is classified into its component parts and their integration with one another is examined. However, no matter how well such a system may work internally, it is also shaped by its relationships within a larger environment, including its funders, resource allocators, auditors, other human service organizations with which it is expected to interact, and key actors in its home community. Therefore, these relationships are also subjected to scrutiny.

The assumption underlying this approach—using either an exploratory or descriptive research design—is that organizations and systems of interrelated organizations are goal-directed, and successful goal achievement is a function of how well organizational structures and functions work together. Information about these important organizational linkages can help explain why programs providing similar interventions to comparable clients can produce quite different outcomes. More often than not, the success of a program in conforming to its intent is more dependent on organizational factors than on the influences typically given maximum attention in the public policy arena. Such information is essential in making useful program modifications (Williams 1976).

The Organization of the Book

The book is organized to express the particular concept of evaluation outlined earlier. This concept views evaluation as a set of complementary approaches that can offer practical information on program implementation and impact for state and local decisionmaking. Evaluation is also seen as requiring a special fiscal, organizational, and political capability, which can benefit the state and local agencies operating social programs.

Chapters 1 through 4 focus on research approaches and methods for carrying out net impact, gross outcome, and process evaluations, respectively. Each set of approaches and methods has its own unique explanatory advantages in providing information useful in improving programs.

Chapter 5 encourages the reader to treat the development of a user-focused evaluation capability as an opportunity to increase staff skills and expand program resources. The author discusses practical planning challenges posed by evaluations conducted at state and local levels, and suggests realistic alternatives for acquiring the funds, expertise, and other resources essential to an evaluation effort.

The final chapter builds on the issues discussed in chapter 5 by proposing ways to strengthen evaluation capability and the use of results, and concludes with a brief overview of the book's major ideas.

Each of the chapters utilizes the same basic format, whose purpose is to assist the reader in absorbing complex material by moving from the general to the specific. This progression begins with an *overview* of the chapter's main ideas, which are relevant to the evaluation of a broad variety of social programs and demonstration projects. This overview is followed by an *application* of these ideas to a contemporary case example, JTPA. Each chapter concludes with a brief exploration of how the ideas in the chapter *relate to and complement* ideas in other chapters, and a *summary* of the main points to be retained by the reader.

In the three technical chapters covering research strategies, the overview in some cases gives the reader a sense of the state-of-the-art regarding the evaluation approach proposed. Where feasible, the application of principles and methods to the JTPA example are presented in a manner consistent with the steps in the research process outlined earlier. Specific illustrations within these chapters are related to the kinds of pragmatic program decisions made by policymakers, administrators, planners, managers, or professionals responsible for program oversight. There is also a commitment to expressing technical concepts in practical language.

In conclusion, it is important to emphasize that looking at the political, organizational, and technical aspects of evaluation recognizes their influence in producing objective information for decisions affecting program evolution. The information user, evaluation funder, policymaker, program professional, and evaluator must work together as a novel partnership to guarantee that the information product justifies its effort and cost. This perspective on program evaluation, stressed throughout the book, acknowledges the reality that research techniques are only one major part of a larger system of influences that shape the form and content of program decisions.

NOTES

1. The decade of the 1970s witnessed a series of large-scale national human service demonstration projects, followed by substantial evaluations of their effects. These were innovative projects designed to test alternative program strategies with particular client groups. Examples are the extensive Seattle/Denver Income Maintenance Experiments, the Carter administration welfare reform projects, the four-state Flexible Intergovernmental Grant Project, and CETA. At the same time, there were a number of net impact studies of more established programs, such as the Work Incentive Program and Head Start. Most evaluations concentrated on the relationship between service interventions and client outcomes, but this decade marked the beginning of interest in the influence of program implementation as well. Social R&D were at their zenith. (See Mirengoff, Barnow, and Gueron for examples of major evaluations in the 1970s and 1980s.)

2. The volumes and their authors are listed in the appendix. Another series of evaluation guides that may be of interest is a set of three volumes for studying local programs under CETA, prepared for Region I, Employment and Training Administration, U.S. Department of Labor in 1978 (Sum et al. 1978). Sage Publications has also produced a series of nine monographs on basic research approaches and methods titled the *Program Evaluation Kit* (Herman 1987).

3. The literature review in chapter 2 is also an excellent source of information about the basis for developing performance standards indicators in employment and training.

4. The three italicized terms, and the discussion of tradeoffs among these characteristics of research, are based on an interesting article by Leslie Kish, a well-known survey research expert, titled "Representation, Randomization, and Control" (1975).

REFERENCES

Barnow, Burt. "The Impact of CETA Programs on Earnings: A Review of the Literature," *Journal of Human Resources* 22:2 (Spring 1987).

Blalock, Ann B., and Hubert M. Blalock, Jr. *Introduction to Social Research.* 2d ed. Englewood Cliffs, NJ: Prentice-Hall, 1982.

Blalock, Hubert M., Jr. *Causal Inferences in Nonexperimental Research.* Chapel Hill, NC: University of North Carolina Press, 1964.

Campbell, Donald T., and Julian C. Stanley. *Experimental and Quasi-Experimental Designs for Research.* Chicago: Rand McNally, 1963.

Cook, Robert, and Lane Rawlins. "The Job Training Partnership Act: New Federalism in Transition," *Publius* (Summer 1985).

Cordray, David S., and Mark W. Lipsey, eds. *Evaluation Studies Review Annual: Volume 11.* Newbury Park, CA: Sage, 1987.

Davis, James A. *Elementary Survey Analysis.* Englewood Cliffs, NJ: Prentice-Hall, 1967.

Gueron, Judith. *Work Initiatives for Welfare Recipients: Lessons from a Multi-State Experiment.* New York: Manpower Demonstration Research Corporation, 1986.

Harrison, Michael I. *Diagnosing Organizations.* Newbury Park, CA: Sage, 1987.

Herman, Joan L., ed. *Program Evaluation Kit.* 2d ed. Newbury Park, CA: Sage, 1987.

Judd, Charles. "Combining Process and Outcome Evaluation," In *Multiple Methods in Program Evaluation,* edited by Melvin Mark and R. Lance Shotland. San Francisco: Jossey-Bass, 1987.

Kish, Leslie. "Representation, Randomization, and Control," In *Quantitative Sociology in the Social Sciences,* edited by Hubert M. Blalock, Jr. New York: Academic Press, 1975.

Lincoln, Yvonna S. *Organizational Theory and Inquiry.* Newbury Park, CA: Sage, 1985.

Lindblom, Charles E. *The Policymaking Process.* Englewood Cliffs, NJ: Prentice-Hall, 1968.

Mintzberg, Henry. *The Structure of Organizations.* Englewood Cliffs, NJ: Prentice-Hall, 1979.

Mirengoff, William. *CETA: Accomplishments, Problems, Solutions.* Kalamazoo, MI: W.E. Upjohn Institute for Employment Research, 1982.

Palmer, John L., ed. *Perspectives on the Reagan Years.* Washington, D.C.: The Urban Institute, 1986.

Patton, Michael Q. *Utilization-Focused Evaluation.* 2d ed. Newbury Park, CA: Sage, 1986.

Pressman, J.L., and Aaron B. Wildavsky. *Implementation.* 2d ed. Berkeley, CA: University of California Press, 1979.

Rossi, Peter H., and Howard E. Freeman. *Evaluation: A Systematic Approach.* 4th ed. Newbury Park, CA: Sage, 1989.

Rossi, Peter H., and Walter Williams, eds. *Evaluating Social Programs.* New York: Seminar Press, 1972.

Simon, Julian, and Paul Burstein. *Basic Research Methods in Social Science.* 2d ed. New York: Random House, 1987.

Smith, H. W. *Strategies of Social Research.* Englewood Cliffs, NJ: Prentice-Hall, 1981.

Suchman, Edward A. *Evaluative Research.* New York: Russell Sage Foundation, 1967.

Sum, Andrew, Katherine Mazzeo, Francis McLaughlin, and Jeffrey Zornitsky. *Evaluating the Performance of Employment and Training Programs at the Local Level.* Boston: Region I, Employment and Training Administration, U.S. Department of Labor, Vol.I-III, 1978.

Weiss, Carol H. *Evaluation Research.* Englewood Cliffs, NJ: Prentice-Hall, 1972.

Wholey, J. *Evaluation and Effective Public Management.* Boston, MA: Little, Brown, 1983.

Williams, Walter, and Richard F. Elmore, eds. *Social Program Implementation.* New York: Academic Press, 1976.

Part II
Complementary Approaches
to
Evaluating Programs

The comprehensive concept of evaluation proposed in Part I gives attention to the important relationship between technical research approaches and the organizational and political context of state and local program evaluation.

The emphasis in this section is on the critical research aspects of evaluation and the significance of producing complementary information about program implementation, outcomes, and impact over a given program planning cycle. Of particular concern is the scientific quality and comparability of information produced by evaluations.

The three chapters follow a common chronology and address the same set of research issues. However, the chapters vary with respect to which research issues are given primary attention. This reflects the different research challenges involved in studying diverse aspects of programs, as well as the contributions different social science disciplines make to program evaluation.

41

2
Evaluating Net Program Impact

Terry R. Johnson
Battelle Human Affairs Research Centers
and
Ernst W. Stromsdorfer
Washington State University

There are many natural social settings in which the researcher can introduce something like experimental design ... which makes a true experiment possible ... Such situations can be regarded as quasi-experimental designs. [We need to] encourage the utilization of such quasi-experiments and to increase awareness of the kinds of settings in which opportunities to employ them occur.

Donald Campbell and Julian Stanley
*Experimental and Quasi-Experimental
Designs for Research*

General Concepts and Methods

In a world of scarce resources and growing federal deficits, it is increasingly important for social programs to document the return that society as a whole receives on its investment. To effectively compete for limited federal, state, and local resources, social programs that have provided services for many years find themselves having to document clearly the benefits and costs of their services.[1] In addition, innovative demonstration projects must properly document their outcomes and costs to compare with existing social programs or alternatives to meet the same goals, so policymakers can make informed decisions on whether the demonstration should be continued in its current form, expanded or reduced in scope, or discontinued. The emphasis on social program accountability applies to all types of social programs, including those that provide health, housing, or income maintenance services to the aged or to children, and has been an integral part of the federal employment and training system for economically disadvantaged youths and adults for the past few decades.

43

The information required to make a decision on whether to expand, contract, or discontinue a social program begins with a *net impact evaluation*. Numerous factors affect the outcomes of participants served by any social program. These factors include the participants' own characteristics, the program environment, and the services provided. Recognizing that many factors may affect program outcomes, a net impact evaluation attempts to answer the fundamental question, what difference does the program make? This is in contrast to a *gross impact evaluation*, which focuses on whether the outcomes of interest for participants are greater after the program than before the program, and does not determine whether the program services *per se* caused the observed differences in outcomes.

A net impact evaluation examines the changes in outcomes from before to after receipt of social services and, in particular, examines whether any change can be causally attributed to the services received. By comparing the outcomes for participants of a given social program with the outcomes that would have occurred if the program did not exist, a net impact evaluation provides valuable information on program benefits that can be combined with cost information to make informed judgments about the cost-effectiveness of the program. In this chapter, we illustrate a general approach to assessing the net impact of a social program by describing how to estimate the net impact of employment and training programs for economically disadvantaged individuals on participants' postprogram labor market experiences.

The details of the net impact evaluation strategy described in this chapter have been tailored to a specific social program, but the key elements of the net impact approach have general applicability to other social programs. For example, the first element of any net impact analysis involves the development of an appropriate *conceptual framework*. This framework identifies the key research questions addressed, the outcomes examined based on those questions, and the participant subgroups and program services delivered to clients.

The outcome measures examined constitute the *dependent variables* for the net impact analysis. The conceptual framework specifies the key relationships investigated between the dependent variables and measures of various causative factors, such as participant characteristics, the economic environment, and the program services. These factors that affect the dependent variables are called *independent variables*. By fully specifying the net impact questions of interest, the conceptual framework identifies the key relationships between the dependent and independent variables to be analyzed.

The second component of a net impact analysis is the development of a *research design* that provides valid answers to the questions of interest. To select an appropriate research design for a particular social program, one should be guided by several criteria. These include *internal validity, external validity, statistical efficiency*, and *feasibility*. Internal validity refers to the ability of the design to yield unbiased estimates of the causal relationship between program services and outcomes; that is, valid estimates of the net impact of the program. External validity refers to the ability of the research design to achieve results that can be generalized to a broader population than the specific samples of individuals upon which the analyses are based. Statistical efficiency relates to the overall sampling strategy and the need to utilize sufficiently large samples to obtain precise answers to the research questions of interest. Finally, feasibility relates to the ability to implement the research design and obtain meaningful results in a timely fashion and within the limited resources available.

Although all of these criteria are important considerations in selecting a research design, the criterion that receives the most attention in the research literature is internal validity, or obtaining unbiased estimates of program impacts. To meet the internal validity criterion, one must be able to compare the observed outcomes for participants with the outcomes these individuals would have achieved in the absence of the program. To do so, one needs a comparable group of nonparticipants to serve as a comparison group.

The key to internal validity is the comparability of the groups being compared. One can obtain valid causal inferences about the net impact of the program only if other factors that affect the outcomes are statistically equal for the two groups. The most effective way to ensure this in a social program evaluation is to use a classical experimental design in which individuals eligible for program services are randomly assigned to treatment or control status. By randomly assigning some individuals to receive services and other eligibles to not receive services, the two groups should be essentially identical on all dimensions that might affect program outcomes. Thus, any observed differences in outcomes can be reliably attributed to the treatment rather than to pre-existing differences in the characteristics of the two groups.

Although this method has often been used to test the effectiveness of new service interventions, it is not generally used to evaluate the net impacts of social programs.[2] This is, in large part, because of ethical, legal, and programmatic concerns. As a result, a matched comparison group approach—referred to as a *quasi-experimental design*—is typically used. Such an approach relies on some matching rule based on measured characteristics. A matched comparison design could involve the matching of service providers, in which one provider offered the treatment and a comparable provider did not; the matching of individuals, in which participants within a given program are matched to comparable nonparticipants; or the design could include elements of both. Because the feasibility criterion in many cases eliminates the use of an experimental design, in this chapter we describe a quasi-experimental net impact evaluation approach. This approach should yield a considerable amount of useful information on the effectiveness of a social program.

A third element of a net impact analysis is the *data collection and analysis plan*. A guiding principle for collecting data is to make sure that the information used is measured comparably for both participants and comparison group members. Thus, if certain data items are obtained from different social service agencies for the two groups, one must review the data collection forms and procedures to determine comparability. In addition, it is particularly important in a quasi-experimental evaluation to obtain extensive historical information on all key outcomes of interest to determine whether the participants and comparison groups are similar on these measures before participants receive program services. If there are major differences in outcomes between the two groups before program participation, this makes it more difficult to isolate the true effects of program services.

Once the data are collected, the next step is analysis. Because the general statistical issues inherent in most net impact analyses are quite similar, the plan for analyzing the data collected for evaluations of different social programs includes many common elements. For example, a key element of any analysis plan is a detailed examination of the likely extent of *selection bias*. Selection bias refers to the potential non-comparability of the participant and comparison groups due to the fact that individuals self-select themselves to become participants. In addition, the analysis plan must include a strategy for estimating the net impacts of the program overall, and for major program services and participant subgroups to answer the questions identified in the conceptual framework.

Finally, although the results of a valid net impact analysis can provide useful information on the extent to which participants are better off as a result of receiving program services, they are not sufficient to directly address questions related to whether the program should continue to operate at the same level, be expanded, contracted, or discontinued. To determine whether a social program is an efficient use of public resources, one must sum the benefits to participants and the benefits that may accrue to other segments of society, and compare the total benefits with the total costs of the program. That is, one must conduct a *benefit-cost analysis*. In practice, this involves measuring the benefits to participants, taxpayers, and government that accrue over time, properly discounting the benefit stream into current dollar values, and comparing the total benefits with the full social costs of the program.

The remainder of this chapter illustrates the key elements outlined above of a quasi-experimental net impact evaluation of a social program with an application to employment and training programs for JTPA-eligible disadvantaged adults. Although the details of the net impact evaluation strategy described in this chapter are specific to employment and training programs, we emphasize the broader applicability of this general approach to other social programs.

Application of the General Concepts and Methods: JTPA

The net impact evaluation strategy described here was designed in response to an increased need for reliable evaluation information at the state and local levels concerning the effects of employment, education, and training programs funded under the Job Training Partnership Act (JTPA) of 1982. The JTPA significantly changed the employment and training system in a way that gave states and local service delivery areas (SDAs) much greater responsibility for program accountability compared to the Comprehensive Employment and Training Act (CETA). This increased the need for reliable information on program effectiveness at the state and local level at the same time that the federal government greatly reduced its role in providing such information.

As a result, states have less access to reliable federal-level data and federally sponsored research to assist them in making informed judgments about program oversight and social policy. To fill the policy research needs of the states, this chapter describes step-by-step how a state can estimate the net impact of its JTPA programs on earnings and welfare dependency and provide valid information on the investment return from the JTPA.

In developing a state-level net impact model of JTPA programs, we were guided by several considerations. First, for the model to assist states in meeting their new accountability responsibilities, it must produce scientifically *valid* estimates of the net impacts of JTPA program activities and services on relevant participant postprogram outcomes. Second, the model must provide *meaningful* and *timely* information that can be understood and used efficiently by a relatively nontechnical audience. Finally, the model must recognize the *resource and other practical constraints* that states and SDAs face. The two most important practical realities affecting the recommended approach are that (1) states and local SDAs will not generally be able to implement an experimental design in which eligible applicants are randomly assigned to treatment vs. control status, and (2) states and local SDAs will not generally be able to conduct follow-up interviews with a large sample of participants and comparison group members.

Because the proposed net impact evaluation model relies exclusively on administrative records from several agencies that collect these data as part of the normal operating process, the model is widely usable. This model supports timely analysis conducted within the economic and political resource constraints faced by states and SDAs.[3] At the same time, it must be recognized that this approach limits the questions that can be addressed and the variables that can be used to adjust for various statistical problems that could threaten the validity of the analysis. Thus, in evaluating other social programs that face different economic and political constraints, one should consider supplementing the research design described here to include primary data collection activities.

The remainder of this chapter describes a detailed approach for estimating the net impact of employment and training programs for disadvantaged individuals. The chronology of the discussion is as follows:

1. We summarize the lessons learned from the research literature on employment and training net impact evaluations.

2. We describe the key elements of the conceptual framework for a state-level JTPA net impact evaluation by building on previous studies. This conceptual framework includes a description of program outcome measures, the trainee subgroups for which impacts should be separately measured, the program activities (services) to be examined, the types of economic and demographic factors that affect these outcomes, and the data that measure these elements.

3. We describe a research design for analyzing the net impact of the JTPA. The research design describes how to select the most reliable comparison group of otherwise similar nonparticipants to approximate what the labor market experiences of participants would have been in the postprogram period had they not participated in the program. This approach to net impact analysis attributes to program participation the *incremental gain* in labor market experiences that occurs over and above what would have happened had these individuals not participated in the program. This is the appropriate concept for providing information on the return on investment of job training programs. The research design also specifies how to select a representative sample of JTPA participants as well as sufficient

numbers of participants and comparison group members to provide statistically valid net impact results.

4. We discuss the steps involved in obtaining and processing the required data. In particular, we describe the elements of a data collection and processing cycle, and indicate potential problems that may arise. We then describe how to organize the various data sources, the types of data cleaning to be performed, and key features of the analysis files to be constructed.

5. We outline a data analysis plan for estimating the net impacts of JTPA programs on participants' postprogram outcomes. Beginning with a description of methods to determine the quality of any comparison group selected, we describe an approach to estimate the overall net impacts of JTPA and major target groups with respect to the key participant postprogram outcomes indicated in the federal legislation. We also discuss potential threats to the validity of the analysis and indicate possible approaches for adjusting for such problems.

6. We describe how to conduct a cost analysis to determine the costs of JTPA services. We also indicate how to combine this information with the net impact results to provide evidence on the return on investment of job training projects.

7. We indicate how the net impact analysis complements analysis strategies described in other chapters.

8. We conclude with a summary of the general concepts and methods applicable to a net impact evaluation of any social program.

Learning from Past Evaluations: Developing the Context for JTPA Net Impact Analysis

In developing a strategy to evaluate the net impact of any social program, it is very important to understand the various approaches that have been used previously and the nature of the results that have been obtained. In an earlier net impact evaluation guide (Johnson 1986), a detailed review of approximately 20 employment and training net impact evaluations was provided. This section summarizes the results of that literature review to set the context for the conceptual framework described in the following section.

With the exception of several recent net impact evaluations of CETA, most of these studies examine the impact of CETA's predecessors, for example, the Manpower Development and Training Act (MDTA) classroom and on-the-job training programs. Some evaluations concern CETA contemporaries, such as the Work Incentive (WIN) program, the Job Corps, or various employment and training demonstrations. Though none of these studies deals explicitly with JTPA programs, and many focus on pre-CETA programs, they are of interest because the programs examined have many characteristics in common with JTPA programs, and the evaluation elements used are the same as those to be developed for a JTPA net impact model.

The previous net impact evaluations of employment and training programs examine the impacts of services on participants' earnings almost exclusively, which is consistent with the policy objectives of federal employment and training legislation.[4] Moreover, Social Security Administration (SSA) records have been the main source of earnings data. Although SSA earnings records have several advantages (e.g., they are a cost-effective source of longitudinal data measured comparably for participants and comparison group members), they have several potential disadvantages, including coverage problems, exclusion of earnings beyond the taxable maximum, and delays of up to three or four years in obtaining reliable data. These delays prohibit a state-level evaluation from obtaining policy-relevant results in a timely fashion. In addition, when SSA earnings are the only outcome measures available, evaluation is limited to estimating impacts on an annual basis.[5]

The results of these studies generally indicate large net earnings gains for women, particularly nonblack women; whereas, the net effect of employment and training programs on the earnings of adult men is less clear. Although almost all studies find the net earnings gains of men to be considerably less than those obtained by women, several recent evaluations find that male trainees never regain the earnings position they held prior to training relative to otherwise comparable nonparticipants. If this is true, why did men continue to enroll in these employment and training programs? Perhaps because of program earnings and the substantial training subsidies offered by CETA.

These results indicate that separate net impact models should be developed for men and women because the relationship between earnings and various socioeconomic and demographic characteristics clearly is different for men and women.

Although the earlier evaluations of MDTA programs focused more on separate net impact models for whites and blacks, more recent evaluations of CETA programs focus on estimating separate models by age groups. Because of the difficulties in developing valid net impact estimates for youth, many recent studies have estimated models only for adult men and women. The problems for youth are twofold: earnings are not the single appropriate outcome measure for youth, as the relative mix of schooling, market work, nonmarket work, and leisure evolves rapidly over time for them; and it is very difficult to draw a reliable comparison group for youth with limited and highly variable earnings histories. As such, it may not be feasible to develop a state-level JTPA net impact model for youth that provides valid results.

Another evaluation element concerns the participant groups chosen for analysis and the variables included in the model to measure the service intervention or treatment effects. For the most part, these studies focus on estimating the average impact of program services on earnings for the selected subgroups. Because in many cases subgroups of interest were participants enrolled in specific program activities (services), this resulted in numerous net impact estimates by program activity or treatment. The only other dimension of the treatment examined in some of these studies was length of program participation. The results indicate that net impacts vary by program activity and length of participation. Although fewer programs are generally offered under the JTPA (as compared with CETA), and the average length of stay in JTPA is less than in CETA, it is still important to develop models that examine these potential differences in outcomes.

Finally, because virtually all of these studies rely on large-scale data bases on program participants developed well before the analysis was undertaken, little information was generally available on the content of the services provided, whether the program services were provided as planned, and the extent to which the services provided varied across sites and over time. To overcome this problem, it is important to conduct a process analysis like the one described in chapter 4.

Developing a Conceptual Framework for Evaluating Net Impact

The conceptual framework is the first major element in the design of a net impact evaluation. This framework answers the question "What is to be learned from the evaluation?" and identifies key research questions to be addressed. These are:

1. Outcomes to be examined and the relationship of these outcomes to
2. program activities or services.
   Participant groups and program activities to be included.
3. Specific definitions of the variables that measure outcomes, program
4. activities, and any other variables affecting the relationship among activities and outcomes.

As such, the conceptual framework guides the development of the research design and analysis method. This section describes a conceptual framework for conducting a state-level JTPA net impact analysis that accounts for the lessons learned from previous studies and is based entirely on available state administrative data sources.[6]

General Evaluation Questions

Although employment and training programs funded under the JTPA can affect different groups, such as participants, employers, the government, or society as a whole, in various ways, the primary goal of the state-level JTPA net impact model is to determine the extent to which JTPA program activities or services improve the labor market experiences of participants relative to what their experiences would have been in the absence of the program. The net impact of JTPA program activities on participants' postprogram labor market experiences provides policymakers with an indication of the overall gains due to these programs.

Although it is important to know whether the mix of JTPA activities on average is effective, for policy purposes it is equally important to identify the relative effects on different target groups. For example, to improve targeting it is important to know whether certain participant groups benefit more from a particular JTPA activity or service than other groups, and whether the net impact of JTPA differs among program activities, by length of participation, and by local economic conditions.

The general objectives of the state-level net impact model can be summarized by the following key research questions:

1. What is the overall net impact of JTPA program activities (services) on participants' postprogram labor market experiences?
2. Do the net impacts change over time? If so, in what way?
3. Which program activities result in the largest net benefits to participants and society relative to their costs?
4. Which groups gain most from participating in JTPA?
5. For a given program activity, do individuals who remain in JTPA longer experience greater net gains in labor market outcomes? Does this effect vary among activities?
6. How does the net impact of the JTPA vary by local program and environmental conditions?

Table 2.1 details the key elements of the net impact conceptual framework that help to make these questions more specific. Each of these elements is discussed below.

Measuring the Factors Involved
in Answering the Evaluation Questions

Participant Outcomes

As table 2.1 shows, the state-level JTPA net impact model focuses on specific postprogram participant outcome measures related to earnings and welfare dependency that are available in automated administrative records in most states. Because unemployment insurance (UI) Wage Records are maintained on a calendar quarter basis, the earnings measures for longer periods can be created as the sum of quarterly earnings amounts. The Aid for Families with Dependent Children (AFDC) grants measures can be calculated as the sum of monthly grant payments. The employment status and the AFDC participation status measures are defined as "dummy" (or indicator) variables. For example, a person is defined to be employed for any period of interest if UI Wage Records indicate positive earnings were received during the period (1 if employed, 0 otherwise).

Table 2.1
Key Elements of the Conceptual Framework
for the JTPA Net Impact Model

Outcome Measures

• Quarterly, semiannual and annual earnings and employment status based on Unemployment Insurance (UI) Wage Records.

• Quarterly, semiannual and annual AFDC grants and AFDC participation status based on public assistance (PA) records.

Participant Subgroups

• Adult men and women: to the extent possible, disaggregate net impacts by sex, age, race or ethnicity, education, and for women, by welfare status.

Program Activities or Services

• Classroom training: when program data are available, estimate separately for remedial education and basic skills versus specific occupational-skills training.

• On-the-job training.

• Job search assistance.

• All other activities or services.

• Combinations of the above activities or services.

Labor Market Conditions

• Unemployment rate.

• Urban or rural location.

Data Sources

• JTPA Management Information System (MIS): participant characteristics, program activities, and placement experiences.

• PA Grants Records: whether received AFDC and size of AFDC grant.

• UI Wage Records: whether employed and amount of quarterly earnings.

• UI Benefit History: whether received UI benefits in preprogram period.

• Local labor market information: the local (or regional) unemployment rate.

These outcome measures are consistent with the major objectives of the JTPA legislation as specified in the law. As the literature review indicates, these measures typically exceed the nature and extent of outcomes examined in previous studies of the net impacts of subsidized employment and training programs. They also capture the range of short-term and relatively long-term impacts that could be observed within, approximately, a two-year program analysis cycle.

The administrative data sources for constructing key participant outcome measures have several advantages for evaluating the net impact of social programs for which earnings and welfare dependency are of interest. First, UI Wage Records are not truncated at some taxable maximum; that is, actual earnings are reported, which reduces measurement error. Second, UI Wage Records are available by calendar quarter, with only a three- to six-month delay in obtaining reasonably complete data. The availability of data by calendar quarter allows considerable flexibility in the choice of a postprogram follow-up period. Third, UI Wage Records are not subject to interviewer bias or respondent error. Moreover, these data are not subject to problems arising from some respondents reporting net (after-tax) earnings and others reporting gross (before-tax) earnings. Finally, they are not affected by response-rate problems.

Monthly AFDC grants from administrative records have several advantages relative to data obtained through surveys. These include timeliness of data availability and the absence of respondent reporting errors, interviewer biases, and response-rate problems. Because these administrative data systems are relatively inexpensive to obtain, our net impact analysis relies on them.[7]

It is also important to recognize the limitations of these administrative data sources. First, although the Deficit Reduction Act of 1984 required all states to become wage-reporting by 1988, there are still a few states that do not report at this time, and will not for the most part be able to use the net impact model to examine earnings impacts.[8] Second, states that do not have automated AFDC Grants Records available at the state level cannot easily use the net impact model to examine JTPA impacts on reducing welfare dependency. Third, because our net impact approach relies heavily on the availability of historical earnings and grants data, states must be able to directly access or retrieve from archives two to three years of UI Wage Records and public assistance (PA) Grants

Records for a given person at any one time. Although most UI Wage Records systems are similar across wage-reporting states and generally contain at least seven quarters of data at any time, there is considerable variation in state and local welfare administration and record-keeping practices, as well as differences in the degree of data automation and retrieval capabilities. These variations present obstacles to implementing this component of the net impact analysis in certain states.

Fourth, UI Wage Records do not generally include employees of federal, state, or local governments, self-employed individuals, or employees in certain other occupations.[9] Finally, because the system is state-based, it is impossible to distinguish individuals who work across the border in a different state from individuals who do not work in covered employment. Thus, one should be very careful in estimating the net impact of the JTPA on earnings for large service delivery areas located near state borders.

Participant Subgroups

The next conceptual issue concerns the participant groups of interest. As table 2.1 shows, the state-level net impact analysis is limited to adults because earnings, employment, and AFDC dependency are not the appropriate outcome measures for youths or those entering the labor market for the first time in their life cycle. Moreover, the more appropriate of these measures, such as schooling attainment and employment competencies, are not contained in any existing program data sets for both program participants and comparison group members. In addition, as discussed above, there is extensive evidence indicating the difficulty in developing a reliable matched comparison group for youths (Dickinson, Johnson, and West 1987(b); Lalonde and Maynard 1987). Because of these problems, the net impact analysis is designed only for adults. States interested in examining youth issues should consider other approaches for conducting a net impact analysis.[10]

A second issue concerns whether separate net impact analyses need be developed for any specific adult groups. Sample sizes and state resources permitting, separate net impact models should be developed for adult men and women because the relationship between earnings and other demographic characteristics is very different for these two groups. In addition, it is desirable to estimate separate net impact models by race and other participant groups, sample size permitting. If no statistical differences are found among any set of population groups, the groups can then be combined for subsequent analysis.

Finally, it is important to investigate whether the impact of JTPA varies by the following participant characteristics:

1. Age—less than or equal to a particular age (e.g., age 35) as compared to over age 35.
2. Ethnicity—whites as compared to blacks and Hispanics.
3. Educational level—at least high school graduate as compared to nongraduates.
4. Welfare status for adult women—welfare recipients as compared to nonrecipients.

The techniques for conducting such analysis are described later in this chapter.

Program Activities: The Service Interventions

The next important element of the conceptual framework is the determination of the key treatments—program activities or services—to be assessed, and the development of consistent definitions of these variables. *Section 204* of the Job Training Partnership Act sets forth a large array of potential activities. However, the major activities provided under JTPA are classroom training (CT), on-the-job training (OJT), and job search assistance (JSA). Nearly 90 percent of adult FY 1984 Title II-A enrollees participated in at least one of these program activities. Although it is important to include in the analysis those participants assigned to all types of activities in order to assess the full range of JTPA activities, as table 2.1 shows, it is most useful to examine the separate effects of CT, OJT, and JSA.[11] A brief description of each of these program activities is provided below.

Classroom training involves basic or remedial education or occupational-skills training to ensure that individuals acquire the ability and knowledge necessary to perform a specific job for which there is a demand. Such programs are usually provided in a classroom or an institutional setting off the job.

On-the-job training emphasizes the development of occupational skills in an actual work setting, ideally in the private sector. The programs are designed for participants who have been first hired by the employer, and the training occurs while the participant is engaged in productive work that provides knowledge or skills essential to the adequate performance of the job.

Job search assistance includes any activity that focuses on the development or enhancement of employment-seeking skills. This service is provided to participants who need practical experience in identifying and initiating contact and interviewing with prospective employers. It is usually conducted in a structured setting and can include approaches such as job-finding clubs or instruction for self-directed job search.

Several complications arise in developing measures of independent variables to represent these program activities. First, there is considerable variation among SDAs in the characteristics of specific program activities, such as length of assignment, occupational category of the training, hours of training per day, and quality of instructional inputs. This makes it difficult to specify variables that represent a uniform treatment. When such a variable is not uniform, it is difficult to interpret its statistical meaning, and biased estimates of net program impact can result. Nevertheless, one must aggregate generally similar activities because it is simply not possible to reliably estimate the net effects of the virtually unlimited variations of a given program activity.

Second, large differences among SDAs in the nature of the program activities provided are likely to occur. For example, even within a state, work experience activities in a particular SDA may resemble OJT programs in another SDA. Finally, the way in which the training activities provided are recorded in the MIS can cause complications. For example, due to the lack of uniform national reporting requirements, some SDAs record participation in a job search workshop as job search assistance, while others record it as classroom training because the sessions are conducted in a classroom setting. Such differences in the content and recording of program activities across SDAs emphasize the importance of conducting a process analysis concurrently with the net impact analysis in order to develop meaningful and consistent measures of program activities.

As indicated above, the ways in which the treatment variables are defined are in large part determined by the structure and content of the SDA Management Information System (MIS) and how standardized definitions are across SDAs. In addition, any variable definition depends on the specific research questions of interest and the population size of individuals who participate in a given program activity. For example, it is desirable to separate classroom training activities that focus on remedial education and basic skills from classroom training activities that provide specific occupational-skills training. However, if the number of individuals participating in each of these programs is too small to produce statistically reliable net impact estimates for separate activities, it may be necessary to collapse these two treatment variables into one that represents classroom training program activities in general.

Thus, although the specific definitions of the treatment or program activity variables depend on several factors, the following variables should be specified to examine overall impacts and impacts by program activity and other characteristics of the services provided:

1. Participant dummy variable: 1 if JTPA participant, 0 otherwise.
2. Classroom training dummy variable: 1 if CT participant, 0 otherwise:
   — remedial education and basic skills dummy variable: 1 if CT program in remedial education or basic skills, 0 otherwise;
   — specific occupational-skills training dummy variable: 1 if CT program in a specific occupational skill, 0 otherwise.
3. On-the-job training dummy variable: 1 if OJT participant, 0 otherwise.
4. Job search assistance dummy variable that includes all employment and placement-related activities: 1 if JSA participant, 0 otherwise.
5. Other activity dummy variable: 1 if not a CT, OJT, or JSA participant, 0 otherwise.
6. Multiple-treatment dummy variable: 1 if a combination of two or more of CT, OJT, and JSA, 0 otherwise.
7. Occupation of training dummy variables: 1 if in specific 1-digit Dictionary of Occupational Titles (DOT) code, 0 otherwise, for each type of occupational skill.
8. Length of program participation in weeks.
9. Total training hours, the product of length of program participation in weeks, and the number of training hours per week.

The Program's Environment

The final conceptual element concerns the program environmental conditions that should be included in the net impact analysis. Here, we refer primarily to characteristics of the labor market(s) within which the program operates, although major SDA characteristics can also be considered.

Little is known about how the net impact of employment and training programs varies by the environmental conditions surrounding a program at a point in time or over time. In addition, because of the nature of local program environmental conditions (i.e., there may be no within-SDA variation on these conditions), it is important to recognize that, at best, it will only be possible to obtain reasonably precise estimates of a few key conditions. However, this can be done only in states that have a large number of SDAs and exhibit considerable variation in the conditions among SDAs.

In conducting a net impact evaluation of JTPA programs, it is most important to control for differences in local *unemployment rates* and *location*, i.e., whether the program participants and their comparison group members are located in an *urban or rural* area. These factors are likely to affect the key outcome measures: the employment and earnings of adult men and women.

The unemployment rate can be obtained from the *Local Area Unemployment Statistics*, published by the United States Bureau of Labor Statistics (BLS). This information is available monthly at the state and county level and for over 1,000 cities with a population of at least 25,000. Aggregate measures of the unemployment rate corresponding to the quarterly, semiannual, and annual outcome periods of interest can be calculated as an average of the seasonally adjusted rates.

In specifying the unemployment rate variable for an SDA, it is also important to recognize that monthly values will not generally be available for the precise area of interest. Depending on the geographic jurisdiction of the SDA, the area it serves may be larger or smaller than the county or the city for which any given information is available. Where the SDA serves multiple counties, one should calculate the appropriate labor market variables by aggregating over the counties served by the SDA. For example, to calculate the unemployment rate one would simply sum the number of individuals unemployed in the various counties served by the SDA and divide by the total number of individuals in the labor force in those counties. In cases where the SDA serves only part of a given county, and where no value is available for a smaller geographical area such as a city, one is constrained to use the county value.

It may also be possible to provide some information on the manner in which the net impact of JTPA varies by different managerial, organizational, or SDA strategies. The service delivery strategies examined should be based on their policy importance to the particular state doing the analysis. Moreover, to ensure that the strategies of interest are distinct and quantifiable, and that there is sufficient variation among SDAs to support the analysis, it is important to conduct a process analysis. Thus, if states with a large number of SDAs (roughly 30 or more) are interested in obtaining information on how the net impact of JTPA varies by a key service delivery strategy, they should first ensure that significant differences in this strategy exist among SDAs.

If it is possible to quantify these differences (usually by means of dummy variables), one could then use the measures of these variables to determine how the net impact of JTPA varies among SDAs. In states with relatively few SDAs, it is unlikely that such an analysis would provide sufficiently precise estimates of the differential effects of the strategy of interest to warrant the analysis.

Developing and Implementing a Research
Design for Evaluating Net Impact

To provide valid estimates of the net impacts of JTPA programs on the earnings and AFDC dependency of adult men and women, the research design must contain several elements. Table 2.2 provides an overview of the key aspects of the research design that are discussed in detail in the next several sections. Although the specific details of this research design are sensitive to the features of JTPA, its basic elements and the issues to be considered in making decisions are applicable to any net impact evaluation of a social program.

Table 2.2
Research Design for the JTPA Net Impact Model

Sample Design

- Samples of JTPA participants (adult men and women) must be chosen so that the results can be generalized to the state level.

- Valid comparison groups must be chosen so that the impact of JTPA can be distinguished from the impacts of other factors that also affect earnings and welfare dependency.

- The size of the participant and comparison samples must be determined so that program impacts can be measured with precision.

Data Collection

- Comparably measured preprogram and postprogram data for participants and comparison group members must be obtained from several different sources, processed, and analysis files developed.

Analysis

- The comparison groups must be examined in detail to determine their comparability to the participant groups and to identify any adjustments that may need to be made to correct for selection bias.

- A comprehensive strategy must be developed to provide valid estimates of the net impacts of JTPA activities (services) on the postprogram outcomes of participants.

The elements of the sample design are discussed below. Data collection and data processing issues are the subjects of the following section. A description of the overall estimation strategy and the specific net impact models to be estimated is provided in the subsequent section.

Sample Design

The sample design is a key element of the overall research design. The sample design involves the selection of the participant samples, a strategy for developing the comparison groups, and the determination of sample size requirements for the analysis. As such, the sample design directly affects the internal and external validity of the analysis, as well as its statistical efficiency. Table 2.3 summarizes the three major elements in the sample design for a JTPA net impact analysis model. In the text we discuss each of these elements in more detail.

Participant Groups

The major issues in selecting the participant group concern (1) the individuals to be included in the sample frame, (2) potential sample exclusions, and (3) the procedure to select participants from the sample frame for inclusion in the analysis. We discuss these issues below.

Sample frame. The choice of the sample frame is an important determinant of the degree to which the findings can be generalized. The sample frame should represent all JTPA participants so the analysis results can be generalized to the state level. The net impact model includes in the participant sample frame all adult male and female JTPA enrollees during a given time interval, as indicated in table 2.3. In

Table 2.3
Key Elements of the Sample Design for
the JTPA Net Impact Model

Participant Group

- Comprised of samples of adult men and women who enroll in JTPA in each quarter of a given program year.

- Individuals will be excluded from the sample frame if they are not from 22 to 64 years of age. Individuals will subsequently be excluded from the analysis samples if they have missing data on key JTPA services received (e.g., program activity, length of participation).

- Quarterly samples of JTPA participants will be selected randomly from the groups of adult men and women enrollees that are included in the sample frame to ensure that the sample is representative of JTPA participants in the state.

Comparison Group

- Comprised of samples of adult men and women who are new ES registrants in offices in the areas served by the SDAs in each quarter of a given program year.

- Individuals will be excluded from the comparison sample frame if they are not from 22 to 64 years of age, if they are not economically disadvantaged, or if they participate in JTPA.

- Quarterly samples of comparison group members will be selected from the sample frame of new ES registrants using a stratified random process to ensure that ES registrants and JTPA participants are similar on certain key characteristics (e.g., welfare recipiency, UI recipiency).

Sample Size

- Because the additional cost of increasing sample size is very small, states are encouraged to include in the analysis as many participants and comparison group members as their staffs and computer resources can handle.

- As a guideline, a total analysis sample of 12,000 cases—divided equally between adult men and women, and between participants and comparison group members (i.e., 3,000 each)—should be adequate to meet most state's analysis needs.

particular, adult men and women who enroll in JTPA in each calendar quarter of a given program year are to be sampled separately. This frame has several advantages. First, it yields a representative sample of JTPA participants in which neither short-term nor long-term participants are oversampled, one which is not sensitive to seasonal differences in the characteristics of participants or program activities. Second, because the time period for selecting each participant cohort within the program year is not too long (e.g., three months), it should be possible to select quarterly samples of comparison group members that closely match participants on the timing of the preprogram decline in earnings. This is particularly important for ensuring valid net impact results. Third, using an enrollee-based sample maximizes the amount of preprogram earnings and AFDC data available for the model. Fourth, this approach accounts for the fact that males and females have qualitatively different labor market experiences.[12]

A participant group comprised of adult men and women who enroll in JTPA in each of the four quarters of a given program year has implications for the timing of project results and the length of the postprogram observation period within an approximate two-year program analysis cycle. With such a sample, one can obtain net impact estimates for the period one year following the calendar quarter after termination only for the first quarter cohort, and only a three-month net impact estimate can be obtained for all four quarterly cohorts in approximately a two- to two-and-one-half-year analysis cycle. Of course, by obtaining additional postprogram outcome records for sample members, one could estimate longer-term impacts by extending the analysis period.

Sample exclusions. Once the sample frame is chosen, one must then determine whether certain types of individuals should be excluded. Although such exclusions reduce the representativeness of the participant sample, exceptions may be indicated for several reasons. It may be desirable to exclude cases that lack data on critical items, or the availability of extremely small samples of atypical treatment or participant groups may engender exclusion.

Most studies incorporate restrictions on participant age. Although there is no universal agreement on the age range to use, participants under age 16 have been excluded because earnings are not an appropriate outcome measure for individuals who are likely to return to school. Participants age 65 and older have been excluded because participation in employment and training programs among individuals eligible for retirement is rare, and a valid comparison group is hard to identify.

Because the net impact model focuses on adults only, we restrict the participant sample to individuals of at least age 22. Because it is difficult to obtain a valid comparison group for older participants, all individuals age 65 and older should be excluded from the participant sample frame. In addition, if the JTPA programs in the state serve very few individuals over age 55, it is desirable to exclude individuals over this age.

Individuals should also be excluded from the sample frame if they have missing data on key variables.[13] A more difficult problem arises when information is missing on the treatment provided by JTPA. For example, one cannot estimate the net impact by program activity or by length of stay for individuals with missing information on program activity or for those who have incomplete data on the start and end dates of their JTPA participation. A few problems concerning the omission of program start and end dates may arise, in part, because length of stay information is necessary for adjusting certain performance standards for JTPA Title II-A programs.   However, since there are no reporting requirements concerning program activity, some cases will contain missing or unusable program activity information.

Moreover, because the quarterly enrollee samples will be selected on an ongoing basis, one cannot know for sure how many cases must be excluded for missing data problems until after the JTPA MIS data are obtained for the sample selected. To compensate for the resulting sample reduction, an expanded participant sample should be selected initially. Individuals who are subsequently determined to have missing data on key JTPA services must be excluded from the analysis sample, provided the reason the items are missing is not systematically related to the impact of the program.[14]

A final issue concerns whether to exclude individuals who participate in JTPA for only a minimal period, such as less than a week. Some studies have included all employment and training participants in the analysis sample while others have imposed arbitrary restrictions that exclude individuals who participate in the program for some minimal period. Note, however, that more-motivated individuals leaving JTPA early because they have found jobs, excluding them from the analysis would result in a negative bias in assessing JTPA impacts. This is because those participants who would do relatively well on their own would be excluded from the participant sample, while the same types of individuals would still be included in the comparison group sample. It is also possible that short-term participants might consist of individuals who would do less well on their own than other JTPA participants. Because similar individuals would remain in the comparison group, excluding the less-advantaged individuals from the participant group would result in a relatively more-advantaged participant group and a positive bias in the estimated program impact.

Either scenario yields a selection bias that threatens the internal validity of the analysis. As such, we recommend that the sample of JTPA participants be kept as representative as possible and that cases not be excluded based on length of stay in the program. It is then possible to examine whether, and in what ways, short-term participants differ from long-term participants to better understand the nature of any selection bias. This, in turn, will help to determine the degree of confidence to attach to net impact estimates by length of program participation.

Selecting the participant sample. Once the exclusions from the participant sample frame have been determined, the next step involves selecting JTPA enrollees for inclusion in the analysis sample. In some states all enrollees in a given program year will be necessary to provide reasonably precise estimates of the average effect of JTPA programs. The sampling issue primarily arises in states that serve large numbers of JTPA participants. We outline a method below for selecting a participant sample from the sample frame described above.

As indicated in table 2.3, the quarterly samples of JTPA participants should be randomly selected from groups of adult men and women enrollees in the sample frame. However, the proportion of males and females varies considerably across SDAs. Therefore, one must first stratify the participant sample by gender before the analysis samples are selected, otherwise there may be insufficient numbers of either men or women for analysis purposes.[15] Choosing random samples in this manner also has the major advantage of providing separate representative samples of adult men and women participants, so that the results can be generalized by gender. Moreover, estimates of the net impacts of JTPA by gender and of the differential impacts by program activity separated by gender can be obtained without weighting the sample. Also, by selecting participants randomly, an analysis of program activities assigned to different types of individuals is possible.

In addition to stratifying the sample by gender, states that want to focus on specific groups, such as female welfare recipients or male high school dropouts, may also consider stratifying the participant sample and oversampling the groups of interest. In general, stratification is desirable only when the research questions of interest relate to groups that occur rarely, or that occur so frequently that their nonoccurrence is rare. Depending on the specific research questions, one could stratify on the basis of participant characteristics or by program activities (services).

For example, because of the wide variation across states and SDAs in the use of work experience programs, states interested in examining the net impact of these programs would probably need to stratify and oversample participants. Moreover, because job search assistance generally constitutes a less intensive treatment and is therefore likely to have a smaller net impact, a much larger sample of participants in JSA is needed to precisely measure the smaller expected effect. Thus, states interested in precisely measuring benefits gained from JSA participation, must sample program participants in greater numbers. States interested in stratifying the participant sample and oversampling certain groups should consult a sampling expert to understand the steps in drawing the information and the implications for conducting the analysis.

Comparison Groups

To estimate the net impact of JTPA on participants' postprogram outcomes, a method is needed to gauge the results participants would have experienced had they not participated in JTPA. The ideal research design for measuring the net impact of any social program involves the use of a classical experimental design to develop a true control group. In such a design, JTPA eligibles would be randomly assigned to either a treatment group that could receive JTPA services, or a control group that could not. With this method, the only systematic difference between the two groups is receipt of program services; any differences in program outcomes are due to JTPA. However, ethical and legal concerns can preclude the use of a randomly assigned control group. Thus, we develop an alternative method that approximates a true control group to the maximum extent possible.

A standard approach for determining the net impact of a program is to compare experiences of persons treated by the program (i.e., JTPA participants) with experiences of otherwise similar persons who are not treated by the program (the comparison group). The comparison group is used to estimate what the experiences of the participants would have been in the postprogram period had they not participated in the program. To ensure that differences between the experiences of the two groups can be attributed to the program, the comparison group must have character-istics similar to participants, particularly in terms of program eligibility. Moreover, available data must be comparably measured for the two groups.[16] One must also verify that individuals in the comparison sample in fact did not receive JTPA services.

As shown in table 2.3, the comparison group should be comprised of new Employment Service (ES) registrants in offices in the areas served by the SDAs. ES registrants have several advantages as a comparison group. First, data are available on several characteristics of interest—including those related to JTPA eligibility—that generally are compara-bly measured with JTPA MIS data.[17] Second, like JTPA participants, new ES registrants have probably experienced a recent decline in earnings.

Finally, also like JTPA participants, ES registrants are in the labor force at the time they apply for assistance. That is, they are either working or actively seeking work. It is important to ensure that participant and comparison group members are similar in their attach-ment to the labor force. Otherwise, net impact estimates can be erroneous. To ensure comparability on preprogram labor force involvement, the comparison group should be drawn from new ES registrants in the same calendar quarter that participants enroll in the JTPA.

Although ES registrants have several important advantages as comparison group sources, certain disadvantages exist. First, because of recent reductions in federal reporting requirements related to the ES, states are no longer required to submit information on the number of economically disadvantaged applicants registered and served by the ES. Because being economically disadvantaged is the major criterion for JTPA eligibility, and given the importance of ensuring that the comparison group be similar to participants on all characteristics affecting eligibility, it is important that the economically disadvantaged status variable be available for the net impact model.[18] Fortunately, many states apparently have continued to collect information on the economically disadvantaged status of ES registrants. States that no longer collect this information will have to modify the comparison group sample selection procedures, as described below.

A second potential disadvantage to using ES registrants as a comparison group concerns limitations in procedures for retaining historical data on these individuals. In the past, most states have kept automated data with individual ES records, including registrant characteristics and ES services received, for a period of three to five years. In some states, however, individual-level data are purged after approximately one year, and archived backup tapes are not very accessible. In such states, it will be difficult to draw the four quarterly samples retrospectively at one time, as comparison group members for the first quarter cohort would already have been purged. Thus, such states must either draw the comparison samples on an ongoing quarterly or semiannual basis, alter their purging practices, or retain historical data for 18 months to two years.

A final complication encountered in using ES registrants concerns the possibility that the ES registrant file may be dominated by UI claimants. In states in which ES offices are co-located with UI offices, or in which the policy is to actively monitor job search efforts of UI claimants, a large proportion of these claimants may be entered in the ES registrant file. Because of the markedly different labor market experiences of the two groups, it is inappropriate to compare the outcomes of JTPA participants with a sample that is dominated by UI recipients. Thus, it is necessary to undersample UI claimants in the ES registrant file in certain states to obtain a comparison sample with a proportion of UI claimants similar to the JTPA population.

In adjusting for this problem, note that UI claimant status, as recorded on the MIS systems for ES and JTPA, may not represent the same concept. In particular, for JTPA participants, being a UI claimant typically means that the person has filed a UI claim and has been determined to be monetarily eligible. The ES claimant status refers simply to the filing of a claim for benefits and does not imply monetary eligibility. Because of this difference, a typical JTPA "claimant" is much more likely to receive UI benefits than a typical ES claimant. To ensure that UI recipiency is comparably measured for the two groups, the UI Benefit History file must be used to determine whether the person was a UI recipient. A decision on the appropriate rate for sampling UI recipients from the ES registrant file would then be based on this measure.

Despite these potential disadvantages, we believe that ES registrants are the best comparison group source among existing state data bases. We now turn to a discussion of additional details related to drawing a sample of ES registrants.

Comparison group sample exclusions. Prior to selecting comparison groups of adult men and women ES registrants, certain cases should be excluded from the sample frame to maintain comparability with participant samples. In addition, it is desirable to exclude those individuals who are clearly not eligible for JTPA and who are likely to have an earnings potential considerably different from JTPA participants. We discuss these sample exclusion considerations below.

To maintain comparability with the JTPA participant samples, the group of ES registrants should be restricted to individuals over 21 and under 65 years of age. If it turns out that no one in the JTPA sample is over a given age (for example, age 55), then the ES registrant sample should be similarly restricted. Also, ES registrants must be excluded from the sample if they are JTPA participants during either the preprogram, program, or postprogram period. This problem, known as comparison group contamination, results in comparing outcomes of program participants with outcomes of other individuals who have participated in the program. Such a comparison yields biased net impact estimates, and results in understating the true impacts of the program. To minimize this problem, one should compare the Social Security Account (SSA) numbers of current and recent JTPA participants with the SSA numbers of ES registrants, and exclude all matches from the comparison sample.

A final issue concerns procedures to ensure the similarity of participants and comparison group members on characteristics related to JTPA eligibility. As indicated above, the primary criterion for JTPA eligibility is that the person be economically disadvantaged. Over the last few years at least 95 percent of adults in Title II-A programs have met this criterion. Moreover, of those who are not economically disadvantaged, or who were not certified to be economically disadvantaged, the act requires that they be persons facing demonstrated employment barriers. Because virtually all adult Title II-A enrollees are economically disadvantaged, the comparison group should also exclude all ES registrants who are not economically disadvantaged at application. This will help ensure that comparison groups are similar to JTPA participants on the key characteristic related to JTPA eligibility.[19]

Selecting the comparison group samples. We recommend that the selection of stratified random samples of adult male and female ES registrants have the same distributions as JTPA participants on certain key characteristics. This approach maintains maximum statistical power for the desired sample design, while ensuring that the participant and comparison samples are similar.[20]

Because of program eligibility considerations and certain practical issues concerning the relationship between the ES, UI, and welfare programs, some of the more important characteristics on which to ensure participant and comparison group comparability are economically disadvantaged status, receipt of UI benefits, and receipt of AFDC benefits. Because comparability between the two groups on economically disadvantaged status will be ensured by excluding from the sample frame for the comparison group all new ES registrants who are not disadvantaged, no additional matching is required on this characteristic.

A simple random sample would probably include relatively too few ES registrants who are AFDC recipients, and relatively too many ES registrants who are receiving UI benefits. For example, nationally, only 9 percent of adult men and 35 percent of adult women JTPA terminees in PY 84 were receiving AFDC at application, and 15 percent of adult men and 8 percent of adult women JTPA terminees in PY 84 were UI claimants at application. On the other hand, it is probable that fewer than 10 percent of all ES registrants are AFDC recipients and, in states in which the Job Service is co-located with UI, the fraction of ES registrants who are likely to be UI claimants could approach 50 percent.

To ensure similarity on these important characteristics, comparison group members should be randomly selected from the sample frames of adult men and women. Thus, for the separate samples of adult men and women, procedures would be used to make certain that the participant and comparison groups are similar on the proportions in the four cells representing combinations of AFDC and UI recipient status. Operationally, for a given total sample size of participants and comparison group members, sampling rates for each cell would be determined to match the two distributions, and then comparison group members would be selected randomly from the cells at the given sampling rates as described in the next section.

Sample Sizes for Participant and Comparison Samples

An important element of the research design is the determination of the appropriate sample sizes for participant and comparison groups. As we indicated earlier, many states will have little choice concerning participant sample size. Because the marginal cost of increasing sample size is very low, even medium to large states should generally use the largest numbers of participants and comparison group members feasible. In states with very large JTPA programs, however, samples should be drawn. This raises the issue of total sample size as well as allocation of total sample among the participant and comparison groups.

The appropriate sample size for the net impact analysis ultimately depends on the size of the impact that is important to detect for policy purposes and the level of statistical accuracy required. With larger sample sizes, one has greater assurance of detecting small differences in overall outcomes between the participant and comparison groups, as well as detecting differences for major participant subgroups or among program activities. The likelihood of detecting a given difference in outcomes also depends on the allocation of the total sample between the two groups and the unexplained variance of the outcome measure, such as earnings or AFDC grants. Thus, although the sample size requirements will differ for net impact evaluations that rely on other outcome measures, in general the more homogeneous the sample, that is, the smaller the variance of the outcome measure, the smaller the number of cases necessary to detect a given difference in outcomes at a specified level of statistical significance.

Based on a number of considerations, a total *analysis sample* of 12,000, divided equally between adult men and women, participants and comparison group members (that is, 3,000 each) should meet most states' analytical needs.[21] This sample size recommendation refers to the final analysis samples and, because some cases will be omitted for various problems described above, initial samples should be somewhat larger.

States interested in obtaining more precise net impact estimates for subgroups of adult men or women, should consider larger sample sizes as needed. In addition, states with relatively small JTPA programs (i.e., fewer than 1,000 adult enrollees per year) should be very careful in interpreting the results, as only very large impacts are likely to be judged as significantly different from zero. As a result, such states might consider pooling samples over time to increase sample size and thereby enhance the reliability of the net impact findings.

Finally, although a total analysis sample size of 12,000 should be adequate to meet most states' needs, the appropriate sample size depends on several factors and there is no size that is correct under all circumstances. States that are unsure as to the appropriate sample sizes to use in a net impact analysis should discuss their concerns with a sampling expert.

Data Collection and Processing Plan

A variety of data collection and processing tasks must be conducted in support of the overall research design. Quarterly samples of participants and comparison group members must be drawn. Preprogram, program, and postprogram data must be obtained from JTPA, ES, UI, and PA (MIS) records. These must be merged with individual participant and comparison group records. All data must be cleaned, and certain cases may need to be excluded. Analytic variables must be specified, and procedures must be implemented to deal with missing information. Finally, analysis files must be developed. This section reviews the various data collection and processing tasks that must be conducted. Readers interested in additional detail are referred to the implementation guide on net impact evaluation in the series of evaluation guides listed in the appendix.

Although none of the data collection and processing tasks outlined in this section is particularly difficult, the overall magnitude of the under-taking is considerable. Moreover, there is a major coordination issue, since many of the tasks must be performed by staff of several different agencies or subagencies. The size and breadth of the data-related tasks have two important implications.

First, there must be active and continuing cooperation and support on the part of several state agencies and subagencies. Because these agencies have different policies and priorities concerning issues such as data confidentiality, any issues of concern must be resolved at the outset. A regular data collection and processing schedule must also be established. Lack of support on the part of any of the agencies involved will considerably reduce the value of the net impact results and could render them useless.

Second, one person should be given the responsibility of managing the full range of tasks and the authority to obtain the necessary staff and computer assistance. The magnitude of the data processing tasks and the involvement of multiple agencies make these conditions particularly important for managing the data processing system. Although managing this effort is likely to be a time-consuming activity in the initial stages, once the system is in place and the individual tasks become routine, the management time required will decline considerably.

Table 2.4 shows the various data collection and processing tasks involved, from sample selection to preparing an analysis file for estimating the net impacts of JTPA. To increase clarity, we have chosen to present as separate steps some activities that could easily be combined into one step. In addition, note that there are likely to be unanticipated data-related issues and problems. To minimize such problems, it is particularly important for researchers and key data processing staff members from each of the involved agencies to meet frequently. Frequent communication helps identify idiosyncracies in the systems, which could produce noncomparable data for certain types of individuals. This communication may produce potential solutions for such problems as well.

Table 2.4
Overview of Data Collection and Processing Tasks

- Select quarterly samples of JTPA participants and obtain, merge, and process preprogram data from various sources for these participants.

- Select expanded quarterly samples of new ES registrants who are economically disadvantaged to serve as comparison group members.

  - Obtain, merge, and process preprogram data from various sources for the expanded samples.

  - Select quarterly comparison groups of adult men and women ES registrants from the expanded samples to match the distribution of participants on four cells comprising combinations of UI recipient status and AFDC recipient status.

- Merge the quarterly preprogram data files that include all of the data obtained in the above steps for the samples of participants and comparison group members.

- Create separate annual preprogram analysis files for adult men and women from the quarterly preprogram data files. This involves merging the quarterly files, editing the data, creating analytic variables, and implementing procedures to handle cases with missing data.

- Obtain program and postprogram outcome data (i.e., AFDC Grants Records and UI Wage Records) for all quarterly samples of participants and comparison group members and create appropriate outcome variables.

- Obtain data on JTPA services for participants in each of the quarterly samples and create appropriate activity or service variables.

- Create separate annual net impact analysis files for adult men and women by merging the preprogram analysis files with the outcome and treatment variables.

Selecting Participant Groups

The first data collection and processing task involves participant group selection. As noted above, samples of adult men and women JTPA Title II-A enrollees must be selected on a quarterly basis. In table 2.5, we list the steps used to select appropriate participant groups for a particular quarter. Minor modifications may be made to accommodate states that desire larger samples.

Although the procedures listed in table 2.5 could be used to select participant groups in any state, some of the steps may not be necessary in certain areas. Some states may need to alter the procedures slightly to meet their needs. For example, because the statistical precision of the net impact analysis is not very sensitive to moderate sample size differences, given the large sample sizes involved, a state that serves adult men and women in JTPA in approximately equal proportions could omit the step involving sample stratification by gender. However, because minimal effort is required to stratify the samples, and the models are to be estimated separately by gender anyway, prestratification by sex is recommended.

The fourth step in this list concerns the procedures involved in selecting the participant samples. Specifically, we suggest that a range of two-digit numbers (00-99) be specified (with the size of the range dependent on the sample size) and that the last two digits of the person's SSA number be used to select the sample, since it is a random number.

Table 2.5
Steps in Selecting the Participant Sample

1. Create a file of all persons who enrolled in JTPA Title II-A programs in any SDA during the quarter that includes SSA number, age, and sex.

2. Exclude those who are under age 22 or over age 64 (or perhaps 55 if serving older persons is rare).

3. Create separate subfiles for adult men and women.

4. Select a random sample of adult men and women from the two separate subfiles using the last two digits of the SSA number, which are random numbers. The size of the quarterly samples should reflect seasonal differences in enrollment and be such that the final analysis samples for the program year, after excluding cases for missing data, include at least 3,000 adult men and women each.

5. Obtain preprogram PA Grants Records and UI Benefit History data and create measures of AFDC recipient status and UI recipient status at enrollment.

Only individuals whose SSA final-digit numbers fall into range would be included in the sample. In addition, to account for potential seasonal differences in JTPA enrollments, one should select a fixed proportion of enrollees in each of the four quarters, using data on enrollments in the prior year to determine appropriate proportions. This is superior to selecting an equal number in each quarter.[22]

Given an estimated 5 percent sample loss due to missing data, the recommendation in step 4 translates into the initial selection of approximately 3,200 adult men and women each to yield an analysis sample of 3,000 each. States with more severe missing-data problems would have to select larger initial samples. Finally, in step 5, key preprogram data are obtained to use in developing the matched comparison groups. The data sources to be used and the specific measures to be developed are discussed below.

Selecting Comparison Groups

As described earlier, the comparison groups are developed from new ES registrants in areas served by the SDAs. Table 2.6 provides an overview of the steps that ES data processing staff could use in selecting appropriate comparison groups of adult men and women for a particular quarter of JTPA enrollees. Repeating these steps for the subsequent three quarters yields matched comparison group members for the entire program year.

The first four steps listed in table 2.6 are designed to yield a sample frame that is somewhat more comparable to JTPA participants than a sample of all ES registrants. Steps similar to these would also be used to develop matched comparison groups. These initial steps mirror the first three steps for selecting the participant samples.

The fifth step addresses the need to expand the initial sample of ES registrants to overcome the sample loss expected at steps 7 and 8. Specifically, the size of the initial samples must be large enough ultimately to yield sufficient numbers of ES registrants who have not participated in JTPA in each of four cells defined by combinations of UI recipient status and AFDC recipient status. This assures that a comparison group with a similar distribution of these characteristics can be

Table 2.6
Steps in Selecting the Comparison Group

1. Create list of all ES offices located in areas served by SDAs in the state.

2. Create a file of all persons who were new registrants in these ES offices during the quarter that includes SSA number, age, sex, and whether the person is economically disadvantaged.

3. Exclude those who are: (a) not economically disadvantaged, (b) age 21 or less, or (c) who are older than the oldest individual in the quarterly JTPA enrollee sample.

4. Create separate subfiles of adult men and women.

5. Select an expanded random sample of adult men and women new ES registrants from the two separate subfiles. As a general guideline, approximately 2,500 each of adult men and women each quarter should be sufficient.

6. Obtain available AFDC Grants Records and UI Benefit History data and create measures of AFDC recipient status and UI recipient status at enrollment for all ES registrants identified in step 5.

7. Exclude persons who are currently participating in JTPA or who participated in JTPA during the prior year based on a match of SSAs.

8. Select separate random samples of adult men and women that match the distribution of participants on the four cells comprising the combination of the comparable measures of UI recipient status and AFDC recipient status.

drawn. Because the expanded initial sample size is likely to vary considerably from state to state depending on individual characteristics, local economic conditions, and the state policies concerning the relationships among the local ES, AFDC, and UI offices, it is very difficult to provide precise guidelines. As a starting point, we recommend initial samples of 2,500 adult men and 2,500 adult women ES registrants be selected in each quarter.

The next step involves obtaining certain preprogram agency data and developing measures of AFDC recipient status and UI claimant status at enrollment. After excluding current or recent JTPA participants from the comparison group sample frame, based on matching SSA numbers (step 7), the final step involves allocating the remaining SSAs to the four recommended stratification cells comprising combinations of UI recipient status and AFDC recipient status. Sampling rates for each cell would be used to match the quarterly distribution of participants on these key characteristics.

These procedures can be used by most states, but some of the specific steps may need to be modified to meet various states' analytical needs, data limitations, or specific circumstances. For example, significant modifications to the procedures may be necessary in states that do not have all of the required data elements in their ES MIS system, in particular, data on whether an ES registrant is economically disadvantaged. Because being economically disadvantaged is the primary eligibility criterion for JTPA, it is important to develop procedures to select comparison group members who are also economically disadvantaged.[23]

In the absence of specific information on economically disadvantaged status, an alternative approach, used extensively in the literature, involves excluding individuals with very high preprogram earnings and then explicitly matching the remaining comparison group members to participants on the basis of preprogram earnings. That is, instead of excluding all persons who are not economically disadvantaged at step 2, one would first obtain UI Wage Records for a much expanded sample at step 5—perhaps up to five times as large if only 20 percent of ES registrants are economically disadvantaged. Then, exclude all persons with high earnings in the immediate preprogram period, who would certainly not be eligible for JTPA. The precise cutoff level is a matter of judgment and depends on the distribution of preprogram earnings in both samples. As a general guide, however, a cutoff level set at the maximum earnings of participants (separately for adult men and women) in the six months before enrollment or somewhat higher (for example, one standard deviation), seems reasonable.

A final issue in selecting the matched comparison groups involves the development of consistent measures of AFDC recipient status and UI recipient status at enrollment. Because ES and JTPA data bases will not generally collect comparable data on these two factors or maintain the enrollment values in the MIS, one must develop consistent measures of these items from the same data set in order to develop appropriately matched groups. The recommended approach for developing these measures is discussed below.

Obtaining Preprogram Data for Participants and Comparison Group Members
An integral step in selecting matched comparison groups for a specific program quarter of JTPA Title II-A adult men and women participants

involves the processing of several different data elements from agency records. In addition to JTPA and ES enrollment/registration data, AFDC Grants Payment Records, and UI Benefit History Records, it is important to obtain UI Wage Records for the preprogram period soon after the participant group is selected. Timely acquisition of these data is necessary because (1) some states do not retain much historical MIS data, thus, the sooner the data are obtained, the longer the preprogram period covered; and (2) some of these preprogram data items are used to develop a profile of individual characteristics that in turn is used to select comparison group members similar in these characteristics.

As a result, though the steps for obtaining data for the preprogram period for comparison group members are identical to the steps for JTPA enrollees, the timing and magnitude of the task differ considerably. The various data elements to be obtained and merged with the quarterly samples of participants and comparison group members are described below. Some problems that may be encountered in this process are also identified.

As indicated in table 2.7, the first two sets of data elements for individuals in the analysis come from JTPA application information and the ES application form. Although only a few items from these forms are used in support of the steps listed in this table (e.g., age, sex, disadvantaged status), it is useful initially to extract *all* application data from the JTPA and ES MIS systems for those individuals selected into the quarterly samples for some analysis purposes. Although only the data items that can be regarded as comparably measured for participants and comparison group members will be used for net impact analysis, all JTPA application data should be obtained in case states are interested in using the net impact design to estimate gross program impacts, or to examine whether assignment of program activities (services) to individuals depends on other measured characteristics available for participants. Moreover, all ES application data should be obtained to get a better sense of the characteristics of this group and how they are likely to differ from the characteristics of the individuals in the participant group.

Detailed preprogram UI Wage Records and AFDC grants histories are particularly important to a net impact analysis. Ideally, three years of

Table 2.7
Obtaining Application and Other Preprogram Data

1. Obtain JTPA enrollment information for each participant: age/sex used in selecting sample (see steps 1-4 of table 2.5); other items used to develop variables for net impact analysis.

2. Obtain ES registration data for each potential comparison group member. Age, sex, and economically disadvantaged status used in developing sample frame for selecting matched groups (see steps 2-4 of table 2.6); other items used to develop variables for net impact analysis.

3. Obtain preprogram monthly AFDC Grants Records for up to three years for participants remaining after step 4 of table 2.5 and for comparison group members identified in step 5 of table 2.6, and create (a) variables measuring quarterly totals and (b) an AFDC recipient-status indicator, defined as 1 if the person received AFDC grants in the month before, during, or after the month of JTPA/ES enrollment or application, and 0 otherwise.

4. Obtain UI Benefit History data for the calendar quarter before and after enrollment for each person in step 3 above, and create (a) total UI benefits received during the quarter prior to enrollment or application and (b) a UI recipient-status indicator, defined as 1 if the person received UI in the month before, during, or after the month of enrollment or application, and 0 otherwise.

5. Obtain up to 12 quarters of preprogram UI Wage Records, and create totals.

preprogram data are needed. There are generally six to 12 quarters of UI Wage Records available at any one time, with approximately a three- to six-month lag before these data are complete. As a result, to ensure that wages for the immediate preprogram quarter are complete for the analysis, it is necessary to update the data for this quarter when the postprogram earnings data are obtained.

One must also obtain AFDC grants received by participants and comparison group members. In addition to obtaining preprogram monthly grants records for up to three years to serve as important control variables in the net impact models, in order to define welfare-recipient status similarly for JTPA participants and ES registrants, data on AFDC grants received for the month after enrollment month must be obtained for all individuals. To minimize problems caused by differences in the length of time from JTPA or ES application to AFDC enrollment, or caused by differences in recording practices among different agencies, a JTPA enrollee (or ES registrant) should be defined as an AFDC recipient if the person received AFDC grants during the calendar month prior to enrollment or registration, the month of enrollment or registration, or during the month after enrollment or registration. Similarly, a UI- recipiency-status indicator can be developed using the same approach with data from the

UI Benefit History file. Although these definitions may differ from JTPA or ES definitions of welfare-recipient status or UI claimant status, they will enable one to generate a comparison group that is statistically similar to the participant group on this important characteristic.

The PA MIS systems in some states may present obstacles to obtaining accurate preprogram AFDC Grants Records for certain types of individuals. For example, in attempting to develop preprogram measures of grants paid, because of changes in household status and other factors, the data base may not allow one to verify that a specific person was in a particular assistance unit throughout the three-year period. This may be true even though it may be possible to identify up to three prior years the preprogram monthly grants paid to a particular assistance unit for a given individual currently in that unit. As a result, the preprogram AFDC history for that unit may not accurately reflect a person's welfare-recipiency status during that period. This is particularly a problem for individuals who experience a marriage or divorce, or who change living arrangements.

To obtain accurate information on the preprogram AFDC status of participants and comparison group members, such problems must be overcome to the extent possible. A potential solution available in Washington State would involve using the "Warrant Roll Extract Files," which contain a record of all AFDC payments made each month, and a list of all SSA numbers in the household that month. These files could be linked over time to determine which assistance unit the person of interest was in, and to obtain the correct preprogram data.

Preparing a Preprogram Analysis File

The next task is to develop preprogram analysis files—created from the annual preprogram data file—for adult men and women. Once the preprogram analysis files are developed, the analytic procedures described in later sections can be implemented to investigate the comparability of the JTPA enrollee and comparison groups in the preprogram period.

Before describing issues involved in conducting these tasks, one important feature of the preprogram analysis file should be noted.

Specifically, because preprogram data elements are defined in terms of their relationship to the *quarter of enrollment*, elements in the same fields on the analysis file will correspond to different *calendar periods* for individuals who enrolled in different quarterly files. For example, data elements for the immediate preprogram quarter, on the file for the enrollees in the first quarter of a program year, will correspond to the period of the second preprogram quarter for individuals who enroll one quarter later. Before comparing dollar amounts in certain preprogram quarters across files, therefore, one must adjust for overall price changes by translating all nominal dollar amounts into real terms.[25]

Editing data files. Although considerable cleaning and editing will have been performed by the respective ES and JTPA data processing staffs as part of their normal procedures, one must conduct edit checks to become familiar with different files and to check data quality. The first type of edit check compares the results of a simple frequency distribution on all variables in each of the annual files with a range of acceptable values.[26] For other data elements, such as UI wages, UI benefits, and AFDC grants, a range of acceptable values should be created that incorporates rough estimates of the maximum amounts that can be received from certain programs in the state.

Although some errors are obvious by inspection of a single data item, other errors may not be apparent except when viewed in combination with another data item. Thus, as a second edit check, limited cross tabulations must be carried out regarding certain items, to identify additional potential data quality problems. For example, cross tabulations of age by education could identify 22-year-old individuals with 19 years of education, an unlikely occurrence. It is also useful to cross tabulate earnings and AFDC grants received in the same preprogram quarters. The presence of individuals with large values for earnings and AFDC payments in a given quarter may be indicative of data errors or other problems.

Specifying analytic variables. The analytic variables specified should be comparably measured for enrollees and comparison group members. For variables derived from a common source, such as AFDC Grants Records, UI Wage Records, and UI Benefit History data, comparability should not be a problem. However, measures of personal characteristics will be obtained from both the ES and JTPA MIS, and differences in the ways in which questions are asked or answers are recorded can present major obstacles to defining comparable variable definitions. Moreover, even when questions and response codes appear to be the same, the information collected may correspond to slightly different concepts due to differences in staff instructions and training. Because of these potential problems, one must review the application forms to both the ES and the JTPA and the corresponding handbooks that provide instructions for recording answers to each question, and resolve remaining issues through discussions with appropriate agency staff.

At a minimum, one should develop comparable measures of age in terms of years, a set of dummy variables for race/ethnicity and sex, a dummy variable for veteran status, and a set of dummy variables for occupation, based on the first digit of the DOT code. In addition, one should develop limited indicators for educational background that are comparably measured. For example, the ES application form in most states generally collects education information in the form of the highest grade of schooling completed (from 0 to 19 years); whereas, the JTPA application form often records an individual's education status in terms of one of the following four codes: (1) school dropout, (2) in school (high school or less), (3) completed high school or received GED, and (4) currently attending or has attended schooling programs beyond high school. With such information, however, it should be possible to recode values from the ES application form to specify separate dummy variables for whether the person is (a) not a high school graduate (i.e., 0-11), (b) a high school graduate (i.e., 12), and (c) has completed additional schooling beyond high school (i.e., 13 or more). Every effort should be made to implement procedures such as these whenever possible to define comparable measures of variables for both groups.

Procedures for handling cases with missing data. In general, the variables used in the analysis should not suffer from major missing data problems. However, in instances where independent variables (e.g., age, education) have missing values, it is preferable to adjust for the missing variable in question rather than exclude all cases that have missing data on any relevant variable. Although there are several alternative procedures that one can use to create substitute values for missing data, the gains from using an elaborate system to fix relatively minor problems is not likely to be worthwhile.[27]

As a result, the mean values of the independent variables—calculated separately for participants and comparison group members, and, of course, separately for adult men and women—should be used for cases with missing data. Thus, as part of the initial analysis task, one should calculate the means of all independent variables separately for participants and comparison group members on the analysis files, and prepare recode statements that set the value of a variable equal to the appropriate mean whenever it is missing. In addition, if differences in the independent variables among the quarterly samples are likely to occur, one should consider using means calculated separately by quarter of enrollment or registration to capture trends in these variables over time. The treatment of missing data in the program participation or service variables is discussed below.

Obtaining and processing during-program and postprogram outcome data. Postenrollment UI Wage Records and AFDC Grants Records must also be obtained for both the participant and comparison groups. Then, appropriate variables must be specified and merged onto the preprogram analysis file. In addition, UI Wage Records must be obtained for the immediate preprogram quarter for all participants and comparison group members to correct for potential measurement error problems due to obtaining data "too early" for that period.

No problems are anticipated in collecting quarterly UI Wage Records in the postenrollment period. The necessary information can generally be obtained from a single request made at the very end of the data collection process. In states that retain only six quarters of UI Wage Records, an intermediate request must be made no later than 18 months after the month in which the first quarter of individuals were enrolled, to ensure that the entire history can be obtained for early enrollees.

With regard to collecting monthly AFDC Grants Records during the program and postprogram periods, it may be preferable to obtain such information on an ongoing basis, rather than only once at the end of the data collection process. In working with PA data systems in which the Recipient History File does not enable one to identify whether a person is in the particular assistance unit throughout the period of interest, it is preferable to obtain the information on an ongoing basis each month to minimize measurement error. Obtaining information on this basis requires that for each of the subsequent months the SSA numbers of participants and comparison group members must be compared with the list of SSA numbers in assistance units that received AFDC payments during the month. The actual values of monthly grants would be included for the SSA numbers that matched, and zeros would be included for those SSA numbers that did not match. Quarterly and annual values would then be calculated as the sum of monthly values.

Note that by stopping the collection of these agency data at a single point, one will obtain eight quarters of UI Wage Records and AFDC Grants Records for participants and comparison group members who enrolled or registered during the first quarter of a program year, seven quarters of data for those who enrolled or registered during the second quarter, six quarters of data for those who enrolled or registered in the third quarter, and five quarters of data for those who enrolled or registered during the last quarter of the program year. Each set of quarterly earnings and AFDC grants data would include one quarter for the actual quarter of enrollment or registration, two subsequent quarters of data that are likely to include program earnings for some participants, and varying postprogram quarters of earnings records. Because of the usefulness of having rectangular analysis files, a common number of postenrollment quarterly values should be created for all individuals onhe file, and missing data codes (e.g., -9s) placed in postprogram quarters for later enrollees for whom data are not yet available. One could, of course, subsequently obtain actual values for these quarters and replace the missing data codes.

Obtaining and Processing JTPA MIS Data

Because individuals can participate in multiple activities, most state JTPA data systems will have a program activity file in which a given individual may have multiple records. To specify consistent analytic variables, program activity records must be extracted for all SSAs in the four quarterly samples of JTPA enrollees. Depending on the archiving procedures followed in a given state, it may be possible for these data to be obtained from a single request made at the end of the data collection process, and hopefully after all or almost all individuals have terminated from JTPA.

After the program activity records are obtained, the next step involves specification of variables to represent services received by JTPA participants. In general, it should be possible to develop relatively detailed indicators of the services received from JTPA, related to the type of occupation and length of training, and whether the person completed training. These variables are described in the conceptual framework section. Once these variables are specified, they should be merged with the preprogram analysis files for participants, and zeros must be entered for comparison group members for all of these variables.

If participants have missing data on key JTPA treatment variables, they should be excluded from the analysis samples, provided the reason the items are missing appears to be random (i.e., not systematically related to the likely net impact of the program). To make this determination, one must compare the characteristics of participants who have missing data on the variables (e.g., length of participation) with the characteristics of participants who have data on the variables. For example, one should compare the age, race, and education of individuals in the two groups of participants to determine if there are major differences.

Moreover, if in the process of collecting data on program experiences one also obtained information on placement status at termination, it is useful to compare JTPA enrollees on their placement status at termination to judge whether having missing data is systematically related to the impact of the program. If enrollees with missing data on JTPA experiences are equally likely to be placed in jobs following the program as enrollees with complete data, this would provide additional confidence that the validity of the analysis will not be compromised by excluding such individuals.

Once the JTPA analytic variables have been developed and decisions made on the treatment of missing data, the final task involves merging these variables and the during-program and postprogram outcome variables to the preprogram analysis files for each individual by SSA number. This results in the creation of net impact analysis files for adult men and women. These files will support all of the analysis tasks described in the next section.

Data Analysis Plan

A data analysis plan must be developed to examine the adequacy of the comparison groups selected, and to use the comparison groups to estimate the net impacts of the program on the outcome measures specified in the conceptual framework. This section presents an overall strategy for obtaining valid estimates of the net impacts of JTPA programs on the postprogram earnings and welfare dependency of adult men and women enrollees.

Before describing the details of the plan, we want to emphasize that the recommended approaches should be quite accessible to all states interested in conducting net impact analysis of JTPA or of other social programs. For example, all of the analysis techniques to be used are contained in standard statistical software packages—such as SAS and SPSS—that should be readily available and familiar to state-level analysts. In addition, after some initial data processing on a mainframe computer, it may be possible to download the analysis files to hard disks that can be accessed by minicomputers. This will minimize the computer resources required to conduct the analysis.

An overview of key elements of the data analysis plan discussed below is shown in table 2.8. We first describe an analysis strategy for examining the adequacy of the comparison groups selected in order to get a better understanding of the direction and magnitude of potential selection bias. We then describe a statistical model that can be used to estimate the average net impacts of JTPA and the impacts for important subgroups. The section concludes with a discussion of potential adjustments for certain data and design deficiencies.

Examining the Adequacy of the Comparison Groups:
Obtaining Evidence on Selection Bias

If the samples of JTPA participants and ES registrants developed through the steps described in the previous sections are similar on both measured (e.g., age, race, education) and unmeasured (e.g., attitude toward work, motivation) characteristics, then valid inferences about the impacts of JTPA programs can be drawn from such comparisons. However, whether an individual participates in a social program is likely to depend on both individual and agency decisions.

Table 2.8
Overview of the Data Analysis Plan

• Examine the adequacy of comparison groups using analysis techniques such as differences in means, differences in distributions, and multiple regression analysis. The adequacy of the comparison groups will be judged in terms of three criteria:

1. Similarity of participant and comparison groups on measured characteristics (e.g., age, race, education).

2. Similarity of participant and comparison groups on preprogram earnings and AFDC grants.

3. Similarity of the relationships between preprogram earnings (and AFDC grants) and measured characteristics for participants and comparison group members.

• Estimate average net impacts of JTPA for adult men and women using an autoregressive model. Net impacts will be estimated for four postprogram outcome measures—earnings, whether employed, AFDC grants, and whether an AFDC recipient—in each of three different postprogram periods: three months, six months, and 12 months.

• Estimate net impacts of JTPA on the various outcome measures for adult men and women and key subgroups using autoregressive models. In addition to sex, the subgroups of interest include:

1. Participant characteristics such as race or ethnicity, age, education, and welfare recipient status for women.

2. Program activities such as CT, OJT, JSA, and all other activities.

3. Program length of stay.

• Adjust net impact estimates to the extent possible for data and design deficiencies:

1. Contamination of the comparison groups.

2. Uncovered earnings.

3. Selection bias.

For example, JTPA participants must decide to apply to the program, meet certain legislated eligibility criteria, be selected by the agency for program participation and assigned a program activity, and decide to accept that assignment and enroll in the program. Although ES registrants do not have to meet any formal eligibility criteria, certain individuals, such as those receiving benefits from government programs such as UI, are required to register with the ES, and some offices follow selective registration policies. Furthermore, whether an ES registrant receives ES services depends on several factors, including the availability of suitable job openings, and the person's qualifications and persistence. Because of these various selection processes, it is unlikely that the resulting samples of JTPA enrollees and ES registrants who do not receive services are truly equivalent on both measured and unmeasured characteristics. This is the issue of *selection bias,* which is highly likely to be present in evaluations of other social programs as well.

All nonexperimental approaches to evaluating the net impact of a social program will probably contain a certain amount of bias. That is, the formal conditions required to ensure unbiased estimates of program impacts are not likely to be met, even if one had extensive data on the characteristics of program enrollees and comparison group members. This is true for the proposed research design. As a practical matter, therefore, one should not focus on the fact that the two groups are not identical, but identify the major dimensions on which the groups differ and determine the extent to which the net impact estimates are likely to be sensitive to those differences.

As indicated in table 2.8, three different criteria can be used to judge the adequacy of the comparison groups selected:
1. Similarity of the JTPA enrollee and comparison groups on measured individual characteristics.
2. Similarity of the JTPA enrollee and comparison groups on preprogram earnings and AFDC grants.
3. Similarity of the relationships between preprogram earnings (and preprogram AFDC grants) and the measured individual characteristics of JTPA enrollees and comparison group members.

Although these are the traditional criteria for judging the adequacy of nonexperimentally derived comparison groups, they are necessary, but insufficient, conditions for overcoming selection bias. Even if the comparison groups selected generally meet these criteria, this should not be interpreted as definitive evidence of an absence of selection bias. With this caution in mind, some analyses are outlined below that can be performed for each of the quarterly samples, and for the annual sample as a whole, to see whether these criteria are met. If they are not met, the analysis identifies the types and extent of differences between the groups. These factors must then be kept in mind when interpreting net impact results.

The first criterion (Criterion 1) is the similarity of the two groups on measured characteristics at enrollment or registration. It is particularly important to compare the participant and comparison groups on available measured characteristics known to affect earnings and AFDC grants. For example, it is particularly useful to determine to what extent the two groups differ on age, race, education, occupation, and handicapped status, and other relevant personal characteristics that are comparably measured for both groups.

Using standard software packages, one would compare the means and the distributions of these measured characteristics for participants and comparison group members (separately for adult men and women) in each of the four quarterly samples and in the overall program year sample.[28] Because the output from standard software analysis packages normally includes the results of *t-tests* and *Chi-square* tests for formally testing the equivalence of the means and distributions of variables in two samples, it is straightforward to compare the similarity of the participant and comparison groups on all measured characteristics.

Similar analyses should be conducted across JTPA program activities. That is, one should not only compare the characteristics of participants to the characteristics of comparison group members, but also compare the characteristics of participants with respect to program activities received, such as CT, OJT, and JSA. This will indicate any additional selection bias arising in estimating net impacts by separate program activity. For example, if one determined that more motivated or energetic individuals were being sent to OJT, the net impacts of this program activity would be somewhat inflated because of this assignment process. On the other hand, if there were relatively few differences in measured characteristics by program activity, this evidence would provide some confidence that no additional selection biases would be introduced in deriving estimates of the net impacts by program activity.

The second criterion (Criterion 2) to judge the adequacy of the comparison groups is the similarity of the key outcome measures of participants and comparison group members in the preprogram period. This involves a test of whether a significant difference exists in the preprogram earnings and AFDC grants of the two groups, controlling for measured characteristics. Such a test provides valuable evidence on whether the two are comparable on the basis of the lagged dependent variables or, in other words, whether there are differences in the outcome variables between the groups in the preprogram period that are due to unmeasured characteristics.

If there are any differences in adjusted preprogram earnings or AFDC grants between the two groups, then this analysis will also provide evidence as to the direction and magnitude of the selection bias. For example, the extent to which JTPA participants have larger (smaller) adjusted preprogram earnings than ES registrants provides some indication as to whether they are more (less) advantaged on the basis of unmeasured characteristics. Moreover, the size of the estimated difference is a reasonable estimate of the amount by which the net program impacts could be overstated (understated) if the difference persisted in the postprogram period.

To formally test for differences in the preprogram earnings and AFDC grants of participants and comparison group members, one would estimate ordinary least squares regression equations (separately for adult men and women) with preprogram earnings and AFDC grants as dependent variables. Multiple regression is a technique that estimates the independent influence of each characteristic on a particular dependent variable, controlling for the influence of all other characteristics in the equation. For example, differences in earnings among individuals may result from differences in education and other personal characteristics, such as age or race, as well as differences in local unemployment conditions. The regression technique controls for the influence on earnings of local unemployment conditions and other personal characteristics, and estimates the independent influence of all these factors as well as program activities on earnings. All standard software analysis packages include multiple regression programs capable of handling the analysis tasks described in this section.

For a given set of outcome measures, the principal task in specifying the regression equations to be estimated is making decisions about which variables to include in a given model. Because the objective of the analysis is to identify whether there are significant differences in the preprogram earnings and AFDC grants of the two groups after controlling for measured characteristics, there are several guidelines that can be used in making decisions concerning the independent variables to be included in the models.

First, include in the model all personal characteristics of the individuals at enrollment or registration who were examined as part of the analysis conducted for Criterion 1 above, such as age, race, education, occupation, and handicapped status. An exception will be those who must be omitted because too few cases exhibit that characteristic, or those who must serve as the "left-out category." For example, it is likely that in many states there will be too few of certain minorities (e.g., Native Americans) to include them as separate variables in the model. As a result, one may need to collapse the five race or ethnicity group variables into three variables, i.e., dummy variables for white, black, and other race or ethnicity status.

Note also that in estimating the regression model, one of the race dummies must be omitted to serve as the "left-out category" (reference category) for comparison purposes. If the dummy variable for white status is omitted from the equation, then the coefficients of the other two dummy variables would represent the effect of being in that particular group, relative to being white, on the dependent variable. For every set of dummy variables included in the regression model to capture the effects of a certain characteristic, one of the variables must be omitted to serve as the reference category for comparison purposes. Because the effects of the included variables are all measured *relative* to the left-out category, the results have the identical interpretation no matter which variable is chosen to serve as the omitted category.

Second, it is important to include previous preprogram measures of quarterly earnings and AFDC grants variables in the model. That is, in examining the comparability of earnings in the immediate preprogram quarter, one should include quarterly earnings and AFDC grants from the second through the twelfth preprogram quarters, given data availability. If, however, one were examining the comparability of earnings and AFDC grants in the immediate preprogram year, then the second, third, and fourth preprogram quarterly earnings and AFDC grants variables would have to be omitted from the regression equation. Such variables are, by definition, part of the dependent variable in this case and, as such, cannot independently affect its value.

Third, variables that are "jointly determined" with preprogram earnings and AFDC should be excluded from the model. Specifically, exclude the dummy variables for AFDC recipient status, UI recipient status, and UI benefit payments in the immediate preprogram quarter from all regression equations estimated over a preprogram period. These variables are essentially other measures of low-income status in the same period and cannot independently affect earnings and AFDC grants in the same period.

A final guideline is to define the variables used according to the appropriate time period. For example, if the dependent variable is earnings or AFDC grants in the immediate preprogram quarter (year), then the unemployment rate in the local area should similarly be defined as the rate for the immediate preprogram quarter (year).

By following these guidelines, one can identify a set of independent variables from those specified, using the procedures described in the data processing section of this chapter. These variables should be included in both the preprogram earnings and preprogram AFDC grants equations. The independent variables to include in a regression model to examine the similarity of participants and comparison group members on earnings (and AFDC grants) in the immediate preprogram quarter are listed in table 2.9. Note that the interactions between the white and the age and education variables are optional and need not be included in the final model. However, they are included in this list to emphasize the importance of controlling for all measured differences between participants and comparison group members.

For each preprogram period of interest, one would estimate four regression equations that included this set of independent variables. That is, separate models would be estimated for adult men and women and for both of the key outcome measures, earnings and AFDC grants. The test for differences in earnings and AFDC grants between the participant and comparison groups in the immediate preprogram quarter would be based on a *t-test* of the estimated coefficient of the JTPA participant dummy variable. On a more intuitive level, because participation in JTPA during a given period cannot have an effect on earnings or AFDC grants in previous time periods, the coefficient of the JTPA dummy variable in each of the regression models described above should not be statistically significant (i.e., should not be significantly different from zero). The extent to which the estimated coefficients are statistically significant and deviate from zero provides evidence on the direction and magnitude of the likely selection bias.

With earnings in the preprogram period as the dependent variable, statistically significant negative (positive) coefficients on the JTPA dummy would indicate that participants were less (more) advantaged than comparison group members in that period on unmeasured characteristics. If this persisted through the postprogram period it would probably result in understating (overstating) the net impact of JTPA on earnings. Thus, if this analysis indicated that after adjusting for differences in measured characteristics the preprogram earnings of JTPA participants were $200 less (more) than the earnings of the comparison group, then one might consider adding (subtracting) $200 to (from) the net impact estimate to adjust for differences in unmeasured characteristics. Note, however, that because preprogram earnings and AFDC grants will be included as independent variables in the net impact model, the extent of this bias should be less in the postprogram period. As such, adjusting the net impact estimate for the total difference in preprogram earnings is likely to overcompensate for the bias due to differences in unmeasured characteristics.

In analyzing the preprogram similarity of earnings and AFDC grants between the two groups, one can examine several different time periods. For the most part, one should be primarily interested in examining the immediate preprogram quarter or year and separate regression equations, like the one described above, could be estimated for both periods.[29] In addition, one could also estimate a regression equation like the one described above for each preprogram quarter and derive a set of estimated coefficients of the JTPA participant dummy. To the extent that including additional lagged values of earnings and AFDC grants in the equation serves to reduce the differences between the two groups, the coefficients of the JTPA dummy variable should be largest (in absolute value) in the early preprogram periods and tend toward zero as the preprogram outcome is measured closer to the date of enrollment.

The third criterion (Criterion 3) used to judge the adequacy of the comparison groups is the similarity of the relationships between earnings (and AFDC grants) and individual characteristics for JTPA participants and comparison group members in the preprogram period. This criterion, which is considerably stricter than the previous two, is quite important because, if the same model is generating earnings (or AFDC grants) in the two groups, it suggests that program impacts will be less sensitive to other potential statistical problems. This would provide additional confidence in our ability to obtain unbiased estimates of program impacts.

To test for differences in the preprogram earnings (or AFDC grants) equations of participants and comparison group members, one would estimate a modified version of the regression equation described above to provide information on Criterion 2. Specifically, one would estimate an equation that included all of the explanatory variables listed above, *plus* each of the variables (except the JTPA participation dummy variable) multiplied by the JTPA participation dummy variable. The formal test of whether the earnings and AFDC grants equations in the preprogram period are different for participants and comparison group members is sometimes referred to as a *Chow test* and is based on an *F-test* of the hypothesis that the coefficients of the interaction terms (i.e., the JTPA participant dummy multiplied by each of the other variables in the model) are all zero.[30]

The three criteria and related analyses described provide considerable information regarding the adequacy of the comparison groups in the preprogram period and the probable biases that must be dealt with. It should be emphasized again that these criteria are relatively strict tests of the comparability of the two groups, and one should not generally expect nonexperimentally derived comparison groups to meet all of them. If the conditions are generally satisfied, then the chances of obtaining unbiased program net impact estimates using standard statistical models are improved. If the criteria are strongly rejected (e.g., F-*statistics* of 10 or 20 when approximately 1.5 is sufficient for rejection), then one should be very cautious in proceeding to estimate net impacts with these comparison groups. Instead, one should first double-check to be sure that the data processing and analysis guidelines described earlier were followed. If the criteria are still strongly rejected, one should then consider obtaining assistance from a researcher familiar with these issues. If, as is most likely, the results are somewhere in between (i.e., preprogram differences between the two groups that are sometimes statistically significant, but not exceptionally large), then one will need to understand the implications of these differences for interpreting and adjusting the net impacts results.

Estimating the Average Net Impacts of JTPA Programs

The four general postprogram outcome measures for the JTPA evaluation are earnings, whether employed, AFDC grants, and whether an AFDC recipient. We will discuss the specific postprogram periods for which these outcomes will be measured for different samples of enrollees, and describe the regression model to estimate average net impacts. A subsequent section will describe how to obtain separate estimates of net impacts for major demographic groups, by program activity and by length of program participation.

Choice of Postprogram Periods and
Implications for Potential Additional Sample Exclusions

The choice of the postprogram periods to be examined depends on the distribution of length of stay in JTPA. For example, if no individuals participated in JTPA longer than six months, then for a given quarterly sample of enrollees (e.g., those who enrolled during first quarter of PY 1985), all such individuals would have terminated from the program by the end of the third quarter of PY 1985. As such, earnings and AFDC grants received during the fourth quarter of PY 1985 would be the outcome measures for the first complete postprogram quarter for these enrollees. If, however, there is considerable diversity in program length of stay and some individuals remain in the program much longer, one would have to decide whether to postpone the analysis and wait until all cases have terminated, or exclude such cases from the analysis samples. Although it is generally not desirable to restrict the participant sample to those who have terminated from JTPA by a particular date (because terminees could differ systematically from nonterminees, which could result in additional selection biases), in most cases it will simply not be possible to wait for all participants to terminate from the program and still provide timely net impact results.

To provide timely results, it may be necessary for states to choose a cutoff date that defines the program period. Any participants who are in the program after that point would be excluded from the analysis.[31] In general, we expect that defining the cutoff date to be six months after the end of the enrollment period for each quarterly sample (e.g., March 31, 1986, for those who enrolled in JTPA during the first quarter of PY 1985) should be adequate to meet most states' needs. This allows a length of stay that is no less than six months for any individual and up to nine months for individuals who enrolled very early in a particular quarter. We expect that such cutoff dates, applied uniformly to participants in all four quarters of the program year, would result in excluding no more than 10 percent of the participant sample in most states. This is unlikely to significantly bias the average net impacts of JTPA, and should not significantly reduce the precision of the estimated impacts.[32]

States that operate JTPA programs that tend to have very long program lengths of stay should consider extending the cutoff date to estimate earnings impacts for the same number of postprogram quarters. On the other hand, in states where JTPA services are relatively brief on average, it may be possible to define a cutoff date that allows for a shorter program period and, as a result, net impacts can be estimated over a longer program period without delaying the analysis.

As described in the conceptual framework, we recommend that the net impacts of JTPA for adult men and women be estimated on each of the four general outcome measures for a three-month, six-month, and 12-month postprogram period. Based on the data collection plan and the strategy to be used to exclude long-term participants (if necessary), the research design enables one to estimate the net impacts of JTPA on these four measures over a three-month postprogram period for JTPA enrollees from all four quarterly samples within approximately a two-year program analysis cycle. It enables one to provide net impact estimates on these outcomes measured over a six-month postprogram period for the first three quarterly enrollment samples. The net impacts for a 12-month postprogram period can only be estimated for participants who enrolled in the first quarter of the program year.[33] Because of the importance of longer-term impacts in making judgments concerning the effectiveness of employment and training programs, some states might consider collecting additional quarters of postprogram information for all individuals for subsequent analysis, and particularly for those who enrolled in the last three quarters of the program year.

Autoregressive net impact models. To estimate the net impacts of JTPA for adult men and women, we recommend that an autoregressive model be used. Using this approach, ordinary least squares regression equations would be estimated for each of the 12 outcome variables, that is, four outcome measures in each of three different postprogram periods, separately for adult men and women. The autoregressive approach is so named because preprogram values of the outcome measures—quarterly earnings and AFDC grants—are also included as independent variables. This approach has the primary advantage of controlling for any differences in measured characteristics between the two groups that remain after the matched comparison groups are selected, which helps to minimize the problem of selection bias.

To control for potential differences in the characteristics of participants and comparison group members to the extent possible, it is recommended that the net impact regression model be a slightly expanded version of the models used to determine whether the comparison groups meet the preprogram comparability Criteria 2 and 3. The only changes in the independent variables to be included in the basic net impact model, as compared to the variables included in the preprogram models discussed above and listed in table 2.9, are as follows:

Table 2.9
Sample Independent Variables to Include in Model to
Examine Adequacy of Comparison Groups

Demographic and Personal Characteristics

Age
Age squared
Black dummy
Other non-white dummy
High-school graduate dummy
Post high-school education dummy
(Age) x (white dummy)—optional
(Age squared) x (white dummy)—optional
(High-school graduate dummy) x (white dummy)—optional
(Post high-school education dummy) x (white dummy)—optional
Veteran dummy—for men only
Handicapped dummy—if measured comparably for both groups

Recent Employment Experiences

Set of eight one-digit DOT dummies: for example, allowing professionals to be the left-out category, the eight occupation dummies would correspond to clerical and sales; service; agricultural, fishery, and forestry; processing; machine trades; benchwork; structural work; and miscellaneous

Preprogram quarterly earnings—separate variables for preprogram quarters two through 12, data permitting

Preprogram quarterly AFDC grants—separate variables for preprogram quarters two through 12, data permitting

Labor Market Data

Unemployment rate during the immediate preprogram quarter
Urban location dummy

Program Participation Variables

JTPA participant dummy (or alternatively, separate dummy variables for program activities)

Other Variables

Set of dummies for the quarter of enrollment or registration: for instance, allowing the first quarter to serve as the left-out category, dummy variables for whether participants (comparison group members) enrolled (registered) in quarter two, three, or four

1. Quarterly earnings and AFDC grants in the immediate preprogram quarter should be included in the net impact model.
2. The net impact model should also include the UI recipient dummy variable, UI benefits earned in the immediate preprogram quarter, and the AFDC recipient dummy variable.
3. The unemployment rate should be defined according to the postprogram period for which the model is being estimated.

Thus, following these guidelines, one can estimate autoregressive models separately for adult men and women, and the estimated coefficient of the JTPA participant dummy variable represents the average net impact of JTPA on earnings and AFDC grants for the three postprogram periods of interest (i.e., three, six, and 12 months). For dependent variables expressed in dollar terms—earnings and AFDC grants—the coefficient of the JTPA participant dummy variable can be interpreted as the average *dollar* impact on a given outcome measure. Dividing the estimated dollar impact by the mean earnings or AFDC grants of comparison group members results in an estimate of the percentage change in earnings or AFDC grants due to JTPA.

For dummy dependent variables (i.e., whether employed in a particular period, or whether receiving AFDC grants during a particular period), the autoregressive net impact model is equivalent to a linear probability model. The model essentially estimates the effects of various factors on the probability of a certain event occurring, for example, having positive earnings in a given postprogram period. As such, the estimated coefficient of the JTPA participant dummy variable can be interpreted as the average *percentage point change* in the probability of working or receiving AFDC grants due to JTPA. By dividing the estimated percentage point change by the mean proportion of comparison group members, one can obtain an estimate of the percentage change in the probability of working (or receiving AFDC) due to JTPA.

Obtaining Net Impact Estimates for Various Subgroups
The models described above focus on providing overall estimates of the net impacts of JTPA for adult men and women. Determining whether JTPA effectiveness varies by the type of program activity and by

personal characteristics has important policy and planning implications.[34] Because JTPA program activities and participant characteristics can change considerably over time, knowledge of how program net impacts vary among them would help interpret time trends in JTPA's impacts. Furthermore, information on which program activities and services work best for given types of participants can provide valuable information for targeting future employment and training programs. Although the approach to estimating net impacts for different groups is formally identical, whether the group refers to the type of program activity or to individual characteristics, additional selection bias is likely to arise. In the next section we describe how to modify the autoregressive earnings and AFDC grants models to estimate the net impacts of JTPA for various groups, and review the additional biases that one must be aware of in interpreting the results.

Net impacts by participant characteristics. In general, specific group effects are estimated by including in the regression equation an interaction term that represents the product of the dummy variable for JTPA participation with the variable for the group of interest. Suppose one is interested in testing whether the net impact varies by a characteristic that is represented by the three dummy variables Z_1, Z_2, and Z_3. One might think of the three variables as representing race or ethnicity categories (white, black, other).[35] Then, the only modification required to the autoregressive model described above involves replacing the JTPA participation dummy variable with three variables that each involves the JTPA dummy variable multiplied by one of the three variables representing the particular group (i.e., JTPA x Z_1, JTPA x Z_2, JTPA x Z_3). The coefficients of these three variables are estimates of the net impact for the three groups of interest.[36]

In attempting to disaggregate JTPA net impacts across groups, it is important that the group characteristics also be included in the model as control variables to account for differences in the general level of earnings (or AFDC grants) across these groups. In our illustration, the three Z_i variables must be in the model separately so that the estimated net impact coefficients only capture outcome differences due to JTPA across these groups and do not also capture the average differences in outcomes due to the Z_i's themselves. In addition, it is also important that the groups be mutually exclusive and exhaustive.

For example, suppose the Z_i's refer to various participant age categories: 22-34, 35-54, and 55-64. Then two types of problems can arise in estimating the net impacts for these age groups:

1. Recoding errors can occur in creating the variables (e.g., ranges of 22-44, 35-54, 55-64) that result in overlapping the age ranges so that individuals age 35-44 would appear in both of the first two groups (i.e., the groups are not mutually exclusive).

2. Individuals in the sample may not fall into any of the three age categories created (i.e., the groups are not exhaustive).

This could occur if some participants were younger than 22, older than 64, or if there were a gap in the age ranges used. If the groups are not exhaustive, then all of the participant observations that do not fall into one of the categories would be treated as comparison group members, which would result in biased estimates of the net impacts of JTPA for the other groups.

At a minimum, we recommend that states examine differential impacts by race, education, age, UI claimant status, AFDC recipient status, and preprogram earnings for those individuals who had preprogram earnings. Because individuals' preprogram characteristics cannot be affected by JTPA, no additional selectivity bias is introduced in disaggregating JTPA net impacts by demographic groups.[37] However, this is not likely to be the case when examining whether JTPA effectiveness varies by program activity.

Net impacts by program activity or service. In principle, to probe beneath the average net impacts of JTPA and provide information on the program activities that contributed to the average effects, one would perform an identical interaction analysis to the one described previously, using Z_1, Z_2, Z_3 and Z_4 to represent classroom training, on-the-job training, job search assistance, and other program assistance respectively. Then, if c_i represents the estimated coefficient for the interaction term between the JTPA dummy and Z_i, then c_1 is the estimate of the average net impact for CT, c_2 would represent the estimated net impact for OJT, c_3 would represent the estimated net impact for JSA, and c_4

would represent the estimated net impact for other JTPA activities. There is, however, potential selection bias that can threaten the internal validity of the by-program activity net impact analysis.

Such bias relates to the nonrandom assignment of JTPA participants to program activities. As described above, the assignment of program activity is likely to be based on the agency's perception of an individual's needs and abilities. To the extent that this assignment process is based solely on the measured characteristics of participants, such as age, race, sex, education, and preprogram earnings, this will not bias the net impacts by program activity, as these characteristics will be included in the net impact model. But if the assignment of program activities is based on unmeasured characteristics, such as motivation and ability, and those unmeasured characteristics also affect earnings, then selection bias results. Thus, one must be very careful in interpreting net impacts by program activity.

Obtaining Net Impact Estimates by Program Length of Stay

To investigate whether the net impacts of JTPA vary by length of stay in the program, one would estimate an autoregressive model like those described earlier, with the overall program participation dummy variable replaced by a JTPA variable that measures length of program stay in terms of total weeks or, more appropriately, total hours. If the effects of length of stay on the outcomes are approximately linear, a convenient specification involves a model with a JTPA participation dummy and the participation dummy interacted (i.e., multiplied) with total weeks (total hours) in the program minus average number of weeks (total hours) in the program. In this specification, the coefficient of the JTPA dummy represents the estimated impact of JTPA at the average length of stay (average total hours), and the coefficient of the interaction term is an estimate of the dollar impact of an additional week (hour) of program participation.

Although the autoregressive earnings model controls for differences in measured characteristics between short- and long-term participants, it is likely that some differences in unmeasured characteristics remain. Individuals who leave the program early may be less motivated or, alternatively, may have found employment on their own. On the other hand, individuals who stay in the program a long time may do so because they have fewer employment opportunities. Length of stay is also likely to depend on the type of program activity and SDA characteristics. Because of these additional selection bias problems, caution is needed in asserting a causal relationship between services and program impacts by length of stay.

Adjustments for Potential Data and Design Deficiencies

In addition to the problem of potential selection bias, there are some deficiencies in the UI earnings, JTPA, and ES data that may affect results. UI Wage Records are incomplete. They do not reflect earnings from jobs that are not in covered employment, or earnings from jobs located across the border in other states. The JTPA and ES data are deficient because there is inadequate information on whether ES registrants participated in JTPA, which may result in a contaminated comparison group. In this section, we briefly discuss the likely extent to which the basic impact estimates will be affected by these data and design deficiencies and the types of adjustments that may be necessary.

In the earlier data processing discussion, procedures were outlined that could reliably exclude those individuals from the comparison group who were currently participating in JTPA, who had participated in JTPA in the previous year, or who participated during the postprogram periods being examined. If it is not possible to implement these procedures, the comparison group will be contaminated to a certain extent. Such contamination would lead to an underestimate of the net impacts of JTPA, since it would dilute the treatment, as some comparison group members would have also received JTPA activities and services.

Although the ES is one source of applicants for the JTPA program, and one might expect that contamination could be high, existing data indicate otherwise. For example, based on data for the State of Washington for PY 1985, only 0.1 percent of all ES registrants active during the year were recorded as having enrolled in JTPA programs. Only 0.3 percent of those who were economically disadvantaged enrolled in JTPA. Although the figures are somewhat higher for enrollment in any training activity (e.g.,

JTPA, Job Corps, WIN, other)—1.0 percent for all applicants and 3.1 percent for those economically disadvantaged—even these participation rates are small enough to be safely ignored.

In states that have higher probabilities of economically disadvantaged ES registrants enrolling in JTPA, and in which it is impossible to exclude those who participate in JTPA from the comparison group before conducting the net impact analysis, it may be necessary to make some aggregate adjustment to the net impact estimates. Specifically, if p (q) is an estimate of the proportion of the adult men (women) in the comparison group participating in JTPA during the period of enrollment through the postprogram period (i.e., from one to two years), the estimated average program net impacts for adult men (women) should be multiplied by $1/(1-p)$ (or $1/(1-q)$) to adjust for this problem.

The second major data deficiency is that UI Wage Records do not include jobs in uncovered employment, or earnings from jobs in other states. However, the omission of earnings due to these problems biases the estimated impact of JTPA only if program participation causally affects the probability of working in uncovered employment or the likelihood of working in another state. Given the focus of JTPA on employment in the private sector, this should be less of a problem for the state-level net impact model. Also, in order to create a meaningful adjustment, one would need information on interview-reported earnings and UI earnings for both groups in the postprogram period, which will not generally be available. Thus, the best one can do is acknowledge the potential problem and indicate that the net impact estimates are based on the reasonable assumption that JTPA does not affect the probability of working in uncovered employment or working across the border in other states.

Cost Analysis and Benefit-Cost Comparisons

The estimated net impacts of JTPA program activities on participants' postprogram labor market experiences can be used to estimate the benefits of the JTPA for program participants and, under certain assumptions, the benefits of the JTPA to society as a whole. To determine whether the JTPA is an effective use of public resources, however, one must assess the costs of providing JTPA activities and compare the costs to the benefits of the program. It is a serious conceptual error to assess a social program on the basis of overall costs or benefits alone. Moreover, to make informed decisions about the design of the program, policymakers must know both the costs and benefits of specific program activities. That is, program activities that yield relatively small benefits may yet be very effective when compared to the costs involved, since what matters is the social rate of return on the dollars invested in each participant, just as it is the rate of return on capital that matters for any private sector investment.

When all costs and benefits are accounted for, a benefit-cost analysis judges the *social* efficiency of a program. It determines whether the value of the goods and services available to society and by extension, to the members of society are greater as a result of the program. To make this determination, the benefits are typically assigned a monetary value, and their present value is compared to the present value of the monetized program costs. Assuming that all present and future benefits and costs are identified, appropriate monetary values are assigned and an appropriate interest rate is used to discount future benefits and costs to their present values. JTPA could be considered a worthwhile use of public resources if (1) the present value of the benefits is larger than the present value of the costs, or (2) the rate of return, that discounts the sum of costs and benefits to zero, exceeds the socially specified rate of return.

Although the process of conducting a benefit-cost analysis is straightforward, there is a variety of issues that limit the validity of such an analysis. Given data limitations and other issues, it will not generally be possible for states to conduct a comprehensive benefit-cost analysis to provide a definitive estimate of JTPA's social return on the investment. Nevertheless, the general approach described below is useful in organizing information on benefits and costs, and enables states to obtain some sense of the effectiveness of the JTPA and the conditions under which JTPA can be regarded an efficient use of public resources.

The discussion begins with a brief description of a benefit-cost framework for analyzing the effectiveness of the JTPA. Then we briefly describe the use of the net impact estimates to measure some of the important social benefits due to the JTPA. We subsequently describe how to conduct a cost analysis to estimate the marginal cost of serving additional JTPA participants and the marginal costs of different program activities. A discussion of the issue of discounting future benefits and costs so that comparisons can be made in present value terms follows. We conclude by considering a few additional comparisons that should be made to determine how sensitive the overall conclusions are to certain assumptions.

Benefit-Cost Framework

The benefit-cost framework presented in table 2.10 lists the major benefits and costs that would ideally be accounted for in conducting a comprehensive benefit-cost analysis. As an aid for keeping track of the different benefits and costs, they are presented from three perspectives: the participant, the taxpayer, and society as a whole. The first class of benefits and costs consists of those benefits received by, or costs borne by, program participants. The participant perspective is important because it sheds light on an individual's incentives and willingness to participate in the program without coercion. The taxpayer perspective, sometimes referred to as the nonparticipant perspective, is important because it reflects the effects of the program on the government budget and the willingness of taxpayers to support the program.

The most inclusive set of program benefits and costs are those accruing to society as a whole. These are simply the sum of benefits and costs received, or borne by participants and taxpayers (that is, all members of society), taken separately. These represent a full accounting of all costs and benefits involved in operating the program. It is important to note that the social perspective ignores transfer payments between segments of society, that is, between participants and taxpayers, and examines instead whether the program results in a net increase in the resources available to society.[38] This is the appropriate perspective for a governmental body to take in examining the overall effectiveness of the JTPA.

Table 2.10
A General Taxonomy of the Benefits and Costs
of JTPA from Different Perspectives

	Participant	Perspective Taxpayer	Social
Benefits			
• Increased output			
- Postprogram output	+	0	+
- Program output	0	+	+
• Reduced receipt of income transfers			
- Reduced welfare payments, regardless of whether still on welfare	-	+	0
- Increased tax payments	-	+	0
• Reduced use of alternative social programs	0	+	+
• Nonmonetary benefits			
- Reduced crime	-	+	+
- Improved work attitudes of participants	+	0	+
- Improved mental and physical health	+	+	+
Costs			
• Program operating costs (e.g., rent, staff wages, and fringes, materials and supplies, and overhead administrative costs)	0	-	-
• Participant opportunity costs (e.g., forgone earnings or home production)	-	0	-
• Transfers to participants (e.g., stipends)	+	-	0
• Costs of participation (e.g., transportation, child care, extra clothing, and food)	+	0	+
• Psychic costs (e.g., stress of studying and being tested, separation from children)	-	0	-

Program Benefits

The major benefit of the JTPA from the social perspective is the increase in output produced by participants. Conceptually, two types of gain should be distinguished: (1) the increase in postprogram output, measured by the increase in earnings of the participants, and (2) the increase in output produced while an individual participates in the program. For the most part, the current-program (as opposed to pre- or postprogram) output due to the JTPA is likely to be small, particularly for participants in classroom training and job search assistance-program activities. Only for OJT programs is the value of program output likely to be positive, and even for these programs it is difficult to assign appropriate monetary values. Because of the difficulties involved in measuring the value of program output, as well as in measuring the value of other nonmonetary benefits, such as reduced crime or improved mental or physical health of participants and their families, we recommend that states do not attempt to directly measure these benefits, but recognize their potential importance when discussing the overall results from the benefit-cost analysis. The primary benefit to be measured, therefore, is the increased postprogram output due to JTPA.

The participant-comparison group differences in earnings in the postprogram period are used to measure the increase in output of goods and services available to society during that period due to JTPA. This is a reasonable procedure provided that JTPA participants do not find jobs in the postprogram period at the expense of other disadvantaged persons.[39] It is beyond the scope of the state-level model to assess the extent of such job displacement. As a result, the benefit-cost analysis is limited to determining whether the social benefits from receiving JTPA activities are greater than the costs to society of providing those activities, as measured by the change in total postprogram earnings due to JTPA activities.

Two issues arise in translating participant earnings gains into a measure of the increase in output of goods and services available to society. First, one must determine how to extrapolate the postprogram gains observed for the periods from three months to one year following termination, into subsequent periods. For example, if the three-month, six-month, and 12-month net earnings impacts imply similar gains per quarter, then it may be reasonable to assume that the gains persist over time. However, based on previous studies, it is likely that the gains decline over time, and information through just the first postprogram year may not be sufficient to estimate reliable time trends for the purpose of extrapolating future gains. This emphasizes the importance of augmenting the basic design with the collection of additional postprogram data to more precisely estimate the long-term gains from the JTPA. If this is not possible, at a minimum the benefit-cost analysis should indicate whether earnings gains observed during the one-year follow-up period are sufficient to make the program worthwhile, and if not, indicate whether JTPA would be viewed as a worthwhile social investment if the gains persisted at their current level for up to five years.[40]

A second issue concerns adjustments that should be made to earnings gains to account for fringe benefits. That is, if the increase in output is equal to the increase in compensation paid to those who participate in JTPA, then although this compensation is primarily in the form of monetary earnings, adjustments for nonmonetary earnings should also be made. Fringe benefits include pensions, health and other forms of insurance, and payments on behalf of the worker for unemployment insurance, workers' compensation, and FICA. As a rough approximation, insurance and pension benefits for workers served by JTPA are estimated to be approximately 10 percent of monetary benefits (Woodbury 1980), and payments to government programs are approximately 10 percent as well. Thus, we recommend that the net earnings gains be multiplied by 1.2 to adjust for fringe benefits in deriving a measure of the social benefits due to JTPA.

To summarize, the benefits to be measured and included in the benefit-cost analysis include only the increase in postprogram output due to JTPA. This is approximated by the increase in postprogram before-tax earnings, as measured by the estimated coefficient of the JTPA dummy variable in the net impact equation—adjusted for potential data and design deficiencies as described in the previous section—and subsequently adjusted for fringe benefits. Procedures will be developed to determine how the increase in earnings over the first year should be extrapolated to yield estimates of increases in postprogram output in subsequent years. These steps will yield an estimated stream of future benefits for both adult men and women. Individual values in these benefit streams will then be weighted by the proportion of men and women served by the JTPA in the particular program year, to generate an estimate of the aggregate benefit stream due to the JTPA.

JTPA Costs

As indicated in table 2.10, there are several different cost components in a benefit-cost analysis. The major cost categories include (1) program operating costs, (2) participant opportunity costs, (3) transfers to participants, (4) costs associated with participating in the program activities, and (5) psychic costs to participants of participating in the JTPA.

The major costs from the social perspective are the program operating costs. These include direct operating costs, such as rent, salaries for instructors, and costs of materials and supplies, and indirect or overhead costs, such as those involved in managing and administering the program overall. Because no fee is charged for program participation to those eligible, the operating costs are not considered as costs from the perspective of program participants. However, operating and administrative costs do involve the use of resources that have alternative uses. They represent real costs from the perspective of the taxpayer and society as a whole. Thus, in table 2.10, such costs are represented as a zero to program participants and as a minus in the other two columns.

A second important component of cost concerns the earnings opportunities and home production that participants forgo while participating in the program. These forgone earnings and home production are clearly costs to participants and, to the extent that less output is produced because workers were participating in the JTPA, the forgone output (as measured by forgone earnings or the value of forgone home production) is a cost to society as well. Although previous studies have recognized forgone earnings and lost home production to be important elements of program cost, because of data limitations these components are almost always excluded from the final benefit-cost comparisons. We also recommend that this cost component be formally omitted from the benefit-cost analysis. Although the social program costs are understated by this exclusion, given the relatively brief length of participation in JTPA and the questionable nature of the assumption that considerable output was forgone when previously nonworking individuals participated in the program, we believe this is justified. In interpreting the results of the benefit-cost comparisons, however, one should indicate to what extent the overall assessment is likely to be sensitive to omitting the social cost of forgone earnings and lost home production.[41]

Other potentially important costs of JTPA from the taxpayers' perspective are transfers to participants in the form of the money value of classroom materials, stipends, transportation, child care, and food or clothing allowances. Although such costs are much less important under JTPA than under CETA, they could be considerable in some cases. Note, however, that such transfers are a cost from the taxpayers' perspective, and a benefit to the participants that receive them. As such, transfers do not affect the cost-benefit analysis from the social perspective because the loss to the taxpayer is cancelled by the gain to the participant.

Other potentially important costs are the direct costs participants incur in participating in JTPA activities as well as any psychic costs. These psychic costs are inherently unmeasurable, and are included in the conceptual framework only for the purpose of completeness. The costs incurred by participants in attending classes or participating in job search activities require data that must be obtained by interview from individual participants. Because of the large expense involved in acquiring such information, and given the fact that these costs are likely to be a small share of the total cost of the program to the individual and to society as a whole, as a practical matter these costs are omitted from the final benefit-cost comparisons.

To summarize, the costs of JTPA to be measured and included in the benefit-cost analysis will be limited to those involved in operating the program, that is, the sum of rent, staff, materials and supplies, and administrative costs. In interpreting the benefit-cost analysis comparisons, however, it is important to recognize that many of the social costs of JTPA have not been measured, and that these unmeasured costs could affect the overall assessment of whether or not JTPA is an efficient use of social resources.

Estimating Program Costs

The benefits from JTPA will be expressed in terms of incremental dollar gains per individual adult participant. Therefore, the cost analysis must similarly estimate the incremental (i.e., marginal) outlay in dollar terms per individual adult participant. Many obstacles exist in deriving reliable estimates of the marginal costs of serving JTPA participants: problems of data omission, inconsistent aggregation, difficulties in allocating input costs among joint outputs, and ambiguity involved in imputing prices of existing agency or SDA resource inputs. However, statistical methods that overcome several of these problems and provide useful information on the marginal costs of employment and training programs are available.

The primary data source for the cost analysis is the *JTPA Annual Status Report* (JASR). The JASR provides for each SDA the characteristics of program terminees and information on program outcomes and costs for Title II-A and Title III programs funded under the JTPA[42] Fortunately, these data are provided separately for adult and youth participants in Title II-A programs.

The JASR data have several advantages. In addition to being in a standardized format with unambiguous definitions of all information items, the JASR contains data on total federal expenditures (but not total social costs) in operating the JTPA, as well as some information on the socioeconomic characteristics of adult program terminees that can be used to standardize the cost analysis. The more important variables are the number of terminees by sex, age, education, race or ethnicity group, welfare-recipient status, limited English language proficiency, and handicapped status, and the average number of weeks participated.

These participant characteristics can be thought of as inputs that enter the employment and training production process and have obvious instructional and resource implications that affect costs. For example, those participants with limited English language proficiency will probably require more program resources to complete training successfully. As such, these characteristics can be used to standardize the relationship between total costs and participants served to obtain estimates of marginal costs as described below.

The JASR contains two major limitations. The JASR does not contain (1) data on the number of terminees by type of program activity, or (2) information on administrative and other costs incurred at the state level in operating JTPA programs. Without information on the number of individuals served by type of program activity, one cannot identify the marginal costs of specific JTPA activities. This precludes comparing the marginal benefits and marginal costs of different program activities and services. As a result, one cannot identify those activities and services that are relatively most effective. One can only evaluate JTPA as a whole. In addition, without information on the costs incurred at the state level, the marginal costs of serving JTPA participants as derived from JASR data are understated.

To overcome these problems, we offer two recommendations. First, every effort should be made to obtain data on the number of adult terminees that participated in various program activities and services during the program year. At a minimum, it is useful to have data on the following: CT-only terminees, OJT-only terminees, JSA-only terminees, terminees who only participated in some other activity, and terminees who participated in multiple activities. This information must be obtained from each SDA for the same period in which the terminee characteristics and program costs on the JASR are reported. One could implement the following steps to obtain the necessary information for PY 1989:

1. Create a working file (on tape or disk) of all persons who terminated from JTPA Title II-A programs in any SDA in the state during PY 1989. The file should include the person's age, data on all program activities and services participated in, and an SDA identifier.
2. Exclude from the file all persons who are 21 or younger.
3. Create variables that represent each type of activity of interest and that may have different cost structures. For example, as indicated above, it is important to differentiate the costs by type of activity as well as costs for those who participate in only one activity vs. multiple activities. This can be accomplished by creating five variables, the first four of which would simply be dummy variables indicating whether the only activity the person participated in was

CT, OJT, JSA, or other, and a fifth variable indicating whether the person participated in any combination of these activities.

4. Create a separate subfile of adult terminees for each SDA.

5. Create counts of the number of individuals in each SDA in each of the five program-treatment types, and merge these counts with the JASR data for each SDA.

Our second recommendation concerns how to handle costs incurred at the state level in the operation of JTPA programs. Conceptually, the actual or imputed JTPA expense incurred at the state level should be added to annual program-year SDA total costs to obtain a better estimate of the overall social costs of JTPA. Provided information is available on the total costs contributed by the state to the operation of JTPA, one can allocate these to the various SDAs. For example, one method is to assume that the overhead costs incurred at the state level in support of various SDAs are proportional to the number of adult terminees in each SDA. Thus, to allocate state-level costs in operating JTPA programs to the different SDAs, one could multiply total state costs by the ratio of the number of adult terminees in a given SDA to the total number of adult terminees in all SDAs. Such a procedure would, in part, overcome the limitation of the JASR data described above. If it is not possible to obtain estimates of costs contributed at the state level to the operation of local JTPA programs, this limitation has to be recognized in interpreting the results of the benefit-cost analysis.

With the basic data set and adjustments described above, one can estimate a program cost function that provides information on the marginal cost of serving JTPA participants. Using ordinary least squares regression techniques, one could estimate a regression equation with total federal expenditures plus allocated costs incurred at the state level (if possible) for the SDA as the dependent variable, expressed as a function of the following variables:

1. Number of adult men terminees.

2. Number of adult women terminees.

3. Number of adult terminees who are:

    black

    Hispanic

other nonwhite

students—high school or less

high school graduates

aged 22-54

welfare recipients

single household heads with dependent children

UI claimants

limited English language proficiency

handicapped

4. Average number of weeks of participation.

With these independent variables in the regression equation, the coefficient of the variable "number of adult men terminees" would represent the marginal cost of serving additional male adult participants in JTPA on average, and the coefficients of the other variables in the model would capture the extent to which the marginal cost varied for serving persons with specific characteristics.

If the procedures outlined above are followed so that data on the numbers of terminees by program activity are obtained for each SDA, then one would estimate a second regression equation like the one above except that the "number-of-adult-men-terminees" and the "number-of-adult-women-terminees" variables would be replaced by the following four variables: the number of CT-only terminees, the number of OJT-only terminees, the number of JSA-only terminees, and the number of terminees that participate in multiple activities. In this formulation, the coefficients of these four variables would represent estimates of the marginal cost for each of the different types of program activities. If there are enough observations, the numbers treated can again be separated by gender, forming eight categories so that costs by activity can be estimated as a function of gender.

These estimates of the marginal costs of serving adult JTPA participants (either overall or by program activity) are then compared to the marginal benefits from the program in terms of increased postprogram output (either overall or by program activity) to state whether JTPA is an effective use of public resources.

One additional potential limitation of the cost analysis should be noted. This concerns the issue of sample size. Since the analysis is based on SDA-level data, the number of observations available in an annual cross-sectional analysis equals the number of SDAs in the state. In relatively small states with few SDAs, working with annual data may yield insufficient observations to estimate a cost model like the one given above and inhibit ability to obtain reliable estimates of program marginal expenses. A solution is to pool quarterly data over a few years and include dummy variables for different quarters to account for seasonal cost differences and other lumpy costs.

Benefit-Cost Comparisons

Three data elements are required to conduct a cost-benefit analysis: estimates of the benefit stream over time, estimates of program costs over time, and the interest rate used to discount future benefits and costs into present dollars.   In this section we indicate how to discount the future benefit stream so that the present value of benefits can be compared to the current program costs, and indicate the criteria to be used to measure the net effectiveness of JTPA as a social investment. The discussion concludes with examples of comparisons that should be made to determine how sensitive the overall conclusions are to alternative assumptions.

Because the benefits of an employment and training program occur over time, one must translate this stream into a common reference period. Conventionally, this involves discounting future dollars into their present value, using an interest rate that approximates the alternative costs of the funds invested. The two interest rates that have been used most often in such processes are the rate of return on investment in the private sector—historically averaging around 10 percent before taxes—or the long-term rate of growth of the economy—historically, around 3 percent. We believe that the lower rate is preferred for evaluating an investment in human capital from the point of view of society as a whole. Because there is much disagreement about which is the more appropriate interest rate to use, however, we also recommend that states examine how sensitive the main results are to using a higher figure such as 10 percent.

Using a 3 percent discount rate, one would measure the net effectiveness of JTPA by calculating a benefit-cost ratio, where the numerator is the present value of the incremental benefits due to the program (i.e., Σ

$B(t)/(1.03)^t$), the denominator is the present value of the costs incurred (which requires no discounting, since all costs are incurred in the current period), t refers to the postprogram years in which benefits are realized, and n is the last year in which benefits are realized. Within the numerous limitations described earlier, the JTPA would be regarded as an efficient use of public resources whenever the benefit-cost ratio exceeded 1.0.

In addition to obtaining the main benefit-cost results described above, we believe it is important that benefit-cost ratios be calculated to demonstrate how sensitive the conclusions are to alternative assumptions. In particular, alternative ratios should be calculated for the following:

1. A 10 percent discount rate.

2. Benefit estimates that do not include adjustments for selection bias or for potential contamination. Since each set of estimates rests on a different set of inherently untestable assumptions, it is important to know how sensitive the overall conclusions are to the size of these adjustments.

3. A range of program benefits and costs that reflects the fact that the main estimates are subject to statistical imprecision. For example, one could construct an upper and lower bound of a 90 percent confidence interval for the net impact of JTPA on postprogram earnings by adding and subtracting 1.96 multiplied by the standard error of the JTPA dummy variable to the estimated JTPA coefficient. By adjusting both the upper and lower bounds for the fringe benefits, one would then obtain an estimate of the upper and lower bounds for the increase in postprogram output due to JTPA. Upper and lower bounds for the marginal cost of JTPA can also be obtained by creating a 90 percent confidence interval around the appropriate regression coefficient (i.e., adding and subtracting 1.96 multiplied by the standard error of the estimated coefficient of the number of adult men/women terminees in the cost equation). Then, by choosing different combinations (e.g., upper bound for benefits and lower bound for costs, lower bound for benefits and upper bound for costs), one can provide useful information on how sensitive the benefit-cost ratios are to alternative assumptions.

These sensitivity analyses, in combination with the main benefit-cost results, should provide useful information on the effectiveness of JTPA programs.

Relationship Among Evaluation Models

Although much could be learned from implementing only the net impact model, considerable complementary information can be obtained by implementing the process analysis and gross impact models described in the companion chapters. In this concluding section, we briefly indicate how the net impact model relates to the other analytic approaches developed to assist states and SDAs in understanding the operations and impacts of their JTPA projects.

The net impact and gross impact analyses are quite complementary. Although both models are designed to address program effectiveness questions, they differ in terms of the types of evaluation questions that can be answered, the range of outcome measures of interest, and the types of comparisons being made. For example, the net impact analysis is limited to adults only, and because it relies exclusively on administrative data sources, there are relatively few outcome measures to examine, and only a limited number of personal characteristics can be included in the analysis.

On the other hand, the gross impact analysis can include youths as well as adults, an expanded set of labor market outcomes, and additional personal characteristics. As such, the gross impact model can be used to address certain relative effectiveness questions for youths served by the JTPA and can possibly provide information on the mechanisms through which the JTPA affects adults' earnings and welfare dependency. Because of the additional outcomes available, a gross impact analysis may be able to provide some evidence on whether the earnings changes are due to changes in wage rates, changes in hours worked per week, or changes in weeks worked per year, although a comparison group is necessary to provide definitive evidence on these issues.

In addition to providing complementary information on different subgroups and outcome measures, information from the gross and net impact models may shed light on important methodological issues affecting the validity of analyses of social-program impacts in general. For example, the gross impact model can use interview-reported earnings, whereas the net impact model relies on UI Wage Records to create measures of earnings. There are advantages and disadvantages to both approaches. By estimating gross impacts, using the net impact design and with the same samples of participants and comparison group members, one can provide evidence on the extent to which the impact results are sensitive to the use of the different data sources. In addition, because the gross impact model has an expanded set of independent variables available, by implementing both models using the same analysis samples it is possible to get some idea of whether the net impact estimates are sensitive to these omitted variables—an important statistical issue. Such comparisons provide important information on the limitations of the different analyses and indicate other independent variables or outcome measures that would be important for subsequent program analysis.

An SDA process analysis is a very important source of information for adding flesh and conceptual relevance to the net impact model. Because of the inherent limitations of the nonexperimental approach in estimating program net impacts, an SDA process analysis is a necessary first step to a valid net impact analysis. In particular, because the validity of the net impact results rests on the similarity of the participant and comparison groups selected, it is critical to understand the JTPA participation-selection process, the factors that govern the assignment of participants to program activities, and differences in the content and recording of program activities across SDAs. A process analysis offers the following information for the net impact model:

1. It will provide a detailed description of the criteria (explicit and implicit) used by SDAs and their subcontractors in screening JTPA applicants to choose individuals for program participation. As such, the process analysis will yield important insights into the type and extent of "creaming" that occurs and the likely differences that may exist between participants and comparison group members that are not possible to control for in the net impact model.

2. It will include a detailed description of the procedures followed in

assigning participants to program activities. It will reflect whether more-advantaged participants are assigned to specific program activities, whether all participants are first assigned to JSA, and whether only those who are not immediately placed are subsequently assigned to CT or OJT. This information helps in determining whether the estimated net impacts by program activity are likely to accurately reflect the relative effectiveness of different activities, or merely represent the fact that more-advantaged individuals are assigned to certain activities, while less-advantaged individuals are assigned to other activities.

3. It can identify major differences in the content of program activities across SDAs, as well as differences in the ways in which similar program activities are recorded in the JTPA MIS. This information is useful in developing meaningful, consistent measures of program activities across SDAs.

4. It will identify variables to include in the model. For example, it can identify SDA characteristics, such as service delivery strategies, which are quantifiable and differ across SDAs, so that they can be included in the model to test whether the net impact of JTPA significantly differs across these dimensions.

In addition to benefiting from the SDA process analysis, note that the net impact model may also produce information that would be of interest to a process analysis. For example, the net impact model may indicate that after adjusting for differences in participant characteristics and local labor market conditions, the net impact of JTPA is considerably different in some SDAs than in others. The process analysis can then examine in detail what it is about the specific SDAs that accounts for such differences. If measures of specific SDA attributes that are potentially responsible for the different net impacts can be developed, they can be included in subsequent net impact models to determine whether they account for the different net impact estimates across SDAs. Such ongoing interaction between the process and net impact analyses highlights the complementary nature of the two analytic approaches and should result in an improved understanding of the factors that affect program effectiveness.

Summary

We have described a general approach to examining the net impact of a social program and illustrated this approach with an in-depth description of how to estimate the net impact of employment and training programs for economically disadvantaged individuals funded under Title II-A of the Job Training Partnership Act. Although the details of the net impact evaluation model have been tailored to a specific social program, the key elements of the approach have broad applicability to other social programs. In particular, any net impact analysis approach must include a conceptual framework, a research design, and plans for data collection, processing, and analysis to answer questions posed in the conceptual framework. Moreover, because a major issue in any social program evaluation is the comparability of participant and comparison groups, it is likely that the concern over selection bias will always be present and the statistical methods described in this chapter are useful in dealing with this potential problem.

Although the results of a valid net impact analysis can provide very useful information on the extent to which participants overall are better off as a result of receiving program services (and, potentially, which participant subgroups benefit most), additional information is required to determine whether a social program is an efficient use of public resources. Specifically, one must use the results obtained from the net impact analysis and other analyses to develop measures of total program benefits, and compare the total benefits with the costs of the program. Although the costs involved in conducting such analyses as part of an ongoing program evaluation effort may be high in the initial stages, once the system is in place the costs should decline considerably and the benefits from the evaluation should be substantial.

NOTES

1. For example, one of the major reasons that the Job Corps education and vocational training program for disadvantaged youth has been able to avoid budget cuts during recent years, despite its extremely high cost per participant, is the availability of considerable research information indicating that corps members receive long-term economic and noneconomic benefits from the program.

2. One exception is the experimental evaluation of employment and training programs for adults and youths funded under the Job Training Partnership Act that was undertaken by the U.S. Department of Labor in 1986. This net impact study involves approximately 15 program operators nationwide, will cost approximately $20 million, and will be completed in 1991 or 1992.

3. Given that the model is usable and provides valid results on important postprogram outcomes, such as earnings and welfare dependency, then an important by-product—*consistency* in application across states—is likely to occur. This will maximize the usefulness of the information obtained from any single analysis by extending all states' knowledge of what is known about the effectiveness of employment and training programs among different state environments.

4. The primary exceptions include Dickinson, Johnson, and West (1987a) who examined CETA net impacts on the components of earnings, including whether employed, the hourly wage rate, hours worked per week, and weeks worked per year, and Bassi et al. (1984), who also examined the impact of CETA programs on welfare dependency.

5. Information on short-term earnings impacts occurring within less than a year can only be provided through primary data collection efforts, or through the use of UI Wage Records.

6. Because the net impact model is based exclusively on available administrative data, the conceptual framework is in large part data-determined. However, even though the conceptual framework is constrained by the features of available state data bases, virtually all previous national studies of the net impacts of employment and training programs summarized in the evaluation guide share several of the limitations of the net impact model described here.

7. Although these administrative data sources are very inexpensive, particularly relative to the costs of survey data, nontrivial data processing costs must be incurred to access the appropriate records from the system. Depending on the size of the files in the state, these costs could range from several hundred dollars to several thousand dollars (or more) per run. Moreover, prior to obtaining these data, it will be necessary to meet any state requirements concerning data confidentiality, and to take steps to maintain data confidentiality (e.g., remove all identifying information and create unique identifier for analysis purposes).

8. Some states that are not formally wage-reporting states have comparable earnings records available that are maintained by their Departments of Revenue and could be used in the analysis if the necessary interagency agreements are made.

9. For example, in some states, UI Wage Records do not include earnings for the following types of employees: certain corporate officers, church employees, individuals paid exclusively on commission, domestics who earn less than a certain amount per quarter (e.g., $1,000), railroad employees, employees of small agricultural firms, casual laborers, and certain barbers or cosmetologists. As a result of these coverage gaps, approximately 80 percent of all state wages are generally included in the UI Wage Records data base.

10. For example, states that are very interested in developing net impact estimates for JTPA Title II-A youth programs might consider implementing an experimental design. Alternatively, states might consider conducting (relatively expensive) interviews of participants and comparison group

members to collect the detailed preprogram and postprogram employment and schooling data necessary for reliable analysis. In either case, the general research design and analysis plans described later in this chapter could be followed. States interested in such approaches, however, should first consult employment and training researchers who are knowledgeable in experimental design issues and questionnaire development to avoid the pitfalls that have plagued previous studies.

11. If, however, work experience or some other program activity is used extensively in a particular state so that the sample sizes are sufficient to support precise net impact estimates, it would also be possible to follow the other procedures outlined later in this chapter to estimate the net impacts for this activity.

12. On the other hand, an enrollee-based sample frame has some disadvantages. To avoid excluding long-term participants from the analysis, an enrollee sample frame causes a delay in analysis findings relative to a terminee-based sample. In addition, because a given group of enrollees may terminate across different quarters, with such a design it is more difficult to estimate earnings impacts that correspond to specific time periods after program termination, such as the three-month period following the quarter after termination. However, alternative sample frames suffer from other problems that are more severe, which led us to the decision to use an enrollee-based sample.

13. The limited amount of missing data is, in part, a reflection of the procedures used by many agencies to assign "default" values when data are missing. Such procedures lead to measurement error, which can also introduce analytical complications as discussed later.

14. It is desirable to examine the missing data problems before making a final decision on whether to exclude such cases from the analysis sample. If the data items are missing for random reasons, then no harm is done by omitting such cases from the participant group. If, however, it is determined that the reason the data are missing is systematically related to the impact of the program (e.g., individuals with missing data on length of stay dropped out of the program and were less likely to be placed), this would reduce the internal validity of the overall analysis. Thus, some simple comparisons of the characteristics of participants with missing data and participants with complete data on program services will be performed as described in subsequent sections before a final decision is made to exclude cases with missing data from the analysis sample.

15. For example, in some SDAs women comprised as little as 25 percent of adult JTPA terminees in PY 84, while in other SDAs women were over 80 percent of all adult terminees in Title II-A programs during this period.

16. According to the JTPA legislation, to be eligible for Title II-A programs, adults must be 22 years of age or older and be economically disadvantaged. The act should be consulted for the exact definition of "economically disadvantaged." To the extent possible, the comparison group should only include individuals who meet the explicit eligibility criteria and who are similar to participants on characteristics emphasized in the legislation.

17. Based on a comparison of ES and JTPA data collected in selected states, the following individual characteristics are generally comparably measured: age, race/ethnicity (white, black, Hispanic, American Indian/Alaskan Native, Asian/Pacific Islander), education (whether received high school degree or equivalent), handicapped status (whether has physical or mental impairment that is a substantial handicap to employment), occupation (primary DOT code of previous job), veteran status (a veteran, a Vietnam-era veteran, recently separated, a disabled veteran), Food Stamps recipient, WIN registrant, and economically disadvantaged status. In addition, preprogram measures of UI Wage Records, AFDC grants, and whether a UI recipient will also be available and comparably measured for both participants and comparison group members. Although this list is not as complete as one would ideally like—measures of marital status, family size, dependent children, ex-offender status, limited English-speaking ability, and detailed data on preprogram employment experiences

are not available—it must be recognized that most of these characteristics were unavailable to previous national studies of the impact of employment and training programs. As such, this is not a limitation that is specific to the model described here.

18. Note that decreased emphasis on the economically disadvantaged measure might introduce additional measurement error into this variable. Not only did ES staff previously have no real incentive to accurately record the status of the applicant (i.e., since ES services do not depend on whether a person is economically disadvantaged), but they now have even less incentive to do so. As a result, it is likely that ES offices under-report serving such applicants. Thus, to the extent that only ES registrants who are recorded as economically disadvantaged are included in the sample frame for the comparison groups, their status should be measured reasonably accurately, which will minimize complications due to measurement error.

19. Several studies exclude from the comparison group individuals with very high preprogram earnings who were clearly ineligible to participate in employment and training programs (e.g., Dickinson, Johnson, and West (1986); Westat (1984)). By matching participants and comparison group members on economically disadvantaged status, however, such additional exclusions should no longer be necessary. Note that if the economically disadvantaged status variable is not available in some states for ES registrants, then procedures to exclude cases with high preprogram earnings must be implemented as described later in this section.

20. The statistical power of any hypothesis test relates to the likelihood of drawing a particular type of incorrect conclusion. The power of a test concerns what is called a Type II error, or incorrectly accepting the null hypothesis (e.g., that there are no significant differences in earnings between program participants and the comparison group) when the null hypothesis is false. Alternatively, the statistical power is the probability of detecting an effect (at the chosen significance level) when the effect of the specified size, in fact, exists (i.e., it is 1 minus the probability of making a Type II error). Because the probability of making a Type II error declines as sample size increases, larger samples are used to minimize Type II errors and maximize the power of the test.

21. With such a sample design we estimate that it will be possible to detect approximately a five (six) percentage point impact on earnings for adult men (adult women) with 90 percent power at a 0.10 significance level. That is, one would have 90 percent power at a 0.10 significance level of detecting an overall net increase in participants' earnings of as small as five or six percentage points.

22. In using enrollments from the prior program year to set the SSA number range in step 4 above, it may be necessary to adjust estimated enrollments to reflect changes in real program resources, that is, changes in federal allocations adjusted for inflation. Such adjustments can be made using information on the percentage change in program expenditures typically incurred for a given percentage change in the number of JTPA participants, which can be obtained from the cost analysis described later.

23. Note that because eligibility for ES services does not depend on economically disadvantaged status, it is likely that this indicator is measured with much more error for comparison group members than for JTPA participants. However, we expect that the error is more likely to be in not identifying some registrants as disadvantaged who in fact are. Thus, by only retaining in the comparison group those ES registrants who are indicated to be economically disadvantaged, the groups should be reasonably comparable on this dimension.

24. Although this would help to ensure similarity in terms of maximum earnings in the preprogram period, in the absence of data on economically disadvantaged status it is also desirable to match the samples more closely in terms of the time pattern and levels of preprogram earnings. For example, based on the preprogram pattern of participants' earnings, one could create specific cells that are

mutually exclusive and exhaustive of all possibilities, and then select comparison group members from these cells to match the distribution of participants.

25. Using quarterly values of the BLS *Consumer Price Index* for all Urban Wage and Salary Earners, one would deflate (divide) the values of the variables expressed in nominal dollar terms by the value of the price index in the same calendar quarter, and create measures of real earnings and real AFDC grants received in each preprogram quarter and real UI benefits received in the immediate preprogram quarter.

26. For data items obtained from ES or JTPA application forms, the range of acceptable values can be specified exactly. That is, if handicapped status is coded as 1 for yes and 2 for no, then any values other than 1 or 2 are clearly errors that likely occurred in entering the data into the MIS. Unless such errors can be readily corrected using other information on the file, they should be set to a common missing data code (e.g., -9) and dealt with as part of the procedures for handling missing data.

27. For example, one can use mean values, a hot-deck or cold-deck procedure, a regression equation, or other more complex methods to deal with missing data problems. In general, as long as the reason a variable is missing is not correlated with the variables representing program participation (e.g., classroom training, length of program participation), no bias is introduced in the estimate of net program impacts, although the standard error of the variable that has been imputed is reduced and the precision of the estimated impacts is overstated.

28. It would also be possible to estimate an OLS linear probability model of the likelihood of participating in JTPA to determine the major differences between the two groups. That is, one would estimate a regression equation with the dependent variable equal to 1 for JTPA participants and 0 for comparison group members, and the independent variables would be all measured characteristics included in the net impact model described later in this section. This approach has the advantage of estimating the independent influence of each measured characteristic, while controlling for the influence of all other characteristics, which eliminates the confounding effects of other variables that may be present when comparing mean characteristics. That is, a comparison of mean characteristics could indicate, for example, that JTPA participants are more likely to be minorities and less educated, whereas the regression approach would account for the differences in education by race and could reveal that, after adjusting for differences in race, there are no differences between participants and comparison group members in terms of education levels.

29. As indicated in the second and fourth guidelines for selecting independent variables discussed above, the only changes necessary in the independent variables in changing the dependent variable from the immediate preprogram quarter to the immediate preprogram year would be to ensure that quarterly earnings and AFDC grants in the second, third, and fourth preprogram quarters were excluded and that the unemployment rate was defined for the entire preprogram year rather than just for the immediate preprogram quarter.

30. Most standard regression programs allow one to perform an *F-test* of such an hypothesis, and also provide the calculated *F-statistic* for the test. Under the assumption that the error terms are normally distributed, the test statistic follows Snedecor's F-distribution with r degrees of freedom in the numerator and N-K degrees of freedom in the denominator, where r is the number of restrictions being tested (i.e., the number of independent variables that have been multiplied by the JTPA dummy), and N-K is the number of degrees of freedom when no restrictions are imposed (i.e., total sample size less the number of variables in the equation). If the test statistic exceeded the critical value for the specified level of significance, then the null hypothesis would be rejected and we would conclude that the preprogram earnings (or AFDC grants) equations for the two groups are not similar.

31. Note that individuals who are still in the program in a given quarter should not be included when analyzing the impact of JTPA on earnings or AFDC grants during that quarter because their earnings

may be unusually low (e.g., for classroom training or job search assistance participants) or unusually high (e.g., for OJT participants), which would bias the estimated overall net impacts.

32. Previous CETA studies indicate that program net impact estimates could be somewhat sensitive to the exclusion of long-term participants, primarily because the excluded individuals tended to be in Public Service Employment programs and were always working (Dickinson, Johnson, and West 1987b). Although this is generally not likely to be the case in JTPA, this suggests that, at a minimum, states should try to obtain longer follow-up data to use in additional analysis that includes all long-term participants to examine how sensitive the results are to this issue.

33. Because of the different sample sizes involved in analyzing impacts for different postprogram periods, the precision of the estimated 12-month net impacts will be less than the precision of the estimated impacts over a three-month period.

34. It may also be of interest to determine how the effectiveness of the JTPA differs among SDAs. This can be determined through including separate SDA-participant interaction terms using the general approach described below.

35. It should be noted that, in principle, similar analyses could be performed to determine whether net impacts vary across local labor market conditions. However, because the labor market variables would take on the same value for all persons in the same local area in a given time period, there is not likely to be sufficient variation to obtain precise estimates of how program impacts vary across local labor market conditions, except in large states, with many SDAs, and where there are considerable differences in labor market conditions across SDAs.

36. To formally test whether the program net impacts differ significantly across the groups of interest, an F-test is used. In this case, the test statistic follows an $F(r, N-K)$ distribution, where r is the number of restrictions imposed by the basic model (equal to the number of groups minus one), and $N-K$ is the number of degrees of freedom in the basic impact model. The hypothesis that the net impacts do not vary across the groups of interest (e.g., across racial groups) would be rejected for $r = 2$ and sufficiently large sample sizes at the 0.05 (0.01) significance level if the test statistic exceeded 2.99 (4.60). Most standard software analysis packages calculate this F-statistic as part of the analysis run.

37. If the characteristics defining the subgroups of interest are not measured equally well for the participants and comparison group members, however, the subgroup impacts will inappropriately reflect these differences. Because the presence of measurement error in an independent variable biases its estimated coefficient downward, if the amount of measurement error on a subgroup characteristic were greater in the JTPA sample, for example, than in the comparison group, the effect of that characteristic on the outcome variable would be smaller in the JTPA sample than in the ES registrant sample. The interaction term would inappropriately pick up such a difference and misleadingly indicate that JTPA impacts were smaller for individuals with that characteristic.

38. Reductions in transfer payments (e.g., AFDC grants) do not represent a benefit from the social perspective, since the increased benefit to taxpayers is offset by the loss of income to recipients, and there is therefore no change in the resources available to society as a whole. Thus, including estimated benefits from reductions in welfare dependency due to JTPA would involve a double counting of benefits.

39. Although very unlikely, in the extreme, the program could produce no net increase in output despite large increases in participants' postprogram earnings by simply reshuffling jobs from nonparticipants to participants.

BIBLIOGRAPHY

Ashenfelter, Orley. "The Effect of Manpower Training on Earnings: Prelimi-
nary Results," in *Proceedings of the Twenty-Seventh Annual Winter Meet-
ing of the Industrial Relations Research Association*, 1975, pp. 252-260.
_____. "Estimating the Effects of Training Programs on Earnings,"
Review of Economics and Statistics, February 1978, pp. 47-57.
Ashenfelter, Orley and David Card. "Using the Longitudinal Structure of
Earnings to Estimate the Effect of Training Programs," *Review of Econom-
ics and Statistics*, November 1985, pp. 648-660.
Bassi, Laurie J. "The Effect of CETA on the Postprogram Earnings of
Participants," *Journal of Human Resources*, Fall 1983, pp. 539-556.
_____. "Estimating the Effect of Training Programs with Non-random
Selection," *Review of Economics and Statistics*, February 1984, pp. 36-42.
Bassi, Laurie J., Margaret C. Simms, Lynn C. Burbridge, and Charles L. Betsey.
"Measuring the Effect of CETA on Youth and the Economically Disadvan-
taged" (Washington, D.C.: The Urban Institute, April 1984).
Bloom, Howard S. and Maureen A. McLaughlin. "CETA Training Programs—
Do They Work for Adults," Joint CBO-NCEP Report, July 1982.
Cooley, Thomas F., Thomas W. McGuire, and Edward C. Prescott. "Earnings
and Employment Dynamics of Manpower Trainees: An Exploratory Econ-
ometric Analysis," in Farrell E. Bloch (ed.), *Evaluating Manpower Train-
ing Programs* (Greenwich, CT: JAI Press, 1979), pp. 119-147.
Dickinson, Katherine P., Terry R. Johnson, and Richard W. West. "An Analysis
of the Impact of CETA Programs on the Components of Earnings,"
Industrial and Labor Relations Review, April 1987(a).
_____. "An Analysis of the Sensitivity of Quasi-Experimental Evalu-
ations of CETA Programs," *Evaluation Review*, August 1987(b), pp. 452-
472.
_____. "An Analysis of the Impact of CETA Programs on Participants'
Earnings," *Journal of Human Resources*, Winter 1986, pp. 64-91.
Fraker, Thomas and Rebecca Maynard. "An Assessment of Alternative Com-
parison Group Methodologies for Evaluating Employment and Training
Programs," report prepared for DOL under Contract No. 20-11-82-15
(Princeton, NJ: Mathematica Policy Research Inc., June 1984).
Heckman, James J. "Sample Selection Bias as a Specification Error," *Econom-
etrica*, January 1979, pp. 153-161.
Heckman, James J. and Richard Robb. "The Longitudinal Analysis of Earn-
ings," Department of Economics, University of Chicago, unpublished
manuscript, June 1982.
_____. "Alternative Methods for Evaluating the Impact of Interven-

tions: An Overview," Department of Economics, University of Chicago, unpublished manuscript, 1985.

Johnson, Terry R., Katherine P. Dickinson, and Richard W. West. "An Evaluation of the Impact of ES Referrals on Applicant Earnings," *Journal of Human Resources*, Winter 1985, pp. 117-137.

Johnson, Terry R. *A Guide for Net Impact Evaluations*, Volume 5, JTPA Evaluation Design Project, Department of Employment Security, Olympia, WA (March 1986).

Kiefer, Nicholas M. "Federally Subsidized Occupational Training and the Employment and Earnings of Male Trainees," *Journal of Econometrics*, August 1978, pp. 111-125.

_____. "The Economic Benefits from Four Government Training Programs," in Farrell E. Bloch (ed.), *Evaluating Manpower Training Programs* (Greenwich, CT: JAI Press, 1979), pp. 159-187.

LaLonde, Robert and Rebecca Maynard. "How Precise Are Evaluations of Employment and Training Programs: Evidence from a Field Experiment," *Evaluation Review*, August 1987, pp. 428-451.

Maddala, G. S. and Lung Fei Lee. "Recursive Models with Qualitative Endogenous Variables," *Annals of Economic and Social Measurement*, December 1976, pp. 525-545.

Mallar, Charles et al. *Evaluation of the Economic Impact of the Job Corps Program: Third Follow-up Report* (Princeton, NJ: Mathematica Policy Research, Inc., September 1982).

Masters, Stanley H. "The Effects of Supported Work on the AFDC Target Group," *Journal of Human Resources*, Fall 1981, pp. 600-636.

Rubin, Donald B. "Using Multivariate Matched Sampling and Regression Adjustment to Control Bias in Observational Studies," *Journal of the American Statistical Association*, 1979, pp. 318-328.

Somers, Gerald G. and Ernst W. Stromsdorfer. *A Cost-Effectiveness Study of the In-School and Summer Neighborhood Youth Corps*, Industrial Relations Research Institute, University of Wisconsin, 1970.

Westat, Inc. "Net Impact Report Number 1 (Supplement Number 1): The Impact of CETA on 1978 Earnings," report prepared for DOL under Contract No. 23-24-75-07, Westat, Inc., Rockville, MD (July 1982).

_____. "Summary of Net Impact Results," report prepared for DOL under Contract No. 23-24-75-07, Westat, Inc., Rockville, MD (April 1984).

Woodbury, Stephen A. "Estimating Preferences for Wage and Nonwage Benefits," paper presented at the NBER Conference on the Economics of Compensation, Cambridge, MA, November 21-22, 1980.

3
Evaluating Gross Program Outcomes

Carl Simpson
Sociology Department
Western Washington University

Some scientists react to the difficulties of establishing cause and effect by withdrawing into their shells and refusing to say that the relationships they find are anything more than correlations . . . But decisionmakers cannot avoid making judgment . . . The decision maker want to know what to change so that he can achieve the effect he wants.

Julian Simon and Paul Burstein
Basic Research Methods in Social Science

General Concepts and Methods in Gross Impact Evaluation

Managers of nearly all organizations — human services and private sector businesses alike—examine the outcomes of their efforts and compare their own achievements with those of other similar organizations. Descriptions of outcomes and comparisons across organizations can be valuable management tools, but can also be misleading. The gross impact evaluation model offers guidance for maximizing the usefulness of these management tools while avoiding errors commonly encountered in the attempt. As Blalock argues in chapter 1, we want to facilitate evaluations that remain closely tied to management information needs, but go beyond program monitoring, both in terms of goals and methods.

The Perspective Taken in Conducting Gross Impact Evaluations

Evaluation research is often viewed as remote from service delivery — as serving distant purposes or as serving no purpose. However, the analysis of data on services and outcomes can be a valuable management

133

tool guiding program development efforts. In addition, with the advent of computerized management systems, such analysis has become feasible in the majority of human services organizations as well as in the for-profit sector. Data systems put in place to facilitate record-keeping and report generation can be extended efficiently to provide a basis for the analysis of service quality and effectiveness. Perhaps these factors help explain why a recent survey finds many service delivery areas (SDAs) in the Job Training Partnership Act (JTPA) system expressing a special interest in systematic self-analysis (Seattle-King County 1985).

Systematic descriptions of program outcomes can focus policy planning discussions. Further, *analysis that compares the effects of program alternatives* can identify strong and weak areas of current services, in terms of their impacts on outcomes. The ability to focus change efforts on low performance areas and to identify high performance approaches as models for planning can enable a continuous improvement of services. It amounts to "technological advance" for service organizations, where effective technology—knowing what transformations produce desired outputs—has been difficult to develop. This capacity to direct change intelligently not only improves program services, but also provides staff with a sense of efficacy—the sense that they are able to affect the quality of their own work. Staff burnout has been identified as an ongoing problem in job training organizations (Franklin and Ripley 1984). One partial solution is putting the tools for more effective management in the hands of local staff.

Even where a foundation of previous research has been laid, analyses by local or state service delivery systems is valuable. Management decisions must be specific: shall we implement services this way or that, place participants with this type of trainer or that, deliver this set of services or that? The local context determines which alternatives are available and also the relative effectiveness of each. Thus, to apply national research findings to local settings, while the only recourse in the absence of better information, is a less reliable management guide than developing local knowledge. For example, Wilms (1980) found no difference between public and proprietary vocational trainers in Southern California, while Simpson (1982) found public schools substantially more effective than proprietary schools for CETA participants in Washington State. To make policy decisions in either area based on research in the other area would be unfortunate.

Gross impact analysis is the study of program outcomes among program participants only. It resembles net impact analysis in that it focuses on outcomes and their probable causes, but it differs from net impact analysis in that no comparison group of nonparticipants is involved. Gross impact analysis provides quantitatively reliable knowledge about program quality and effectiveness, with the goal of guiding program development. The method builds efficiently on already-existing data collections adding data elements as required, to improve validity at a reasonable cost. Postprogram follow-up surveys are used to measure program outcomes. Program qualities tested for their possible influence on outcome levels are measured using available management information systems (MIS) and, where applicable, by collecting additional data describing services delivered to specific individuals and forms of program implementation developed by various service providers.

Questions Gross Impact Analysis Cannot Address

Among the wide range of *possible* impacts of any human services program, only a smaller set can be addressed using the gross impact approach. Several important *society-wide goals* of employment-related programs are essentially impossible to study *definitively*, because legislation that improves the situation of some individuals may be creating or overlooking problems among other individuals. These impacts include (1) increasing national productivity, (2) reducing total national unemployment, (3) reducing average job turnover time, and (4) improving the skill level and, therefore, the flexibility of the overall labor force.

In addition, gross impact analysis cannot draw any conclusions concerning the *types or degree of change caused by participation* in a particular program. This question can only be addressed by *net impact studies*, which compare program participants with similar individuals who did not participate in the program (see Johnson and Stromsdorfer, chapter 2). Gross outcomes refer to total postprogram outcomes; net impacts estimate the proportion of total outcomes that may be uniquely attributed to participation in the program intervention. This means that gross impact studies cannot estimate the extent to which participation in a program changes individuals, the cost-effectiveness of a program, the time it takes for participants to repay the cost of a program in taxes generated by program success, or the impact of the program on reducing other costs such as welfare supports.

Questions Gross Impact Analysis Can Address

There are two broad categories of analysis goals for which the gross impact approach is well-suited: (1) *describing a broad range of program outcomes*, and (2) estimating the *unique impact on outcomes produced by alternative methods of delivering services*. The statistical assumptions underlying these and the power of the conclusions which can be drawn from them are so different that the remainder of this chapter will refer to them separately, as *gross outcomes analysis* and *differential impact analysis*. The first term avoids the word *impact* as a reminder that no cause-and-effect impact can be estimated using descriptive analysis.

The Description of Gross Outcomes

The description of gross program outcomes does not allow the evaluator to infer causation—to assume that the program or some aspect of the program is responsible for the outcomes observed. This type of analysis is well-suited to describing a wide range of outcomes for participants, employers, or others, with results available in a relatively short time. Descriptive findings *in themselves* imply no success or failure, but can be evaluated against managers' expectations. Descriptive data may also help establish reasonable new baseline expectations for outcomes not previously measured systematically. Descriptive gross outcomes can also be used as tools to identify problem areas that deserve more detailed analysis. Finally, the ability to measure relatively numerous and detailed outcomes provides a way to describe the range of program outcomes, and how programs are achieving their impacts. For example, job training program outcomes can include such issues as whether employment is training-related, whether fringe benefits are provided, whether promotions are likely, and whether employers are satisfied with the programs.

Gross outcomes may be described for one office, one organization with multiple offices, or a system including more than one service delivery organization. However, where more than one organization or office is described, caution must be exercised in interpreting any comparisons that are made. Outcome comparisons tend to be interpreted by research consumers as if caused by differences in program effectiveness—an error, given the limitations of descriptive analysis.

The careful description of program outcomes is often a necessary element of process evaluations (discussed by Grembowski in chapter 4 of this volume). Two foci of gross impact evaluations—broadening the scope of outcomes measured and exercising technical care during measurement—are therefore particularly valuable to process evaluations. By the same token, a process analysis can be extremely valuable in identifying the particular outcomes that are appropriate to measure as part of a gross impact evaluation for a given organization.

Differential Impact Analysis

The second type of analysis proposed here does involve the estimation of cause and effect. Differential impact analysis is a method for rigorously *comparing program variants*—alternative service strategies and alternative approaches to implementing service delivery. Different program services and implementation forms can be compared to assess whether, other things equal, *one or more alternatives are more effective than others in producing desired outcomes*. That is, the unique impact of each program variant can be estimated in comparison to all other program variants being used in a program during the analysis. Participants experiencing each program variant *act as a comparison group* for those experiencing other variants. This opens the way to a wide range of analysis questions that might be asked by managers. The specific questions depend on what program variations exist in a particular service delivery system, and on the areas in which managers are most interested in developing information. The term *program variants* is used here as shorthand to include all existing program alternatives in services assigned to individual clients and in forms of implementation found among service providers in the service delivery system.

Within the constraints of sample size, these same questions can be asked for *particular populations of participants*: which treatment modes are most effective for target group A, and which for group B?[1] Comparisons can also be made among *service providers*. This means that states can improve the reliability and meaningfulness of comparisons made among local agencies, and can also identify especially valuable directions for program technical assistance efforts, as long as the influences of environmental conditions and other important differences among agencies are taken into account.

Differential impact analysis is especially well-suited to program development efforts because of its ability to identify program variants that influence the program's ability to produce desired outcomes *within the limits of the particular clients it serves* and *within the range of treatments available* to it. It cannot tell us whether a program is worth retaining. However, given that a program exists, it can point the way toward making it operate more effectively.

Differential impact analysis recognizes that the most serious threat to reliable comparisons among program variants is *selection bias*. Clients who select or are selected for different program variants often differ from each other in ways that influence probable postprogram success. The impact of such client background differences must be accounted for before the unique impact of program variants can be identified. Otherwise, estimates of program variants are *biased*. Although no set of measures could ever estimate all selection effects, it is possible for analysts who know a particular service delivery system well to construct measures that will prevent a considerable proportion of the bias that can be caused by unmeasured selection. Each additional investment in such preventative steps improves the validity of the research findings.

The second major threat to differential impact analysis is from *confounded program variants*—service strategies or program implementation modalities that completely overlap one another. If all clients assisted through a particular service provider are assigned services that differ in, for example, three ways from services given all other clients in a system, it is impossible to determine which of these three might account for a higher or lower success rate by that provider. The treatments overlap so completely that they cannot be separated statistically; they are confounded with one another.

Similarly, any time one service delivery organization implements program variants that are entirely unique, the analyst encounters at least two factors that are confounded: whether participants experienced the specific program variant in question, and whether they enrolled through the specific organization in question. Thus, completely overlapping implementation by more than one provider as well as completely unique implementation by any provider constitute confounded program variants, which make fully accurate differential impact analysis impossible. This means that the differential impact analysis of treatment variants becomes possible only when the treatment system being studied includes a sufficient number of service providers or service tracks that implement services differently, but not completely differently, from each other.

The Types of Factors Measured During Gross Impact Evaluations

Both descriptive outcome analysis and differential impact analysis require measures of program outcomes. These may be recorded by service providers, reported by participants during follow-up surveys, or reported by employers. In addition, differential impact analysis requires the measurement of program variants and "control variables." Program variants may be measured at the individual level, indicating which specific services each participant received, or at the service provider level, indicating how programs are implemented for the average client. Control variables include a wide range of selection factors that can bias findings if excluded from the analysis.

An overview of the various types of measures that may be involved in gross impact designs is provided in exhibit 3.1. Measures are grouped according to the source of each measure, and the purpose each measure serves in an analysis (outcome, program variant, control variable). The intersection of each type of outcome variable with each type of program variant shown in the exhibit indicates a major *relationship* studied using this approach. In exhibit 3.1, these relationships are indicated by letters A through N. Any given differential impact analysis involves the relationship between one outcome variable and some number of test variables (program variants) along with the control variables included to protect against selection bias or other sources of error. Within this structure, each test variable represents an "hypothesized" effect on the outcome in question.

Exhibit 3.1 also indicates the most likely sources for each type of measure, recognizing that measurement decisions depend on the nature of each service delivery system. Outcomes are measured through observation of participants or relevant others. Some outcomes are observed by service providers, while others require special data collection. Surveys of service providers are inexpensive because their numbers are small compared to participants; however, they can measure only implementation variants, not individual service variants. Participant service records kept by service providers are both more reliable and less expensive than measures included during follow-up interviews of former participants.

Exhibit 3.1
Nature and Sources of Measures That May Be Included
in Gross Impact Analysis

	The Purpose of Each Measure and Its Relation to JTPA				
	OUTCOMES FOR		**PROGRAM VARIANTS**		**Controls**
Data Source	**Participants**	**Others**	**Implementation**	**Service treatment**	**against bias**
Survey of service providers			F		J
Participant treatment kept by service providers		D	G*	H	K
Standard MIS files	A				L
Participant follow-up surveys	B			I**	
Follow-up surveys of others, such as employers	C	E			M
Published data by locality					N

* Individual service treatment records may be aggregated to indicate typical agency patterns.

** Selected treatment variants can be measured through participant follow-up surveys, although these require retrospective reports

Variables measured as *controls against bias* can come from many sources, depending on the specific design of the analysis. Service providers, participants, and others, such as employers or referral agencies, can provide valuable data concerning the selection process. Service providers also implement policies that affect selection bias. This does not mean the analyst should ask service providers for their interpretation of their own selection processes. Rather, it means that once the analyst has identified specific selection policies and practices likely to affect outcomes, these will be measured most validly through reports from those directly implementing or experiencing the process. In addition, MIS files and published demographic and labor market data report standard variables known to affect labor market success and are, therefore, necessary to include in differential impact analyses. One strength of the gross impact approach is its *flexible ability to measure multiple indicators of selection into particular service treatments.*

The Design of Gross Impact Evaluation Studies

Nearly all modern human services organizations have committed records of client characteristics at intake and services received to the electronic memory banks of micro- or minicomputers. The relatively ready access an analyst has to these MIS records lays the initial base for inexpensive, yet valid, gross impact evaluation studies. Client populations can be defined and samples drawn from these MIS records, with individuals identified for inclusion in a study at either entry or termination from the program. Once the population—all clients who participated in the particular programs to be analyzed—is defined, representative samples can be assured by using a variety of convenient random selection methods. The population should include clients enrolled throughout a calendar year if the program experiences seasonal fluctuations in outcomes, and should proportionately represent all geographic areas from which clients are drawn.

MIS records may be augmented to improve the power of a given study to evaluate specific aspects of program services. In addition, standard survey research methods can be employed to perform short-term follow-up data collection on program participants or other relevant actors such as employers, treatment facilities, or school administrators. For longer-period follow-ups, the problem of noncompletions reduces the value of the survey approach. For programs with mobile clientele, establishing good locater information on clients will be critical to the success of follow-up survey efforts. The construction of surveys, drawing of samples, and conducting of survey interviews are tasks about which much is known, making guidance readily available (e.g., Fink 1985; Babbie 1989; Rossi, Wright, and Anderson 1983; Frey 1983; Dillman 1978). In addition, the availability of university-based survey research centers, as well as private research firms, makes expert guidance readily available in most areas.

Analysis of gross impact data often can be performed on the same computers used to store MIS data, using one of the readily available statistical analysis packages. Any package that calculates percentage distributions, *chi square* with percentaged tables, analysis of variance tests comparing means, and multiple regression is adequate for the needs of nearly all gross impact evaluation efforts.

The Application of Gross Impact Evaluation Concepts and Methods to the Case Example: JTPA

The remainder of this chapter illustrates the gross impact analysis approach by offering methodological guidance tailored specifically to one program, the Job Training Partnership Act. Much of what is said here applies to any job training program, and with a little translation, to any human services program. Conceptualization, design, measurement, and analysis issues in gross impact evaluations, however, are illustrated within the vocabulary of JTPA services and the JTPA service provider system. This section begins with a discussion of the proper uses of descriptive outcome analysis, then moves on to differential impact analysis and the study of employer outcomes.

The Uses and Limits of Descriptive Gross Outcomes Analysis

Descriptive analysis takes its name from its goal of examining outcomes without making causal attributions. Descriptive patterns may be reported on the basis of data covering all participants or estimated from a sample of participants. Where sampling is involved, proper procedure will generate unbiased estimates of patterns characterizing all participants as well as information on how accurate those estimates are.

Descriptive data are relatively easy to collect and report, but also easy to misinterpret. This discussion, therefore, takes two directions: (1) identifying ways to make gross impact description most useful to JTPA managers, and (2) identifying the major limits on its valid interpretation.

Avoiding Interpretations that Imply Causality

As the term *description* indicates, the primary limitation on descriptive data analysis is that it involves none of the research design or analysis techniques designed for explaining causal relationships. The major reason for this limitation is that descriptive analysis offers no comparisons. For example, if we learn that employers are highly satisfied, we cannot know whether the reason is the friendly service, the quality of participants placed with them, reimbursement they may have received, a general tendency to answer positively, or a variety of other possibilities. We can guess, but the research findings offer no guidance until comparisons are made—in this example, comparisons between employers training more- and less-qualified participants, with higher and lower reimbursement levels.

This limitation does not mean that managers must refrain from interpretation. We all interpret the world daily. It means that managers *must not assume that the findings themselves imply a particular interpretation.* Thus, the first of the following two statements a JTPA manager might make is flatly incorrect, while the second could be correct.

1. "We find employers to be highly satisfied with JTPA, proving that we are sending them the types of employees they want."
2. "We find employers to be highly satisfied with JTPA. In my opinion, this is true because we are sending them the types of employees they want."

Statement 2 avoids incorrect causal attributions, while also stating a possible interpretation that could be examined through further analysis. The value of the descriptive finding is that it *identifies the facts the manager may work with and may attempt to explain.* We can learn how satisfied employers are. The limitation is that the findings do not themselves offer any causal explanation for the level observed.

The most common error in interpreting descriptive data on job training programs is to assume that outcomes described after the completion of a program are caused by the program. In the heat of political battle, I may say, "Look what our program has accomplished; we have 84 percent placement rates!" In so stating, I may be taking credit for upswings in the economy, for individuals who recovered from temporary unemployment, and for random change, as well as for cases where employment was produced by the program.[2] Similarly, if I claim that one service provider is "better" (causes greater success) than another on the basis of descriptive findings, I err by assuming that the difference was produced by program services alone, which cannot be demonstrated using descriptive statistics. Such claims are problematic not only because they are subject to self-serving interpretations, but also because they often tend to mire program development efforts in the most obvious and least useful interpretations—some vague improvement in "management," "creaming" efforts, economic shifts, and so on.

Broadening the Range of Outcomes Measured

The most basic way in which descriptive analysis can improve a program manager's information base is by taking advantage of its flexibility to enlarge the range of outcomes measured. We are too often wedded to the narrow range of outcomes readily available from agency records or required by government performance standards. These measures should be included in any descriptive analysis, but the addition of further outcome measures offers considerable benefits: the identification of unrecognized areas of program quality or problems, and the expansion of managerial decisionmaking into quality-enhancement rather than program-compliance only.

A hierarchy of outcomes may be arranged according to the extent to which each is required for a meaningful analysis of JTPA. Some states or SDAs may wish to include only a minimal core set of measures, making the follow-up as brief and inexpensive as possible and limiting

Exhibit 3.2
Prioritized Participant Outcome Measures

1. **Required postprogram performance standard standards**

   • Employed during 13th week after termination?
   • Earnings during 13th week.
   • Number of weeks worked, during 13-week follow-up period.

2. **Other core measures explicit in JTPA mandate**

   • Employment, including:

     — Hours per week employed at follow-up.
     — Pre- to postprogram change in hours per week and percent weeks employed.

   • Earnings, including:

     — Hourly wage rate at follow-up.
     — Total earnings from termination to follow-up.
     — Preprogram to postprogram change in wages and earnings.

   • Welfare dependency, including:

     — Whether receiving public assistance at follow-up.
     — Monthly dollar amount of public assistance at follow-up.
     — Total public assistance received between termination and follow-up.
     — Preprogram to postprogram change in public assistance received.

3. **Measures of skill transfer and utilization**

   • Whether employment is in training-related field.
   • Proportion of the work utilizing skills from training.
   • For employer-based interventions, retention with that employer.

4. **Measures of job quality**

   • Benefits (medical, retirement plans; paid vacations; sick leave).
   • Likelihood of layoffs or reduction in hours.
   • Likelihood of promotion and/or raises.

5. **Measures characterizing those not employed at follow-up**

   • Why termination job was lost or left, if applicable.
   • Whether participant is seeking work, and if not, why not.

6. **Subjective orientations of participants**

   • Intention to make use of the JTPA intervention (career orientation).
   • Personal evaluation of JTPA program services.
   • Personal evaluation of postprogram job.
   • Personal comparison of postprogram job with preprogram job.

their analysis options accordingly. Others may wish to mount a more comprehensive analysis, once the decision is made to expend initial set-up costs. The marginal increase in cost from inclusion of all six types of measures discussed below is small, making it logical to measure all. Nevertheless, some measures add information without being necessary to the research effort. With this distinction in mind, exhibit 3.2 displays outcomes in six categories, from highest (1) to lowest (6) priority.

The most basic outcomes focus on the *explicit JTPA mandate* that JTPA be considered an investment in individual lives—an investment in human capital. As such, it should show returns in higher probability of employment, higher earnings, and lower dependence on public assistance. Three measures are required by the Department of Labor. Beyond those, the survey method allows various components of employment and earnings, such as hours worked and wage rate, to be specified.

Although measures indicating *skill transfer and utilization* are not explicated as outcomes in the legislation, they are clearly implied. They represent the most direct impact of training-based interventions, and are especially sensitive to program variants, making these outcomes particularly useful to managers who wish to develop their programs based on differential impact analysis. They are also particularly useful for descriptive analysis, because findings indicate, in and of themselves, the extent to which outcomes are being produced via the method presupposed for all training programs.

In addition to wages, various intangible benefits from employment and indirect forms of income, such as medical benefits, are important aspects of *job quality*. A prime indicator of probable long-range employment success is whether the overall quality of each job places it into the category sometimes characterized as the "primary labor market" or into the "secondary labor market" (Doeringer and Piore 1971; Vermeulen and Hudson-Wilson 1981). Primary labor market jobs are relatively stable, include gradually improving income and benefit levels, are usually full time, include the possibility of promotion, include fringe benefits and are, in general, the types of jobs that can reasonably become a career. Secondary labor market jobs seldom include benefits, possibility of promotion, or a system of pay increments, are often part time, and are subject to layoffs. Even where a short-term follow-up shows participants retaining employment, jobs in the secondary labor market represent a poor risk for long-term employment stability.

Finally, the lowest priority outcomes are measures of *participants' satisfaction*. They are lower priority than other measures because their meaning is less clear, they are less reliably measured than other outcomes, and they have been excluded from most job training legislation and evaluation studies. Nevertheless, they are much to be recommended. They can offer valuable information to JTPA program operators, and they are inexpensive to add to participant interviews. In particular, subjective indicators of job adjustment may be extremely important to measure in cases where the transition into the workforce is expected to be especially problematic, e.g., in the case of long-term welfare recipients. Job satisfaction has surprisingly little correspondence to earnings, but is considerably influenced by job quality and skill use, making this subjective measure useful for assessing quality of program placements.

Asking Questions

One important approach to both limits and potentials of descriptive analysis is to ask meaningful questions without demanding more complex comparisons than allowed. Some questions involve no interpretation; they simply seek *baseline descriptive information*. Other questions may be worded specifically enough that a descriptive answer will assist the analyst in *developing or confirming explanations*. The following questions illustrate this point:

1. Does it appear that program goals are being met? If I know roughly which *levels of program outcomes* are expected, measuring outcomes lets me know whether I am in condition red, yellow, or green. Descriptive levels do not tell me why outcomes are higher or lower than expected, or whether my program itself has much to do with producing those outcomes. However, they tell me whether I need to look for factors creating low outcomes, whether high or low outcome levels are concentrated in particular program activities, and whether my organization is in better shape with regard to some outcomes than others. That is, descriptions of outcome levels can let managers know whether to worry, and which program areas to worry about most actively.

For some postprogram outcomes—those mandated as postprogram performance standards—clear expectations will be established. When expectations are unclear, descriptive measures can help establish reasonable baseline expectations. These would constitute first approximations that might be improved upon in subsequent

2. Does any service provider appear worth learning more about? One particularly useful application of descriptive analysis as a first approximation is the *comparison of SDAs or subcontracting service providers*. Such comparisons should be interpreted with great care, since agency performance levels are influenced by factors over which program operators have no control, such as the local economy, or may result from policies not intended by the act, such as increasing performance rates by serving those with least need. Descriptive differences point out where further investigation might be most useful, helping to *pose questions correctly rather than answering them*.

3. Is there any apparent change over time? Descriptive outcome figures kept over time—each month for example—can be used to form a baseline series indicating stability or change in services provided and program outcomes. Such a "time series" can sometimes alert managers to unexpected changes. It can also provide a relatively inexpensive first approximation of the effects of major program changes made during the time series.

Investigating Specific Propositions

One major strategy of multivariate analysis is to test a particular interpretation by seeing whether competing explanations for the observed findings can be eliminated. This tactic is not available for descriptive analysis. However, the same general strategy may be followed by posing questions thoughtfully and specifically enough to logically *reduce* the range of findings that would be consistent with the particular explanation proposed.

There is little value in asking broad questions such as: does on-the-job training (OJT) produce more placements than classroom training (CT)? Too many different interpretations could reasonably explain either positive or negative findings. However, specific propositions direct expectations to only a few findings. *If* the expected finding occurs, then we have greater faith in the correctness of the proposition guiding the analysis.[3]

For example, if I identify some JTPA program activities as skill training programs, I will expect that a disproportionate number of postprogram job placements will be in the skill area. I have no *a priori* way to set expected levels, but descriptive findings are nevertheless interpretable. If only 2 percent of workers in my area are cashiers, and only 6 percent of my CT participants have previous experience as cashiers, then a finding that 65 percent of employed graduates from my cashier training class are cashiers suggests that the program is working in the way I envisioned. This does not indicate how well the program works, only that my proposed explanation about the way it works is supported.

Another example involves the question: what accounts for nonretention of jobs held at JTPA termination? Several specific propositions are easy to imagine, each suggesting its own specific measures. For example, if JTPA participants lack the ability to learn complex skills, instances of nonretention should occur most often when the training or the job involved complex skills or where the participant's preprogram skills were weakest. Similarly, employers should often report that the participant was unable to perform complex tasks. If these variables are measured along with others indicating alternative explanations, managers can assess which explanations account best for the patterns observed.

As a final example, one may argue that JTPA should move participants into primary labor market positions (Taggart 1981). One could examine the degree to which this occurs by measuring qualities of postprogram jobs that define the primary labor market, as shown in exhibit 3.2. Findings would not indicate the degree to which JTPA treatment caused the job quality mix observed, but they would recommend greater or lesser concern about program quality, depending on the number of jobs exhibiting the desired qualities.

Perceptions Held by Employers and Participants

Some questions are inherently descriptive. If I wonder what importance employers place on various qualities of individuals they hire, I can ask them to tell me. Although it is always possible for data on such perceptions to be limited by incorrect self-knowledge or by misleading responses, these perceptions are appropriately interpreted in their descriptive form. The same is true of participants' job satisfaction or other participant perceptions in which JTPA managers may have interest. Similarly, employers' satisfaction with JTPA and their perceptions of the costs and benefits of participating in OJT or Work Experience may be taken at face value, as long as one recognizes that the information indicates no more than perception, and that perceptions do not necessarily reflect program impact.

Illustrations of Informative Descriptive Analyses

Several illustrations of descriptive findings are reported here, all taken from one statewide study of CETA OJT conducted in Washington State (Simpson 1984a). The findings displayed in exhibit 3.3 illustrate that measuring training-related employment as well as overall employment

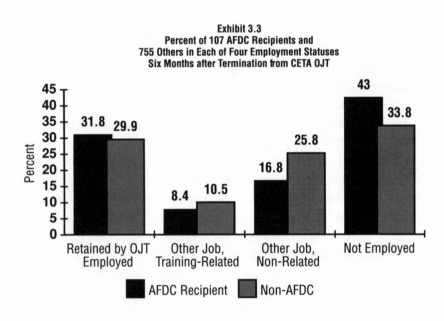

Exhibit 3.3
Percent of 107 AFDC Recipients and
755 Others in Each of Four Employment Statuses
Six Months after Termination from CETA OJT

at follow-up helps avoid jumping to an erroneous conclusion. If only the percent employed or not employed at follow-up were displayed, we would observe the expected pattern: AFDC recipients are employed at a rate about 9 percent below the rate for non-AFDC participants. We might, therefore, be led to conclude that AFDC recipients are less job-ready or less personally stable, and therefore fail more often than others to retain their OJT jobs. A program manager might consider imposing more counseling on AFDC participants, offering more support services during OJT contracts, or placing fewer AFDC recipients in OJT, although it is widely known to produce the highest postprogram placement rates.

However, when the outcome is presented with a slight increase in specificity, these interpretations no longer appear logical. AFDC and non-AFDC participants retain their OJT jobs at equal rates. They also move to other, training-related jobs at equal rates. The entire differential in employment is produced by the fact that among the 60 percent of participants who did not remain with their OJT employers or in the field of their OJT positions, non-AFDC recipients were two-thirds more likely to find work outside the OJT field. Now the most likely interpretation is that AFDC recipients are much less able to *locate jobs* without the assistance of the job training program, as shown by their relative lack of success once they leave the positions into which they were leveraged by OJT subsidies. However, once the program assisted their job entry, they *retained* their positions as often as their more employable colleagues. This means that the OJT program is doing well at equalizing the chances of AFDC people in the short run, but it also means that the OJT program effects are not carrying over to later job search success.[4]

Exhibit 3.4 illustrates the value of an extremely basic analysis of follow-up data. A group of OJT participants is followed from the beginning of their OJT contracts through contract completion and nine months beyond. The percent of the initial group who remain employed with their initial OJT employer has been calculated at several points during the OJT contracts, and monthly after termination. The findings graphed in exhibit 3.4 fall into three segments, so clear as to be quite valuable in their descriptive state.

During the OJT contract, some gradual attrition occurs, so that on the

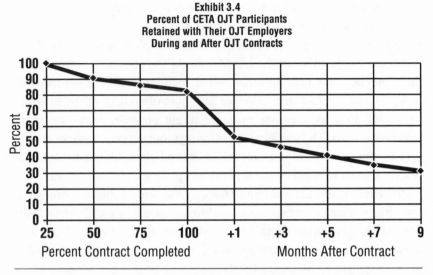

Exhibit 3.4
Percent of CETA OJT Participants
Retained with Their OJT Employers
During and After OJT Contracts

date of contract completion, only 83 percent of the original placements remain.[5] Then, a full 30 percent of all OJT jobs are lost or left in the month following the termination of the contract. Following this stage, attrition once again becomes gradual, with another 21 percent of jobs being left over a nine-month period. When the findings graphed here are combined with an official "entered employment at termination" rate of 78 percent, we also learn that the great majority of jobs lost during the first month following the OJT contract were counted as program successes. Despite their simplicity, these findings speak unambiguously about the value of postprogram follow-ups and the way in which the OJT system at that time and place was working.

The final illustration of descriptive findings offered here comes from a small recent survey of OJT employers in one SDA. The figures here suffer a relatively large error margin since they are based on only 78 interviews. However, employer responses were so extreme that the small numbers cannot obscure the basic thrust. Exhibit 3.5 reports one set of employer perceptions relevant to an interpretation of employer cost or benefit from participating in the JTPA OJT program. Aside from the wage subsidy OJT employers receive, the greatest cost or benefit they receive from participation in OJT is the work produced by the participant. If the participant is less skilled, slower to learn, less productive, or less tractable than normal non-OJT hires, the placement represents a cost. Indeed, the wage subsidy is supposed to offset such costs. For this reason, employers were asked to compare their OJT participants, at the point of their initial hire, with the typical non-OJT hire for the same position.

The results shown in exhibit 3.5 make clear that in this SDA, the great majority of employers perceive that they have benefited from hiring an OJT participant. Over 80 percent say their OJT hire is easier to supervise than other hires, and over 60 percent say the OJT hire is a more productive worker than non-OJT hires. The same pattern holds for all the specific ratings save one: 31 percent of employers report their OJT participant needed greater-than-average training, while only 11 percent say they needed less. Even here, in the area assumed by definition to represent a cost to OJT employers, the majority say OJT and non-OJT hires are identical.

This descriptive finding is chosen to illustrate both the value and the limits of descriptive findings. Program planners can feel assured of the

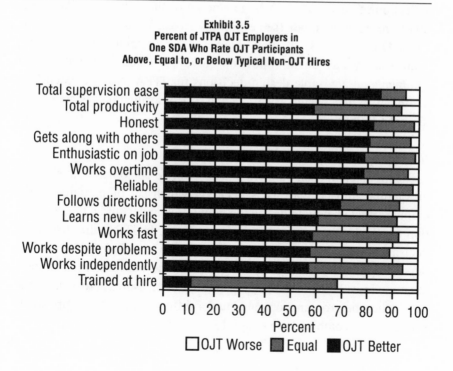

Exhibit 3.5
Percent of JTPA OJT Employers in
One SDA Who Rate OJT Participants
Above, Equal to, or Below Typical Non-OJT Hires

satisfaction with which their OJT program is being greeted, can use these results in marketing OJT to other employers, and can rest assured that their assessment and assignment system is locating successful workers. Yet, they cannot know how much of this employer satisfaction stems from excellent matching of particular employer needs and particular participant strengths and weaknesses, how much from the general employment maturity, which is by policy required of all OJT participants, and how much from "over-selection" of the most employable individuals to be placed in OJT. Many policy implications depend on these alternatives, although some implications are clear in any event, such as the feasibility of reducing wage subsidy without inducing employer perceptions that OJT is too costly.

Minimal Research Design for a Participant Follow-Up Analysis

Whether analysis will remain descriptive or move on to differential impact, certain minimal research design requirements guide the proper collection of survey data. A large amount of literature is available on survey research methods (see especially Rossi, Wright, and Anderson 1983; Dillman 1978). In this chapter, a set of topics that must be addressed by any client follow-up survey is listed with only brief comments on advisable design decisions for JTPA. A more extensive treatment of the design issues facing JTPA evaluations is found in Simpson (1986).

Identifying the Population to Be Analyzed

The *first* step in designing either a descriptive outcomes analysis or a differential impact analysis is deciding which set of participants to include—that is, how to define the *population* under study, the population to which conclusions will be generalized. In JTPA, the first such decision involves which authorizing titles are to be included. This choice depends primarily on managers' goals for the analysis. In addition, attention must be paid to the comparability of measures across title and to whether the programs operated under different titles are comparable enough to be combined meaningfully.

The second decision regarding which population to study is whether the population should include the following: all of those found to be eligible for JTPA services, all of those who were enrolled in JTPA, all statuses at termination, or only participants who were employed at termination. Studying all eligibles would be required for a full analysis of selection into the program. However, for a descriptive analysis of gross outcomes or a differential impact analysis of the effects of program service or implementation variants, only participants receiving services need be included.

There is sometimes a temptation to reduce data collection costs by including in the study population only individuals who terminated with employment. However, there are several reasons why *gross impact analysis designs should include all termination statuses* in the population to be studied.[6] The only outcome that can be measured with a population limited to participants who were employed at termination is "retention of the termination job." Estimates of other standard outcome measures--average wage, proportion employed, etc.—would be badly inflated by excluding the group least likely to be employed at follow-up—those unemployed at termination. On the other hand, to estimate this group's follow-up employment and earnings at zero (their status at termination) would underestimate program success by ignoring delayed employment. Further, including all termination statuses allows the evaluation to examine why some individuals gain less than others from the program, insures comparability with cost data, and guards against differences in service providers' methods of defining termination status.

Deciding Whether Data Collection Should Be Longitudinal

In order to analyze *change* in employment, earnings, life satisfaction, and the like, the same individuals must be measured before and after the program intervention. In some situations, program eligibility data partially satisfy this need by detailing work history as well as individual background characteristics. When these data constitute adequate preprogram measures, an evaluation may be "added on" efficiently by identifying a sample at the point of program termination and measuring postprogram outcomes parallel to the preprogram measures already available.

A wide range of preprogram data may be informative concerning client characteristics. The important issue regarding the analysis of change is that the preprogram measures be similar enough to postprogram measures to be comparable. If the range of program outcomes is widened, additional preprogram measures may be required. However, pre- and postprogram measures need not be identical, as discussed later in this chapter.

Determining the Duration of the Study

While it would be convenient to concentrate data collection into a few months, this shortcut endangers the validity of the research, introducing known biases and others less easy to identify. The population to be studied should, therefore, be defined to include *all enrollees or terminees throughout the full year.*

This definition prevents bias due to seasonal variations in the labor market. Similarly, in classroom training, some institutions tend to end courses during particular months, so that the proportion of terminees who are program completers vs. those who are dropouts varies monthly. Third, different service providers develop different policies concerning when to commit their funds, in total or for particular services, and how long to hold unsuccessful participants before terminating them when required to by the expiration of agency contract periods. All these factors produce seasonal differences in the likelihood of program success.

Defining the Size of the Study Sample

Once a population is selected for analysis, the question becomes how *large* a sample should be in order for calculations to estimate accurately the patterns within the entire participant population. Assuming a *representative* sample, the primary determinant of error margin (i.e., of the accuracy of conclusions) is the number of cases upon which estimates are based. A conclusion that one program variant has 10 percent higher retention rate than another means little if the margin of error for that estimate is 20 percent. Therefore, the first decision must be how many cases are needed in order to generate a level of error acceptable to those who will use the analysis results.

One essential reason that survey research has become such a widely used method is that the accuracy of estimates rises rapidly as we move from very small samples to samples of modest size; yet, samples of modest size are nearly as accurate as very large samples. This occurs because error decreases as a function of the square root of the sample size. More precisely, the estimated error associated with any measure depends on the *standard error* of that measure. For random samples, the standard error equals the standard deviation of the measure divided by the square root of the sample size *(i.e., se = sd ÷ sqrtN)*. Thus, if an income measure has a standard deviation of $4,000, the standard error is about $800 with a sample of 25, $400 with a sample of 100, $200 with a sample of 400, and $100 with a sample of 1,600.

One can see the danger of relying on a very small sample. However, it is equally evident that the marginal improvement from each increase in sample size is quickly reduced as sample size becomes larger. In the example above, adding 375 to a sample of 25 reduces error by $600, from $800 to $200. However, another 1,200 cases would be required to trim a further $100 off the standard error.

This phenomenon explains why many state and local surveys with limited funds choose sample sizes in the range of 350-500. Efficiency (accuracy gained per increase in data collection cost) rises rapidly below that level, but more slowly afterward. In addition, when percentages (e.g., percent "yes") are reported, samples in this size range produce error margins at or under 5 percent, a round number and error margin typically satisfactory for most purposes. However, sample size decisions should always be made after analysis goals are clearly established.- Planners will be well-advised to consult one of several thorough texts on sampling (e.g., Kish 1965; Sudman 1976) or to employ a sampling specialist in cases where sampling appears problematic or in order to determine the most cost-efficient sample.[7]

One additional consideration must be included in planning sample size: not all members of the initial sample selected will be contacted. Therefore, the number of specific individuals selected for inclusion in the sample must be greater than the number of completed interviews desired. The number to be selected is calculated by dividing the desired number of completed interviews by the planned survey completion rate. For example, to complete 400 interviews at a completion rate of 70 percent would require that 571 names be identified in the initial sample (400 ÷ 0.7).

Stratifying Samples

Populations are sometimes divided into subgroups, or strata, each of which is sampled separately. Strata may be sampled in proportion to their numbers in the population, or disproportionately. Although some believe that samples must be proportionately stratified to insure the proper number of members with various background characteristics, this belief is in error. Proper sampling procedures insure a representative sample. No reason exists to consider *proportionate stratification* in gross impact analysis.

There are several conditions under which *disproportionately stratified* samples are sometimes recommended (Sudman 1976). Only one of these is applicable to gross impact analysis, but that one reason is central to statewide differential impact analysis as well as to analyses of subcontractor performance within large SDAs. The need for disproportionate stratification of gross impact samples arises when the analyst's emphasis is on comparing or reliably characterizing subpopulations rather than on characterizing the entire population of participants. This occurs in the case of JTPA postprogram performance standards, where welfare recipients are treated as a separate stratum. In addition, statewide analysis aimed toward comparisons among SDAs, or SDA-level analysis comparing service providers, should consider stratifying to insure reliable characterization of smaller units. For such comparisons, the operative issue is not total sample size, but sample size for each subunit being compared with any other.

Identifying Members of the Sample

The sample of participants who are interviewed must be *representative* of the population being studied; i.e., each element of the population must have an equal chance to be included in the sample. *None of the claims for sample efficiency or reliability holds when samples are not representative.* Sample selection procedures must guarantee equal probability of inclusion, eliminating any purposeful or accidental selection. The only way to guarantee equal probability of inclusion is to select from the population into the sample at random. The classical approach is to select each individual from an ordered list, using a table of random numbers. Two, more convenient methods, however, are equally valid.

First, the last three digits of participants' social security numbers are random with respect to any meaningful characteristic of individuals. Therefore, sample members may be selected by identifying a range of three-digit numbers that would produce the required sample size, and including all participants with numbers falling in that range. If, for example, 25 percent of the names are to be sampled, the lower end of the range is chosen at random, and the upper is set at 250 higher. The second method is *systematic sampling based on a random start*. If 25 percent of the population is to be sampled, a list of names, typically a computer file, is prepared. One of the first four is chosen at random, and then every fourth name is included in the sample.

Participants may be selected into the sample at either *program entry* or *termination*, as long as the full population of participants is available for the sample. From the practical research administration viewpoint, it is often preferable to identify the sample at termination. However, if the data collection plan requires the addition of individual treatment measures throughout the program, it would be most efficient to identify participants for inclusion in the analysis *upon entry*. At that point, they could be specially tagged for collection of individual treatment data and inclusion in the postprogram follow-up.

Establishing a Follow-Up Period for
Measuring Postprogram Outcomes

In addition to outcomes measured at program termination, postprogram outcomes are especially valuable for assessing program quality. In the case of JTPA, a three-month follow-up is required, making that period the obvious choice for a first, and perhaps only, follow-up. The majority of any survey costs occurs before the first question is asked— recording locater information, identifying a sample, keeping records on that sample, tracking hard-to-locate former participants, hiring and training interviewers, setting up interview phone banks, making multiple calls to locate the participant, and introducing the purpose of the call. Therefore, the most efficient design is to add questions to a pre-existing survey.

In addition, the issue of selecting a follow-up period should be examined on its own merits. The major question is whether three months is too short a follow-up lag period. Factors weigh on both sides of the question.

There is value in extending the follow-up time period. Recent studies testing how well various follow-up measures predict long-term net impact of JTPA find three-month follow-ups much stronger than termination data alone, six-month follow-ups stronger than those at three months, and nine-month periods stronger than those at six months (Geraci 1984; Zornitsky et al. 1985). While the gain from each additional delay is smaller than the one before, each does offer improved validity.

Costs are also involved in extending the follow-up period. Follow-up surveys are subject to serious *sample attrition* if the first or only interviews are conducted very long after termination. Since sample attrition introduces unknown biases, it is preferable to conduct shorter-term follow-ups and achieve higher completion rates. In addition, a three-month follow-up is minimally acceptable. That delay is long enough to allow the rate of employment after classroom training to stabilize. It is also long enough for OJT placement to stabilize after the postcontract drop-off, even where 30-day delayed performance payments may delay that drop-off. Three months is also long enough to eliminate most inconsistencies introduced by the tendencies of some service providers to make more extensive use than others of the "administrative hold for job search assistance" category following the program.

Given the costs and inefficiencies of long-term follow-up surveys, states or SDAs planning to do longer-term follow-up may wish to consider using unemployment insurance (UI) wage records if they are available. Once access to the UI data base is established, a one- or even two-year follow-up is as easy to perform as a six-month follow-up. (UI system use is detailed by Johnson and Stromsdorfer in chapter 2 of this volume.) One factor, however, limits the usefulness of these data as a *gross* impact measure: UI data cover only individuals who maintain residence within the state. In the net impact approach, movement out of state is assumed to be equivalent for treated and untreated groups. However, gross outcomes are measured only for participants, making movement out of state a serious problem. One cannot determine whether a record of zero earnings represents continuous unemployment or movement out of the state. Use of this approach is recommended only if a separate tracking effort—to estimate the proportion who moved out of the UI reporting area—is mounted for those individuals with zero UI income. That estimate could then be used to adjust estimated job retention rates.

Choosing the Data Collection Method

Gross impact analysis involves data collection through follow-up surveys of participants and employers. The rapid expansion of the survey research industry has been accompanied by a growing literature on how to conduct surveys, the strengths and weaknesses of surveys, and the relative strengths and weaknesses of in-person interviews, mail questionnaires, and phone interviews (e.g., Dillman 1978; Rossi, Wright, and Anderson 1983). Survey research technology will not be detailed here; it will suffice to make the following summary claims:

1. Correctly conducted, surveys have proven highly reliable.
2. Surveys suffer much less response bias than once feared, as long as the respondent believes the interviews are conducted by a neutral party,[8] and interviewers converse in a natural style (Bradburn 1983).
3. Bias from nonresponse can be problematic, but can be guarded against by achieving relatively high response rates and either insuring relatively equal response rates from all key subgroups or statistically adjusting subgroup response rates during analysis.
4. Given the cost of in-person interviews and the high nonresponse rate and possible educational bias in response with mail questionnaires, phone surveys are usually recommended for program evaluation.

Conclusions Concerning Design

When the research design decisions just discussed have been made, the basic structure of the evaluation effort is in place. These issues have been touched on only briefly, as they are so basic. However, detailed treatments are available in various standard texts (e.g., Rossi and Freeman 1982), making further comment here unnecessary.

Differential Impact Analysis: Estimating Influences on Program Outcomes

The primary goal of differential impact analysis is to reliably describe differences in postprogram outcomes across program services and forms of service delivery implementation, so as to identify the *probable causes* of those differences. In nonexperimental research, identifying causal relationships is problematic. However, quasi-experimental research designs, such as those recommended by Campbell and Stanley (1966), can considerably increase our confidence in having reliably identified the major causes of differences we observe. (See also Campbell and Cook 1979; Caporaso and Roos 1973.) For purposes of program development, managers will wish to gain information about the differential effectiveness of *program variants*—options available to managers in the services assigned to individuals and in forms of program implementation. These variants may be altered on the basis of evaluation findings in order to improve program effectiveness.

Formal, quantitative differential impact analysis is a relatively underdeveloped field, as is well-illustrated in Borus's (1979) program evaluation primer. After listing 44 specific participant characteristics known to affect labor market success, he turns to the question of "program component independent variables." His one-paragraph discussion of this topic begins by saying that "It would be extremely useful in modifying existing programs and in the planning of new programs to know which of the (program) components is most effective for various types of participants" (Borus 1979, p. 70). Two measures are suggested: program length, "... and, if possible, a measure of quality." A review of previous studies using a differential impact analysis approach to evaluating job training programs is included in Simpson (1986).

Identifying probable causal connections is valuable to program managers because changing a factor that has a causal influence on program outcomes is likely to change the level of those outcomes. While formal causal modeling may seem the domain of esoteric social science, it is essential to research on the basis of which investment decisions may be made. Let us suppose that a weak analysis confirms higher success rates among individuals who receive shorter intake procedures and concludes that brief intake causes improved program performance. Let us further assume that a more solid causal analysis would have learned that the most highly employable participants entering the system were given brief intake because they had little need, and that it was their employability rather than the intake that affected their postprogram success. Ironically, if an SDA were to base decisions on such weak research and overhaul its intake system to offer only short intake, its performance would not improve and might deteriorate, because those participants who needed, and previously received, the longest intake no longer have that opportunity.

The goal of each of the steps involved in differential impact analysis is to increase our confidence that we have identified those program variants that do have a direct influence on program outcomes and are therefore useful to program managers in improving their programs. This chapter can only summarize some major characteristics of nonexperimental research designed to increase the analyst's ability to identify causal relationships. There are also useful references available on this complex subject (e.g., Blalock 1964; 1985).

Research into causal relationships begins with *comparisons*. To determine whether program option *A* is better than option *B*, one must identify a criterion of comparison (e.g., job retention) and compare options *A* and *B* on that dimension. Options could be basic program activities, such as OJT, classroom training, or work experience, or optional variants within the same activity, such as OJT assignments developed by the participant, developed by the service provider, or initiated by an employer. These comparisons should be selected so that a causal interpretation is reasonable. This is where past research findings, economic theory, and managers' knowledge of programs come into play. If answering a question in causal terms would fly in the face of logic or of established information, the question probably should not be posed as part of a differential impact analysis.

In addition, to convincingly establish that a relationship is causal, findings from our comparisons must hold up after competing explanations have been eliminated. Each time we identify a plausible competing explanation, test it, and find that it does not explain away the difference between options *A* and *B*, we increase our confidence in the causal association between program variant *A/B* and the outcome in question. For example, our confidence in finding that public classroom trainers perform better than proprietary trainers (or the reverse) would be increased by learning that the difference in performance could not be accounted for by differences in participants' literacy skills or prior job experience, by differences in the fields for which each type of school trained participants, etc.

The goal of quasi-experimental research is to eliminate the effects of all important measurable alternative explanations. That goal is never reached, but we can eliminate *many* important alternative explanations. These include both factors of interest to the analyst, such as other *program variants confounded with the one being tested*, and *control variables*, such as age or gender, known to affect the outcome in question.

Classical experiments attempt to eliminate competing explanations by controlling variants other than the *A/B* comparison of interest and by randomly assigning individuals to variants *A* and *B*, hoping thereby to produce groups equivalent in all regards except for the variant under study. Quasi-experimental research occurs in settings that allow neither the control of variants other than those directly under study nor the random assignment of participants to program variants. Instead, multivariate statistical techniques are used to determine whether alternative explanations are able to undermine our confidence in findings.

The primary strategy of differential impact analysis is to *utilize each program variant as a comparison group for each other variant*. Except where program variants are too highly correlated with each other or with participant background characteristics, multivariate analysis can estimate the unique effects of each. This same approach has guided recent research on the impact of college (Astin 1977). In the case of college impact, no untreated comparison group exists, making net impact studies impossible. However, comparisons among colleges, with each acting as comparison group for the other, are possible given careful measurement of differential selection into each college. The same logic applies to differential impact analysis, where the decision is made to structure research that cannot ask net impact questions but which can, nonetheless, reliably compare different treatments and treatment contexts.

Combating Bias That Threatens the Validity of Differential Impact Analysis

The comparisons demanded by the analysis goals and the data collection method—surveys in this case—determine the major threats to the validity of differential impact analysis. These risks are summarized below. Each is a source of *bias,* as opposed to *random error.* The term bias refers to error that consistently misdirects research results. Like a compass with a metal object nearby, readings from the analysis are distorted in a consistent direction. To correct the findings, one must remove the object or adjust for its influence. Random error differs from bias in that it takes no particular direction. Random error can be as serious as bias if it is large. However, techniques for minimizing random error are well-developed in survey research (i.e., careful measurement techniques and properly constituted samples).

Some types of bias can also be dealt with through standard survey research techniques. These include bias from censored samples, nonresponse bias, and response bias. They can be prevented by selecting samples correctly, achieving high response rates across all major groups in the sample, and wording questions properly. The two types of bias defined in exhibit 3.6, *selection bias* and *bias from confounded program variants*, are combated during multivariate analysis. This means that descriptive gross outcomes analysis, which does not employ multivariate techniques, is always subject to serious bias. Differential impact analysis is able to reduce, but not eliminate, these biases during analysis.

Bias is reduced when equations include measures indicating selectivity and program variants that overlap with the program variant being tested. However, many selection biases are unknown or cannot be measured, making statistical adjustments difficult. Therefore, selection

Exhibit 3.6
Two Types of Bias Especially Problematic
to Differential Impact Research

Selection Bias

When participants who select or are selected into different program variants differ in ways that affect program outcomes, observed outcome differences between program variants could be produced either by program qualities or by participant characteristics. If participant characteristics are not taken into account, estimates of program impact will be biased. For example, preprogram employment experience influences postprogram employability and may also influence which program service is assigned. If employment history is not measured, the analyst cannot adjust for its impact on postprogram outcomes, producing biased estimates of the differential impact of service assignment. Since many such differences may exist but not be measurable (e.g., subjective motivation), some degree of selection bias is always present in differential impact analysis.

Confounded Program Variants

When two program variants are correlated with each other, the unique effects of each can be estimated if both are included in the same equation. However, if one is omitted, then the estimate for the included variant will absorb the effect of the omitted one, biasing conclusions in that direction. For example, if in a particular service delivery system, service providers who exercise especially careful quality control over employer sites acceptable for OJT assignments also conduct more elaborate intake assessment of job maturity prior to OJT assignment, and if both of these improve OJT postprogram outcomes, then both must be included in the analysis, or the estimated impact of either one alone will be inflated.

---

bias is the most serious analytical problem as well as the most difficult to diagnose.

Minimizing Bias from Nonrandom Selection

Reducing the effects of selection bias follows the general logic of causal analysis. Each source of selection bias is an alternative explanation that can be countered only by inclusion in multivariate equations of variables which identify the selection process. The discussion below identifies four major sources of selection bias. For each, the aspects of differential impact analysis most likely to be affected and the measurement strategies most able to minimize the bias are indicated.

Sources of Selection Bias

1. *Legally eligible individuals may or may not apply to JTPA* because of differences in information available, personality or motivational differences or geographical differences in services available. This selection process is critical for net impact studies, but seldom biases differential impact analysis, which involve only comparisons among individuals already enrolled in JTPA. However, if this type of bias

differs across SDAs, then statewide differential impact comparisons among SDAs will be affected.

Little protection from this type of bias is available to analysis that does not include an untreated comparison group. However, SDA-level measures of program availability and participant measures of motivation for applying to JTPA may help assess possible differences between SDAs. In addition, standard demographic background characteristics may be correlated with motivational characteristics, allowing their inclusion in differential impact analysis to act as a partial proxy for direct measures of motivation.

2. *Participants may or may not be enrolled into JTPA after eligibility is determined.* If the reasons are correlated with program outcomes, bias will result. The source of this type of selection may be program policies and practices such as targeting, a participant's choice after learning of program options, or failure to locate a program placement of the type decided on for that participant.

Measuring the source and nature of the selection is the appropriate tool for reducing bias from these sources. It is possible to measure implementation policies such as targeting, which are intended to determine which eligible individuals are enrolled. In addition, measures of participants' demographic and work history characteristics may act as a proxy for agency selection or may indicate which participants best fit the agency's desired targets. Beyond that, the key measures of agency selection involve the proportion of eligibles for each provider who fail to enroll and the reasons why they have made that choice. Given some JTPA managers' reported emphasis on enrolling the most qualified participants, statewide differential impact analysis will be well-advised to include agency-level measures of intended and, where possible, actual selectivity by service providers.

3. *Participants may request a particular treatment aside from the decision to enroll in JTPA.* If the reasons for that request also predict that participant's likely program outcome, this self-selection can bias estimates of how program activity affects outcomes. This is especially likely to occur where employers select desirable job applicants and then send them to JTPA to request OJT enrollment,

or where schools send their best students to JTPA for support to complete a program. Participant requests are most likely to involve a basic program activity, or a particular school or employer. Analysis comparing these most basic treatment variants is, therefore, the most likely to suffer from this source of bias.

The best protection against bias from self-selected treatment is measuring participants' route into JTPA: whether they requested particular services, and if so, which ones and why. In particular, the route from employer or school to JTPA should be identified, since it involves a type of self-selection most likely to affect postprogram success. One could also measure the degree to which particular service providers control the assignment to treatment vs. allowing participants to elect their own treatment.

4. *Participants may also be assigned to particular treatments by program managers.* If treatment A rather than treatment B is assigned on the basis of factors that also influence program outcome, selection bias is present.

This source of bias has potentially pervasive effects on differential impact analysis because rational service provider policy offers the most intensive services to those with the greatest need. That is, many JTPA services are intentionally compensatory. Since "greatest need" often translates to "least employable," the selection of services on the basis of need can bias estimates of treatment impacts on employment outcomes in studies that do not include measures of need in the analysis. To identify compensatory effects of treatment, one must have measures of both the need and the treatment. Since these two factors have opposite effects, they cancel each other out and neither effect is visible without joint analysis of both variables.

Measurement Approaches to Combat Selection Bias

When differential selection cannot be prevented, it must be identified by measuring the selection process and decisions. Differential impact analysis has the advantage of attacking from two different angles, using *individual-level measures* of preprogram characteristics and of the selection process experienced by each individual participant, and also employing *agency-level implementation measures* of selection policies and typical practices. Individual-level measures have several advantages for combating bias:

1. Ideally, they can include the agency's diagnosis of each participant's need and its service prescription for each participant as well as the treatment each individual actually received. Both the participant's true level of need and the agency's perception of each participant's need are important potential sources of selection bias.

2. They offer information on the explicit selection process by the JTPA agency. For example, we can learn how much intake time the agency spent with each particular participant. It is one thing to know what "full" intake includes (an agency-level measure) and another to know that individual A received only a "fast track" intake review, while individual B was judged to require extensive pre-employment services.

3. They can include the route each specific individual takes into training. This proves to be one primary indicator of selection bias.

4. They allow precise measurement of program variants, increasing the power of the measures most important to any differential impact analysis.

Agency-level variables also exhibit two particular strengths in combating selection bias.

1. The problem of compensatory treatment cannot be fully solved by individual-level measures, because no precise measures of need or assistance exist. Agency-level measures indicate resources *available* or provided *on average*. They are, therefore, much less influenced by compensatory treatment. For example, if agency A provides job search assistance to only 5 percent of clients while agency

2. B does so for 40 percent, it is almost certain that many individuals of equal need will receive this service in agency B but not in agency A. Agency policies directly affect selection. Targeting decisions, policy toward "creaming," policies regarding single vs. multiple activity treatments, and the like, have some consistent effect on selection across all participants enrolled through a particular agency. Such agency policies can indicate selection on difficult-to-measure criteria such as how participants present themselves interpersonally.

The Potential for Severe Bias in
Analyses of the Most Basic Program Divisions

Perhaps the two most basic program divisions managers might wish to analyze using the differential impact analysis approach are different service providers within a service delivery system and different program activity assignments. Unhappily, these divisions are the most likely to be affected by selection bias as well as by bias from confounded program variants. Implementation policies vary most widely across service providers and across basic program services. Service providers are likely to want control over which participants are assigned to each basic service. Similarly, participants are more likely to exercise choice regarding preferred basic services than about more specific implementation policies. Service provider implementation and service mix involve basic resource allocation decisions and are, therefore, likely to be affected by geopolitical concerns.

Different Service Providers

SDAs, and to a smaller extent their subcontractors, are located in different labor markets and political atmospheres. Although one can account for some of these differences through measures of the labor market environment and agency policies, many will remain unmeasured. Therefore, some unknown degree of bias will persist in analysis across service providers, especially SDAs. The fuller and more accurate the measures of labor market environment and agency policies concerning recruitment and selection, the smaller the remaining bias.

Basic Program Activities

Basic service treatment options are designed, in part, to accommodate differences in participant needs and qualifications. In particular, job search assistance assumes job readiness, OJT assumes minimum acceptability to employers, and work experience assumes an absence of even the most basic job experience. Selection bias is likely to be especially serious in such cases, because differential selection on the basis of employability is explicitly called for. In addition, different treatments produce outcomes through different mechanisms, making them complex to compare directly. For example, true training interventions are intended to produce skill transfer and employment, leading to a career line. These outcomes have little relevance, however, for an intervention based on securing employment through the leverage of a payment made to employers.

These concerns lead to the recommendation that (where resources allow) sample size should be large enough to accommodate separate analysis within each basic activity, along with tests performed across all activities. In addition, differential impact analysis should include "membership-identifier" variables indicating enrollment in each of the most common program activities and in each SDA included in an analysis. These variables will absorb the effects of basic program activity and also some unmeasured selection effects, thereby reducing bias in estimates of other effects.

Although these problems appear overwhelming, and are never solved completely, each additional measure of selection improves estimates. The analyst, therefore, has the power to produce highly useful and quite accurate estimates, which should, nevertheless, always be interpreted as imperfect. Simpson's (1989) analysis of one SDA illustrates the value of measuring selection into program activities. Without controls, it appeared that enrolling participants in multiple-sequenced activities produced only a slight improvement in job retention at 13 weeks. However, after including in the analysis a set of competency benchmarks measured at program entry, a large benefit became observable for those enrolled in sequenced activities. These competencies had been used as a basis for assigning multiple services, so that participants with greatest need received most intensive treatment. These two factors tended to cancel each other out, so that the effects of each could be observed only when both were included in the equation.

Measuring Potential Influences on Outcomes

Differential impact analysis tests the impact of program variants and control variables on postprogram outcomes. In particular, managers may test whether particular forms of implementation produce greater or lesser success and whether assignment to particular program services or to services with particular qualities improves an individual's chances of experiencing postprogram success. Basic categories of factors may be tested to examine their possible impact on these outcomes. They are shown in exhibit 3.7.

As discussed earlier, the analysis of how program implementation and treatment influence outcomes is one of the most neglected areas of

Exhibit 3.7
Types of Factors to be Tested as Possible Determinants
of Program Outcomes, with Examples

Types of Determinants		Examples
Program variants: Forms of program implementation	Basic oganizational components	• Form of contracting used • Program cost • Size of program
	Service delivery framework	• Targeting (selection) policies • Typical intake procedures • Quality control procedures • Exit practices
Program variants: Individual services (treatment) received	Membership identifiers	• Basic service assigned to (OJT, CT, etc.) • Service provider enrolled through
	Variable descriptions	• Intake screening intensity or method • Treatment intensity (length, complexity) • Characteristics of the trainer • Job search assistance received
Control variables	Client characteristics	• Age • Employment history • Educational attainment
	Selection processes	• Indicators of "creaming" • Referrals involving prescreening
	Labor market characteristics	• Unemployment rates across place/time • Median wage across place/time

research in employment and training. Implementation studies do not include estimates of impact on outcomes. Outcome studies typically work with the very limited base of treatment measures derived from accessible agency records. This means the thoughtful measurement of program variants is the key to creative advances in program development based on differential impact analysis.

Of the factors shown in exhibit 3.7, those labeled "program variants" are identified by choice, because the analyst hopes to learn whether particular implementation forms or particular individual services enhance program outcomes. Program variants include the basic organizational arrangements and the service delivery framework established to implement delivery of services, and the specific treatment received by each participant. Treatment includes both *variable descriptions* of the services received, such as the length of a training program, and measures identifying only whether or not a participant was a member of some particular set, such as recipient of classroom training or enrollee through a particular service provider.[9] A third set of factors, "control variables," is required in order to insure that effects estimated for program variants are as accurate as possible. These measure participant background, selection processes, labor market qualities, etc. When these are analyzed together, it becomes possible to isolate estimates of the unique effects of each on a given program outcome.

The conceptualization phase of measuring treatment and implementation is critical. The criteria summarized in exhibit 3.8 offer some guidance. Criteria 1 and 6 are essentially technical, and may be honored without much knowledge of JTPA. However, criteria 2 through 5 require knowledge of the state or local JTPA service delivery system, making input from program managers critical to successful analysis. *As a general principle, differential impact analysis becomes useful to guide program development only when measures are developed in collaboration between researchers and program directors.* Measures are also suggested by JTPA implementation studies (reviewed by Grembowski, chapter 2 in this volume) and some excellent analyses of CETA implementation (Levitan and Mangum 1981; Snedeker and Snedeker 1973; Franklin and Ripley 1984).

Exhibit 3.8
Criteria Useful When Selecting Implementation
or Treatment Variables for Analysis

1. Can the variable be measured reliably?

2. Is there reason to believe it varies across individuals or service providers?

3. Is there reason to believe it represents a nontrivial program impact?

4. Does the variable measure a program variant under the control of program managers; that is, is it a policy-relevant variable?

5. Are program managers open to changing the program variant to be measured?

6. Given cost and time constraints, can the measure be integrated into a data collection scheme?

Service Provider Surveys to Measure
Program Implementation Variants

In exhibit 3.7, the first sets of measures characterize program implementation—aspects of the organizations put in place to provide JTPA services. These measures characterize the entire organization—its structure, policies, and practices—rather than any one participant's treatment. Most program implementation variants are best measured through surveys of service-providing organizations. Data for each service provider can then be attached to the computer files of all participants who enrolled through that provider. In this way, data collected inexpensively by surveying a limited number of service providers can be used to analyze program impacts on all individual participants in the sample.

Depending on the nature of the measures, agency directors may be able to answer reliably, or agency staff may need to compare notes or consult records in order to characterize typical practices accurately. With easy-to-answer questions, phone surveys may be used. For more demanding measures, however, a written survey, which allows time for data gathering, is preferable. The recommendation here is to use a written survey of each service-providing organization, with a backup telephone contact person who can clarify questions as they arise.

One problem with service provider surveys is that agencies may *intend* one form of implementation but actually carry out another, making self-descriptions inaccurate. This can be partially remedied by a second form of implementation measurement: *aggregated agency characteristics.*

Aggregated variables are measured with the individual participant as unit and then summed, percentaged, or averaged across all participants within each agency. For example, agency surveys could report whether policies emphasize training women for nontraditional occupations. The aggregated form of measurement for this same issue begins by constructing the individual-level variable. Nontraditional training fields for women are identified, and the training field of each female participant in the sample is coded as traditional or nontraditional. That individual variable is then aggregated for each agency, producing an agency-level variable, "percent of female participants trained in nontraditional fields," which may be used to double-check agency reports.

Suggested Measures of Program Implementation

Program implementation variants can be divided into *basic organizational components,* such as forms of contracting and staffing, and *service delivery framework* within which intake, service assignment, provision of basic services and support services, and program exit occur. The latter are most likely to have a direct influence on program outcomes, because they affect the nature of services provided and the selection process through which individuals are assigned to treatments. Yet basic organizational components are inexpensive to measure and may influence outcomes *indirectly,* by affecting various aspects of the service delivery framework. They are also important as control variables, to protect interpretations from alternative explanations after the research is completed.

Basic Organizational Composition

Forms of contracting. SDAs may or may not use requests for proposals (RFPs) as part of the subcontracting process. For both service provider contracts and trainer referral contracts, use of fixed-price, performance-based contracts may be contrasted with other approaches to contracting.

Staff qualifications. Franklin and Ripley (1984) argue strongly that staff qualifications represent a key to success, although they are not specific about what constitutes good qualifications.

Staff turnover. One might assume that staff stability (low turnover) would predict success, although during the late CETA era, one study found the reverse to be true (Simpson 1984a).

Staff workload and division of labor. Client-to-staff ratio, ongoing staff training, and the division of staff between direct service, administration, and development work can influence intensity and effectiveness of service delivery and, therefore, client outcomes.

Service provider history. The age of service providers, how much their services have changed over time, their relations with the private and public sectors, and their rate of growth or decline may be useful to identify, although JTPA implementation studies suggest these factors have little differential impact on program outcomes.

Size. The size of SDAs or subcontractors (amount of grant, number of participants, size of staff) may also be included as control variables.

Program costs and cost-related policies. Program costs are usually very difficult to measure precisely for individuals or for specific services. However, total cost-per-participant can be measured as an implementation variable, and analyzed either as outcome or as one possible influence on outcomes, when different SDAs or different service providers are being compared. In addition, policies toward use of support services, rate of employer reimbursement, and length of training can be measured. Aggregated measures, such as the proportion of participants receiving support services or the average length of OJTs, may also be useful.

Service Delivery Framework

Many of the same factors Grembowski poses as key to understanding organizational process (see chapter 4) are also valuable measures of program implementation for differential impact analysis. These may serve as program variants or as controls against bias.

Explicit selection processes. Agency selection is critical to measure, both as a service quality issue and also because *selection bias can be partially addressed with such measures.* Agency policy may emphasize enrolling the most job-ready, those with greatest need, or those whom the program is most likely to benefit. Agency selection policy may reserve some activities, such as short OJTs, primarily for those who are most easily served. A greater or smaller proportion of participants may have been referred initially by employers or schools, adding an issue of preselection.

Intake procedures. Procedures used during intake for selection, diagnosis, information giving, and counseling may differ in intensity and type. They may affect how well the agency treatments match the abilities and needs of each participant to the labor market. They may also act as indicators of the agency selection process.

Possible measures include length and intensity of typical intake; proportion of participants who get full intake; number of "hurdles" participants must pass, as an indicator of selection for motivation; whether intake is centralized or conducted by subcontractors; whether intake is conducted individually or in groups; what diagnostic tools are *available* and how often various tools are used, policies regarding targeting and other screening criteria; and what proportion of placements with employers were initiated by the employers.

Quality control over referral and program activity mix. Service providers may exercise strict control over the development of participant assignments, including rigorous screening of schools, agencies, or employers involved in treatment, or they may take the *laissez faire* approach, offering information and encouraging participants' self-directed search for assignments, but exercising little control. This issue promises to be one of the most valuable areas for agency-level measurement, because referral represents the pivotal point of agency influence over treatment.

Possible measures of agency control include whether employer referrals are encouraged, giving control to employers, or carefully reviewed and screened, retaining agency control; whether policy encourages "open contract" referral arrangements, whereby employers agree to fill all openings for certain job titles by choosing among a set of eligibles sent for review by JTPA, giving service providers great control; whether the agency conducts formal quality reviews of employer-trainers or classroom-trainers, increasing control; and whether a large proportion of assignments are developed through participants' self-directed search, which decreases agency control.

The second half of the quality control issue is *how quality is defined.*

Among those agencies that perform explicit quality control reviews over potential referrals or placements, what *criteria are used to define quality?* Some possible measures include the following: previous JTPA placement or retention track record, if applicable; in the case of employer-based interventions, employer stability or growth, typical non-JTPA turnover rates, typical wage rates, amount and quality of training likely to occur in OJT assignments, employer's ability to supervise constructively; in the case of schools or community-based trainers, staff quality, ability to handle special student needs, placement assistance for graduates, and credibility among employers.

Exit practices. The final element of treatment is the set of program completion and job search options implemented. Exit practices are especially important to measure at the agency level. Individual measures of job search assistance suffer from the compensation problem: those least able to locate jobs on their own are most likely to receive job search assistance, creating the appearance that postprogram employment is *negatively* correlated with receipt of job search assistance. Agency-level measures of the *average availability* of assistance are not affected by the compensation problem. Measures may include availability of job clubs or job search workshops, proportion of staff time devoted to postprogram job development, proportion of trainers who include formal job placement assistance, and method of placement, i.e., centralized or handled by subcontractors.

Individual Measures of Treatment Variants

The nature and intensity of services received by different participants in a program vary widely *within* service providers as well as between them. These differences among individual experiences require individual level measurement. In addition, individual-level measures offer several advantages, as listed in exhibit 3.9.

Some individuals' treatment experiences are routinely recorded as part of agency MIS files. Others may be recorded by agency staff as the treatments occur, or may be included in participant follow-up surveys, measured through participants' recall of the services they received. The preferable form of measurement is agency recording. Agency staff can

Exhibit 3.9
Major Advantages of Individual Level Measures

- They tie program services to outcomes for the same specific individuals, offering precise analysis of the degree of association between the two.
- They tie specific services and outcomes to specific individual background characteristics, providing direct tests of control variables.
- Normally, they vary more widely than agency level measures, strengthening statistical tests.
- Normally, they suffer less overlap with other test variables than agency level measures, strengthening statistical tests.

---

record services as they occur, avoiding recall errors, and including sequence. Staff are also more able than participants to identify which services are administered. Agency measurement is also less expensive, as measured in terms of dollars, since it avoids telephone interview time. It is, however, more expensive in terms of staff time and often in terms of staff resistance to data recording.

Gathering such information through participant surveys also has certain advantages: less lead time is required; it is the only option available when samples are identified at termination; and state or multi-SDA analyses may not reflect information necessary to coordinate data collection by large numbers of local direct service personnel, making measurement at follow-up the only viable option.

Intake Services, Screening, and Selection

Since intake intensity should be compensatory, with greatest intensity reserved for those with greatest need, good intake will tend to equalize the chances for success of those with greater and lesser need. Accurately estimating the impact of intake on program outcomes, therefore, requires both measures of intake *experiences* and also measures of participants' *need* for intake assistance. The best approach to measuring need is to identify specific barriers to employment via the competency-bench-marking approach developed most thoroughly in the area of youth competencies (Simpson 1989).

Measures of individual intake experiences can include both the nature and intensity of intake diagnosis and services. One approach would measure time in intake (individually or in workshops), specific intake diagnostics such as testing, and intensity of specific types of intake services such as career counseling. Another approach would identify *separate paths taken by individuals enroute to program enrollment*, such as employer-initiated OJT contracts.

Delay Between Eligibility and Enrollment

The time lag between eligibility and enrollment may be a component of selection bias. Enrollment that is almost immediate typically indicates a referral initiated by an employer or a school, and therefore involves preselection. Beyond that, up to some point, delays tend to weed out the least motivated. Very long delays, however, probably discourage those most qualified and motivated.

Assignment to Basic Program Activities

Clearly, one measure of individual treatment must be the basic program activity or activities to which each individual is assigned or referred. These are normally available through MIS files, although comparability of data elements may be an issue where multiple service providers are included in the analysis. Information on multiple activities and sequencing will often require an additional data collection effort beyond the standard MIS. It is especially important to distinguish between (1) *multiple-sequenced activities planned in advance,* such as an orientation workshop followed by classroom training, followed by OJT in the same skill area; and (2) *"second chance" activities* assigned to individuals who failed to utilize their first service successfully and are more likely to fail the second time also.

Treatment Intensity and Completion

In addition to the type of program activity, the *length and intensity* of the activity should be measured, along with whether participants *complete* their programs. The most common measure here, length of time enrolled in JTPA, is easy to obtain from MIS files, but confounds several incompatible measures: length of planned treatment, completion of treatment vs. dropout, addition of "second chance" treatment, treatment vs. dropout, addition of "second chance" treatment, and extension of enrollment in a postprogram administrative hold while employment is sought. For some of these factors, shorter enrollment indicates probable employment failure; for others, longer enrollment indicates probable failure. They must, therefore, be measured separately to produce unambiguous results.

Unfortunately, no precise measures of *training intensity* per-time-period exist. However, partial indicators of intensity can be measured once the intended nature of the intervention is identified. These might include whether the intervention results in a credential, in fields where one exists; how many hours of formal training and of "hands-on" training are provided; whether formal training is "mainstream" (satisfying state certification, taken by nondisadvantaged individuals also); and if the intervention involves employment, how complex the job is and how much *new* material it presents for participants to learn.

Perhaps the most important form of treatment intensity to measure is the presence or absence of multiple program activities assigned in sequence to address multiple barriers to employment. If process analysis indicates that serving the hard-to-serve is a priority for the organization, then this approach is especially important to analyze.

Characteristics of Trainers

Although factors such as trainers' methods or organizational arrangements can seldom be changed by JTPA, knowledge of which types of trainers most effectively produce desired outcomes can improve quality control and referral decisions. In addition, information on effective training approaches may be of interest to schools and especially to employers, since relatively little is known about how to train effectively on the job.

Some measures describing trainers can be gained from participant follow-up surveys (Simpson 1982). However, the most reliable measurement sources are trainers themselves, i.e., schools or employers. In classroom training, the easiest measures are *typologies of trainers*, e.g., trainers who enroll primarily JTPA participants vs. mainstream trainers, or trainers who are public, proprietary, or community-based. In addition, trainers vary in size, mix between experiential ("hands-on") and formal learning, inclusion of internships, and a great range of other characteristics. It is advisable to construct such measures in collaboration with local vocational educators, who are most aware of variations in available training variants.

In the cases of employer-based treatment, i.e., on-the-job training and, to a smaller extent, work experience and youth tryout, a wide range of measures is available. Relatively little research has been done, however, on such measures. Simpson's (1984a) Washington State OJT research identified characteristics of the trainer and OJT positions, including employer's growth rate, typical non-JTPA turnover rate, the industrial sector, including whether public or private, the quality and complexity of the job, the use of relatively formal training methods, and *range of tranferability of skills* gained from training, i.e., do they apply to a wide range of jobs or are they "firm-specific"?

Expenditures per Individual Participant

The primary marginal cost for each JTPA participant, is the *direct cost of training*. Although other costs are typically impossible to consider during a gross impact analysis, marginal training costs for each participant are usually available through contracts with trainers or employers. (See Zornitsky et al. 1985.) This means that the major program costs attached to each specific participant could be analyzed if these records can be integrated with the basic data set being used. However, such analysis is not to be confused with benefit-cost analysis. (See Johnson and Stromsdorfer, chapter 2 in this volume.)

Another cost issue that also represents an agency policy issue is *ancillary support services*. Except for the issue of stipends offered during classroom training, there appears to be no cogent reason to detail specific support services. However, the total amount expended per person could be recorded at little cost. Such services might affect program completion, although no postprogram impact would be expected beyond that caused by completion.

Needs-based payments are complex to analyze. Income from any source has the potential to affect life stability, personal stress, and other factors, which can in turn influence postprogram labor market experiences. Therefore, a precise analysis of the impact of needs-based stipends *per se* requires measurement of total income during training as well as income from stipends.

Program Exit and Job Search

Agency implementation variables, discussed earlier, measure the availability of various supports at termination. Individual-level measures indicate who makes use of which support services and provide the basis for aggregate agency-level variables. Possible measures include a number of job search services: enrollment in job club or less extensive job search courses, receipt of specific job referrals from trainers or JTPA staff, and receipt of less formal job search assistance from JTPA staff. It is also useful to measure *when* the services occurred. If a job search workshop occurred during or prior to training, all participants have had benefit of it by the time they have to look for work. If the workshop occurs after the end of training, the most successful participants will not enroll because they will have found jobs already. This creates a "compensatory effect," which is extremely difficult to analyze validly.

In addition, participants' *job search behaviors* may be important to measure. These include the importance participants place on finding or retaining work, using the skills learned during the JTPA treatment, and the extent to which a participant is "place bound" (unable to relocate). The expressed importance of working in the training area can be used as a control variable, but can also be analyzed as an intermediate program outcome. Those intending to use such analysis may wish to measure the same variable at enrollment in order to allow an estimate of change during training.

Measurement of Control Variables

As discussed earlier, the approach differential impact analysis takes to prevent bias involves measuring "control variables" for inclusion in multivariate statistical analysis. Many of the most important protections against bias, such as measuring selection criteria, intake procedures, and exit practices, are also of interest as implementation and treatment variants. Analysis of such measures serves the *dual* purposes of testing their impact on program outcomes and also testing whether their exclusion from multivariate equations would bias estimated impact of other program variants. Individual measures, such as preprogram barriers to employment and the route into the JTPA training activity, are also of interest for programmatic reasons, but in differential impact analysis they operate primarily as control variables.

Other control variables fall into two categories: *individual background characteristics* and the *labor market environment*. These measures are not analyzed in the hope of improving programs by changing them; most of them cannot be changed by program managers, or will not be changed, since they are part of the program mandate. They are important because they are likely to affect program outcomes and to differ across service providers, program activities, or other program variants. Therefore, unless they are measured and included in differential impact equations, the estimated impact of program variants of interest to program managers can be biased.

Several individual background characteristics affect program outcomes: *inherited characteristics*, such as gender and ethnicity; *previously achieved characteristics*, such as education level and work experience; and *life cycle situation*, such as marital status and number of dependents. Some mix of these measures is normally available in management information systems. Where factors known to affect labor market experiences are omitted from MIS files, or where measurement is truncated to distinguish only program eligibles from noneligibles, MIS files must be augmented. Borus (1979) provides a detailed enumeration of individual background measures found to influence employment status. Readers are referred there for information on the development of control variables measuring individual background.

One difficulty with preprogram measures is establishing their proper *time frame*. "Preprogram dip" in earnings and employment has been grappled with in much detail, making clear that information running back as far as three years before the program can be useful (Bloom and McLaughlin 1982; Johnson and Stromsdorfer, chapter 2 in this volume). That period may be too costly for agency data collection, but it is clear that too short a preprogram period, such as three or six months, will underestimate the long-term earning potential of many participants and will fail to distinguish those with temporary problems from others.

Measures of labor market characteristics are quite powerful in national studies. They appear to have less effect on training outcomes in a single state or locale. Even so, any study comparing service delivery in more than one geographic area must test the possibility that differences in unemployment levels, average salary levels, or demand for particular types of jobs may affect estimates of differential impact analysis. Aside from census and employment data, the availability of labor market measures depends primarily on the role each state has played in developing reliable occupational outlook data. Most SDAs have compiled this information during their planning periods.

Construction of Category Identifiers

The simplest but most important form of data any differential impact analysis requires is a *set of code numbers that identifies individuals and their membership in various categories*. These categories include sets of service providers, specific trainers, and types of services. Each category to be identified during analysis must have a unique identification number. These are required—

1. To merge data from different sources, allowing the construction of data sets that include the full range of test and control variables, and allowing inexpensive service provider data to be integrated into individual-level analysis.
2. To organize the data set and know what original records to consult in cases where errors on the computer file must be corrected.
3. To construct membership identifiers. These variables are the vehicle required before differential impact analysis can test the impact of membership in particular organizational units, activities, or fields. (The construction of such variables is discussed below.)

The identifiers listed below should be included in any analysis which utilizes data from each source mentioned. The precise nature of each identifier depends on the common practice in the state or SDAs mounting the analysis effort.

Participant identifiers. Codes identifying individual participants are the basic data-file organizing unit and are also necessary in order to merge data from MIS files, follow-up interviews, and individual treatment records. The best participant identifier is a social security number, which is unique and normally required if official data such as UI, welfare, or criminal justice information is to be combined with JTPA data.

Employer identifiers. If employer interviews are conducted, data must be collected under an identifying code, unique for each employer, which is also recorded on each participant's file. In this way, the appropriate employer data may be added to the files of each individual. If agencies have not yet developed employer identification codes, they will also find them extremely useful for organizing employer relations and marketing information and assessing use patterns and retention track records of participating employers.

Classroom trainer identifiers. If special data are collected on classroom trainers, they must be catalogued under identifiers also included on participant records to allow data merging. In addition, trainers enrolling a sufficient number of participants in a sample may be tested using either/ or membership variables, if each trainer has a unique identifier.

Training field identifiers. The field in which participants trained or gained work experience should be identified. This allows description of outcomes by field, construction of either/or membership variables where the number of cases allows, and introduction of labor market data tied to training field.

SDA and subcontractor identifiers. When an analysis combines SDAs, each must be uniquely identified in order to test for differences in outcomes produced by each and add labor market data to individual computer files. The same is true for subcontractor comparisons within one or more SDAs. If subcontractors are numbered within each SDA, unique identifiers can be formed by combining SDA and subcontractor identifiers.

Time period identifiers. The simplest reliable way to calculate time periods, such as lag between eligibility and enrollment, is to record the date of each event, including eligibility, enrollment, treatment start, planned treatment end, actual treatment end, termination, and follow-up. If dates are expressed in compatible units, time periods can then be calculated by subtracting one from the other.

Measures That Place Special Demands on Sampling

The measures of program variants just reviewed may be placed into four categories, in order to focus on two types that make special demands on the *size or structure* of samples. These four approaches are shown in exhibit 3.10. The term "variable description" refers to measures that may take a range of values, for example, percentages, amounts, or degrees of some quality. These are the most common types of measures, explaining why measures are often referred to as *variables*. They are distinguished from "membership identifiers," which always take only two values. The individual (1) does or (2) does not belong to that category.

Standard sampling considerations are structured for variables measured at the individual level. The two-program implementation measures in exhibit 3.10 place special demands on the sample. The demands differ depending on whether the measure is a *membership identifier*, indicating whether or not a participant was served via some specific treatment context, or a *variable description* of some particular aspect of program implementation. Membership identifiers, which indicate whether or not individuals received services via a particular organizational or treatment activity provide an effective way to locate impacts on postprogram outcomes, but not to explain why they are located where they are. Variable descriptions of program characteristics, on the other hand, measure specific qualities that vary across all service providers or program activities, rather than separating each as a whole from the others. This approach does not pinpoint concrete contexts where differ-

Exhibit 3.10
Four Approaches to Measuring Program Variants,
With Examples

	Program Implementation (Measured via a Survey of Service Providers)	Measure of Individual Treatment
Identifier of membership in a specific context	Enrolled through N.W. corner SDA, subcontractor No. 3 versus all others	Trained in community college program versus all others
Variable description of program characteristics	Percent of services performed in-house	Planned length of participant's training program

ences occur. However, it helps explain why they occur, a quality which makes them especially helpful for program development. The particular demands placed on sampling differ between the analysis of membership identifiers and the analysis of variable program descriptions.

Membership Identifiers

Measures that identify membership in particular treatment contexts place little restriction on the number of service providers or other treatment contexts required. If two contexts are identifiable, they may be compared by entering the membership identifier into an equation that also includes the appropriate control variables. However, this simplicity is gained at some cost. First, *explanatory power is no greater with 20 contexts than with two.* Each context is compared individually with all others. Second, *reliability of such comparisons depends on the number of participants enrolled in each membership group.* Thus, no matter how large the total sample, estimates for membership in a category containing very few participants cannot be reliable. This means that analysis of this type may require large, disproportionately stratified samples.

Membership in highly specific contexts, such as particular schools or employers, is usually immune to analysis because so few individuals belong to each context. Membership in larger units, such as SDAs, is entirely possible to assess given that a large enough sample is drawn from each SDA. This limitation on the analysis of specific treatment contexts is of greatest interest for states and large SDAs, which may wish to assess relative performance among different units within the system.

Variable Descriptions of Program Implementation

The sampling demands made by variable descriptions of implementation are directly opposite to those made by membership identifiers; they require multiple treatment contexts, but not larger samples within each. Since participants in each context receive a specific value on some measurement scale, the number of participants in each context matters little. Thus, sample stratification is unnecessary. That advantage, however, is purchased at the cost of requiring *multiple treatment contexts* to be included in the sample.

Imagine that two service providers have been measured on two variables—intensity of intake procedures and the degree of job search assistance provided. If we find that the two providers differ in outcome level, how can we decide which of these variables accounts for the difference? For that matter, how can we claim that either of these, rather than some other variable, explains the difference? To assess whether intake or placement had the impact, we need to compare situations characterized by thorough intake but little job search assistance, and vice versa. With only two organizations, however, that is not possible. These two agency characteristics, as well as any others one can imagine, are by definition perfectly correlated and cannot be disentangled. (In statistical terms, only one degree of freedom is available.)

This same problem faces research comparing more than two contexts, where the variable in question happens to differentiate only one from all others. An analysis reported by Franklin and Ripley (1984) illustrates. They report that program performance was lower in CETA prime sponsors characterized by "crisis management" style. While this finding appears reasonable, only one prime sponsor in their sample was so characterized. Their conclusion, therefore, was based on a comparison between one prime sponsor and 14 others. Consequently, any number of other qualities of that one prime sponsor could have produced the differences they observed.

In the case where three service providers are included in a sample, it is very likely that the problems discussed above will remain. However, there is now a possibility that, in unusual circumstances, one variable characteristic of service providers would have such a strong and consistent impact that a statistically reliable effect would emerge. The principle of parsimony—using the simplest explanation consistent with the facts—becomes the guide to interpretation here. If the differences among outcomes in the three contexts closely fit a single linear treatment measure, but no others, then it is parsimonious to explain findings with that one factor. If, however, they vary far from a linear fit, or if more than one variable fits equally well, the less tidy, but more accurate interpretation must be used; namely, that each unit differs from the other for reasons we cannot demonstrate.

If we introduced a second treatment characteristic variable into the analysis based on three contexts, we would automatically revert to the case in which it is impossible to distinguish among competing explanations. In statistical terms, the number of variables that may be uniquely estimated may not be greater than the degrees of freedom, which equal the number of cases minus one. Since these variables are measured only at the organizational level, the number of cases we are speaking about is the number of service-providing organizations in the analysis.

Extending this line of thought, it is apparent that analysis including many SDAs or analysis of large SDAs including many service providers can be especially valuable for local program development. The larger the number of different agencies in the analysis, the more feasible the tests of agency implementation variables. More variables can be handled simultaneously, and each is tested more reliably and less ambiguously. That is, other things equal, the more separate service providers included in a sample, the lower the covariance among implementation variants is likely to be, strengthening the ability of multivariate analysis to estimate the unique effects of each.

This general rule, that the larger the number of contexts, the firmer the analysis of variable program characteristics, leads to a practical question: what is the minimum number of service providers required for a reasonable differential impact analysis of agency-level implementation measures? The answer is twofold. First, the bad news. The answer depends on many factors: variance in each independent variable, variance in the outcome variable, covariance among independent variables, and covariance between independent variables and the outcome variable. Therefore, no precise minimum can be set forth. One might reasonably say that there is little point in pursuing analysis of variable program implementation measures with fewer than six or seven service providers. In many cases this would be too few, while in others, it would be sufficient.

Second, the good news. There is an analysis procedure that can in most cases protect against incorrectly attributing too much importance to variable descriptions of program characteristics. This procedure involves jointly testing the variable program characteristic measures along with membership identifiers indicating enrollment in each particular service provider in the sample. After identifying variable program characteristics that appear statistically reliable, the analyst then adds to the equation the set of membership identifiers indicating enrollment through each specific service provider.[10]

If the variable program characteristics retain their statistically reliable effects, then our confidence in the initial findings remains high. If their effect in the equation is eliminated by the addition of the membership identifiers, then we must conclude either that some service providers differ from each other, but we do not know why, or that the initial test procedure was inappropriate. With small numbers of units, the latter is always a strong likelihood.

Analysis Procedures for Descriptive Outcome and Differential Impact Evaluations

This chapter makes no attempt to provide instruction in the use of statistics. However, a brief overview of analysis strategies for descriptive gross outcomes analysis and differential impact analysis may be useful.

Descriptive analysis involves quite basic statistical tools. The value of descriptive analysis rests more on the thought that goes into the questions the analyst asks than on statistical sophistication. Descriptive analysis begins with univariate (one-variable) averages or percentage distributions. Beyond that, bivariate (two-variable) associations can be calculated, as long as the analyst bears in mind that descriptive associations can be produced by many factors other than the two being analyzed. Exhibit 3.11 describes conditions under which different bivariate statistics are most appropriate.

Differential impact analysis can be performed satisfactorily with standard multiple regression techniques, except for one particular situation, which is discussed. The strategy of multivariate analysis is straightforward. One outcome is analyzed, with multiple potential influences tested simultaneously to estimate the unique impact of each on the outcome. In this instance, the goal is to ascertain whether and how much policy variables of interest affect the outcome after taking into account the possible effects of other factors such as selection. However, the statistical techniques required to implement that strategy require specialized training. Parts of the discussion that follows assume prior background in multivariate analysis.

Analyzing Various Types of Measures

A wide range of statistics is available in various software packages. However, nearly all statistical tests required for descriptive gross impact analysis or differential impact analysis can be performed with four basic tools: *chi square*, analysis of variance (ANOVA), Pearson correlation, and ordinary least squares (OLS) regression. Why these are typically adequate is laid out in a highly readable form in Bjornstadt and Knoke (1982). Which of these is used depends on the nature of the analysis and the way in which the variable was measured—commonly referred to as the level of measurement. Exhibit 3.11 suggests appropriate statistics for different levels of measurement and for different analysis goals.

The critical distinction regarding level of measurement is between *ordered* and *nominal* variables. Ordered variables are those for which values assigned to each category of the variable form a logically defensible sequence from smaller to larger, lower to higher, etc. Ordered variables include age, level of satisfaction, costs, ratings on various descriptive scales, and the like.

Variables that cannot be ordered are termed nominal variables. The categories of variables like marital status or SDA identification codes cannot be placed in a meaningful hierarchy or sequence. The results of tests that require ordered variables would be meaningless if applied to nominal variables such as these.

Dichotomous variables, those taking only two values, such as "yes" and "no," occupy a special status in that they are by definition ordered, even when they appear logically nonorderable. Any variable that includes only two values can be expressed as a yes/no question. In the case of one SDA vs. others, for example, the variable becomes "Did this participant enroll through SDA #1?" The responses "yes" and "no" are interpretable as ordered, with yes greater than no. It is this quality of dichotomies that makes membership identifiers especially powerful in differential impact analysis.

Statistical assumptions vary somewhat for dependent (outcome) vari-

Exhibit 3.11
Suggested Statistics for Different Levels of Measurement

Type of Analysis	Type of Variable		Suggested Statistic
	Independent (e.g., a program variant)	Dependent (an outcome)	
Bivariate	Ordered	Ordered	Correlation [1]
Bivariate	Ordered	Dichotomous	Treat as type C [2]
Bivariate	Dichotomous or nominal	Ordered	ANOVA (F test) [3]
Bivariate	Dichotomous or nominal	Dichotomous or nominal	Chi square
Multivariate	Ordered or dichotomous	Ordered	Ordinary least squares multiple regression
Multivariate	Ordered or dichotomous	Dichotomous	Varies. See text
Multivariate	Any	Nominal	Log-linear Analysis [4]
Multivariate	Nominal	Ordered or dichotomous	Transform independent to dummy variables

[1] If ordered variables contain few (3 – 6) categories, it may also be advisable to observe relation ships in tabular form. However, the chi square statistic would typically underestimate the likeli hood of a reliable relationship because it ignores information on order.

[2] In this case it is convenient to treat the independent variable as the dependent, and vice versa, so that ANOVA may be used.

[3] In the dichotomous case, the t-test is equivalent to the F test used in ANOVA.

[4] If available to the analyst, recent developments by Goodman (1972) make limited multivariate analysis of nominal variables possible. (See also Davis 1974.) Goodman's program is named ECTA (Everyman's Contingency Table Analysis). SPSSx has also installed a version.

---

ables vs. independent (predictor, explanatory) variables. Therefore, the choice of statistical tools depends on the level of measurement for each. Exhibit 3.11 reflects this requirement. Analysis goals are separated into bivariate (two-variable) and multivariate (one dependent variable, more than one independent variable) cases, with measurement indicated for both independent and dependent variables.

Multivariate Analysis with a Dichotomous Dependent Variable

Every statistic is developed on the basis of mathematical assumptions. In the case of ordinary least squares regression, many of the original restrictive assumptions have proven unnecessary. That is, the statistic is highly robust; data can be structured in ways not fully satisfying statistical assumptions, yet the statistic produces accurate and efficient estimates. Even so, in the case where the dependent variable is dichotomous and is highly skewed (unevenly distributed), assumptions are violated severely and error can result.

Happily, recent work with statistics based on log-linear transformations of dichotomous dependent variables—and using "maximum likelihood *chi square* goodness of fit" tests—avoid the problems faced by ordinary regression. This means that appropriate conservative multivariate methods to analyze dichotomies, such as whether or not participants are employed at follow-up, do exist. Regression tests have been compared with these more conservative methods, with the result that we can now be quite certain when we are required to use the more conservative, but also less convenient, methods and when the simpler regression analysis is appropriate. (See Knoke 1975; Goodman 1976; Gillespi 1977.) The following guidelines summarize this knowledge:

1. If a dichotomous dependent variable is split relatively evenly (between 75 percent/25 percent and 25 percent/75 percent) OLS regression may be used.

2. If OLS regression cannot be used and all or many independent variables are ordered, Logit or Probit transformations of the dependent variable are advisable.

3. If OLS regression cannot be used and many independent variables are dichotomous or nominal, Goodman's Multiway Contingency Table Analysis may be used.

Constructing and Testing
Membership Identifiers ("Dummy Variables")

Some extremely valuable factors to include as independent variables in multiple regression analysis are measured as nominal variables, which are not admissible in a regression equation. Nominal variables may be analyzed, however, after they are transformed into dichotomies that are tested in place of the original variable. These dichotomies, known as "dummy variables" in formal statistical analysis, are called membership identifiers throughout this chapter to indicate their nature, i.e., they measure whether or not a participant belongs to a particular category. For example, MIS systems may include a measure of ethnicity, including values for each of five or more major groups. If membership variables are constructed for each of these groups (e.g., a variable named "othwhite," and scored 1 for all originally coded "other white" and 0 for all others), these new dichotomies may be tested as independent variables in regression analysis.

Regression slopes that result from tests of dummy variables, if statistically reliable, indicate that members of the named group (e.g., those enrolled through unit *A*, "other white" participants, or OJT participants) are the estimated average amount higher or lower on the outcome in question than all members of other groups. All but one of the dummy variables created from an original nominal variable may be tested in a single equation.

Constructing and Testing Interaction Terms

One useful type of question for JTPA program managers may be addressed by using interaction terms. This question is Do particular groups of participants, more than others, experience greater success from some program variants than from other variants? For example, is classroom training (CT) more successful than other treatments in erasing the deficit produced by previous low educational attainment? In an interaction, two variables *combine* to produce a joint effect different from that which both acting independently would produce. In the example, dropping out of high school reduces postprogram outcomes and CT may, in itself, produce higher or lower than average outcomes. In addition, the interaction hypothesis suggests that the impact of educational attainment on postprogram outcomes is stronger when the treatment is not classroom training than when it is. To test such an hypothesis, one must construct an interaction term that would be scored 1 for dropouts who enroll in CT and 0 for all others. This interaction term, the product of the other two, identifies those individuals who were in a position to have some portion of their educational deficit eliminated by participation in CT.

Normally, the interaction term, appropriate control variables, and the original variables from which the interaction was constructed must all be included in one multiple regression equation (Blalock 1965). Since the interaction term will include portions of both original variables, an effect of either or both original variables would erroneously be carried by the interaction term alone. Only when the original terms are both included in the test can we be certain an effect of the interaction term is not spurious.[11] If such a test produced, for example, a slope of -0.20 for dropout status and +0.10 for the interaction term, then the proper interpretation would be (a) that being a high school dropout, in itself, reduces postprogram employment 20 percent, and (b) that CT erases half of the education effect among dropouts, so that dropouts who enrolled in CT experience only a 10 percent lower placement rate (-0.20 +0.10).

Reporting Standardized or Unstandardized Regression Coefficients

Standardized regression coefficients, termed "Betas," are often re-ported because they indicate the *relative power of each variable in one equation to account for variation in the dependent variable.* Betas have a commonsense meaning similar to that of a correlation: a Beta of 0.5 always indicates a "stronger" effect than a Beta of 0.4. Unstandardized coefficients (regression slopes) are expressed in terms of the metric of the independent and dependent variables, and are much more precise but often less intuitively satisfying. If, for example, education is scored using a four-point scale, a slope of 0.10 indicates that *each* step of that education scale raises the outcome variable by 0.10. The lowest step compared with the highest, three intervals above, has an estimated 0.30 higher level. If the dependent variable is employment status, 0.30 translates to 30 percent. If it is hourly wage, 0.30 translates to 30 cents.

These considerations make slopes somewhat more complex than Betas to communicate when findings are reported. When results of research are being applied to program development efforts, however, unstandardized slopes are the preferable estimate because they give a direct estimate of the *amount of change in an outcome that is produced by a given change in the input.* Is it more helpful for me to know that education, which I cannot control, is more powerful than program activity? Or am I better served by estimating that after the effects of education are accounted for, my OJT program produces postprogram wages an estimated 47 cents lower (or higher) than my CT program? Clearly the latter, unstandardized report is preferable.

In addition, unlike standardized Betas, unstandardized slopes are not influenced by the variance of a particular variable within a sample. This can be important when relatively small subgroups are being analyzed. If only 10 percent of my sample enrolled in work experience, even if WEX participants are employed only half as often as others, the variable "enrolled in WEX?" can explain only a limited portion of the variation in employment experienced by the entire sample. However, the unstandardized slope indicates how much less often this minority is employed than are other participants. The slope remains the same whether 10 percent or 50 percent of participants are enrolled in work experience.

In general, unstandardized regression slopes are both more useful and easier to report when (1) the dependent variable is naturally interpretable, as in the case of income or a dichotomy that translates to percentages, and (2) the independent variable is a dichotomy, allowing statements like "participants in category *A* are *X* percent higher than those in category *B*." In other cases, the analyst must choose between reporting ease and managerial usefulness. For a full analysis, both forms augment each other. For example, a report might indicate that a particular program service has a negligible impact on variation in outcomes for an entire SDA, but go on to show a large impact on a few clients.

Estimating Change

For descriptive analysis, change may be indicated by subtracting the preprogram value from the postprogram value of an identically measured variable. This procedure is simple and the results are often taken at face value. However, the descriptive report of change is especially problematic because change is heavily dependent on the original base figure. If, for example, a sample includes many students or displaced homemakers with zero earnings during the preprogram year, then regardless of program impact, that group is likely to generate higher *change* in earnings than a group including primarily high previous earners. At the other end of the scale, displaced-worker programs will typically show negative change figures—a reduction in earnings—not because they are less effective than other programs, but because preprogram earnings were especially high. This problem is especially severe if preprogram values vary more widely than postprogram values, as is more often the case in highly successful programs than in less successful programs.[12] For this reason, presentation of *descriptive* change results can be seriously misleading.

In *multivariate* differential impact analysis, the goal is to estimate unique causal effects of each factor tested. Since the preprogram level of an outcome variable clearly affects change in that variable, any analysis of change must include that level as a predictor in the regression equation. This necessity leads to an approach that considerably improves the ease and usefulness of change analysis. Predicting change with preprogram level produces awkward results, i.e., higher preprogram levels of any variable produce lower rates of change. However, it is possible (and preferable) to replace change with postprogram level as the outcome being predicted. Since change is calculated as postprogram minus preprogram level, any two of the following variables is sufficient to produce the third via simple mathematical operations: (1) *the preprogram level*, (2) the *postprogram level*, and (3) *change*. Therefore, the equation is satisfied regardless of which two are used.

It is preferable to use the two that produce the most sensible results: the postprogram outcome as dependent variable and the preprogram measure of the same outcome as a control variable. In such a case, the effect of preprogram on postprogram level (the autoregression term) indicates stability over time, i.e., the tendency for those most employable before the program to be most employable after the program also. *Other* variables in the equation that show a reliable impact on the postprogram outcome may be correctly interpreted as indicating factors that increase or decrease (change) the outcome in question from the preprogram to the postprogram period.

These considerations open another possibility. It is a short step to conclude that the multivariate analysis of change is hurt very little if the preprogram measure differs slightly from the parallel postprogram measure. The analysis still indicates which factors increase or decrease the outcome controlling for preprogram level of approximately the same factor. Identical pre- and postprogram measures are desirable. However, the analysis of change remains possible with less-than-exactly parallel pre- and postprogram measures.

Analyzing a Large Number of Potential Influences on Outcomes

Multivariate analysis is straightforward in studies where only a few theoretically derived variables are tested. All are entered into the equation and the results reported. In cases where many measures are to be tested as independent variables, however, it is no longer possible or advisable to include all in a single test. Such attempts can make undue demands on the sample size, a problem that becomes especially serious if the sample size is reduced by the accumulation of missing cases from each of the many variables involved. This produces the problem of how to move through multiple tests efficiently without distorting or overlooking effects. The following suggestions may assist in that endeavor. Performing such analysis, of course, requires prior statistical background. This "cookbook" summary is not meant to imply otherwise. It only suggests steps to make analysis relatively efficient.

Step 1. Insure that variables are in the proper form for multivariate analysis and that variation is sufficient to make analysis meaningful. For data management purposes it is advisable to construct a "codebook" listing all variables and showing for each the level of measurement, number of useable cases, and an indicator of variation.

Step 2. Select the appropriate dependent variable for each analysis.

Step 3. Separate variables according to their importance to the analysis. Those that are most important, because they are known to affect the outcome and must be included to prevent bias or because they hold special program development interest, should be given priority during analysis.

Step 4. Separate variables according to missing cases. In particular, questions asked only of subsets of participants, such as job qualities or reasons for unemployment, should be analyzed separately from other questions applying to all. The safest form of multivariate analysis is based only on cases for which full information on all variables is present. Under that approach, any case with a single missing value is eliminated from the entire analysis.

Step 5. Compute correlations between all independent variables and the dependent variable being analyzed. Correlations are the basis for the calculation of multiple regression coefficients, making them the appropriate bivariate test building toward regression analysis.

Step 6. Identify those variables that are appropriate in terms of missing values and have high priority as control variables—those required to protect against biased estimates. Observe their correlations with the outcome(s) in question. Select from this set those variables exhibiting a reliable association with the outcome being analyzed.

Step 7. Enter the variables selected at the conclusion of step 6 into a multiple regression equation, to identify the subset of these variables that have reliable multivariate effects on the outcome. For simplicity, analysts may use a stepwise procedure, which automatically selects reliable effects. This produces a minimal set of control variables which must be included in subsequent runs. Other variables from these tests may be set aside for the moment with the knowledge that were they included in the regression equation, their effect would be too small to alter findings noticeably.

Step 8. Identify the most important test variables, i.e., program variants of special policy interest. Observe their correlations with the outcome in question, selecting those showing reliable association. Enter these singly, or in appropriate sets, into equations that include the minimal set of control variables identified in step 7.

Step 9. In addition to variables tested in step 8, analysts may wish to *explore* other program variants, hoping to discover useful unexpected relationships. Group measures according to policy area, such as intake, quality control, or trainer characteristics. Correlate these with the outcome being analyzed and enter those which are reliably greater than zero into an equation including the minimal set of control variables identified in step 7.

Step 10. The procedures outlined above for reducing the set of reliable effects ignores the possibility of *suppression*, a situation in which two variables are correlated with each other but have opposite effects on the dependent variables and, therefore, tend to cancel each other out in bivariate tests. These effects become visible only when both independent variables are tested jointly. They are, therefore, overlooked when only reliable bivariate correlations are forwarded for test in regression equations, as in steps 6-9.

Short of a full exposition of this issue, one step may be suggested to guard against most errors of this type. Suppression of the type the analyst most wishes to uncover occurs only when some variable is correlated with one of the variables identified during steps 8 and 9 as reliable predictors. Correlations should, therefore, be calculated between each of these reliable effects and other independent variables. Where reliable correlations are found, the variable in question may be added to the reduced set of reliable effects located after step 8 or 9. Relatively few changes will be produced by such a procedure, but it does guard against the most damaging errors from undetected relationships. These tests may be facilitated by using a backwards stepwise elimination of unreliable effects, where statistical packages include this option.

Step 11. Membership identifier variables, such as service provider, industrial sector, and similar others, should be examined if they have not already been included as program variants. These may be added to the reduced sets of reliable effects identified in steps 8, 9, or 10. Findings may prove useful for future contracting or marketing. Also, such tests protect against spurious findings of program effects.

Step 12. Finally, having identified reduced sets of the most powerful and unique effects on each outcome being analyzed, the analyst will be well-advised to return to the data set in order to examine *what measures are associated with these key effects.* Such analyses may be conducted formally, using these key effects as dependent variables in their own right, or may be undertaken as less formalized examinations of patterned associations. Such further analysis can corroborate or challenge initial interpretations, or can help the analyst develop interpretations of initial findings by detailing the apparent nature of the variables found to have greatest impact on the outcome.

Combining Data from Different Sources

One complexity of effective differential impact analysis is the need to combine data from several different sources into a tailor-made data set. The combination of data also provides two of the method's strengths: the ability to protect against selection bias from several angles, and the ability to measure different types of variables in the most reliable and efficient manner.

Aside from the availability of appropriate computer facilities, the key to combining (merging) data is to include the correct identifiers in each data set to be merged. It is advisable to produce a *master identifier cover sheet* to become part of each participant data file. This sheet should include all the identifying information required to merge data: participant social security number, SDA identifier, agency (subcontractor) identifier, employer identifier, etc.

For differential impact analysis, *all data should be merged into individual participant records*, since the participant is the unit of analysis. All identifiers must appear in the participant's original data file. Each of the other original files must contain only the particular identifier required to correctly merge into the participant file. For example, implementation program variants are measured at the agency level. Each participant who enrolled through the agency with the ID code "10" will receive values on all implementation variables which were provided by that agency. The agency identifier will appear on those participants' master identifier sheets and also on the appropriate agency implementation data reports, allowing the match of identifiers, followed by the combination of data.

Once data sets are merged, statistical tests will be calculated on the basis of the number of participants (or employers) in the data set, not on the basis of the number of service providers or geographical regions that may have supplied particular data elements. The analyst must, therefore, remain aware of limitations surrounding the number of separate treatment contexts required for reliable differential impact tests (discussed earlier).

Research Design for an Employer Follow-Up

With the advent of JTPA and the expansion of private sector involvement, interest in measuring employer benefits has risen. The popularity of this issue among service providers is no doubt connected to a concern for marketing JTPA services and products to employers. The perceptions of OJT or WEX employers are useful to indicate which program approaches are relatively effective, which are distasteful to employers, and what steps might encourage or discourage future participation by employers (e.g., Wentling and Lawson 1975; Minnesota Office of Statewide CETA Coordination 1979; Simpson 1984b). Employers may be interviewed primarily as a marketing tool. In addition, employer interviews can be valuable program evaluation tools. They may be used to assess the effectiveness of participant services or to assess employer benefits, both central to JTPA program development. How these goals translate into a research design depends on the relation of the employers being studied to JTPA, in particular, whether they are *participating employers* or *termination employers*.

Termination employers are those who employed participants at their termination from any program activity. They are consumers of JTPA's "products." Some hire former JTPA participants without knowing that the training their new employees received was supported by JTPA. Others have participated in providing training or experience to the participants they subsequently hire at termination.

Participating employers are those who participated in the delivery of services, through on-the-job training, work experience, or tryout, regardless of the termination status of the participants involved. Many become termination employers also. However, many employers participate in contracts that end prematurely, or complete a contract but choose not to hire the JTPA participant following his or her participation in JTPA.

For termination employers, surveys may ask *direct marketing questions,* such as how the employer came to hire a JTPA product, or may address *indirect marketing goals*, such as measuring employer satisfaction with the former participant hired, with the goal of demonstrating program success to future employers. For participating employers, marketing questions may be expanded to include willingness to continue or expand future participation. In this case, the goals of marketing the program and assessing employer costs or benefits overlap. The major marketing tool for engaging new employers in service delivery is evidence that past participating employers feel that the benefits of participating have outweighed the costs.

For termination employers, the goals of assessing participant services and employer benefits are nearly identical. Employer costs or benefits occur entirely because participants are or are not well-prepared for their jobs. In the case of participating employers, reports of costs and benefits can include not only ratings of the participant, but also evaluations of the JTPA programs and personnel and direct perceptions of participation as beneficial or costly.

Employer surveys are unique in that many employer reports may be taken at face value and are, therefore, especially useful for descriptive analysis. The employer's role as consumer of JTPA products (participants), makes employer ratings of participants valuable to JTPA program operators regardless of the factors influencing them. Because JTPA agencies wish to have the most effective participating employers repeat their involvement, employer satisfaction with agency policies or personnel is critical. Similarly, employers' perceptions that they have benefited from participating in delivering JTPA services are meaningful descriptive estimates of employer costs and benefits.

In addition, information gathered from employers can be valuable to the analysis of participant outcomes. Employers are in a unique position to report subtle job quality outcomes, certain forms of selection, and for participating employers, individual-level measures of training provided or other qualities of the program intervention.

Identifying Employer Population to
Be Analyzed and Designing the Sample

The most basic of all employer design questions is whether the population being studied includes all termination employers, all participating employers, or both. In addition, managers who wish an in-depth analysis of one specific program activity may prefer an even more specific definition, such as all OJT employers. Aside from modest differences in cost, these decisions should be made on the basis of policy objectives. To which programs do managers wish to apply the results? Are specific services earmarked for further development? Is descriptive material on the range of all employers' experiences needed? The research design should be shaped by these decisions; it should not drive them.

Any analysis of participating employers must include all participating employers within the program services to be analyzed. In the event that one participant is placed with more than one employer before program termination, both employers must be included. To identify the sample of participating employers only from the population of those who were the "final" employers, is to bias the employer sample by eliminating a group of placements that worked out especially poorly—those that ended prematurely and were followed by transfer to further treatment.

Sample Size
Only one issue differentiates participant and employer sampling with regard to sample size: the completion rate for employer surveys will probably reach 80 percent or more. Therefore, the initial sample of employers required to produce a target sample of completed interviews *is smaller than that required with participant samples.* For example, if we decide to aim for 400 completed interviews and expect an 80 percent completion rate, an initial sample of 500 will suffice. For a participant survey with 70 percent completion rate, the figure would be 571.

Integrating Employer and Participant Samples
Combining employer and participant data is recommended for any but the most basic marketing study or descriptive analysis of employer benefits. If both employer and participant follow-up analyses are conducted, samples should overlap as much as possible. The validity of each in no way depends on the degree of overlap between the participant and employer samples; it depends on the *representativeness* of each sample. A sample of participants selected at random will produce some proportion with employers—those employed at termination, or those in employer-based programs, depending on whether the employer survey is of termination or participating employers. This sample selection also

produces a random sample of the program's employers, and insures a substantial number of cases in which both participant and employer data are available for joint analysis.

Follow-Up Period

Employer surveys should allow a lag time after hire, long enough for the employer to observe the former participant's work and decide whether to retain the individual, but short enough to allow employers to retain clear impressions of participants who remained on the job only briefly. Lag time should also be short enough for impressions of working with JTPA to remain salient. Since most positions gained by JTPA graduates have relatively short probationary periods, *a three-month follow-up survey* should be adequate for an employer survey. This also gives participating employers who hire participants at termination enough time to observe their new workers under full-wage conditions. In cases where OJT positions involve a posttermination performance payment, follow-up should occur at least one month after the final performance payment to avoid distortion from expected payments.

Data Collection Methods

Most employers rely heavily on telephone communications and respond well to telephone interviews, especially if they are scheduled beforehand. Agency personnel who work with employers may resist interviewing, feeling that the intrusion on employers' time jeopardizes good will. Experience with CETA and JTPA surveys shows, however, that brief interviews are usually accepted and the majority of employers are pleased that JTPA staff care enough about the quality of their program to check with those who consume their products.

In-House vs. Third-Party Data Collection

Because JTPA staff work closely with many employers, there are program development advantages in having staff conduct the interviews. These interviews are efficient because they occur along with other employer contacts. They also allow staff to enhance their program development and employer quality review by integrating them with employer data collection. Staff interviews may introduce response bias problems, however, because participating employers may wish to participate again and may be less than candid about their costs and benefits from participation.

Viewed from the standpoint of measurement validity, research efforts must be neutral. If the results of an employer analysis are to be disseminated publicly, both the employers responding to the survey and the research consumers must be assured of the neutrality of the measurement and analysis, and of the confidentiality of individual responses. Similarly, if employers themselves are being assessed, a third-party research team should collect data, with guarantees of confidentiality.[13] If employer surveys are conducted in-house, efforts can be made to ensure the perception of neutrality (see Dillman 1978; Bradburn 1983); however, these measures cannot successfully emulate third-party neutrality.

Estimating Employer Costs and
Benefits Using the Gross Impact Approach

Job training programs have an impact on employers as well as on participants. Employers may be viewed as *direct beneficiaries* of the job training system and in some cases, as *incurring costs* of providing services to that system. In fact, it is often difficult to separate benefits to employers from benefits to participants and society. When a placement works well, all benefit. When an employer provides training, the participant can become more employable (either within the firm, or generally), and the employer can gain a more productive worker. Similarly, the wage subsidy employers receive is rewarding to them and also to the participants, who receive full pay for a period of partially subsidized work. For measurement purposes, employer costs and benefits may be treated as if they accrued only to employers. However, interpretations of research findings should recognize that the most effective systems can probably benefit all actors—employer and participant benefits need not be mutually exclusive.

Employer outcomes are not specified in JTPA legislation. Nor is there a long tradition of past research focusing on and defining them. Indeed, our initial directions in exploring possible measures are the result of two major limits to measurement and research design in this case: the lack of prior development in this area of research, and the inability of gross impact research to estimate net impacts.

Employer Estimates of Their Own Costs and Benefits

Within the limits of the gross impact approach, the true net impact of JTPA on employers cannot be estimated. That would require comparisons with employers hiring non-JTPA participants. Nevertheless, we can *ask employers to give us their estimates of their costs and benefits.* This may be accomplished by specifying a *break-even point* for each measure of cost or benefit, and asking employers to report whether their experience with JTPA or with specific JTPA participants fell above or below that point. The break-even point differs by type of measure and is discussed below. The strategy in each case is to express the measure in terms simulating true or perceived net cost or benefit, by wording the measure in terms of break-even point and offering responses on either side of that point.[14]

Although such an approach is far from true net impact, it may provide knowledge of employer outcomes and how they combine or offset each other. This, in turn, will build a knowledge base required before conceptualizing a net impact analysis. In particular, we can analyze the degrees of association among different measures of cost or benefit and assess the relative importance employers assign to these factors. However, the main value of this approach is that it allows approximations of employer costs or benefits useful for guiding program development.

Measurement Strategy in a New Area of Study

As a relatively new area of study, employer benefits cannot be measured definitively. It is possible to specify a *range of probable benefits and costs,* but too little is known about each or about their relative worth to employers to develop a precise, meaningful accounting. Some of these costs and benefits, such as the OJT wage subsidy, can be expressed in precise monetary terms. Others may be equally important to analyze, but impossible to quantify or even to conceptualize clearly.[15] They include the following:

1. The major indication that hiring a JTPA participant was rewarding to an employer is a decision to retain the participant. It might also be possible to estimate how far above or below a break-even point (a point of indifference, neither costly nor rewarding) each participant's performance falls; however, such estimates would remain speculative.

2. Fear that JTPA participants may have serious problems not easily observed before hire is impossible to quantify in precise monetary terms, but is a very important cost for many employers (Simpson 1984b). Even when no problems arise, the perceived risk that they might occur represents a cost.

3. Provision of training is costly to participating employers. Assigning quantitative values to employer training, however, is difficult because most training is informal; more training may be planned than occurs; most training would be offered to all new employees regardless of JTPA involvement; and much of the training may be so specific to the particular employer that it binds the worker to that job rather than transferring to other employment situations, introducing a hidden benefit.

Other elements of the JTPA program are complex to conceptualize because they may act as either costs or benefits. For example, employee screening can be a service to employers, but giving partial control over screening to an agency whose goal is serving the disadvantaged may be costly. Similarly, hiring the disadvantaged is typically assumed to be one cost to participating employers. Yet, one study of CETA OJT employers found that over one-tenth of the respondents listed the knowledge that "you are helping others with need" as *the major reason* for participating in OJT (Simpson 1984b).

We face these measurement challenges primarily because little work has been completed in this area, and many of the most important costs and rewards to employers are inherently perceptual and, therefore, not readily susceptible to monetary quantification. The approach suggested by gross impact analysis is to develop multiple measures of potential costs and benefits to employers and investigate the extent to which each is *perceived by employers* to act as a cost or a benefit in their specific cases. The following are some examples:

1. Once we learn *which aspects* of JTPA employers estimate to be most costly and most rewarding and *how important they perceive different costs and benefits to be*, analysts can begin to define and prioritize employer outcomes.

2. We can analyze whether particular types of employers have different perceptions of the costs and benefits of JTPA, and whether these ideas are associated with greater or lesser program success for participants.

3. We can test ideas about the ways in which JTPA is rewarding or costly to employers. Rather than assuming that particular JTPA services, such as client screening, are costly or rewarding to employers, we can examine the extent to which the implementation of these services increases or decreases the rewards or costs perceived by employers.

4. We can *analyze the association among different measures of cost and benefit*. Are costs of providing services higher where benefits, such as the subsidy to participants' wages, are higher? Do employers who receive high levels of one type of benefit tend to receive less of others, or is JTPA implementation such that some agencies reward employers across-the-board more than others do?

Outcomes for Termination Employers

Any employer's major costs or benefits from hiring are the job performance qualities of the new employee. For termination employers who did not participate in delivering JTPA services, this is the only source of cost or benefit relevant to JTPA. The question for them is whether the new JTPA-trained employee will function in the job *as well as* other appropriately trained new workers. *There is no reason to expect JTPA participants to be better trained than others;* the goal of JTPA is to eliminate participants' previous deficits.

Each area of worker performance of importance to the employer represents one dimension, or scale, of cost or benefit. How many days' work will the new employee miss during the first month? How much employer training will be required before the worker becomes productive? How much supervision time will be saved by a "self-starting" worker? Cost and benefit represent two ends of each scale. The break-even point lies at the point on the scale that represents the average new (non-JTPA) hire for that job in that labor market, as perceived by the employer. If the average new-hire misses four days' work per month, hiring a former JTPA participant who misses an average of two days represents a benefit to the employer.

For employee qualities that are not naturally quantified, the former JTPA participant may be compared with the average non-JTPA hire for that same job, using a rating scale such as "much better," "a little better," "about the same," "a little worse," "much worse." Qualities to measure include skill level, speed and quality of work productivity, indicators of supervisability, and indicators of adjustment to the job.

In the case of any one participant, job performance may be better or worse than average for reasons unrelated to JTPA participation or referral. However, if, over a large number of employer interviews, the average JTPA hire proves to be more satisfactory to employers than their average non-JTPA hires, we have reason to claim a role for JTPA in producing that benefit to employers.[16]

A second possible benefit to termination employers is a former participant's job retention record throughout the follow-up period, and whether further retention is likely. Retention implies that the worker is productive and adjusted, and also wishes to remain employed. Unless job loss results from cutbacks forced by declining business, laying off a trained worker indicates a cost to the employer: the cost of hiring and retraining another worker, and loss of productivity during the training period. (See Vermeulen and Hudson-Wilson 1981.) Whether these costs occur because participants perform poorly or because they quit is also valuable to explore.

Outcomes for Participating Employers

An employee's productivity and tractability during the training con-tract represent major costs or benefits to employers who take part in the JTPA program. After the contract, they may become termination em-ployers by hiring the participant they trained. At this point all the benefits discussed above apply. Beyond these, the most obvious benefit is the *subsidy to participant wages.*

By far the most common reason employers give for participating in OJT is the subsidy. Other explanations commonly reported include eliminating the need to screen large numbers of applicants, the ability to expand or to stabilize without mounting the full cost for the new employee, and satisfaction at being able to assist deserving individuals (Simpson 1984b). Commonly reported costs include the time and supervision required to train, the potential of greater-than-average worktime lost to personal or family problems, the possibility that maximum performance after training will not match that of other employees, and the possibility that JTPA employees might turn over faster than others would.

One element of employer costs has declined dramatically since early CETA programs: the degree of constraint experienced by the employer. O'Neil's (1982) analysis of employer hesitance to use "targeted jobs tax credits" demonstrates that the sheer fact of being constrained can be costly to employers. Earlier CETA programs protected their right to serve participants with greatest need, but in so doing, raised the employer constraint expenses above the threshold allowing participation.

Some of these costs or benefits have break-even points of zero. For example, the OJT wage subsidy cannot be costly in and of itself, and paperwork requirements cannot be seen as benefits; they can at best pose zero cost. Other benefits and costs to participating employers are meaningful only when a break-even point is defined in comparison to typical employees who would be hired were it not for the JTPA program. The two major outlays JTPA wishes participating employers to accept are hiring individuals who appear to be less qualified for the job than typical non-JTPA hires, and providing extra training beyond that required by typical non-JTPA hires. The issue is not, for example, whether the OJT employer loses five or 10 weeks of productive time during training, but whether the *difference in training time* for typical non-OJT hires vs. the OJT hire is zero, five, or 10 weeks. A difference of zero weeks represents a break-even point on that particular measure.

There is no *a priori* method to establish a balance between major costs and benefits for participating employers. Program policymakers must decide whether they are satisfied with the differences employers report between JTPA participants and other hires, given the JTPA reimbursement they receive. Data on employer benefits and costs simply make decisions such as setting the level of OJT reimbursement more rational.

Even so, such interpretations may be less obvious than many program managers suppose. In particular, it is not always the case that employer-based programs work best for participants when employers receive maximum benefit from participation, as demonstrated by economic theory regarding nonsubsidized on-the-job training (Maranto and Rodgers 1984; Hoffman 1981). Employers always engage in *introductory OJT,* specific to the firm and to the job. This training represents part of the *employer's investment* in hiring any new employee. The typical sequence is hire with intention to retain, invest in training, and retain as planned.

The subsidized OJT situation differs from this typical sequence in that the *training occurs before the decision to retain,* and the *training may not be the result of a decision to invest in training.* If the total cost of training a JTPA participant is greater than the income derived from the wage subsidy, the employer must decide to invest in training, which in turn implies a commitment to hire if possible, so as not to waste the investment. If, however, an SDA offers subsidies equal to or larger than the employer's cost, the employer may participate without ever having decided to invest in the participant. The reason may be kind—"Now I can afford to help this person." Or, it may be hard-nosed—"I make more money hiring OJTs, even if I increase turnover by letting them go after the contract ends."

At the extreme, some participating employers use the federal wage subsidy without incurring the expense of providing any services. In-depth interviews with CETA OJT employers located some who explicitly stated that they provided no training and refused to alter their hiring practices at all, choosing instead simply to gather the windfall wherever one of their new hires happened to be OJT eligible (Simpson 1984b). Therefore, service providers are presumably well-advised to balance costs and benefits for participating employers in such a way that outcomes are positive, but not so positive as to protect employers from making an investment in each participant they train.

Outcomes Measured through Agency Records

The most basic benefits accruing to participating employers are financial, and may be recorded directly from JTPA contracts. This form of measurement is preferred because it is highly reliable, it indicates both planned and actual expenditures, and it avoids the awkwardness of asking about money during telephone interviews. In addition, agencies may be able to estimate the amount of screening and referral time they provided, thereby offsetting employer hiring costs. The question of how effective the screening was is separate, and must be measured during employer interviews.

Outcomes Measured through Employer Surveys

In addition to measures listed earlier for termination employers, participating employers incur a number of costs during their contracts, and also experience the potential costs and benefits of working with JTPA agencies. These may be measured through follow-ups, in the form of employer reports of their activities or perceptions of JTPA. Presumably the most basic costs incurred in the case of OJT are training costs. Although small employers seldom estimate training costs, they can report length of typical training for a given position, length and intensity of JTPA training compared to non-JTPA training, whether specialized methods, curricula, or personnel are used during training, etc.

Measures of perceived participation risk. Participating employers face the costs of accepting risk or constraint from their involvement with JTPA. Although particular JTPA participants may prove to be ideal workers, a program offering subsidies in exchange for hiring particular individuals has some implied risk. Employers may fear that the employee could be a poor worker, an alcoholic, or a thief. This felt risk may loom larger than the actual costs experienced when a particular worker performs poorly. The JTPA agency could also attempt to constrain the employer's behavior, or unexpected paperwork demands could develop. These *possibilities* may be expensive in employers' perceptions.

At the other extreme, the employer could reduce risk by retaining control over the hiring process. In the most extreme case, employers make firm hiring decisions before sending their new employees to apply for the OJT subsidy. Since this practice undercuts the hiring-incentive role of OJT wage reimbursement, employer reports may be somewhat biased, depending on guarantees of confidentiality. At a more intermediate level, JTPA staff, recognizing employers' fear of risk, may screen so carefully that the risk factor is neutralized. Thus, valuable knowledge may be gained from measures of employers' "felt-risk," employers' control over screening, and the degree to which JTPA staff screen out participants least job-ready (and therefore most in need).

Measures of employers' direct assessment of participation costs and benefits. Employers may also be asked for their direct assessments of the costs or benefits of participating. Most of the measures suggested thus far have been indirect, in that they ask employers to rate a particular JTPA participant or placement experience. This approach has the value of defusing employer concerns about being evaluated, i.e., clarifying that it is the employee who is being evaluated, and it allows aggregation of quite precise information regarding a representative sample of participants.

Certain employer outcomes, moreover, are best estimated in a direct form. Employers can be asked to evaluate JTPA services and staff, and to indicate how beneficial or costly they found specific aspects of participation to be. Some measures, such as the subsidy to wages, help in enlarging or stabilizing the work force, or the good feeling of helping others, can logically represent only some degree of benefit. Others, such as JTPA applicants' screening, may represent costs or benefits, depending on their quality.[17]

The Characterization of the Employment
Establishment and of the Participant's Position within It

When one goal of employer surveys is to perform differential impact analysis of participant outcomes, employment-establishment characteristics and participant-selection-and-training characteristics should be included among employer measures. The following three levels of measurement specificity are encountered:

1. Measures characterizing the entire employment establishment, such as number of employees, industrial sector, or referral patterns established with JTPA.

2. Measures applying to any employee with the same job held by the JTPA participant, such as job complexity, qualifications required for that job, or training level of typical non-JTPA hires.
3. Measures applying specifically to each JTPA participant, such as the length of training received, or employer's ratings of that participant.

In cases where SDAs envision repeated local employer follow-ups, efficiency can be increased and nuisance to employers decreased by treating categories 1 and 2 as once-only measures analogous to those for service providers. Category 1 measures could be taken during an initial work-up with each new employer. Category 2 measures would be gathered once for each separate job title into which each employer accepted JTPA participants. Such measures are easily integrated into program operation where employer *or* participant analyses are envisioned. They can be combined with participant data for analysis as long as both employer and participant data include an identifier for each employer.

An Illustration of Differential Impact
Analysis Including Employer Data

A summary of selected findings from the Washington State CETA OJT study discussed earlier will serve to illustrate the application of differential impact analysis (Simpson 1984a). That study analyzed data from a nine-month follow-up of 881 OJT participants and 517 OJT employers who trained them. In addition, data from participant MIS files, state labor and industry sources, and surveys with all OJT service providers in the CETA system were combined with data from the two follow-up surveys. Selected findings relevant to one program development issue—quality control over OJT placements—are summarized here.

There is a continuing question concerning the extent to which OJT represents a training intervention, with employers reimbursed for additional training costs demanded by their program participation, or a hiring incentive program in which employers provide little service except to hire from the list of eligibles. In addition, during the period immediately preceding the 1982-83 data collection for this analysis, the State of

Washington had decided to rather dramatically expand its OJT program, raising the question of whether pressure to enlarge the pool of new employers led to a deterioration in the quality of OJT placements.

While gross impact analysis cannot assess the net impact of OJT for participants, we were able to test a series of propositions comparing forms of OJT implementation that placed greater or lesser emphasis on quality control. We were also to compare specific OJT placements that appeared to provide service to participants of greater or lesser quality. The following summarizes findings from differential impact analysis of these implementation and treatment variants on postprogram outcomes. All of these reports are for the outcome variable most clearly affected by programmatic variables—whether or not one retained employment with the original OJT employer.[18]

1. Various qualities of OJT implementation and treatment explain far more variation in outcomes than do the full set of participant background characteristics included in MIS files and augmented by measures on the follow-up survey, although age and employment history have considerable impact. This was true in part, we learned, because so many OJT positions were entry level, making such minimal demands that some highly qualified OJT enrollees left voluntarily, thus undermining program success.

2. Service provider measures indicating the degree to which strong quality control procedures were a part of their OJT program implementation proved strongly associated with the rate at which participants retained their OJT positions through the nine-month follow-up. A number of factors raised OJT retention: more demanding quality review for new and old employers, a policy demanding higher than minimum wage for OJT placements, and a willingness to hold some money back because an insufficient number of satisfactory employers were available for OJT. We estimated a 28 percent difference in OJT retention rates, above and beyond other factors, between agencies placing most and least emphasis on quality control.

3. Consistent with the interpretation that OJT in this system was suffering from low quality control, a set of measures designed to measure the quality of participant training also indicated higher OJT

retention where training had been more intensive. In particular, employers who reported offering any special instruction for OJT participants, who used more formal preparation along with informal OJT, and who had more personal involvement in the training retained their participants more often. The impact of these factors was modest because training intensity overlaps with two other powerful predictors of retention: the complexity of the job, and the participant's enthusiasm for the work.

4. While it is common to worry about OJT participants' ability to meet their job demands, the reverse proved much more problematic in this study. The less background the participant reported having in the area of the OJT job and the more complex the employer described the job as being, the higher the OJT retention (after adjustments for participant background characteristics). We found that only 7 percent of the participants were fired for inability to do the work, while 10.3 percent gave boredom with the job or getting no training as the main reason they quit, and another 14 percent left for a better job. In all, 31 percent quit, while 21.7 percent were fired or left by mutual agreement with the employer.[19]

5. The three strongest predictors of OJT retention were the employer's rating of how enthusiastic and cooperative the participant was, the employer's rating of how fast the participant worked, and the participant's felt importance of retaining a career in the type of work represented by the OJT job. All these turn out to be much higher when the job is more complex, when OJT positions provide more training, when participants are moving into a new area of work rather than being placed in a job about which they know a great deal, when employers more frequently provide evaluative feedback to participants, and where service providers emphasize quality control. The higher the quality of the OJT placement, the more likely participants were to like the job and treat it as a career they valued, and in turn display behaviors employers wanted to see.

These findings conclude that in that particular OJT system at that time the program needed to develop quality control over the nature of the OJT site, i.e., the services offered by employers. One other troublesome finding consistent with this concern for quality was the discovery that some employers in that sample were explicitly using the OJT reimbursement as windfall profit.

Although employer-initiated OJTs were quite common in this sample (45.8 percent of all OJTs), most of these represented referrals by knowledgeable employers who made no hiring decision until eligibility was established. Postprogram success in these cases was no higher than average. However, one-sixth (17.3 percent) of the employers we interviewed said they first made a firm hiring decision and then sent the participant to CETA to see if a wage subsidy could be gained.[20] This phenomenon represents both a poor expenditure of training dollars and a selection mechanism likely to bias outcome estimates. Among these participants, retention was 12 percent higher, after adjusting for other factors.

This set of findings was chosen to illustrate the value of differential impact analysis because many separate tests lead consistently to the same conclusion, and because that conclusion is in essence opposite to the normal interpretation of weak program performance. When one service provider performs at a higher (descriptive) rate than another, nearly all analysts will ask whether that difference was produced by "creaming," i.e., whether the finding represents selection bias. Few will ask, however, whether participants were *too highly qualified*, relative to the quality of the OJT jobs and training. Yet, careful quantitative analysis of program implementation and treatment confirms the latter interpretation in this one service delivery system.

How Gross Impact Analysis
Complements Net Impact and Process Evaluations

The most valuable uses of the gross impact evaluation method—and also its major limitations—may be placed in relief by a brief examination of the ways in which the three approaches in this volume complement each other. The gross impact approach exploits its measurement flexibility to enlarge the range of outcomes analyzed as well as the range of factors considered as influences on outcomes, yet the quantitative nature of its measures helps insure that conclusions are reliable.

In the Washington State CETA OJT example, the gross impact analysis provided no knowledge of the net value of that OJT system to its participants. If we had employed both the net and the gross impact approaches, the major value of the gross impact findings would have been to broaden the range of measures analyzed—both outcomes and programmatic factors that might have influenced the net impact. These measures would have *increased our ability to explain how the system works to produce the high or low net impacts* we identified, providing guidance on improving net impact. Without a net impact evaluation, we do not know how urgent the need for system improvement is. Without the gross impact evaluation, we have less guidance regarding the mechanisms needed to improve a system.[21]

At the other end of the continuum lies process analysis. Its detailed analysis of program implementation feeds gross impact analysis by identifying measures worthy of quantification. Only when the analyst understands the process by which organizations operate will meaningful outcomes be selected for measurement, or will the analysis of program-variant effects upon outcomes be meaningful. The centrality of implementation factors to differential impact analysis means that gross impact analysis is in part quantified process analysis and should always be preceded by at least a partial process analysis.

In addition to its focus on outcomes, gross impact analysis adds four major complements to process analysis: (1) *postprogram* outcome measures, (2) quantitative precision of measurement, which allows reliable estimates of the impact of program variants on outcomes, (3) reliable comparisons across multiple service providers or treatments, and (4) measurement of *individual service treatments* as possible influences on outcomes, along with measurement of the implementation factors also emphasized by process analysis.

Because process evaluation avoids the limits of formal, quantitative data collection, it can be flexible, creative, and unique. However, for the same reason, i.e., process analysis does not collect quantitative data, conclusions from process analysis are subject to considerable error, which can be reduced by subjecting the conclusions of process evaluations to a gross impact analysis. Such interpretations can be tested in multiple contexts and can include a range of measures indicating individual treatment as well as program implementation. Thus, for example, a process evaluation conclusion that an organization is less effective than it might be because of some particular element in its internal structure can be tested by comparing outcomes, as indicators of effectiveness, among organizations differing with regard to that structure.

The CETA OJT study, discussed in order to illustrate differential impact analysis, began its conceptualization phase with an informal process analysis. Our aim was to identify alternative theories regarding OJT system operation, program variants likely to impact outcomes, and program variants that could be changed if policymakers decided to use our findings to improve program performance. While standard variables for such research were also measured, several analyses that proved to be most fascinating involved variables that emerged from the process analysis. Had the research ended at the process analysis stage, these ideas could not have been tested and could not have generated quantitative estimates of the impact which program variants can have on outcomes.

Chapter Summary

The major goal of the gross impact evaluation approach presented here has been to improve the technology available to managers of human services organizations. Technology, in this case, is knowing how to operate programs that effectively produce the desired outcomes—transforming clients with given needs at intake into postprogram success stories. Gross impact analysis approaches that goal with two distinct analytic strategies: the analysis of descriptive gross outcomes, and differential impact analysis. These analyses are performed using data from several possible sources: MIS files, participant interviews, data from service providers on individual treatments and program implementation, and data from others, such as employers, who may be closely involved in the operation or outcomes of the program.

The analysis of descriptive gross outcomes is useful because it is simple. It is also dangerous, for the same reason. The following steps may be taken to enhance the usefulness of descriptive outcome measures: (1)

broadening the range of outcomes studied, to provide fuller interpretations of how the program is functioning; (2) tailoring measures and analysis questions to make findings more meaningful; (3) measuring views of those whose perceptions have *prima facia* meaning (e.g., employers); and (4) insuring high technical standards during data collection and analysis. Analysts can also protect against misuse of descriptive reports by limiting the nature of their interpretations to those merited, given the limitations of the analysis.

The second analytic approach, differential impact analysis, is more expensive and also more useful for program development. This method increases the level of technology available to managers by testing the relative effectiveness of alternative forms of program implementation or service treatments provided to individuals. That is, differential impact analysis estimates the degree to which difference in postprogram outcomes is *caused* by any given program variant. Each alternative is tested against other alternatives which are in place in the service delivery system.

Further, differential impact analysis attacks the problem of selection bias, the primary factor limiting the validity of descriptive gross outcome reports and inhibiting causal interpretations. By using a variety of sources to measure selection processes as well as client characteristics predictive of postprogram success, the most powerful "alternative explanation" facing all program evaluation—that outcomes were produced by client characteristics or selection rather than by the program—can be greatly mitigated, if never completely eliminated.

Thoughtful preparation of survey data collection tools and appropriate use of analysis techniques, available in a wide range of statistical packages, can make differential impact analysis a powerful tool for improving program performance on mandated outcomes. At the same time, the wide spectrum of measurable and describable gross outcomes can be used to improve or maintain the quality of service while core outcomes are being maximized. Findings apply directly to the state or local service delivery systems in which the evaluation was conducted, directing managers to increase some services or retain some implementation forms, while reducing others. Local applicability of findings, protection against selection bias, and testing of alternative program variants provide the basic components of quasi-experimental causal analysis, so that careful differential impact analysis produces results that can more accurately identify factors influencing program effectiveness. Changing these factors is, therefore, likely to produce improvement in effectiveness.

NOTES

1. Whether each group is better off because of participating in the program is a net impact question. Gross impact analysis identifies which services work better for each group.

2. The range of available alternative explanations may be identified by asking managers of programs that are performing poorly to explain their organizations' weak showing.

3. The aim of all research is to increase or reduce our confidence in particular conclusions or interpretations. To reject new information because it is imperfect is as foolish as to embrace unreliable findings wholeheartedly. The analyst must assess the value of any research finding. Structuring the research so that findings are firmer improves the value of the research, even if the method remains considerably less than perfect.

4. Since these results are descriptive only, this interpretation is also subject to error. It could be, for example, that more AFDC recipients leave their OJT positions because they are unstable, while non-AFDC recipients leave in order to move to higher paying jobs in nonrelated areas. Such possibilities can be tested if the researcher has entertained them early enough to make the data available. In this case, for example, more non-AFDC people did quit for better jobs, but not enough more to invalidate the initial interpretation offered in the text.

5. This figure and others in this series may be somewhat lower than typical since Washington was experiencing rather serious recession during this study.

6. Above and beyond the obvious reason that JTPA now requires such a definition.

7. One topic of particular interest to small SDAs involves the correction downward of the sample needed for a given error margin when the population from which the sample is drawn is very small.

8. This does suggest one possible pitfall of low-budget program evaluation: if surveys are conducted in-house, respondents may bias their answers in a positive direction. Sophisticated external consumers will therefore tend to question findings based on surveys, unless they are conducted by third parties and guarantee confidentiality.

9. These membership identifiers also serve as extremely important control variables under conditions discussed later in the chapter.

10. The term "membership identifier" has been used throughout this chapter to refer to what statisticians typically call "dummy variables." The standard rules governing proper analysis of dummy variables should be followed during the analysis described here. If all membership identifiers are entered simultaneously, only $n-1$ may be included. For example, if 15 service providers are included in the sample, membership identifiers (dummy variables) indicating 14 may be included in a single regression equation. If the analysis involves a forward stepwise procedure, n (all) membership identifiers may be included.

11. It should be noted that because interaction terms are highly correlated with their constituent variables, analysts should consult the change in variance explained ($\underline{R^2}$) rather than relying on t or F scores for each individual variable within the model.

12. When programs are most successful, nearly all participants are employed after the program. Variance in earnings is greatest when a large proportion of participants earns nothing.

13. Optionally, a written form with anonymous return could be administered by staff, but not without the problems of return rate and secretarial overload which accompany mail surveys.

14. Examples of such questions as they appear in a survey are available in Simpson (1986).

15. For a set of specific suggested measures that have been pre-tested among JTPA employers, see Simpson, 1986.

16. One difficulty with survey data emerges here. Respondents often tend to bias their reports in a positive direction, so that the midpoint of any set of answers is always a bit above the face validity midpoint. Thus, if a group of employers were asked to rate all their employees, the average employee would be rated somewhat above average. Analysts should bear this in mind when interpreting employer ratings. However, no precise information exists with which to estimate to what extent responses are inflated, making adjustments imprecise.

17. See Simpson (1986) for specific measurement suggestions for this issue as for other employer issues.

18. One of our more intriguing findings was that the ability to regain other employment once the OJT position was lost was almost entirely immune to interpretation via program variables. That is, the impact of the OJT program—or, rather, any variations in its implementation—extended only to getting and retaining the original OJT job.

19. For valid measurement of issues such as this one, it proved especially useful to have data from both the employer and the participant.

20. Presumably, employers were so candid with us because we were a neutral third party. Some employers even offered explicit statements that they viewed the entire process, cynically, as a windfall.

21. It is possible in theory, and at great expense, to conduct net impact evaluations that include a broad range of outcome measures. The cost-efficient design suggested in this volume by Johnson foregoes this possibility to make the research feasible for states and large SDAs. Any quantitative analysis of a wide range of program variants automatically becomes a gross impact analysis because these measures are meaningful only among participants. An untreated comparison group must, therefore, be omitted from such an analysis.

REFERENCES

Astin, Alexander. *Four Critical Years: Effects of College on Beliefs, Attitudes, and Knowledge.* San Francisco: Jossey-Bass, 1977.

Babbie, Earl R. *Survey Research Methods.* 5th ed. Belmont, CA: Wadsworth Publishing Co., 1989.

Bjornstadt, George W., and David Knoke. *Statistics for Social Data Analysis.* Itasca, IL: F. E. Peacock Publishers, Inc., 1982.

Blalock, Hubert M. *Causal Inferences in Nonexperimental Research.* New York: W. W. Norton and Co., 1964.

Blalock, Hubert M. *Causal Models in the Social Sciences.* Rev. ed. Chicago: Aldine, 1985.

Blalock, Hubert M. "Theory Building and the Statistical Concept of Interaction." *American Sociological Review* 30 (1965): 374-380.

Bloom, Howard S., and Maureen A. McLaughlin. *CETA Training Programs— Do They Work for Adults?* Government report by the Congressional Budget Office and the National Commission for Employment Policy (1982).

Borus, Michael, and William Tash. *Measuring the Impact of Manpower Programs: A Primer.* Ann Arbor, MI: Institute of Labor and Industrial Relations. The University of Michigan-Wayne State University, 1979.

Bradburn, Norman M. "Response Effects." In *Handbook of Survey Research,* edited by Peter Rossi, James D. Wright, and Andy B. Anderson. New York: Academic Press, 1983.

Campbell, Donald T., and Thomas Cook. *Quasi-Experimentation: Design and Analysis Issues for Field Settings.* Chicago: Rand McNally, 1979.

Campbell, Donald T., and Julian C. Stanley. *Experimental and Quasi-Experimental Designs for Research.* Chicago: Rand McNally, 1966.

Caporaso, James A., and Leslie L. Roos. *Quasi-Experimental Approaches: Testing Theory and Evaluating Policy.* Evanston, IL: Northwestern University Press, 1973.

Dillman, Don A. *Mail and Telephone Surveys: The Total Design Method.* New York: John Wiley & Sons, 1978.

Doeringer, Peter B., and Michael J. Piore. *Internal Labor Markets and Manpower Analysis.* Lexington, MA: D. C. Heath, 1971.

Fink, Arlene, and Jacqueline Kosecoff. *How to Conduct Surveys: A Step-by-Step Guide.* Newbury Park, CA: Sage, 1985.

Franklin, Grace, and Randall B. Ripley. *CETA: Politics and Policy, 1973-1982.* Knoxville, TN: The University of Tennessee Press, 1984.

Frey, James H. *Survey Research by Telephone.* Newbury Park, CA: Sage, 1983.

Geraci, Vincent J. *Short-Term Indicators of Job Training Program Effects on Long-Term Participant Earnings.* U.S. Department of Labor, August 1984.

Gillespi, Michael W. "Log-linear Techniques and the Regression Analysis of Dummy Dependent Variables: Further Bases for Comparison." *Sociological Methods and Research* 6 (1977): 103-122.

Goodman, Leo A. "A Modified Multiple Regression Approach to the Analysis of Dichotomous Variables." *American Sociological Review* 37 (1972): 28-46.

Hoffman, Saul D. "On the Job Training: Differences by Race and Sex." *Monthly Labor Review* 104 (1981): 34-37.

Kish, Leslie. *Survey Sampling*. New York: John Wiley & Sons, 1965.

Knoke, D. "A Comparison of Log-linear and Regression Models for Systems of Dichotomous Variables." *Sociological Methods and Research* 3 (1975): 416-434.

Levitan, Sar A., and Garth L. Mangum. *The T in CETA: Local and National Perspectives*. Kalamazoo, MI: W. E. Upjohn Institute for Employment Research, 1981.

Maranto, Cheryl L., and Robert C. Rodgers. "Does Work Experience Increase Productivity? A Test of the On-the-Job Training Hypothesis." *The Journal of Human Resources* 19 (1984): 341-357.

Minnesota Office of Statewide CETA Coordination. *Private Sector Experience with CETA On-the-Job Training*. St. Paul, MN: Minnesota Department of Economic Security, August 1979.

O'Neill, Dave. "Employment Tax Credit Programs: The Effects of Socioeconomic Targeting Provisions." *The Journal of Human Resources* 17 (1982): 449-459.

Rossi, Peter H., and Howard E. Freeman. *Evaluation: A Systematic Approach*. 3d ed. Beverly Hills, CA: Sage, 1982.

Rossi, Peter, James D. Wright, and Andy B. Anderson. *Handbook of Survey Research*. New York: Academic Press, 1983.

Seattle-King County Private Industry Council and Snedeker Scientific, Inc. *JTPA Evaluation Issues, Priorities, and Contingencies at the SDA Level*. Technical Report for the JTPA Evaluation Design Project, Washington State Employment Security Department, 1985.

Simpson, Carl. *Vocational Classroom Training Outcomes Project: Final Report*. Olympia, WA: Washington State Employment Security Department, 1982.

Simpson, Carl. *CETA On-the-Job Training Study Final Report*. Olympia, WA: Washington State Employment Security Department, 1984a.

Simpson, Carl. *CETA On-the-Job Training Employers: A Survey of Employers and OJT Officers*. Olympia, WA: Washington State Employment Security Department, 1984b.

Simpson, Carl. *A Guide for Gross Impact Evaluations*. Olympia, WA: JTPA Evaluation Design Project, Washington State Employment Security Department, 1986.

Simpson, Carl. "Competency-Based Assessment and Remediating Barriers to Employment: A Quality Analysis of One SDA." *Evaluation Forum* 4 (1989): 24-26.

Snedeker, Bonnie, and David Snedecker. *CETA: Decentralization on Trial*. Salt Lake City, UT: Olympus Publishing, 1973.

Sudman, Seymour. *Applied Sampling*. New York: Academic Press, 1976.

Taggart, Robert. *A Fisherman's Guide: An Assessment of Training and Remediation Strategies*. Kalamazoo, MI: W. E. Upjohn Institute for Employment Research, 1981.

Vermeulen, Bruce, and Susan Hudson-Wilson. "The Impact of Workplace Practices on Education and Training Policy." In *Jobs and Training in the 1980s: Vocational Policy and the Labor Market*, edited by Peter Doeringer and Bruce Vermeulen. Boston, MA: Martinus Nijhoff Publishing, 1981.

Wentling, Tim, and Tom Lawson. *Evaluating Occupational Education and Training Programs*. Boston, MA: Allyn and Bacon, Inc., 1975.

Wilms, Wellford W. *Vocational Education and Social Mobility: A Study of Public and Proprietary School Dropouts and Graduates*. Los Angeles: University of California, 1980.

Zornitsky, Jeffrey et al. *Measuring the Costs of JTPA Program Participation*. Cambridge, MA: Abt Associates, Inc., 1984.

Zornitsky, Jeffrey et al. *Post-Program Performance Measures for Adult Programs Funded under Titles IIA and IIIA of JTPA: Early Findings Prepared for the U.S. Department of Labor's Performance Standards Advisory Committee*. Cambridge, MA: ABT Associates, Inc., 1985.

4
Evaluating Program Implementation

David Grembowski
Department of Health Services
University of Washington
with
Ann Bonar Blalock
Washington State Employment Security

What describes does not explain; patterns are not processes but are the results of them.

Constance Perin
Everything in Its Place

Process evaluations differ from outcome studies in the kinds of questions asked, the nature of the data collected, and the range of methods used to gather and analyze information to answer these questions. These differences are the basis for giving more emphasis in this chapter to issues that *cut across* social programs, and for providing a less intensive treatment of these issues in the case example, JTPA. In general, the chronology of this chapter follows that of chapters 2 and 3. The first section explores a conceptual framework for process evaluations, the second examines measurement challenges, the third focuses on methodology, and the fourth illustrates some of these issues through JTPA.

The emphasis on generic issues in this chapter fits the nature of studies of program implementation. Such studies have a substantially shorter history within applied research, the influences and relationships to be studied are not as well-identified or as easily defined, and a much broader range of methods can be used. Unlike outcome evaluations, there is no established set of traditional conceptual frameworks or research strategies on which to rely. The evaluator must *develop* a framework and draw from a wide spectrum of methods in tailoring a research approach and strategy to fit the particular questions guiding an evaluation, within the research resources available in a given setting.

A Conceptual Framework for Process Evaluations

Social programs are created to carry out social policies. More specifically, they are to achieve certain outcomes through the use of particular interventions, or change agents (Pressman and Wildavsky 1979; Shortell 1984). The typical reasoning is: "If we provide X, then Y will result, where X is the service(s) and Y is the intended outcome(s)." These "if-then" relationships are a program's "theory of cause and effect." This theory proposes that particular kinds of program interventions will produce certain desired outcomes. In chapter 1 it was proposed that two kinds of program interventions, or "strategies," are involved in this causal theory: an *implementation strategy* and a *service strategy*. The service strategy is frequently the intervention for which a program is best known. However, the way in which this service intervention is delivered, organizationally, is also an important part of the theory's explanation of cause and effect.

In the past, program evaluations have focused mainly on the important relationship between the service intervention and program outcomes. Consequently, little empirical knowledge has been produced about the influence of the organizational context in which services are provided. Yet, those involved in the operation of social programs have long recognized that implementation structures and methods have significant effects on outcomes and are often more open to modification than is the more politically visible service strategy. Fortunately, a new interest in evaluating program implementation has developed over the past decade, stimulated by practitioner information needs and interests, and by the broadening of the applied research repertoire.

In this chapter, the success of a social program is assumed to be dependent on both the appropriateness of its theory about the relationship between interventions and outcomes, and how well this theory works when applied in a pragmatic program setting. It also assumes that it is possible that a program's service intervention may be appropriate to the problem the program is to address, but the implementation strategy may be flawed, or that the implementation mode may be a feasible one, but the services provided are not appropriate to the problem.

To achieve the outcomes desired, it is assumed that both the implementation strategy and the service strategy must be appropriate to the problem and operate as intended. Furthermore, it is understood that problems in implementing a program and problems in exposing clients to the service intervention are directly amenable to change—that is, to modification—if sufficient information is available about the nature of these problems.

Although few implementation studies are designed specifically to test a program's cause-effect theory, there is a new appreciation of the importance of implementation studies, the complementary nature of information from process and outcome evaluations, and the utility of these different information sources in making policy recommendations and program improvements. In fact, the exploration of how a program's implementation and service interventions are being applied in local settings is now considered an integral part of comprehensive evaluations of social programs.

While impact evaluations inform us about the influence of a program's service strategy on outcomes, they do not explain why these outcomes occurred. Process evaluations fill this knowledge gap by analyzing the implementation strategy that contributed to the outcomes observed. A primary goal is to answer questions about how and why programs are working or not working as intended.

This chapter presents one approach, among a number of possible approaches, for conducting process evaluations. It is based on a simple principle: because most social programs are implemented by organizations, understanding what goes on inside and between organizations involved in the operation of a program is vital to explaining program performance. These organizational relationships are the "black box" that has traditionally been neglected in studying programs. In the approach taken here, *a social program is viewed as an organizational system composed of interrelated parts that must work together to produce the outcomes desired.*

In carrying out a process evaluation, the organization is broken down into its parts, and each part, as well as the relationship among parts, is examined to learn more about implementation generally, or more specifically, the reasons for a particular level of performance. When process evaluations are used regularly to evaluate of social programs, they are an essential management tool for explaining outcomes and resolving implementation problems, as well as for improving the general functioning of programs.

Consistent with this approach, a model of an *organizational system* and its *environment* is presented as a guide for evaluating implementation. There are alternative approaches for studying organizations, but the dominant approach is systems analysis, which is the basis for the model used here. This model (figure 4.1) is a synthesis of a variety of systems analysis approaches (Lyden 1975; Mintzberg 1979, 1983; Hollingsworth and Hanneman 1984; Grembowski 1983, 1986, 1989). The different components of the model are the "parts" of the system. The linkages represent the flow of resources and relationships among the parts. The model's perimeter is the larger environment in which the organizational system operates.

Some of the parts of the organizational system, such as authority hierarchies, are *structural,* and some, such as actual organizational practices in utilizing program resources, are *functional.* The underlying assumption in the model, and in most system models, is that organizational effectiveness and efficiency depend on the *degree of integration,* or consistency, among the system's parts, and between the system and its external environment. Therefore, the way in which a program's implementation and service strategies are actually being applied can be studied by analyzing the characteristics of these components and their interrelationships, and the relationship between this organizational system and its environment.

The model may seem to have an air of finality about it, as if it perfectly matches what actually occurs in social programs (Mintzberg 1983). This impression is not intended. All models are simplifications of reality, which assist the evaluator in managing the study of inherently complex phenomena. Conceptual models of this kind sharpen the major features of organizations, making them easier to understand and analyze.

This chapter will give special attention to this framework for process evaluations, focusing more intensively than do the net impact and gross

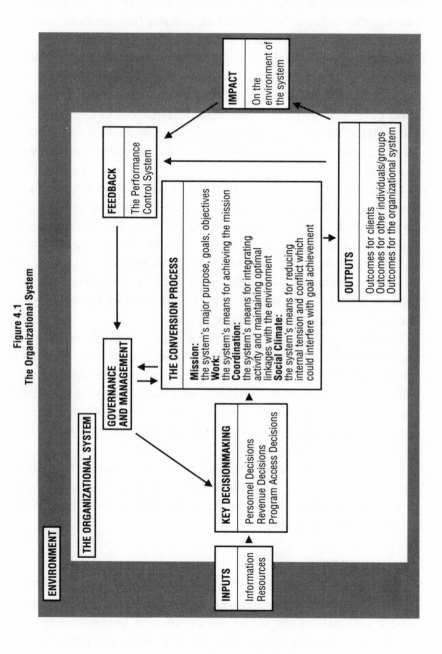

Figure 4.1
The Organizational System

ENVIRONMENT

THE ORGANIZATIONAL SYSTEM

GOVERNANCE AND MANAGEMENT

FEEDBACK
The Performance Control System

IMPACT
On the environment of the system

THE CONVERSION PROCESS

Mission:
the system's major purpose, goals, objectives
Work:
the system's means for achieving the mission
Coordination:
the system's means for integrating activity and maintaining optimal linkages with the environment
Social Climate:
the system's means for reducing internal tension and conflict which could interfere with goal achievement

KEY DECISIONMAKING
Personnel Decisions
Revenue Decisions
Program Access Decisions

OUTPUTS
Outcomes for clients
Outcomes for other individuals/groups
Outcomes for the organizational system

INPUTS
Information
Resources

outcome chapters on this first *theoretical* step in the research process. This attention is justified by the lack of guidance from previous research about what should be studied in analyzing implementation, and the multiplicity of conceptual options from which an evaluator must choose. The general framework for an evaluation provides a context in which specific research questions can be developed. These questions then direct the selection of a research design and methods of data collection and analysis. Therefore, *the development of a framework for research is the first and most important issue that must be addressed in any process evaluation.*

The evaluator conducting net and gross outcome studies can draw from previously tested and refined frameworks that suggest a fairly circumscribed set of alternative research questions. Relating services to outcomes can be very complex, but the nature of the variables and relationships to be studied are often relatively straightforward. This is not the case in studying implementation. A wide variety of variables and relationships can be the subject of study, and there are few established frameworks to guide this kind of analysis.

The questions to be answered in net impact and differential gross impact studies require rigorous methodologies that are more dependent than process studies on the use of advanced statistical methods. On the other hand, because many process variables can only be measured qualitatively, process studies can draw from a broader continuum of established methods of data collection and analysis, such as the case study and the social survey.

Consistent with the strong emphasis in this chapter on the framework for conducting process evaluations, the components, or organizational parts, of the organizational model presented above are briefly described in the sections that follow.

The Environment

An organizational system can be viewed as having a *boundary* that separates it from the larger environment in which it operates. Everything outside this boundary can, for purposes of analysis, be considered part of the environment of the system. In this model, the organizational system refers to those organizations within a particular service delivery area that are responsible for a program. These will be referred to here as *program organizations*. The system may involve one central organization with both administrative and service delivery functions, or it may involve an administrative organization with a number of subcontractors who deliver services, these arrangements being dependent on a program's particular implementation strategy.

The *environment* includes other organizations in the same service delivery area which operate related programs or deliver related services, and organizations within and beyond the service area—such as state and federal agencies—that affect the system through such mechanisms as laws, policies, plans, regulations, or administrative directives. Because the environment normally involves influences over which program organizations have less than optimal control, it often represents fixed conditions that act as constraints on decisions and action, to which the organizational system must adapt in order to maintain itself. Information about the environment is, therefore, useful in understanding how external circumstances shape program implementation, why certain kinds of organizational behavior and program outcomes are defined as problems, and what impact the program may be having on the environment itself.

Inputs, Key Decisions, and Outputs

The environment is the source of *inputs* that the organizational system uses to achieve its goals—i.e., the goals of the program, and also its goals as a system. Inputs consist of *resources,* such as funds, staff, and clients, and *information*, such as data on the local economy.

The flow of inputs into the organizational system is governed by three kinds of key decisions: *revenue, personnel,* and *program access* decisions. Revenue decisions determine issues such as budget allocations for achieving goals. Personnel and access decisions determine issues such as who is hired and fired, and whether consultants are needed to provide expertise in certain areas. Access decisions determine issues such as the characteristics of clients entering the system. The system utilizes, or *converts,* inputs to produce desired *outputs,* such as the number of clients whose social or economic problems have been reduced after being exposed to the program. Outputs, in turn, have an *impact* on the environment, either by ameliorating or exacerbating the problem a program is meant to address.

Governance, Management, and Feedback

The conversion of inputs to outputs is directed by *governance*—that is, by those individuals with ultimate responsibility for a program's performance and the actions they take. Operational responsibility is usually delegated by governance to program management. A primary function of governance and management is to establish the goals of the organizational system and make sure they are achieved. Together, the output and impact components of the model measure program performance. Through the *feedback process,* program outcomes and their influence on the program's environment inform governance about how well the system is performing. If governance receives information indicating that the system operating the program is not achieving its goals and objectives, the conversion process—the utilization of resources—may be altered to increase performance. If the impact of the system on its environment is problematic, new relationships may need to be developed with organizations outside the system.

The Conversion Process

The *conversion process* can be studied along four dimensions: *mission, work, coordination,* and *social climate.* In the model, the mission dimension consists of the goals and objectives of the organizational system, which in many cases are developed by governance through a formal *planning process.* The *mission component* has an important influence on the conversion process as the interface between the external environment and the other functions involved in the utilization of resources. Governance must interpret the system's environment, define the system's purpose in this environment, and design its work, coordination activities, and social milieu to accomplish that purpose. If gross errors are made with respect to defining the mission, these errors are often repeated in designing and monitoring other functions.

The working assumption here is that if the organization is to operate properly, a "fit"—or consistency—must be maintained between the environment and the mission of the system, and between the mission and the other dimensions of the conversion process.[1] An essential part of studying the conversion process is determining the extent to which a proper fit exists, and identifying what factors are enhancing or acting as deterrents to maintaining consistency among components. The concept of integration or consistency will be discussed in more detail later in the chapter.

The *work dimension* is an organizational system's major means for goal achievement, i.e., the major activities it undertakes to achieve its mission. This dimension includes responsibilities such as the procurement of resources, the development of work flow procedures, the design and maintenance of the pathway clients follow through the system, and the provision of services to these clients. The work dimension, representing essential organizational and service delivery functions for achieving key goals, is critical to study in examining the implementation of a program's distinctive service delivery strategy.

As suggested previously, the *coordination* dimension addresses the necessary integration of an organizational system's mission with its work effort to produce the intended outcomes. In studying this dimension, the evaluator would analyze, for example, the allocation of responsibility among various divisions and personnel within the system, communication patterns within its authority structure, and processes for developing policies and procedures. In many social programs, coordination also involves a number of other factors: internal mechanisms for coordinating the activities of an administrative agency with those of subcontractor organizations providing services; service delivery activities across subcontractors; and the system's administrative and service delivery activities with those of important organizations in the environment. The way in which coordination is handled is considered to have a strong effect on the operation of the system and is, therefore, a significant area for study.

The last dimension, *social climate*, refers to the interpersonal internal environment of the organizational system, such as the social norms and professional orientations of staff, staff and client morale, the motivation of staff to achieve the mission, and the level of tension and conflict within the system. This dimension has a special relationship to the other three parts of the conversion process: to achieve its goals and survive in its environment, the system must define its purpose, determine what kinds of efforts are required to realize it, and apply these strategies with a minimum amount of interdivisional and interpersonal strain (Lyden 1975).

Conflicts inevitably occur as resources are utilized. Such conflicts can undermine a system's effectiveness and threaten its continuation. Therefore, organizational systems operating programs seek to maintain tensions and conflicts at reasonable levels through various mechanisms, such as involving clients and other interest groups in planning processes, or pursuing an "open-door" management style. Inasmuch as the social climate dimension plays an important role in accomplishing organizational missions, its investigation provides useful information to the evaluator.

In summary, an analysis framework is proposed that treats the organizational system operating programs as composed of a number of essential parts that articulate with one another and with the outside environment to affect the way in which programs are implemented. Process evaluations can usefully focus on each of these component parts, and on the level of integration and consistency across them.

In the next sections, measurement and methodological issues in applying this, or any other, model in process evaluations are discussed.

Measurement Issues in Process Evaluations

Several factors frequently motivate process evaluations: the desire to resolve a specific performance problem, such as increasing the number or changing the composition of clients served; the desire to carry out a comprehensive review of a program's operations prior to the beginning of a planning cycle; or the wish to explain the results of an outcome evaluation. In some cases, process studies will be limited to those aspects of organizations that have received the most political attention. Some evaluations may be confined to particular components that are known to be problematic. Other process studies may emphasize components that are working well, with the purpose of identifying and learning more about those features that are most critical to replicate elsewhere. The more comprehensive process evaluations will look at all components of the system and their interrelationships.

Regardless of the rationale for conducting process studies or establishing their comprehensiveness, there is a key difference between process and outcome evaluations that has an impact on the measurement of implementation influences and on the methodologies used in studying them. Two goals of all program evaluations are (1) to sort out what is *most responsible* for program outcomes and *how* these influences may be affecting outcomes, and (2) to make recommendations for correcting, sustaining, or improving outcomes by making changes in these critical factors. In most programs, despite the simplicity of their descriptions in legislation, these influences are enormously complex. Both the implementation strategy and the service strategy involve an array of more specific treatments. The relationships among these treatments-within-treatments are also complex.

In conducting outcome studies, evaluators have been able to use previous research to narrow the range of variables studied, with some confidence that the most significant factors have been included. Even so, there has been a tendency in some outcome studies to assume that this carefully selected set of variables, representing particular client characteristics, services, and outcomes, are the only ones of importance. In truth, the effect of a program's implementation strategy on outcomes can never be totally separated from the effect of its service strategy. Implementation factors are inevitably confounded with service treatments in producing program effects. Therefore, comprehensive evaluations look jointly at both kinds of interventions.

The selection of the most important influences in implementing a program have not benefited from the long research history characteristic of outcome evaluations. A host of factors is involved, and evaluators have not had enough experience in studying them to conclude, with the same level of confidence, which of these influences tend to be the most important in producing outcomes—either independently, or in combination with the service treatments.

If we are not able to distill a set of variables for studying implementation, then process evaluations must, of necessity, be approached quite differently than outcome studies in terms of the questions directing them, the measurement of the influences implied in these questions, and the methodologies used in answering such queries. Otherwise, the evaluator will be making premature judgments about the critical influences, and may select the wrong ones to study.

Given this context, it is still essential in process evaluations to formulate a manageable set of general research questions, determine how feasible it is to answer them in terms of staff, data, and cost, and consider the measurement and methodological issues involved. A conceptual model, such as the organizational model suggested here, is a useful tool for focusing a process evaluation, highlighting those aspects about which there is some knowledge or clue, and tailoring the study to the concerns and interests of evaluation sponsors and users.

Measurement Approaches

The choice of variables, or influences, to study in process evaluations flows from the research questions being asked. Looking at the components of the model, it is obvious that even though the research questions may be clear-cut, the definition of "organizational parts" and "relationships" is a very difficult task.

Although the definition of treatments and outcomes presents problems in outcome studies also, another difference between process and outcome evaluations involves the ease with which the variables selected for study can be defined and measured empirically. Again, outcome studies can rely on previous research, which typically directs the evaluator to a circumscribed set of quantitative indices. Many of these are accessible from ongoing administrative data systems—i.e., treatments, such as "classroom training" and "on-the-job training," and outcomes such as jobs obtained, hours worked, wages received. These indices can be extracted and inserted readily into bivariate (two-variable) and multivariate (multiple-variable) statistical analyses. In this respect, outcome studies can more efficiently simplify the complex relationships between service interventions and outcomes than process studies can simplify the complex relationships among different aspects of program implementation. Although process evaluators may be able to develop measures that are just as accurate representations of implementation variables as indices used to define service and outcome factors, they do not have the luxury of using ready-made, easily obtainable indices that economize the research effort.

Therefore, *the first challenge in using the model, and one of the greatest research hurdles in implementing process evaluations, is the definition and measurement of those characteristics of the components of the organizational system that are the major focus of a particular evaluation.* As with the development of a conceptual framework, this challenge must also be resolved at the front end of the research process. The research questions based on this framework should clearly direct the evaluator to those organizational components and relationships of greatest interest. Then the issues are: how will the major variables be defined, how will indices to represent them be developed, what research designs are appropriate, and what methods can be used in studying an organizational system?[2]

In general, process evaluations pose different measurement and methodological issues than do gross outcome or net impact evaluations because of differences in research purposes and information uses, the kinds of data collected, and the range of methods used to analyze these data.

Evaluation Purposes

Social programs are abstract concepts until applied in actual settings. In the process of translating these abstractions organizationally, the intended implementation mode and service strategy are inevitably molded by organizational forces. It is the purpose of process evaluations to examine how well a program's implementation strategy and service intervention have been put into practice within the intent of a program's authorizing legislation, and to make a judgment of the role of implementation in producing program outcomes. The information obtained from such an examination and judgment provides a basis for decisions not only about *what* needs to be changed in improving a program, but *how* changes might best be made.

As Patton (1987) points out, however, choosing questions to answer in process studies requires the acceptance of a tradeoff between *breadth* and *depth*. A few questions may be studied in great depth or many in less detail. The former may provide clear results on specific issues but fail to address other important concerns. On the other hand, collecting less data on a wider range of issues often reduces confidence in the findings. Breadth is often sacrificed for depth when the goal is to explain an outcome or gain insight into the cause of a problem. Identifying a few important questions to study may be critical if it is felt that these issues affect other characteristics of implementation.

The purpose of outcome evaluations, in contrast, is to determine the specific relationship between the service strategy and outcomes—ideally, whether the service intervention has been responsible for the outcomes or these outcomes have been due to some other set of influences or to chance. The information from outcome studies informs policymakers and administrators about the effectiveness of the service intervention, which is critical to decisions about who should be served in the future, and with what mix and sequence of services. This purpose and use is essential, but narrower in scope than the focus of most process evaluations.

Qualitative vs. Quantitative Measures

The task of developing *operational definitions* and *indices* for key variables in studying the components of a program's organizational system is also much more difficult in process evaluations because a great deal of the data on implementation are *qualitative* in nature.[3] Depending on the purpose of the evaluation, the attitudes and behavior of significant participants within and outside the system may need to be defined and measured. Ways to measure the content of decisions, the characteristics of decisionmaking entities and processes, and the nature of service delivery policies and practices also may be necessary. The personal attributes and actions of clients, management, and other actors may need to be defined and classified.

For example, "profiles" of individuals and services may have to be developed using a combination of indices of different variables, such as profiles of the different kinds of clients entering the service delivery system, those provided services, and the combinations of services they received. Defining the "hard-to-serve" client population, for instance, may require the development of a set of weighted social and economic indicators that can be quantified.

However, quantifying variables that are normally described by using qualitative measures, such as the hard-to-serve, require the evaluator to make arbitrary decisions about which indices are the most valid and useful, how highly correlated are these indices with one another, and which should be given more weight than others in representing the phenomenon being studied? Many implementation factors, such as service delivery practices, cannot or should not be quantified. The tradeoff is that qualitative information is necessarily classified and analyzed more subjectively, with less reliance on the use of the statistical methods that characterize many outcome studies.[4]

Therefore, implementation evaluations cannot depend as much as outcome studies on existing management information systems (MISs). The measures in these automated information systems tend to be simple quantitative data elements that satisfy reporting needs. They are often restricted to a small number of variables and are frequently limited to single indices for these variables. But an MIS can be an important resource for outcome evaluators. For certain aspects of implementation, ongoing monitoring/reporting systems can be of some assistance to process evaluators as well. Certain aspects of implementation are quantifiable—particularly the characteristics of the client flow through the service delivery pathway. Some characteristics of the client pathway, such as the number and kinds of clients enrolled, assessed, and assigned services, are already being collected in these information systems. Additional questions on intake and follow-up forms can capture some of what is currently absent from these MIS systems.

Statistical analyses of these data can then be carried out to determine some of the details of the conversion process (see figure 4.1). The chapter on gross outcome evaluations covers this aspect of process studies, and will be discussed in more detail later in this chapter. However, despite the ability to use quantitative measures for studying certain elements of implementation, the fact that many of the variables studied in process evaluations cannot be measured quantitatively means that the evaluator must use innovative measurement approaches and make a careful selection of a combination of methods for analyzing this information (Patton 1987; Shortell 1984).

In summary, there are several critical measurement issues in studying implementation: (1) the extent to which useful, valid, and reliable quantitative data elements are available for defining important variables; (2) the extent to which a program's ongoing MIS contains reliable, extractable, and accurate data on these variables; and (3) the extent to which useful qualitative definitions and indices of variables can be developed and collected for factors that do not lend themselves to quantification.

Methodological Issues in Process Evaluations

Performing a process evaluation within the organizational approach proposed is much like assembling a jigsaw puzzle. After the evaluation's questions are identified, definitions and measures of the important factors are developed, a research design is selected to guide sampling, data collection, and data analysis, and information is collected about each component of the system and its environment, the process evaluator must *integrate* this information to provide insights about interrelationships within the organizational system and the system's relationship to its environment. These insights will help the evaluator make a judgment of the efficiency and effectiveness of program implementation, and its probable influence on outcomes.

The integration of this kind of information by a researcher or research team is a combination of art and science, since precise statistical estimates cannot be made about most of these relationships. It is important, given this constraint, that the researcher select the most rigorous methodology possible, in order to make sound judgments based on the information available, and to have a credible basis for defending these judgments. Therefore, *the selection of a research design is the second challenge in planning studies of program implementation.*

The purpose and scope of the evaluation, the nature of the research questions, and what is already known about the key variables and their relationships effectively shape the choice of a research design that will guide the sampling of subjects, data collection methods, and methods of information analysis. Other important considerations are the kinds of data available, their quality and accessibility, and their appropriateness for statistical analysis. Whether information to answer the research questions must be freshly collected, such as through questionnaires or interviews, or is available from existing administrative data systems is also a determinant of design decisions.

The Research Design

A prerequisite for deciding what research design is most appropriate and feasible is a clear understanding of the research questions to be answered. This includes decisions about what factors are to be studied and what relationships between them are to be analyzed. In chapter 1, research designs that guide evaluation activities in answering the research questions are classified into four general categories: exploratory, descriptive, quasi-experimental, and experimental. The guide for research that most closely approximates scientific principles is *experimental* design, which involves the random assignment of research subjects into "program-treated" and "nonprogram-treated" groups. The outcomes of these two groups are compared statistically to determine whether the program's service intervention is producing intended results.

Experimental designs are appropriate, however, only when there is substantial knowledge of the key independent and dependent variables, which can be measured quantitatively with little error. Otherwise these designs may be inefficient and may direct research attention to the wrong variables. These designs are the preferred choice for net impact studies in fields such as employment and training. The U.S. Department of Labor's current national field study, the JTPA Experiment, is an example (Bangsor et al., 1988). In some programs, however, such as certain mental health programs, the literature may be equally extensive but some of the critical outcomes—increased self-esteem, more realistic life expectations, and improved quality of life—are very difficult to measure and quantify.

Experimental designs are not always appropriate for studying the effects of service interventions on outcomes in such programs. In some cases the evaluator may be forced to develop quantitative "proxies" for mental states and behavior that have questionable accuracy. In other programs, new interventions may be tested for the first time and lack a substantial history of evaluation. Experimental designs are not appropriate where the major variables of interest are yet to be identified or clearly defined.

With many social programs, *quasi-experimental* designs employing a comparison group are a useful fall-back when the political or organizational context of a net impact evaluation precludes withholding a service treatment from one group of eligible clients. These designs are no more appropriate than experimental approaches, however, if either the services or the outcomes are difficult to measure and cannot be incorporated easily into statistical analyses.

In practice, process evaluations primarily utilize *exploratory* and *descriptive* designs. These designs reflect a wide range of research approaches, from very simple case studies to very technical social surveys. Any given process evaluation is likely to involve a customized design that combines more than one type of approach within these two general types of designs, based on the questions directing the study and what organizational components and relationships are of greatest interest.

For example, customizing an evaluation of the implementation of a basic educational skills program might involve an exploratory design for studying program decisionmaking, a simple descriptive design for studying the nature of program participation, and a more sophisticated design involving statistical analysis of client flows. Studying governance and management, for instance, involves a range of organizational behaviors—negotiating, decisionmaking, selecting rules and regulations, and monitoring compliance. It also involves structures that permit and shape this behavior—official policymaking bodies, power structures, policy statements, manuals, and reporting requirements. To study this component of the model, the evaluator may initially want to identify key factors by conducting in-depth interviews of governance and management. This may be followed by a more specific and detailed descriptive survey of program decisionmakers, i.e., those whose decisions have an effect at the client level, and clients themselves.

An innovative, customized approach is essential in conducting a comprehensive process evaluation that focuses on all the components of the organizational model and key relationships among them. This may involve an integration of several different exploratory or descriptive designs focusing on different aspects of the organizational system to be studied. The information yielded by this customized approach must then be utilized by the evaluator, based on clearly defined criteria, in judging the "fit" achieved among the different parts of the organizational system and the relationship between the program organization and its environment. This requires a great deal of research and program experience, creativity, and a consideration of all the methodological options.

In conclusion, exploratory process evaluations are important predecessors of outcome studies, for they can identify influences in the organizational system that affect program outcomes. Exploratory designs are also useful in identifying key implementation variables for inclusion in subsequent impact evaluations. The goal of these exploratory studies is to refine the research questions that could subsequently be studied, and to pin down the most important influences to study, using more rigorous designs that rely on quantitative methods.

Sampling

In studying program implementation, we are not only interested in individual program participants, who are usually the focus of most outcome evaluations. The research subjects in process evaluations may be program staff, such as directors, planners, managers, and caseworkers, or individuals outside the program's organizational system who interact with participants or the system but are not formal targets of the program's interventions, such as participants' families, other service providers, employers, or school personnel. Or the "subjects of study" may be far less tangible aspects of the system or its environment, such as the components and processes of the organization. Therefore, the question—who or what is to be sampled—requires a more complex answer in process evaluations than in outcome studies. Most process evaluations seek information on a *combination* of human subjects and a *range* of organizational phenomena.

When individuals are the subject of study, it is often more economical in terms of time, effort, and money to study a small group of individuals who represent the larger population of interest, such as a sample of personnel who are representative of a program's entire case management staff, or a sample of program participants who are representative of a particular subpopulation within the target group. The way in which the evaluator selects these "representatives," and how many are selected, is critical in preventing bias and in obtaining accurate estimates, as discussed in chapter 1. If the process evaluator wants to draw a sample of those individuals who best represent a larger group, basic sampling principles are necessary to reduce bias and allow for the generalization of results to the same program in a different setting, or to other similar programs (Kish 1965).

Probability sampling is an efficient method to use in studying client flow along the service delivery pathway, mainly because of the large number of clients involved and the ability to list all individuals in the population of interest. This form of sampling assures the evaluator that results are representative of the larger population.

Where the general characteristics of the entire caseload are the main interest, *simple random sampling* is useful. This allows each case in a population—and all combinations of these elements—an equal chance of being included in the sample.

More often, the evaluator will want information broken down by demographic, labor force, or other characteristics. In this case, a *stratified random sample* is appropriate. Here the population is divided into various categories, or "strata," and a simple random sample is drawn from each stratum. These subsamples are then joined to form the total sample. For example, in studying the characteristics and patterns of client flow through a service delivery system, the process evaluator may want to know the experiences of different client groups. Each group serves as a stratum, and a separate random sample of clients is drawn from each stratum.

Probability sampling, however, is not appropriate for gathering much of the information needed in process evaluations. Studies of program implementation may focus on only a small number of individuals or organizations; for instance, those policymakers or organizations that appear to have the broadest effect on a program. In this situation, a wide variety of nonprobability sampling techniques will be more appropriate and useful. *Purposive sampling* is often the most feasible choice (Patton 1987). This involves a careful selection of each individual or entity to be included in the study sample using a set of criteria based on the purposes of the evaluation and the questions to be answered by it. This is a more subjective strategy but is often better suited to the information needs of process evaluations. For example, selecting a "panel of experts" who the evaluator has reason to believe is representative of individuals knowledgeable about a given phenomenon can be more economical, convenient, and useful than questioning a larger group selected through random sampling.[5]

The problem with nonprobability sampling, however, is that the evaluator has little basis for estimating how representative the information obtained really is.[6] Interpreting the results of evaluations confined to this kind of sampling must therefore be properly qualified. In practice, process evaluations usually involve a combination of the two basic kinds of sampling methods. Integrating information obtained by these different means requires inductive thinking and often produces insights not otherwise available. A wealth of excellent beginning texts is available on sampling issues, strategies, and specific techniques. Some of these are listed in the reference section following this chapter.

Data Collection and Analysis

As discussed earlier, studies of implementation tend to utilize an exploratory or descriptive design, and more often, a combination of these approaches. The purpose of exploratory designs is to gather beginning ideas about a particular phenomenon, identify its most important elements and interrelationships, and formulate more precise questions for further study. Although some of the characteristics of program implementation have been studied fairly extensively, such as management and service delivery, the more distinctive features of a program—i.e., those characteristics intended to be novel, such as the use of performance standards for monitoring program outcomes in JTPA—may not have been well-studied. These new features are expected to have a greater effect than previous program strategies and, therefore, are an important area of inquiry. Exploratory approaches are most useful in examining these unique program characteristics.

An exploratory design calls for relatively unstructured methods for collecting data and usually nonstatistical methods for analyzing this information. Data collection methods such as participant-observation, oral history techniques, and panel-of-experts strategies, which resist reliance on prior assumptions and preconceived frameworks, are examples of standard data-gathering strategies appropriate to exploratory studies. The information collected in this way is processed, distilled, and integrated by the evaluator within the questions of interest.

Where knowledge of a phenomenon already exists, a continuum of descriptive designs can be used in answering process questions. In general, the purpose of descriptive studies is to determine *associations* among important factors—how these influences are *related*—which goes beyond the intent of exploratory studies, but stops short of determining cause-effect. Relationships may be assessed using statistical or nonstatistical evidence. Which source of evidence is the more "truthful" depends on the quality of research design: whether the right variables were studied; whether these factors were appropriately defined and measured (either quantitatively or qualitatively); whether these measures were collected reliably and in accordance with the sampling strategy; and whether the resulting data were appropriately analyzed.

The least sophisticated descriptive studies can be illustrated by relatively informal surveys of selected participants, staff, or relevant others, using flexible *interview schedules*, or the use of a small set of general interview questions chosen to gather in-depth information related to the overall evaluation questions. Collecting this kind of "open-ended" information requires a flexible classification scheme for analyzing data and, ultimately, a great of deal of study and integration of information by the evaluator. The advantage of data collection and analysis flexibility is that the evaluator can make immediate adjustments in both the structure of an interview, based on how an interview is unfolding, and in the way information from interviews is coded or classified, based on the nature of the data emerging from the interviewing process.

The most sophisticated descriptive designs, which permit advanced statistical analysis, require much more structured forms of data collection—for example, standardized questions with quantitative response categories. A number of different survey techniques are possible. Examples are one-time surveys that measure a study sample at only one point in time, and panel surveys—often referred to as longitudinal surveys—that measure the same group of individuals or organizations at various points over an extended period of time. Surveys can differ substantially in terms of the number of people studied, the sophistication of the information-gathering mechanism, the complexity of the information obtained, and the kinds of analysis techniques that are appropriate.

The automated management information systems in social programs used to inform governance, management, and funders about the organizational system are essentially surveys based on intake questionnaires filled out by clients and update forms completed by staff. In client surveys, information is typically gathered on each client at standardized decision points along the service delivery pathway. A new feature of many programs is a one-time, follow-up panel survey of clients (and sometimes others, such as family members or employers) utilizing questionnaires or telephone interviews. These standard administrative data collection techniques typically produce a narrow range of information. Their advantage, however, is that the data are quantified and can be analyzed using statistical techniques.

It is clear, however, that the data collection and analysis choices that must be made by the evaluator are more complicated in process studies. The options are greater, there are different sets of risks and benefits (in terms of bias and utility) involved in each decision, and it is difficult to identify all the important variables at the outset; i.e., many must be discovered as a study progresses. For example, if the researcher wants to study the content of and motivation for particular policy directives affecting implementation, administrative records are an important source of information. Some of this information can even be quantified, such as how many decisionmakers took a particular position, how many policies were issued and on what subjects, and how many of these were actually implemented.

In many cases, however, information from records must be extracted laboriously, using only a general framework for identifying the relevant influences. The evaluator can supplement this information by interviewing program policymakers, or gathering information from decisionmakers outside the system who are likely to have a special knowledge of program policies and policymakers, using open-ended or more structured techniques. Most typically, the evaluator will choose a *mix of data collection and analysis strategies*. The nature of the mix depends on the kinds of information available, the kinds of evaluation resources that exist for gathering and analyzing this information, and the quality of data in automated program information systems (Patton 1987; Mintzberg 1983b).

Statistical analysis techniques are powerful tools in the researcher's mix of strategies. Therefore, opportunities to obtain high quality quantitative data must be exploited. Statistical techniques can provide the following kinds of information: (1) information about central tendencies, such as what staff attitudes may be most typical; (2) information about variations, such as whether clients are similar or different regarding self-selection into a program or some other characteristic; (3) information to compare central tendencies and variations across groups, such as how the rate of self-selection may vary between white and minority clients; and (4) information about relationships, such as whether selection into a program may be *related to* (but not necessarily caused by) staff attitudes and behavior.

As in outcome studies, it must be kept in mind that statistically significant relationships are statements of probability, not certainty. Making causal inferences requires evidence beyond establishing the existence of a relationship, or an association. In nonexperimental studies, such as most process evaluations, the evidence is not sufficient to claim causality, even though findings may be statistically significant. Since process studies typically involve a combination of statistical and nonstatistical techniques, the evaluator must be careful to judge the importance of statistically significant results in the context of the results obtained by other means, such as through content analysis or some other form of classifying information for analysis.

In summary, a wide variety of data collection and analysis methods can be useful in process evaluations, since the issues studied are substantially different and considerably broader than in most outcome studies. The process evaluator must be familiar with the full research repertoire, selecting a combination of methods that best fit the nature of the questions being asked and the kinds of information desired from a particular evaluation. Because there are many more methodological choices available than in outcome studies, the researcher must take an inventive approach in customizing sampling, data collection, and analysis to the specific purpose of an evaluation. The interpretation of findings yielded by this customized approach will usually necessitate a unique integration of information by the evaluator within an overall analysis framework. Fortunately, process evaluators now have an abundance of methodological material in the research literature to aid them in this task (see references for selected sources).

Application of the Organizational Model
to the Case Example: JTPA

It is now important to illustrate how a process evaluation can be conducted by applying the organizational model to an existing program. This illustration will focus exclusively on Title II of the federal job training legislation, which is JTPA's major employment and training program for adults and youth. The Title II program is implemented in local service delivery areas (SDAs). Governance occurs through a Private Industry Council (PIC), composed of members from the public and private sectors but dominated by the latter sector as mandated by Congress.

The administrative agency of an SDA, which is responsible for operating the JTPA program, frequently decentralizes service delivery to other organizations in the community through performance-based or other kinds of contracts. Sometimes PICs and administrative entities are one and the same. Where a PIC and an administrative entity have separate functions, the PIC is primarily responsible for local employment and training policy, coordination, and program oversight, and the administrative organization has operational responsibilities. Mayors are expected to work with PICs as part of a public/private partnership.

Typically, the PIC/local-elected-official partnership, the administrative agency, and the contracting private and nonprofit community agencies that may deliver services comprise the local organizational system of greatest interest in process evaluations. These are the organizations ultimately responsible for program implementation and performance. The main features of JTPA implementation are described in the appendix. To add to the reality and increase the utility of the application of the organizational model, insights and examples from actual studies of program implementation will be woven into this application. (Comptroller General 1985; Cook et al., 1984a, 1984b; Walker 1984, 1985.)

Each component, or group of components of the model, will be discussed separately, in the same chronological order as they were introduced in the first section. Among the many potential influences, measures, and methods that deserve consideration, only a selected few can be covered under each set of components. Three kinds of issues will be addressed under each part of the model: *conceptual, measurement, and methodological.* Because of its importance, the greatest attention is given to the conversion process.

Studying the Environment

Conceptual Issues

The environment of an SDA includes local conditions, such as the local economy, as well as other JTPA agencies at the local, state, and federal levels. These agencies form a complex web of organizational relationships that often influence—and, at times, dictate—how the SDA's programs are implemented.[7] Specific aspects of an SDA's environment that should be included in a process evaluation are reviewed briefly below.

The Immediate Environment of Programs

The chief task of the evaluator in studying influences emerging from the environment is to identify the factors that operate closest to the program and, therefore, have the greatest effect on its resources. This level of the environment is the city, town, or rural area surrounding the organizations implementing the program. The most important community influences are social, economic, and political, such as labor market characteristics, market trends, demographic characteristics, incidence of social problems, and attributes of local government.

For example, information on the area's poverty population, labor force, and wage structure provides a context for understanding the practical limits placed on program implementation, how program organizations accommodate local conditions and circumstances, and the significance of program outcomes. If, for instance, wages are generally depressed for women, or high-paying jobs scarce, it may be unrealistic to expect that changes in program implementation will improve female participants' situations.

The Inter-SDA Environment

Local organizational systems are influenced also by relationships among SDAs, which may range from a high level of coordination and cooperation to severe tension and conflict. Good relationships among local-level organizational systems may support greater independence for SDAs *vis-a-vis* the implementation of state policies. Disruptive competition for state incentive money, for example, can undermine collaborative action to pursue local-level goals. Therefore, process evaluations should explore the nature of this particular set of relationships and its potential impact on program operations.

The State Environment

Studying state-level organizations as a source of environmental influences should again involve an investigation of social, economic, and political characteristics. A major emphasis, however, should be on the network of state organizations that develop state program policies, assume state-level administrative responsibilities, craft state program plans, formulate criteria for monitoring coordination among state agencies and institutions relevant to employment and training programs, make statewide assessments of local performance, and sometimes evaluate SDA program implementation and outcomes.

The Federal Environment

As with state-level organizations, the study of federal environmental influences involves questions such as the following:

1. What social, economic, and political influences are operating nationally to affect federal employment and training policy and practice?
2. What are the specific purposes, policies, rules and regulations, administrative directives, and the actual organizational practices of relevant agencies at this level, such as, the federal agencies and the Congress, which have an impact on SDA implementation?

Although most evaluations of local-level program implementation cannot afford to devote much time to federal-level influences, it is important to acknowledge the larger framework within which implementation occurs.

Interaction Between the Organizational System and Its Environment

The model assumes that program outcomes and what happens in implementing programs are not totally at the mercy of the environment. The characteristics of local implementation have an impact on the environment as well. While this reciprocal relationship is difficult to study, it is a significant aspect of comprehensive process evaluations.

Measurement and Methodological Issues

Measurement Issues

Two kinds of environmental influences, among a wide range of potential variables, are important to define and measure: (1) socioeconomic and political factors, and (2) structural and functional characteristics of state and federal organizations. Table 4.1 provides examples of environmental indicators for these dimensions.

Demographic information on the area's poverty population and labor force, and labor market information on the wage structure of local jobs

Table 4.1
Examples of Environmental Indicators

I. Demographic and Political Indicators

Economic	Social	Political
A Local economy Unemployment rate Per capita income Average wage rate Inflation rate Unemployment insurance caseloads Number unfilled jobs	A Demographics Total population Population by • age • race/ethnic group • sex • education • religion	A Priority given to employment training by government B Relationship between government
B Market trends building permits new businesses business closings	B Social problems Crime rate Alcoholism/drug abuse rate School dropout rate Households with female head (%) Households receiving state/federal assistance (%)	and business, service agencies, and client advocacy groups

II. Bureaucratic Characteristics of Agencies and Councils

Characteristic	Indicator/Source of Information
Decisionmaking hierarchy	Organization chart showing accountability patterns
Policymaking process	Policy statements
Exercise of regulatory power	Written regulations
Administrative procedures	Service plans Administrative directives
Coordination with other agencies	Cooperative agreements
Monitoring	Written protocols Sanctions levied

provide a context for judging the meaning of program outcomes, and the constraints placed on program implementation in resolving outcome problems. Many program organizations regularly document the kinds of conditions suggested as part of their planning process. Normally, indicators of political and bureaucratic conditions are qualitative, designed to capture influences exerted by political and organizational forces on program implementation. While the lists in table 4.1 are incomplete, the intent is to construct a set of indicators of the relevant conditions affecting the local organizational system, as a useful measurement tool. This helps the evaluator understand, for example, why a wage differential between men and women may have occurred, and why this outcome may be considered problematic.

While many of the variables in table 4.1 can be measured quantitatively (e.g., local wages and unemployment rate), others can only be measured qualitatively (e.g., a written history of state policies regarding a local problem). Although numerous indicators can be constructed, the evaluator's choice is usually determined by the purpose of the evaluation. For example, a process evaluation examining low placement wages for female participants might focus on local wage rates, while an evaluation of job satisfaction among staff might focus on relationships between the state and the local administrative agency.[8]

Methodological Issues

Federal and state employment and training agencies regularly collect data on some of the variables in table 4.1 through their ongoing automated management information systems. The Bureau of Labor Statistics and the U.S. Census collect additional data on a regular basis. A number of national longitudinal surveys provide environmental data. Governors' offices and state employment and welfare agencies analyze state-level socioeconomic and labor market information. Some states conduct periodic social surveys providing a range of information on employment, training, and related programs, and their environments. These quantitative data are relatively accessible for sampling and statistical analysis purposes. Multivariate statistical analyses can be performed to determine which variables are most important, and how they may be associated.

Obtaining and analyzing information on political influences, and on the characteristics of federal and state organizations, are more difficult tasks because of the qualitative nature of the data. Studying organizational structures and processes often requires an analysis of administrative records within a framework devised by the evaluator, supplemented by informal or structured interviews with key actors to provide greater information depth and accuracy.

Studying how a program's organizational system has, in turn, influenced its environment will involve some of the same data sources. For example, the evaluator may want to identify SDA resistance to state incentive policies and how this resistance may lead to modifications in performance standards. Or, the researcher may want to study the influence of exemplary SDA performance in increasing support for testing alternative solutions to problems such as the male/female wage differential.

In summary, much can be learned unobtrusively about the environment from information already available to the evaluator from automated systems and records, some of which lends itself to statistical analysis. Other kinds of data will have to be freshly collected within specific information purposes, using purposive samples, employing questionnaire or interview formats designed with attention to analysis options, and building in ways to reduce bias.

Goverance and Management

Conceptual Issues

The conversion of resources into the human, organizational, and fiscal "products" of a program is directed by *governance*. Governance refers to the body of decisionmakers who develop and communicate the goals and means to be used by the organizational system in achieving its purposes, the rights and responsibilities that guide the behavior of these decisionmakers, and their actual attitudes and behavior in carrying out their roles.

Management refers to the hierarchies of personnel, under the guidance and supervision of governance, who are responsible for the day-to-day operation of organizations within the system, their duties and privileges, and their actual attitudes and behavior. The pronouncements and actions of these major program actors influence the form and substance of program implementation. In JTPA, governance is the responsibility of the SDA's Private Industry Council (PIC), the SDA's top elected official, and its administrative organization. This arrangement is similar to the state-level governance and management structure headed by the governor, State Job Training Coordinating Council, and JTPA administrative agency.

Through a feedback process referred to in the model as the *perform-*

ance control system, program outputs inform governance and management about the efficiency and effectiveness of the organizational system. The control system will be discussed later, after looking more closely at the conversion process for translating organizational resources into program outcomes.

In JTPA, subcontracting for administrative or client services, and monitoring subcontractors' performance are special functions of governance and management. There is an emphasis in JTPA on "performance-based contracting," which commits governance and management to regular assessments of subcontractor performance, and leads subcontractors to engage in self-monitoring activities.

Measurement and Methodological Issues

Measurement Issues

Two kinds of variables are particularly important to examine in studying governance and management: (1) the characteristics of the power hierarchies directing the system, and (2) the kinds of decisions made at different levels of this hierarchy. The evaluator must distinguish between the kind of hierarchy intended in a program's implementation strategy and the one actually utilized, and the areas of decisionmaking expected to be given highest priority and those actually given the most attention by decisionmakers.

A distinguishing feature of JTPA implementation is the use of a public/private governance partnership. Therefore, an important implementation question is "How well is this partnership between local elected officials and the PIC actually working?" Here, key areas of investigation are the level of cooperation and collaboration, and the merging of expertise and other resources to create a program responsive to the private sector job market. The composition of the partnership and control of decisionmaking are authorized in the legislation. More difficult to define are the partnership's intended functions and actual activities.

The JTPA legislation commits governance to a number of general responsibilities, such as setting job training policy, reviewing job training plans, overseeing performance and monitoring coordination. The criteria for formulating policies and regulations to carry out these responsibilities, and actual decisionmaking behavior, must be specifically defined. The literature on organizational theory and behavior is a useful resource for measures, but the evaluator will frequently need to develop his or her own indices and criteria based on the data already available and the data that is feasible to generate in a given program setting (Blau and Schoenherr 1971; Simon 1957, 1977; Mintzberg 1979, 1983).

Methodological Issues

Studying governance involves an exploratory or descriptive approach. A traditional data collection device for understanding who is most influential in making particular kinds of decisions in given areas of activity, and through what means, is the selective interviewing of known decisionmakers, using largely open-ended questions. A content analysis of this information is useful in sketching the nature of decisionmaking. On the basis of this preliminary information, more structured interviews can be held with key decisionmakers, and a more thorough study of their documented positions can be made. In analyzing such information, the evaluator will want to look for discrepancies between the intended governance and management strategy and actual practices, and the influence such discrepancies may have on other components of the system—particularly service delivery and outcomes. However, since most of the data on this component will be qualitative, statistical analysis techniques will not be feasible, and the evaluator will need to develop a scheme for classifying data that fits the questions to be answered.

Inputs and Key Organizational Decisions

Conceptual Issues

The environment is the source of needed resources and information. It is also the source of constraints to goal achievement. The myriad inputs coming into the system are sorted and prioritized for use by governance and management, resulting in critical revenue, personnel and access decisions that influence implementation.

Revenue decisions govern the flow of money and other resources into and through the system. In JTPA, federal allocation formulas determine the nature of monetary resources, but SDAs are permitted to supplement JTPA funds with state and local revenues.

Personnel decisions govern the flow of specialized knowledge and technical expertise into the system. These decisions affect the quality of personnel, which directly influences program success or failure (Franklin and Ripley 1984). In JTPA, for example, managerial, service delivery, contracting, information system, and monitoring capability are needed.

Access decisions in JTPA govern the flow of program participants, employers, and educators into and out of the system. Given the limitations on funds, only certain individuals among those eligible for the program will enter the system and be exposed to its interventions. This affects the nature of implementation and influences a program's "distributive" outcomes—that is, the outcomes experienced by different groups of clients, such as women vs. men, minorities vs. nonminorities, youths vs. adults. Contracting decisions influence which employers and educational providers will participate in the system, be coordinated with it, and be affected by that relationship. These are examples of the kinds of input and decisionmaking variables to be studied in examining implementation.

Measurement and Methodological Issues

Measurement Issues

Those resources with the greatest potential influence on implementation and outcomes need to be defined and indices for them developed. Variables involved in funding, such as monetary vs. in-kind contributions, must be defined more specifically. The loan of staff or equipment from a state agency may supplement federal funds in a significant way. Pinning down different kinds of nonmonetary resources is, therefore, important. Job qualifications for staff must be specified in terms of education, experience, and compatibility with political and organizational agendas.

The characteristics of the personnel actually hired and assigned to various responsibilities must be broken down into useful indices. Both formal client access policies, such as eligibility requirements and recruitment rules, and informal access practices, such as the way in which staff handles outreach and intake functions, must be defined. The division of labor within the system, the structure of decisionmaking and the nature of revenue, personnel, and access decisions must also be defined operationally and studied over the course of the program. In many instances, the evaluation research literature will not provide substantial help, and the evaluator will need to take an innovative approach in defining these variables for study.

The relationship between inputs, revenue, personnel, and access decisions and other components of the organizational system must be defined. Since resources limit possibilities in the conversion process and provide a context for maximizing the use of resources within this process, relationships between resource allocation/utilization and elements of the conversion process are an essential focus in process evaluations.

Methodological Issues

What happens to monetary resources is somewhat simpler to track quantitatively than what occurs with the acquisition and use of personnel or the recruitment and selection of clients. Focusing on relationships among these system parts and other components requires a combination of exploratory and descriptive research designs and a variety of data collection and analysis methods.

For example, management information systems can be useful sources of data on participant access. A random sample of clients can usually be drawn from a particular historical cohort to determine typical outreach, intake, appraisal, and service assignment patterns. However, few JTPA information systems record information at the beginning of the service delivery chronology—particularly at outreach, recruitment, intake, and eligibility determination points—where the initial and more subjective access decisions are made.

Some of the more significant characteristics of the attitudes and behavior of staff, other providers, and clients regarding access are not retrievable from information systems, program documents, or client files, and must be inferred from observations and discussions, or from interviews with these individuals. There is an extensive literature on personal, telephone, and mail survey research that can aid the evaluator in this task (Dillman 1978; Fowler 1984; Yin 1984).

Because different forms of data collection will yield a combination of qualitative and quantitative information, analysis methods will necessarily involve both statistical and nonstatistical techniques. As in all qualitative analyses, the goal of inductive inquiry is to discern underlying patterns in the data (Patton 1987). These patterns and the results of quantitative analyses, together, form a basis for understanding what is happening in this component of the system, and for determining the fit between this and other parts of the system. The integration of this diverse information must be guided by the specific research questions directing a particular evaluation.

The Conversion Process: Mission

Conceptual Issues

Goals

The mission component describes the goals of the organizational system. In JTPA, Congress established three common goals for all SDAs regarding "economic disadvantaged" youth and adults: to increase employment, to increase wages, and to reduce welfare dependency. However, Congress also granted SDAs the discretion to tailor these goals to local employment and training problems. Within the legislative mandate, each SDA develops its own set of goals in response to environmental constraints, the agendas of PIC members, and other considerations. Once these goals are formulated, the objectives that are subsumed under each goal are specified. These serve as "indicators" that inform governance and management about the level of SDA goal achievement.

Because SDAs have considerable autonomy in developing goals, the directives driving the program vary across SDAs. Studying implementation within a particular SDA organizational system, or across SDAs, therefore, requires careful identification and description of organizational goals, or the mission of the SDA system. Without this important definitional step it is virtually impossible to investigate the influence of a given SDA's distinctive mission on other components—particularly the work component—on other parts of the system, or on outcomes.

A major task in studying goals is distinguishing between *manifest* and *latent* goals. For analytical purposes we can think of goals formalized in legislation or in written policy statements as a system's manifest goals— i.e., those goals presented to the system's environment as its primary guiding principles. These may indeed be the goals that have the greatest influence over the system's activities. Given SDA autonomy, however, other powerful agendas, or latent goals, may actually take precedence. These less tangible goals may represent the major influence on action. Organizational development inevitably results in the emergence of goals idiosyncratic to a particular system.

A second task is establishing how priorities are set among these manifest and latent goals, and what these priorities are. This is essential in understanding decisionmaking processes, other aspects of the conversion process, and the significance of a system's outcomes. For example, in JTPA clients must ultimately be matched with employers in local labor markets. The emphasis an SDA places on employers vs. clients often varies. This is sometimes apparent in mission statements. For example, the two goal statements below are taken from the files of two SDAs.

Client-Oriented Mission

To provide comprehensive employment and training services required to prepare and place eligible SDA residents into subsidized employment. Specific emphasis will be placed on selecting employment and training opportunities that will increase the earned income of clients and will result in secure, full-time unsubsidized jobs.

Employer-Oriented Mission

To assist local businesses to solve employment-related business problems, allowing both business and individuals to increase productivity and profitability. To support local economic development efforts by the preparation of low-income, unemployed area residents as a workforce for new or expanding business and industry.

These priorities move program implementation in quite different directions.

A third task is to determine how internally consistent or conflicting a system's set of goals may be. Sometimes a system's manifest and latent goals are similar, or at least compatible. In other cases they may be in continual competition or severe conflict. An SDA may have a manifest goal of providing comprehensive services, but a latent goal of providing lower-cost services that meet employer needs. Or SDA goals may be at odds with subcontractor goals.

SDAs typically contract with a variety of organizations—public schools, private industry, the employment services, private sector training organizations, and community-based organizations. An SDA subcontractor may purport to share an SDA's goals, but because subcontractor organizations frequently deliver JTPA services as only one activity among others, agendas independent of the SDA may be the primary influence, and these agendas may or may not be compatible with the SDA's. The less dependent on the SDA a subcontractor is for resources to survive, the more its goals may differ, and the further its implementation of the program and performance may stray from what the SDA intended. Also, the actual goals of the PIC may not be compatible with those of the SDA's administrative agency.

A fourth task is to understand how the system's most important goals—those actually being pursued—are influencing the methods used to achieve them, that is, how goals affect means, or the work component. Some process studies of client selection and service assignment practices in SDAs have suggested extensive "creaming" of job-ready clients, resulting in a neglect of the hard-to-serve (Walker 1984, 1985; Orfield and Slessarev 1986). This has been linked to the mandated use of performance standards, which some studies suggest force SDAs to choose between conflicting goals—serving the disadvantaged vs. meeting standards—with the result that SDA missions have sometimes turned toward the latter in order to secure incentive bonuses.

In summary, the relationship between formally articulated goals and those which must be inferred from organizational activity, and the level of consistency between these sets of goals, have a significant effect on other components of the system. They condition judgment of the system's compliance with a program's intended implementation strategy and the effectiveness of that strategy in producing desired outcomes.

Planning

Most organizational systems engage in *planning* to develop their goals and define the means for achieving them. The plan resulting from this process is based on three kinds of planning decisions: (1) who will be given the program's treatment, or service intervention; (2) what the nature of the treatment provided will be; and (3) how funds will be distributed in order to deliver the treatment.

In JTPA, decisions about who is to receive the program's service strategy determine the general target group of this strategy, and the specific subpopulations of clients to be exposed to the treatment. The Congress establishes general eligibility and target group requirements, which act as screening and sorting mechanisms for assuring that services are provided to those who need them most. In some SDAs, these mechanisms may fulfill this purpose (Walker et al. 1984, 1985). However, client populations involve a range of "job readiness" or "need," and as discussed earlier, the pressures of performance standards sometimes act as powerful incentives to serve those whom staff view as most likely to obtain the higher paying jobs. This phenomenon is an important element to be studied in gaining knowledge of the actual practices of the organizational system.

Treatment decisions direct which general set of services are to be received by clients, and which mix and sequence of services is considered more appropriate for one subpopulation than for another. Distributive decisions regulate the flow of resources to the service delivery system and to clients. They determine what combination of money, personnel, equipment, and support will go to whom. These are political decisions that involve weighing competing claims against an agency's resources by various interest groups, each seeking decisions in their favor (Franklin and Ripley 1984).

In JTPA these may be subcontractors or organizations in the program's environment. Studies suggest that failing to satisfy such groups has often led SDAs to engage in defensive maneuvers rather than to seek an integration of services related to local needs. In practice, SDA governance tries to strike a balance among competing demands—i.e., the service needs of clients and employers, performance objectives, costs, and politics. Decisions are also made about entering into coordination agreements with other organizations to increase the efficiency of service provision or expand the scope of available services.

In studying planning, it is important to remember that plans may accurately reflect intentions, but organizational systems characteristically remold plans in the process of carrying them out, and sometimes plans are deliberately circumvented. Both the attributes of formal plans and the characteristics of activities flowing from these plans are significant subjects of study.

Measurement and Methodological Issues

Measurement Issues

Distinguishing between manifest and latent goals inevitably involves qualitative information. The evaluator can identify manifest goals from legislation and recorded policy pronouncements, but these are frequently abstract and require considerably more specification by the researcher. Answering questions such as the following may be of assistance in the measurement process:

1. What is the source of a particular goal statement, and what priority in the hierarchy of goals does it enjoy? For example, it is important in judging the influence of manifest goals to know whether the statement is mandated in the program's legislation, is unique to the organizational system's top decisionmakers, or is an interpretation of the legislative mandate by administrators.

2. What information can be inferred from a particular goal statement? For example, the evaluator may want to classify goal statements along the following dimensions: the content of the statement, who is to be most affected by the goal, what outcomes are implied in the goal, and how the goal articulates with other goal statements.

Even more subjective, latent goals are exceedingly difficult to define and measure. Information must be obtained from the self-report of decisionmakers or inferred from organizational activities. Consider the goal of "increased wages" for clients. The evaluator can draw insights about the meaning of this goal by studying resource allocation. If an SDA allocates resources so as to meet both federal performance standards regarding wages and organizational goals that are sensitive to the educational and training needs of certain clients, or if the SDA forgoes the possibility of meeting or exceeding standards in order to provide richer pre-employment services, this difference in allocation priorities will help define the mission component. This illustrates how interrelated the information is that must be developed by studying different components of the system. In this case, the evaluator seeks clues about the latent mission from information about the utilization of system inputs, the nature of governance and management, and the work component of the conversion process.

Measuring goal consistency is essential, but equally difficult. Consistency can be defined in terms of whether different goals imply different means, or different courses of action. Attributes of goals, such as compatibility, competition, or conflict, must also be defined more precisely. The evaluator must usually develop his or her own definition and indices, tailored to the program being evaluated.

The planning process may also pose measurement problems. Some aspects of planning are relatively simple to measure, such as the composition of planning bodies, the characteristics of planning policies and procedures, and the content of plans. Others are more difficult. For example, a chief concern of governance in most organizations is the difference between planned and actual performance. However, in some social programs governance and staff develop a written plan as a prerequisite to obtaining funds, but once these funds are awarded, management may pay little attention to the plan. In this case, the most difficult measurement problem is to classify actual activities in such a way that they can be compared against the plan. Some of these activities are captured by quantitative data in information systems; others must be inferred from observation and interviews.

Methodological Issues

Clearly an exploratory or descriptive design is most appropriate in learning about the mission component. An analysis of documents, observational techniques used at meetings of decisionmakers, open-ended interviews with selected policymakers and administrators, and a study of organizational activities, such as the characteristics of the planning process, are examples of useful data collection techniques.

An analysis format must be developed in advance of qualitative data collection, based on the research questions guiding the evaluation and the variables selected for study within the mission component. Once information is collected from different sources, the challenge is to integrate these data to provide an accurate picture of the key goals of the system, which, in turn, affect the means selected for goal achievement and how well the program's implementation strategy is carried out in practice.

The Conversion Process: Work

Conceptual Issues

Studying the means a system uses to achieve its mission reveals the distinctive characteristics of the actual mode of program implementation. As indicated earlier, "means" refers to the activities a system engages in to achieve its goals and objectives. To illustrate some of the conceptual issues involved in studying the work component, we will focus on subcontracting and service delivery.

Subcontracting

An important aspect of identifying a system's means for goal achievement is deciding what functions or services will be performed or provided by the SDA, PIC, administrative agency, or organizations under contract to one or another of these entities. In JTPA, subcontractors are an important element of the organizational system. All three of the planning decisions discussed earlier are reflected in the nature of subcontracting entities, the criteria guiding contracting arrangements, and subcontracting processes. Since subcontracting introduces another set of organizations into the system, it increases its complexity. The emphasis on performance-based contracting in JTPA further complicates the work component.

Subcontracting, however, may increase the efficiency of resource allocation by giving SDAs the opportunity to choose among competitors. It may allow a PIC to reap the benefits of successful program performance while spreading the risks among a number of organizations. It may spur the SDA to make specific decisions about which services are to be provided and to which target groups, and how service delivery is to be coordinated. Or accountability may be the paramount concern in awarding contracts, that is, transferring partial accountability from a council or administrative agency to subcontractors (Walker et al. 1985). The organizational politics of subcontracting is, therefore, an important area of study in process evaluations.

There are usually two basic kinds of contracting for services in JTPA: (1) *market* subcontracting and (2) subcontracting by *function*. In the former, the subcontractor organization focuses on a particular client group, or geographical region, such as youth, women, minorities, or particular counties within an SDA. In the latter, funds are divided among subcontractors according to a particular service or occupational area, such as the provision of on-the-job training or training in the area of financial services. Both the choice of a subcontracting mode and the selection of subcontractors reveals important features of the system's goal achievement strategy.

In a decentralized system, accountability for performance is transferred downward through the vehicle of subcontracting. Through a request-for-proposal process, potential subcontractors are informed about SDA expectations: number of clients to enroll, services they should receive, and number of clients expected to achieve the desired outcomes. In subcontracting by function, the PIC or administrative agency is typically accountable for the access, treatment, and distributive decisions incorporated in the contract, while the subcontractor is typically responsible for meeting the performance standards in the contract through its own similar kinds of decisions.

In market subcontracting, organizations may be given greater freedom to decide how their training funds are to be allocated among the services authorized in the contract. A chief task of process evaluators is to study the planning decisions reflected in contracts, the extent to which they are honored in terms of subcontractor activities, and how these influences affect the overall implementation of the program and its outcomes. For example, the initial decisions subsequently included in a contract may have been problematic or poorly communicated. Or, subcontractors may have been only weakly monitored for compliance with the contract, or may have simply ignored SDA expectations for performance. Key issues in contracting are (1) the level of coordination and cooperation among subcontractors, and between the PIC or administrative agency and the subcontractors; and (2) the extent to which SDA goals are successfully implemented or gradually displaced by the changing power relationships within a decentralized service delivery system. Competition and dissension in this area have often subverted a program's intended implementation strategy (National Alliance of Business 1984; Walker et al. 1985; Orfield and Slessarev 1986).

Figure 4.2
Client Pathway*

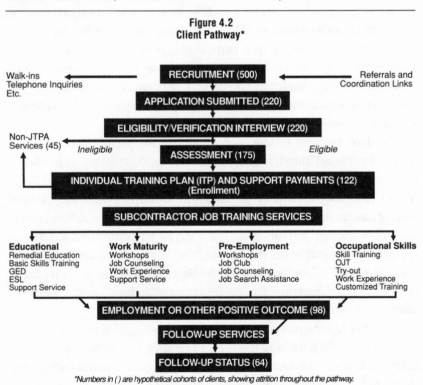

*Numbers in ( ) are hypothetical cohorts of clients, showing attrition throughout the pathway.

The Service Delivery System

Within the larger organizational system, the service delivery system implements the program's service strategy. That is, the service delivery system is the part of the model that actually provides services to clients. The service strategy is a set of services, and sometimes subsidies. For example, the provision of on-the-job training to clients involves subsidies to employers. In both instances, the intervention is expected to change the behavior of the recipient; the client is to increase his or her work experience and occupational skills, while the employer is to give more attention to hiring the disadvantaged. However, implementation and service strategies rarely work precisely as intended. On-the-job training provided by some employers may be little more than unsupervised "make work." Employers may lay off other, more highly skilled workers in order to acquire subsidized workers. The study of program implementation must capture these nuances.

In virtually all social programs, clients receive services in a standardized sequence of steps, frequently termed the *client pathway* (Patton 1986). Each step, from entry to exit, is a necessary condition for the one that follows. Each involves certain underlying assumptions that link this chain of activities together. Figure 4.2 illustrates JTPA's client pathway. Table 4.2 suggests common assumptions.

The way stations on the pathway outlined in figure 4.2 represent decision points in the movement of clients through a progression of activities, which ultimately expose them to the program's service interventions and lead to the achievement of outcomes—outreach, recruitment, intake, eligibility determination, assessment, plan development, service assignment, case management, referral, placement, and followup. Each step in the chronology needs to be studied and analyzed with respect to the following factors: the nature of the policies and management directives guiding what happens to clients; rewards and sanctions for staff and clients in adhering to these guidelines; staff and client attitudes and behavior; the attitudes and behavior of other key individuals interacting with clients within the pathway, such as employers and the personnel of other programs to which a client may be referred; and relationships between staff, clients, and others involved in the pathway with those outside the organizational system.

Table 4.2
The JTPA Service Delivery System:
A Hierarchy of Program Objectives and Validity Assumptions

Hierarchy of Objectives	Linking Validity Assumptions	Some Points Where Client/Employer Matching Occurs
I. Immediate		
1. Recruit individuals to participate	Program must have adequate supply of appropriate individuals to achieve ultimate objectives and performance standards	Employer needs a specific number of individuals trained to perform a specific task(s). A training program is developed to meet the employer's needs, or qualified participants are referred through placement/job search services. SDA may recruit individuals or draw from applicant pool to meet employer needs. SDA may recruit employers to participate in OJT, institutional training, or other programs
2. Determine eligibility for JTPA services	Services must be targeted to those who qualify to achieve ultimate objectives and performance standards	
3. Enroll individual if eligible		Employer refers individual (who may or may not be an employee) to JTPA for training. Individual is enrolled if eligible.
II. Intermediate		
4. Determine participant needs	An individual's employment barriers can be determined reliably	
	Treatments have greatest impacts when targeted to remove an individual's employment barriers	
5. Determine appropriate program (treatment) for participant as allowed under JTPA	Skills, attitudes, and behavior are malleable and can be changed by JTPA services	

Table 4.2 *(Continued)*
The JTPA Service Delivery System:
A Hierarchy of Program Objectives and Validity Assumptions

Hierarchy of Objectives	Linking Validity Assumptions	Some Points Where Client/Employer Matching Occurs
II. Intermediate *(continued)*		
6. Learn new skills, change attitudes, improve employability skills consistent with aims of program and participant needs	Programs cause behavioral and attitude changes only when completed	Employer hires on-the-job training participant, contigent on successful completion of program
7. Complete training (treatment) program	Credentials are needed to enable participant to compete in labor market	
8. Receive credentials documenting achievements		
III. Ultimate	Completion of program and credentials will enable participant to find employment	
9. Achieve positive proximate outcomes (placement, increased earnings, welfare dependence, performance standard, etc.)	JTPA services enable participants to retain employment over the long-run	Employer hires participant
10. Achieve positive final outcomes (employment retention, increased earnings, welfare dependency, performance standards, etc.)	Long-term employment of participants resolves nation's manpower problems as defined by Congress	
11. Accomplish JTPA purposes as specified in the legislation		

For instance, studying recruitment may involve determining the effect of scarce resources on the use of outreach services, and ultimately on those served by a program. Important to study is the nature of entry into the service delivery system, i.e., whether a client can enter the system at a single point of contact in a single visit, or whether several appearances at numerous offices are required.

Intake staff often act as system "gatekeepers," making discretionary decisions about access within organizational goals, planning decisions and clients' circumstances (Nagi 1974). An activity as apparently straightforward as eligibility determination can be complicated by conflicts in system goals or staff prejudices and management preferences, which influence the kind of clients who subsequently experience the interventions and are expected to produce the outcomes desired.

Client appraisal and service plans hold another key to the way in which program resources are used to achieve organizational missions. These latter activities are unusually vulnerable to the personal ideologies and agendas of staff, and the self-assessment and communication skills of clients. The actual assignment of clients to services may be conditioned by screening processes designed to determine client motivation, and on assessments linked to satisfying unmet performance standards. The actual provision of services may be fragmented across a number of subcontractors, with the possibility that clients may fail to experience a coordinated mix and sequence of intended services. Or, the assignment of clients may be affected by a "pigeonholing process," which classifies client's needs within a standardized set of categories (Mintzberg 1983a).

This standardization of aspects of the pathway simplifies service delivery and conserves resources, avoiding the customization of decisions at each step. However, predetermined diagnostic tools are not perfect and frequently lead to faulty judgments. The way in which assessment and other semidiscretionary decisions are controlled by predeveloped formats has an important effect on client selection, what services clients receive, how they are treated in the pathway, and their outcomes.

It is also important to analyze changes in clients as they move through the pathway. Attention should be given to whether a service intervention actually reduces or eliminates a client's needs, and how much service integrity is involved, that is, to what extent the client received the services formally prescribed in the service plan, or received fewer or less intensive ones, or ones substituted by the subcontractor for those planned.

In summary, these are only a few of the many factors that can be studied in focusing on the work component of the organizational system. Again, the emphasis in a given process evaluation will depend on the research questions that direct the research.

Measurement and Methodological Issues

Measurement Issues

Given the broad range of variables involved in studying the work component and its relationship to other parts of the system, it is clear that some factors pose minimal measurement problems, some pose many. For example, developing categories to measure the type(s) of subcontracts in an agency is often relatively simple. However, measuring the variation in monitoring procedures, compliance protocols, and enforcement of penalties across types can be difficult and often can only be done qualitatively.

Data collected for reporting purposes can assist the evaluator in measuring the characteristics of the service delivery system. Management information systems selectively describe the client pathway, which permits descriptive analyses of client flows through the pathway. Unfortunately, few MISs contain information on program applicants or precise descriptions of the particular services and subsidies provided to individual participants or to different target groups. These systems rarely contain information on others affected by a program, such as employers. Also, some MISs do not permit easy access to a client's entire program history, focusing instead on the production of aggregated data.

Therefore, although quantitative measures for some variables are readily available in MISs, a combination of indices routinely used in information systems and data from other sources—both quantitative and qualitative—will be needed in studying the service delivery system and its relationship to other parts of the conversion process. Measures of the service delivery system suggested in the survey research literature can be useful in supplementing data in information systems.

Methodological Issues

Exploratory and relatively unstructured descriptive designs are the choices for studying subcontracting. A review of documents supplemented by interviews with key actors may be the most useful data-gathering techniques (Burstein et al. 1985). A format for analyzing this qualitative information, consistent with the research questions, must be developed by the evaluator.

More rigorous descriptive designs can be used in studying the service delivery system. Documenting what occurs at each major step in the client pathway, and what validity assumptions are involved, is a first step in studying the service delivery system. Determining the nature of attrition as a cohort of clients traverses this pathway, based on figure 4.2, is important, since this identifies the points at which particular kinds of service delivery problems may be occurring. For example, in tracing the origins of a wagedifferential between male and female participants, the attrition patterns for the two sexes can provide significant clues about the sources of wage differences.

Much of what is happening along the pathway is available for analysis in an MIS or case files. For greater information detail, interview or questionnaire techniques can be used with staff, clients, and key others.[9] If response categories are scaled, statistical analyses of this information can be performed. However, qualitative data from in-depth interviews can often yield more useful insights.

The Conversion Process: Coordination

Conceptual Issues

Implementation studies can identify coordination mechanisms and assess their effects on other parts of the organizational system. There are numerous ways to coordinate activities and other phenomena in organizations. One strategy is *standardization,* which often takes the following forms (Mintzberg 1979):

1. *Standardization of outputs* through the use of performance standards. Although subcontractors may emphasize different methods for producing outputs, performance standards set parameters that coordinate activities.

2. *Standardization of staff skills.* Because professional skills are needed in program organizations, staff members have considerable autonomy and discretion in applying their skills. Standardizing these professional skills lets each staff member know what to expect from others, which supports coordination.

3. *Sandardization of tasks* to be performed. For example, subcontractors responsible for youth services may make the assumption that all youth have similar needs and, therefore, require the same services. While this assumption may not be valid, standardizing the service coordinates activities for youth.

4. *Informal communication* among staff performing a particular set of tasks. Sometimes the most important coordination activities are the product of informal communication networks.

5. *Direct supervision and monitoring* of staff. Coordination can also be achieved through management of staff.

Through strategies such as standardization, the efficiency of the organizational system is increased in terms of *work flow* and *productivity*. Some issues that process evaluation can usefully address in this area are the following:

1. *Matching of clients with employers, or the labor exchange function.* The key issue of interest is control over the matching process. If the majority of clients find jobs on their own rather than through the placement efforts of staff, clients are in control of employment outcomes. If most clients are placed through staff job-development efforts, staff have greater control over the matching process. Identifying these differences can alert the evaluator to problems in coordinating the labor exchange function.

2. *Relationships with subcontractors, and organizations in the environment to which clients may be referred for service.* While service delivery may be more effective when responsibilities are distributed among a number of organizations, decentralization requires increased coordination efforts. Problems may occur when it is unclear who is accountable for what responsibilities, which occurs more often when subcontracting is carried out by function (e.g., when accountability for meeting a performance standard is distributed

across many subcontractors). Accountability, which involves effective coordination, is stronger under market subcontracting. If only one organization is providing services to the hard-to-place, for example, it is clear who is accountable for the performance of programs oriented to that group.

3. *Provision of multiple services delivered by different subcontractors that require coordination over time.* In this case, clients must be appropriately linked to a series of services in the correct sequence. Case management systems can increase the coordination of a client's sequence of service treatments. If the MIS stores the client's service plan, the MIS can be used to alert staff about changes in service or service provider before their scheduled occurance.

4. *Coordination of intake with other steps in service delivery.* If intake is the responsibility of the administrative agency, and other organizations provide the services, it is important to know how smooth and timely the flow of clients is from agency to contractors, and whether these organizations share validity assumptions. Do they define clients' needs and barriers similarly and agree on the kinds of service to be provided to a given individual? The evaluator needs to determine how problematic the relationship is between the two organizations and how this situation affects the referral network for clients.

5. *Displacement of SDA goals.* Subcontracting can distract an administrative agency from its goals by shifting attention to contracting and monitoring (Mintzberg 1979, 1983). Process studies can determine to what extent goal displacement is occurring.

All organizational systems must coordinate their activities to survive. Governance and management set the coordination agenda in the process of defining the organizational mission and decentralizing the service delivery system. The evaluator's task is threefold: to identify those areas of the system that are likely to require the greatest coordination, to describe coordination policies and practices, and to examine the effectiveness of coordination strategies in the context of other elements of the conversion process (particularly service delivery) and other components of the system. Coordination issues clearly cut across all components of the model.

Measurement and Methodological Issues

Measurement Issues

Defining and measuring the standardization of client outcomes, staff skills, and organizational tasks involve both qualitative and quantitative indices. Tasks and skills require the development of profiles that involve both kinds of data. Studying *work flow, volume,* and *productivity* inevitably requires the same combination of data. Some client outcomes, on the other hand, are measured quantitatively in an MIS.

Work flow can be measured in terms of client time, such as the average time required for a client to move from one point to another in the client pathway, and/or worker time, such as the average time required of staff to complete paperwork or procedures associated with a given step in the pathway. Volume can be measured in terms of performance ratios related to costs, staff, and time. Costs can be measured by units of service or activities, such as cost per counseling session. Staff productivity ratios can be related to workload standards, such as the number of clients per case manager. Time ratios can be based on the frequency of a program activity in a given time frame, such as the number of clients screened for eligibility per month.

Many of the variables and relationships describing different aspects of coordination can only be measured qualitatively, such as staff communication patterns and the characteristics of the referral network. The evaluator can rely on the organizational literature in identifying key variables, but will frequently need to develop his or her own definitions and indices.

Methodological Issues

The kinds of research designs and the range of data collection and analysis methods discussed under other parts of the conversion process apply to the study of coordination. An exploratory design may be most appropriate when the SDA organizational system is complex, with extensive decentralization of responsibilities to subcontractors, and when little is known about the level of coordination. In simpler systems, or where studies of coordination have been conducted previously, evaluations can use fairly sophisticated descriptive designs. Methods will depend largely on the ability to obtain and analyze reliable, appropriate quantitative data. For example, in studying coordination between organizations within the system, and between the system and organizations in the environment, data on the number and kinds of clients referred to/from these organizations, and the distribution of services within that network, can be accessed from an MIS.

The Conversion Process: Social Climate

Conceptual Issues

The level of *satisfaction* felt by staff, clients, and others is important to the achievement of organizational goals and is as indicator of the efficiency of program implementation. Retaining high-quality, motivated staff is critical to organizational functioning; therefore, identifying the reasons for dissatisfaction and turnover is a significant task for process evaluators. The reasons for staying or leaving may vary by job qualifications, position, amount of training, and other factors. Factors to consider include the degree of job satisfaction and compatibility with professional colleagues (and with the system) regarding values and goals. Sources of stress that may encourage turnover include the use and enforcement of performance standards, personal conflicts over work decisions, and disparities over what is "best" for clients. An employee's perception of the availability of better job opportunities, or nonwork factors such as family ties, friendships, community relationships, and finances may influence retention and turnover (Flowers and Hughes 1973). In performing this review, the evaluator should also determine whether mechanisms, such as an "open-door" style of management, exist for solving staff grievances as they arise.

In JTPA, employer satisfaction is essential to encourage, since the supply of training and jobs is dependent on good employer relations. In chapter 3, issues related to employer satisfaction are suggested in the discussion of employer surveys. Examples are employers' overall satisfaction with the program, with program staff working with particular clients, and with the clients they hire or train.

Client satisfaction is frequently studied in terms of the client's perception of the quality of the program's services, the manner in which these services are provided, and the nature of staff-client relationships. A study of CETA classroom training programs illustrates the importance of client attitudes for organizational goal achievement (Simpson 1984a,b). Although clients generally reported high satisfaction with the program, more detailed survey questions revealed that the quality of training received was the key reason for their satisfaction. The following training characteristics had an impact: training that was based on a clear-cut plan; training that felt like employment; instructors who encouraged independence and gave positive feedback about performance; the ability to communicate and negotiate problems with the instructor frequently. The role played by the instructor also was a key factor.

This study also suggested, however, that low client satisfaction was not positively associated with noncompletion of a program. Financial problems, job opportunities, and a change in vocational goals were major reasons for dropping out. In fact, a substantial number of dropouts were quite satisfied with the program. In this sense, studying the reasons for dropping out has implications for the sorting and screening process at the beginning of the client pathway. These findings also have implications for service design and implementation, by either the administrative agency or the subcontractor.

In evaluating satisfaction levels, factors within and outside the organizational system, such as the adequacy of resources to serve all eligible clients, must be studied. Client pathways may create dissatisfaction through waiting lists at intake, attendance requirements in training, and other sorting mechanisms that tend to separate clients on the basis of motivation and satisfaction. The adequacy of job opportunities at the end of program participation can also condition client satisfaction by forcing an organizational system to focus on clients' shortcomings and their "repackaging" to better compete for jobs. This "reform" may produce high employer satisfaction but low client morale.

Measurement and Methodological Issues
Measurement Issues
The definition and measurement of variables such as satisfaction, motivation, and morale involve attitude measurement, a major area of

concentration in social psychology. Although one thinks of attitudes as qualitative variables, the field of attitude scaling involves quantification of response categories in highly structured survey instruments, such as questionnaires and interviews, which are designed specifically to obtain information on the values, beliefs, and emotional states of respondents.

Attitude scaling has often been confined to outcome studies, partly because of their more rigorous nature and longer research history. Process studies have tended to rely on qualitative information obtained by more open-ended surveys. The substantial literature on attitude measurement, however, offers the process evaluator an opportunity to use a combination of indices, which can expand the knowledge base on program implementation (Edwards 1957; Upshaw 1968).

Methodological Issues

The collection and analysis of information on attitudes, regardless of the level of rigor, are complicated by the inevitable measurement errors involved in self-reporting. All surveys depend on respondent honesty, openness, and insightfulness. The more sophisticated data collection and analysis techniques used in studying attitudes tend to force choices, and may not permit the respondent to fully express the true range or intensity of feelings, to explain the context in which they occur, or to provide the reasons for feeling them.

Open-ended survey questions afford more opportunities to probe for this kind of detail. Statistical analysis of scaled data and content analysis of more informally collected data have different tradeoffs. Again, the status of previous knowledge about the research questions of interest, and the willingness of the evaluator to accept different degrees and kinds of bias, will determine the methodology used in studying this aspect of the conversion process.[10]

Outcomes and Impact

Conceptual Issues

Several kinds of outcomes can be produced in the JTPA conversion process: (1) mandated outcomes for clients, in particular, increased employment and earnings and reduced economic dependency; (2) potential outcomes for employers, such as lower employee recruitment and training costs; (3) required outcomes for the organizational system itself, in terms of meeting performance standards, achieving local goals, and increasing the efficiency of program operation; and (4) possible outcomes for other systems, such as reduced caseloads and costs in the welfare and/or unemployment insurance systems.

As indicated in table 4.2, achieving long-run impacts that go beyond immediate program outcomes is the ultimate aim of JTPA. Outcomes for clients measured at follow-up points beyond program exposure may not be as positive as outcomes at program completion. The effect of the program on its environment may be minimal. For instance, the program may not have reduced unemployment in the community. The number of economically dependent clients making demands on other programs may not have been decreased. Referral networks among service providers may not have experienced better coordination. Implementation may not be the source of problems, but the process evaluator will want to look for possible relationships between components of the organizational system and long-term impacts.

Measurement and Methodological Issues

Outcome measurement has been covered in chapters 2 and 3, in terms of outcomes at program exit and outcomes at follow-up points. The impact of the environment on the program has been recognized in outcome studies, but defining variables and developing measures describing the impact of the program on its environment have traditionally been neglected, largely because of data accessibility and the difficulty in sorting out the separate effects of implementation and service strategies from forces in the environment. In most cases, estimating a program's effects on the environment is beyond the scope of process evaluations.

Feedback: The Performance Control System

Conceptual Issues

Some kind of mechanism for keeping governance and management continually informed about program outcomes and the broader impacts of a program is necessary if the organizational system is to be fine-tuned or modified to increase efficiency and effectiveness over time. The *performance control system* is designed to accomplish this task (Mintzberg 1979). It consists of two parts: (1) a plan describing desired outputs and impacts within mandated performance standards and local goals, and (2) management controls to determine whether the plan has been achieved. The performance control system is, therefore, a *monitoring* mechanism used by governance to manage program and organizational performance.

In a highly decentralized system involving multiple subcontractors with considerable autonomy, administrators usually lack the authority, and sometimes the resources, to control subcontractors' means for producing outputs. Therefore, monitoring strategies are limited to checking on a narrow range of outputs that can be quantified in an MIS, or relatively easily coded and analyzed from program forms or questionnaires.

To be effective, the monitoring function has to involve rewards for compliance with the plan and sanctions for nonconformance. In terms of state-level performance control systems, the reward is increased funding to the SDA, which can be used for its own purposes within broad state guidelines. The sanction is compulsory technical assistance provided by the state to the SDA in order to identify and correct performance problems. In the case of the SDA monitoring system, the reward can be renewal of a subcontractor's contract or provision of a bonus or increased autonomy, and the sanction can be technical assistance provided by the PIC or administrative agency to the subcontractor, or cancellation of a contract.

Monitoring systems represent a way to reinforce an organizational system's compliance with goals and a means for judging the system's success in accomplishing its mission. However, monitoring can also be intrusive and disruptive, creating tension between the monitor and the monitored (Mintzberg 1979, 1983). Performance control systems that extend beyond basic oversight—checking on the meeting or exceeding of performance standards, verifying expenditures and conformance with basic rules and regulations—can also consume excessive administrative resources and reduce staff morale.

For example, technical assistance in JTPA sometimes involves a managerial technique, such as imposing more goals or increasing the intensity and frequency of monitoring. At the SDA level, this increased administrative pressure frequently engenders resistance and can redirect subcontractors toward compliance-oriented activities, which may further interfere with successful overall performance. SDA staff may be driven to ignore the social consequences of their decisions in order to meet performance standards, which can result in a neglect of those most in need of service. If the competence of subcontractor staff is the problem, tougher monitoring techniques can be a waste of the SDA's administrative energy.

Monitoring is also ineffective if the performance control system does not include a commitment to *reporting*, or providing feedback to governance and management. The quality of monitoring and reporting affects decisions about modifying the system. Faulty feedback can lead to flawed changes. In general, although performance control systems are essential, overdeveloped systems can stifle innovation, encourage conservative program management, and overemphasize easily quantifiable economic outputs, such as earnings, while downplaying less easily measured social outcomes, such as increased employability.

The use of an MIS may contribute to these potential problems. MISs appear to be the most efficient way to manage such information, but, in fact, reliance on them restricts the content of monitoring plans and limits monitoring strategies. As a result, governance and management may misjudge the underlying causes of performance problems. Therefore, actions that the system's leadership takes to ameliorate these problems may be based on misleadingly sparse or unrealistic information.

Measurement and Methodological Issues

As mentioned earlier, a key task is classifying the content of written monitoring plans and procedures, which includes the following dimensions: (1) goals and rationales, (2) alternative courses of action to be taken regarding compliance, (3) rewards and sanctions, and (4) information to be reported to governance and management. The same process can be applied to the monitoring strategy practiced by the agency, which includes (1) activities used to identify various forms of noncompliance, (2) actions taken to correct compliance problems, (3) activities involved in rewards and sanctions, and (4) information actually reported to governance and management about these activities. Discrepancies between the written plan and actual practice may point to potential breakdowns in the operation of the feedback system.

Monitoring and reporting involve the judgment of information about program outcomes and the impact of these outcomes on a program's environment, and the communication of this information to those responsible for adjusting program implementation and performance. A basic question is whether administrators are actually receiving *and* using information from the performance control system in decisionmaking. Descriptive designs and qualitative methods are most useful in answering this question. In-depth interviews of an SDA's monitoring staff and decisionmakers in the PIC, administrative, or contract agencies can supplement content analysis of monitoring and reporting documents.

Studying the "Fit" Among Parts

At the beginning of this chapter, a model of an organizational system was presented to be used in evaluating program implementation. An underlying assumption of the model is that organizational effectiveness and efficiency depend on the degree of integration, or consistency, among the system's parts (Lyden 1975; Harrison 1987). Thus, after collecting information about program implementation, a chief task is to determine the degree of consistency among the following elements in the model's conversion process:

1. Between the mission component and the environment.
2. Between the mission and work components.
3. Between the mission and coordination components.
4. Between the mission component and the feedback system.

Two other factors must also be assessed. First, organizational systems cannot perform well if the mission, work, or coordination components are "missing" from the conversion process. For example, organizations without goals (a mission component) or a well-defined client pathway (work component) often have poor performance records. Information collected during the course of the process evaluation is used to make this assessment.[11] Second, the social climate of an organizational system is an indicator of how well the system is operating. Thus, the degree of satisfaction and tension in the system must also be assessed, as discussed earlier.

These are the major, initial points of inquiry. If the evidence suggests that inconsistencies exist, *or* that components from the conversion process, *or* that staff morale is low, further data collection analysis is often necessary to discover the underlying reasons for these problems. Process evaluations have distinct cycles: a *macro* cycle to assess the

Table 4.3
Summary of Major Findings: An Example

Component	Conversion Process	Proper Fit
Mission	**Satisfied.** Goals are well-defined and governance actively manages the SDA through the performance control system	**Satisfied in part.** Goals and access decisions are consistent with local conditions. Performance standards and treatment decisions are consistent with each other but are inconsistent with local conditions
Work	**Satisfied in part.** Steps in the client pathway are interrelated with each other, but staff show little awareness of intake procedures mandated by governance	**Satisfied in part.** Work component is consistent with mission component's goal to provide comprehensive services, but dominance of performance standards in mission component forces SDA to rely on screening mechanisms to sort out less qualified clients. Females seem to fare worse than males
Coordination	**Satisfied.** Responsibilities well-defined and managed	**Satisfied.** Mechanisms exist to coordinate the SDA's activity with the subcontractors' activity
Social Climate	**Satisfied.** Although outcome differences exist, no differences in satisfaction among male and female clients	**Satisfied in part.** Stress in enforcing subcontractor performance standards.

overall operation of the organizational system, and one or more *micro* cycles targeted at specific issues discovered at the macro level.

Are the Parts Consistent?: An Example

An example may clarify these points of inquiry. An evaluator has just completed a process evaluation to determine why female clients have lower placement rates and wages than male clients. The first task is to compare the information collected for the environment and each component of the conversion process. The goal of this inductive analysis is to discover common patterns by performing the consistency checks described above.[12] The major results of this effort are organized to help compare findings across components of the model, as shown in table 4.3.

In our simplified example, a lack of fit appears to exist between the mission component and the work component. Given this source of the performance problem, a second round of micro-level analyses could be targeted at discovering its likely cause(s), such as poorly designed screening procedures, inadequately trained intake staff, or simply that few females with work experience apply to the program.

In summary, in the course of this investigation the evaluator has taken the following steps:

1. Reviewed the research literature to learn more about issues the program is meant to address.
2. Become thoroughly familiar with the program being evaluated.
3. Developed a clear understanding of the research questions of major interest and the use to be made of the answers.
4. Collected trustworthy information on the separate influences and components of the system.
5. Utilized applied research skills innovatively in integrating this diverse range of information.
6. Relied on inductive judgments about "fit," qualifying the assumptions underlying these judgments honestly and fully.

In documenting this process in the final report, any alternative (but less convincing) interpretations of the data should be presented to demonstrate that a thorough analysis was conducted. Recommendations for changing the parts of the system to achieve a proper fit among its parts should also be included. In our example, performance standards might be lowered to increase the consistency of the mission and work components. In addition, new intake procedures might be installed along with better management controls to assure proper selection of clients.

Did the Implementation Strategy Work?

Once the above analysis is completed, the evaluator can examine the merits of the program's underlying implementation strategy. As mentioned at the beginning of the chapter, each social program involves a theory regarding program implementation. The actual implementation of the program may differ from the theory. For example, the public-private partnership in JTPA, which increased the role of business in the governance of employment and training programs, was intended to increase client placements, but this might not happen in practice.

In interpreting the findings of process evaluations, two overriding potential questions are, therefore, "Is the theory valid, and does the implementation strategy work?" (Scheier 1981). In practice, process evaluations tend to ignore the first question and concentrate on the second. If possible, process evaluations should seek clues about both. If information from an evaluation suggests that the theory itself is problematic, then improvements are indicated in the social ideology or policy on which the theory is based. If the theory appears sound but the implementation strategy does not seem to be working as intended, then improvements in the way the program is organized and operated are indicated. Sorting out the information from process studies along these lines provides important guidance in planning change.

Conclusions

A complementary relationship exists between process and impact evaluation. Impact evaluation, which is part of an organization's feedback system, determines the results, or outcomes, produced by the program. However, by their methods, impact evaluations typically treat programs as "black boxes"; what goes on inside the program (or box) to produce the results is rarely assessed. Process evaluations fill this gap by analyzing the processes that produce program results.

Findings from a process evaluation often provide direction for conducting impact studies (Patton 1987). A process evaluation might be conducted to discover important issues and develop hypotheses, which are tested using the gross impact model in the previous chapter. For example, qualitative results may suggest that participants receiving a thorough needs assessment have better outcomes than those who are not assessed. This hypothesis could be tested in a gross impact model by including a dummy variable indicating whether the participant received a needs assessment. Shapiro (1973) provides an example of how differences between quantitative and qualitative results were resolved in a study of elementary education.

In summary, there are several characteristics of process evaluations that should be remembered. Compared to outcome studies, process evaluations require that much more consideration be given to the development of research questions and a study design capable of answering them. This requires a much more deliberate selection process for focusing evaluation activities on those influences and relationships of greatest interest and relevance for information users, within the constraints imposed by a sparse research literature, the difficulty in defining and measuring some of the key variables, and the necessity of collecting qualitative data that are not designed for statistical analysis.

Second, in designing a process evaluation, a unique mix of data collection and analysis methods must be carefully selected to fit the research questions to be answered.

Finally, because of greater difficulty in measuring implementation variables and heavier dependence on qualitative data, the process evaluator usually has more discretion than the outcome evaluator. This methodological freedom has a cost, however, for it makes the task of integrating and interpreting the range of information collected during the course of the study much more complex.

NOTES

1. Harrison (1987), Grembowski (1983), and Lyden (1975) propose this approach for assessing organizational performance.

2. Patton (1987) presents methods for addressing these issues in evaluating program implementation, which may be applied to the analysis of an organizational system.

3. Differences between quantitative and qualitative data are also discussed in chapter 1 as well as in Patton (1987), Schwartz and Jacobs (1979), and Mintzberg (1983a), among others.

4. If the quantitative approaches are subject to measurement error (and most of them are), the tradeoff may be greater accuracy. In this case, qualitative data may be the more accurate source of information.

5. Patton (1987) describes a variety of purposeful sampling strategies that may be employed in evaluations of program implementation.

6. The possible bias associated with nonprobability sampling may be reduced by collecting information from multiple samples. If the information is consistent across samples, a degree of convergent validity may be obtained.

7. Some programs are implemented directly at the state or federal level, such as special programs under JTPA for dislocated workers operated by states, and programs for Native Americans operated by the federal government. Studying program implementation in these instances involves the same general variables and relationships, but primary attention is given to the level at which the most important aspects of implementation occur, treating the other levels as "the environment."

8. The literature on studying program environments is sparse. However, a useful resource is a recent special issue of one of the American Evaluation Association's journals, which is listed in this chapter's references. (See) Conrad and Roberts-Gray (1988: 40)).

9. Simpson (1986) provides questionnaires for clients and employers in the JTPA program.

10. Simpson (1986) and Grembowski (1986) present questions for measuring client, employer, and staff satisfaction in employment and training programs.

11. Sometimes organizations emphasize one component over others at different stages of their development (Lyden 1975). For example, at start-up an organization's chief concern might be to produce tangible results. It, thus, puts emphasis on the work component, which later shifts to the coordination component as confusion mounts. Later, attention might shift to the mission component as questions are raised about whether the organization is making a difference in the outside world.

12. A key concern in this and all analyses is the validity, or accuracy, of the findings. Patton (1987) explains how "triangulation" can be used to verify the initial results of this exercise.

REFERENCES

Austin, Michael. *Evaluating Your Agency's Programs*. Beverly Hills, CA: Sage, 1982.

Bangsor, Michael, Michael Borus, Howard Bloom, and Larry Orr. "The National JTPA Evaluation." *Evaluation Forum* 1 (1988):23-24.

Blank, William E. *Handbook for Developing Competency-Based Training Programs*. Englewood Cliffs, NJ: Prentice-Hall, 1982.

Blau, Peter M., and P.A. Schoenherr. *The Structure of Organizations*. New York: Basic Books, 1971.

Burstein, Leigh, Howard E. Freeman, and Peter H. Rossi. *Collecting Evaluation Data*. Newbury Park, CA: Sage, 1985.

Comptroller General. *Job Training Partnership Act: Initial Implementation of Program for Disadvantaged Youth and Adults*. U.S. General Accounting Office Report. GAO-HRD-55-4, 1985.

Conrad, Kendon J., and Cynthia Roberts-Gray. "New Directions for Program Evaluation." *Evaluating Program Environments*. 40 (1988).

Cook, Robert F. et al. *State Level Implementation of the Job Training Partnership Act*. Rockville, MD: Westat, Inc., May 16, 1984a.

_____. *Early Service Delivery Area Implementation of the Job Training Partnership Act*. Rockville, MD: Westat, Inc., June 15, 1984b.

Dillman, Don A. *Mail and Telephone Surveys*. New York: John Wiley, 1978.

Dunn, William. *Introduction to Public Policy Analysis*. Englewood Cliffs, NJ: Prentice-Hall, 1981.

Edwards, A.L. *Techniques of Attitude Scale Construction*. New York: Appleton-Century-Croft, 1957.

Elmore, Richard F. "Backward Mapping Implementation Research and Policy Decisions," *Political Science Quarterly* 94 (1980):601-616.

Filstead, William J. *Qualitative Methodology: Firsthand Involvement with the Social World*. Chicago: Markham Publishing, 1970.

Flowers, Vincent S., and Charles L. Hughes. "Why Employees Stay," *Harvard Business Review*. (July-August 1973): 49-60.

Fowler, Floyd F. *Survey Research Methods*. Newbury Park, CA: Sage, 1984.

Franklin, Grace A., and Randall B. Ripley. *CETA: Politics and Policy, 1973-1982*. Knoxville, TN: University of Tennessee Press, 1984.

Grembowski, David. "A Systems Approach to Solving Patient Flow Problems," *Journal of Dental Education* 47 (1983):181-187.

_____. *JTPA Evaluation at the State and Local Level: A Guide for Process Evaluations*. Olympia, WA: Washington State Employment Security Department, March 1986.

_____, Ronald Andersen, and Meei-Shia Chen. "A Public Health Model of the Dental Care Process," *Medical Care Review* (December 1989).

Harrison, Michael I. *Diagnosing Organizations: Methods, Models, and Processes.* Newbury Park, CA: Sage, 1987.

Hollingsworth, J.R., and R. Hanneman. *Centralization and Power in Social Service Delivery Systems.* Boston: Kluwer-Nijhoff, 1984.

Kish, Leslie. *Survey Sampling.* New York: John Wiley, 1965.

Levitan, Sar A., and Garth L. Mangum. *The T in CETA: Local and National Perspectives.* Kalamazoo, MI: The W.E. Upjohn Institute for Employment Research, 1981.

Lyden, Fremont J. "Using Parson's Functional Analysis in the Study of Public Organizations," *Administration Science Quarterly* 10 (1975): 59-70.

Miles, Matthew B., and Michael A. Huberman. *Qualitative Data Analysis: A Source Book of New Methods.* Beverly Hills, CA: Sage, 1984.

Mangum, Garth, and John Walsh. *Employment and Training Programs for Youth: What Works Best for Whom?* Washington, D.C.: National Council on Employment Policy, 1978.

Millar, Annie, and Rhona Millar. *Developing Client Outcome Monitoring Systems: A Guide for State and Local Social Service Agencies.* Washington, D.C.: The Urban Institute, 1981.

Mintzberg, Henry. "An Emerging Strategy of "Direct Research." In *Qualitative Methodology,* edited by John Van Maanen. Beverly Hills, CA: Sage, 1983a.

_____. *Structure in Fives: Designing Effective Organizations.* Englewood Cliffs, NJ: Prentice-Hall, 1983b.

_____. *The Structure of Organizations.* Englewood Cliffs, NJ: Prentice-Hall, 1979.

Morris, L.L.. and C.T. Fitz-Gibbon. *How to Measure Program Implementation.* Beverly Hills, CA: Sage, 1978.

Nagi, Saad Z. "Gate-Keeping Decisions in Service Organizations: When Validity Fails," *Human Organization* 33 (1974):47-58.

National Alliance of Business. *What's Happening with JTPA? Highlights of NAB's 1984 Survey Data.* Washington, D.C.: National Alliance of Business, 1984.

Ntiri, Daphne Williams. "Training the Economically Disadvantaged," *Training and Development Journal* 34 (1980): 97-103.

Oetting, Gene, and C.D. Miller. "Work and the Disadvantaged: The Work Adjustment Hierarchy," *Personnel and Guidance Journal* 56 (1977):29-35.

Orfield, Gary, Helena Slessarev. *Job Training Under the New Federalism.* Chicago: University of Chicago, Illinois Unemployment and Job Training Research Project, 1986.

Patton, Michael Quinn. *Utilization-Focused Evaluation*. Beverly Hills, CA: Sage, 1986.

_____. *How to Use Qualitative Methods in Evaluation*. Newbury Park, CA: Sage, 1987.

Pressman, J.L., and A. Wildavsky. *Implementation*. 2nd ed. Berkeley, CA: University of California Press. 1979.

Rossi, Peter, and Howard Freeman. *Evaluation*. Beverly Hills, CA: Sage, 1982.

Scheier, Mary Ann. *Program Implementation*. Beverly Hills, CA: Sage, 1981.

Schwartz, Howard, and Jerry Jacobs. *Qualitative Sociology: A Method to the Madness*. New York: Free Press, 1979.

Shapiro, E. "Educational Evaluation: Rethinking the Criteria of Competence," *School Review* (1973): 523-549.

Shortell, Stephen. "Suggestions for Improving the Study of Health Program Implementation," *Health Services Research* 19 (1984): 117-125.

Simon, H.A. *Administrative Behavior*. New York: Macmillan, 1957.

_____. *The New Science of Management*. Englewood Cliffs, NJ: Prentice-Hall, 1977.

Simpson, Carl. *CETA On-the-Job Training Study: Final Report*. Department of Sociology. Western Washington University, Bellingham, WA, 1984a.

_____. *Final Report on the Vocational Classroom Training Outcomes Projects, Volume 1*. Demographic Research Laboratory, Department of Sociology, Western Washington University, Bellingham, WA 98225, 1984b.

_____. *JTPA Evaluation at the State Level: A Guide for Gross Impact Evaluations*. Olympia, WA: Washington State Employment Security Department, March 1986.

Suchman, Edward A. *Evaluation Research*. New York: Russell Sage Foundation, 1967.

Taggart, Robert. *A Fisherman's Guide: An Assessment of Training and Remediation Strategies*. Kalamazoo, MI: The W.E. Upjohn Institute for Employment Research, 1981.

U.S. Department of Labor. *Job Development and Placement: CETA Program Models*. Washington, D.C.: U.S. Government Printing Office, 1978.

_____. *On-the-Job Training: CETA Program Models*. Washington, D.C.: U.S. Government Printing Office, 1978.

Upshaw, Henry S. "Attitude Measurement." In *Methodology in Social Research*, edited by Hubert M. Blalock, Jr. and Ann B. Blalock. New York: McGraw-Hill, 1968.

Walker, Gary et al. *An Independent Sector Assessment of the Job Training Partnership Act, Phase I: The Initial Transition*. New York: Grinker Walker & Associates, MDC, Inc., March 1984.

_____. *An Independent Sector Assessment of the Job Training Partnership*

Act, Phase II: Initial Implementation. New York: Grinker Walker & Associates, MDC, Inc., January 1985.

Webb, Eugene, and Karl E. Weick. "Unobtrusive Measures in Organizational Theory: A Reminder." In *Qualitative Methodology,* edited by John Van Maanen. Beverly Hills, CA: Sage, 1983.

Weiss, Carol H. *Evaluation Research.* Englewood Cliffs, NJ: Prentice-Hall, 1972.

Williams, Walter. *The Implementation Perspective.* Englewood Cliffs, NJ: Prentice-Hall, 1972.

Yin, Robert K. *Case Study Research.* Newbury Park: Sage, 1984.

Part III

Organizational
and
Political Issues
in
Evaluating Programs

State and local program evaluations take place in an environment vulnerable to numerous political and organizational pressures. The most bias-free and comprehensive evaluation plan may fail to yield information that is useful to and usable by decisionmakers in improving programs, if the implementation of the plan is flawed organizationally.

In this section, the authors examine an integral part of the state and local evaluation process, one frequently ignored or given only minimal attention; that is, the development of a sufficient organizational commitment and professional capability to evaluate programs that support vigorous and useful program evaluations.

5
User-Centered
Evaluation Planning

Deborah Feldman
Washington Employment Security Department

An evaluation can no longer be seen merely as a creature of the evaluator's own choosing. Insofar as we are dealing with the intent of being used in a political environment, the choice of the program to evaluate and the types of policy questions to be asked must reside with the decisionmakers.

Eleanor Chelimsky
Evaluation Forum

Basic Concepts

Three major complementary approaches to evaluating social programs have been outlined in the previous chapters. Taken as a whole, these approaches are meant to provide a comprehensive view of evaluation possibilities at the state and local level. In order to supplement these more technical descriptions of evaluation models, this chapter examines the practical *evaluation planning* issues that cross-cut all three approaches: how to effectively initiate, staff, and fund an evaluation, how to support its proper implementation, and how to insure that it is well-utilized once it is completed.

The chapter is presented in several sections. This introductory section presents some key concepts about the nature of the *evaluation planning process* and the important role played by the *evaluation planner* in that process. The central ideas expressed suggest a general framework for planning the evaluation of social programs at both the state and local level. Later sections expand upon this framework, using the JTPA program as a continuing example.

Effective planning for evaluation requires an expansive view of the planner's role and the planning process. In this view, the focus of the

301

planning effort is not narrowly centered on the research aspects of the evaluation. Rather, attention is more broadly focused on developing and sustaining organizational support for the evaluation and utilizing its results, as well as on implementing the evaluation. The planning process for the evaluation grows out of important preliminary *organizational work* that sets the stage for later successful implementation of the evaluation, dissemination of useful information, and utilization of the results.

The overarching principle emphasized in this chapter is that of a *user-focused approach* to evaluation planning. This concept begins with the premise that if evaluation is to be truly useful in improving social programs, evaluation planning must start with the anticipated users of the results and their particular information needs, and then build from this essential base. Ideally, the user-focused planning approach consists of a series of sequenced steps as outlined in chart 5.1.

CHART 5.1
Steps in the User-Focused Evaluation
Planning Process

Preliminary Planning for a User Focused Evaluation

• Identifying users and their information needs.
• Assessing the organizational supports to and constraints on the evaluation process.
• Making a preliminary assessment of resources required.
• Developing a beginning support network for the evaluation.

Developing a Specific Evaluation Strategy

• Identifying users' key evaluation issues and questions.
• Determining the feasibility of the questions.
• Choosing a manageable set of researchable questions.
• Selecting an appropriate evaluation approach and feasible methodology.

Planning for the Implementation of the Evaluation

• Developing an implementation plan.
• Assessing the resources needed and their costs.
• Developing a staffing strategy.
• Acquiring the necessary resources.

Implementing the Evaluation

• Collecting and analyzing data.
• Developing conclusions and recommendations.
• Disseminating the evaluation information to users.
• Utilizing the evaluation information for decision making.

The chronology in chart 5.1 suggests a neat, logical progression of steps. In practice, the chronology will not be so clear-cut. The process may require that multiple tasks be coordinated and carried out within the same time frame, rather than in a clearly defined sequence. Nonetheless, outlining the ideal helps us think about and sort out the broad array of planning tasks that will be needed to support and sustain program evaluation. The second section will expand upon key components within this framework, using JTPA as the case example.

The integrating principle tying these tasks together is the assumption that the primary purpose of state and local program evaluation should be to provide information that *informs decisionmaking*. It should be relevant to the users, written and packaged in a way that invites use, and available at the most opportune time from the decisionmaker's perspective. Otherwise, the investment in evaluation may be wasted. The planning process must, therefore, begin with the user and his or her perceived information needs, remain cognizant of these needs throughout, and end with information that is actually put to use in improving a program.

In the user-focused planning process, the role of the evaluation *planner* is distinct from the *evaluator* and central to the effort. In some instances, in smaller organizations, the person planning the overall evaluation effort may also act as the evaluator, i.e., the one who designs the evaluation, oversees its implementation, and analyzes and reports on the findings. Nonetheless, the planner's role in this process is separate and distinguishable.

The planner plays a key organizational role that complements and supports the more technical research activities of the evaluator. The planner acts as a crucial communicator and coordinator among three major groups involved in the evaluation process: the evaluation research staff who must design, implement, and analyze; the administrators and other decisionmakers who need the evaluation information; and the program staff and clients who may be affected by and, in turn, affect the evaluation process and its outcomes.

Evaluation does not occur in a social vacuum. Just as political and organizational factors influence a program's design and operation, so will such factors influence the nature, scope, and ultimate utility of an evaluation. A chief challenge for the planner will be to accurately assess and creatively build upon the *organizational context* in which the evaluation is to take place.

At each stage of the process, the planner will want to anticipate organizational *constraints* to and *supports* for evaluation and adjust planning activities accordingly. For example, in the initial stages the planner should focus on defining specific evaluation users and uses. How might the organizational context influence the interest and participation of potential users? Will inter- and intra-agency conflicts hinder efforts to bring certain users together? Given differing organizational agendas, what kinds of accommodations to others and support for the evaluation will different decisionmakers be willing to make? And, most important, what kind of benefits will users expect in return for their participation?

The planner must also carefully assess organizational factors that may affect the actual evaluation process. How well the evaluator and evaluation activities are received by program staff, clients, and others involved in the process will depend largely on the quality of advance organizational work undertaken to prepare, educate, and appropriately involve these concerned parties. In the role of organizational communicator and coordinator, the planner can help anticipate staff concerns about the evaluation and work collaboratively with the evaluator and his or her team to address these concerns.

Frequently, a major organizational constraint to evaluation is lack of staff expertise and other resources. In an era of scarce resources for social programs, the evaluation planner must unavoidably be preoccupied with resource acquisition and planning. What kinds of expertise will be required, and how can that expertise best be obtained? What kinds of financial support and other resources, such as computer services, will be necessary?

In the evaluation planning process, the final principles to stress are *collaboration* and *partnership*. The importance of the planner's role in working closely with researchers, other staff, and evaluation users has already been emphasized. The planner is further challenged to go beyond the immediate user circle to seek creative funding partnerships in both the public and private sectors. The collaborative funding approach is an organizational investment that extends beyond the life of the individual evaluation effort. In seeking funds outside the immediate program to be evaluated, the evaluation planner creates new networks of contacts and new possibilities for outside community support and involvement in the program. Such support and involvement are likely to enhance not only the evaluation effort, but also the ongoing program effort.

An amplification of the central themes presented above follows. The evaluation planning chronology, as outlined earlier, serves as the general framework for elaborating on the planning process and the evaluation planner's role in that process. Within this framework, the chapter focuses on the first three major planning stages leading to the actual implementation of the evaluation:

1. Preliminary planning for user-centered evaluation.
2. Developing a specific evaluation strategy.
3. Planning for implementation of the evaluation.

Within each of the major stages, the more important planning tasks will be highlighted. As in previous chapters, the JTPA program is used as a case example for illustrating key features of the process.

Preliminary Planning for a
User-Centered Evaluation

Even before specific evaluation questions are delineated or an evaluation approach settled upon, important preliminary planning issues must be considered. This preliminary work revolves around the following interrelated questions concerning the organizational setting in which the evaluation will occur:

1. Who will be the chief users of the evaluation results?
2. What kinds of evaluation activities are most feasible?
3. How will the fiscal and organizational context influence the evaluation effort?
4. How can organizational support for the evaluation best be developed?

The manner in which these questions are dealt with will have long-range consequences for the implementation of evaluation and its ultimate integrity as a useful planning, policy, and management tool within JTPA. This first section focuses on these preliminary planning concerns and the role of the evaluation planner in developing organizational support for evaluation.

Defining the Users

If evaluation is to be pragmatic, i.e., provide useful information to decisionmakers for improving social programs, then the evaluation planning process must begin by anticipating and identifying the evaluation *users* and their *information needs*. These factors should drive the initial formulation of the evaluation project and the planning steps that follow (Patton 1978; Davis and Salasin 1975). This kind of user-centered planning approach increases the likelihood that evaluation results will be useful and, in fact, used.

A user-centered approach implies that the evaluation planner should play an activist role in identifying, educating, and involving potential users in the evaluation process. In this preliminary planning stage, for example, the planner has to target potential customers and supporters of evaluation and initiate contact, rather than wait for these parties to involve themselves. In collaboration with technical staff, the planner assists users in articulating their specific requirements, and suggests ways in which evaluation might fulfill these needs.

The proactive planner needs to *market* evaluation on several levels. In addition to information, evaluation offers side benefits of which potential users should be made aware. These benefits, such as improved agency coordination and cooperation and increased political credibility, are often intangible and not easily measured. Evaluation can also be marketed as a capacity-building investment in the organization, yielding improved staff capabilities for future evaluation or related research activities. It can lead to an enhanced Management Information Systems (MIS) or other data collection system, and increased access to contact in research, professional, and private sector networks outside the organization's normal sphere of communication.

Potential users of evaluation need not be narrowly defined. While the interest and commitment of program policymakers and administrators are key, other users, both in and out of the program, should not be overlooked. Additional candidates include planning and operations staff, whose input in shaping and refining the focus of the evaluation inquiry is valuable. Decisionmakers and staff from related programs or agencies who might benefit from the evaluation results should also be considered.

In the case of JTPA, where legislation mandates coordination between employment and training and welfare and educational agencies, joint support of evaluation activities is an important possibility to explore. Users from these coordinating agencies may have substantive contributions to make in the form of data, staff expertise, and political or fiscal support. There can be a beneficial return on such contributions to these people in the form of useful evaluation findings, or increased recognition and credibility as an evaluation participant.

Finally, potential users may include a variety of groups outside JTPA, such as elected officials and legislators, clients and client-advocates, researchers, local business and labor groups, and the general public. While not all such users may be involved directly in the evaluation process, it is important to consider how their interests and their information needs might affect the ultimate focus of the evaluation.

In identifying a range of potential users and their needs early on, the planner establishes a better position for garnering a broad base of organizational support essential to the evaluation effort. How information needs ultimately translate into a specific research design will be picked up in a later section.

Determining Feasibility

Before considering a specific research plan, evaluation planners must study the *feasibility* of evaluating a particular JTPA program. Are some kinds of evaluation efforts more likely to succeed than others? Is the timing appropriate, or would an evaluation yield better results at a later date? To answer these kinds of questions, a number of experts have suggested that evaluation planners begin with an "evaluability assessment" of the program in question (Rutman 1980; Schmidt 1978). Such a preliminary assessment, which may require assistance from an outside specialist, will help an organization accomplish the following goals:

1. Define the appropriate scope and timing for an evaluation.
2. Avoid wasting time and planning effort that will not produce useful results.
3. Identify evaluation barriers that need to be removed before evaluation can take place.
4. Lay the groundwork for doing further evaluation planning when circumstances are more conducive to such efforts.

Some of the most obvious barriers to useful evaluations of JTPA programs are related to resource or technical constraints. In the following sections, some of the major implementation issues concerning funding, staffing, and managing JTPA evaluation efforts will be presented in greater detail. These concerns are briefly mentioned here as they touch on program evaluability.

Financial constraints. Are sufficient funds available to ensure successful completion of the evaluation effort? If not, can additional funds be obtained within an acceptable time frame? A scaled-down, but well-supported evaluation effort, providing quality information in a few key areas, may prove to be the most useful interim option.

Staffing constraints. In-house staffing of an evaluation effort is one way to overcome financial constraints, but if staff resources are thinly stretched, or if staff lacks the necessary technical expertise, this strategy may end up compromising the quality and usefulness of the evaluation. An in-house evaluation may also lack sufficient credibility if the effort is perceived as self-serving.

Evaluation time frame. To be most useful, evaluation results must be available to users within a time frame that supports their decisionmaking needs. In JTPA, for example, evaluation activities should ideally mesh with the two-year program planning cycle to produce information for decisionmakers at key junctures within that cycle.

Data collection problems. Insufficient, inaccessible, or unreliable data may also limit the nature and scope of an evaluation effort.

Program Features Affecting Evaluability

Another set of factors affecting evaluability has to do with the *contours of the program itself*. A social program may exhibit certain characteristics that make evaluation outcomes more difficult to interpret and utilize effectively. Typically, a *process* study may be necessary to elucidate such features before an organization considers evaluating. The process model presented in chapter 4 suggests key organizational components that might be useful in determining program evaluability. For example, *program goals* are a central feature affecting evaluability. Explicit program goals provide a predetermined standard against which program processes and accomplishments can be measured. When a program's goals are unfocused or constantly changing, the task of evaluation is more difficult. How do you measure your achievements if you are not sure about what you are trying to achieve?

Alternatively, program goals may be well-defined, but inconsistent with each other, complicating the task of evaluation. For example, the goal of achieving a high placement rate at a low cost per placement often conflicts with other goals, such as significant participant skill development or long-term retention of trainees in their placements. Such goal conflicts are inherent to many JTPA programs. The issue is not to completely eliminate such conflicts, but to make the evaluation approach as sensitive as possible to the constraints placed on achieving program outcomes.

The manner in which program services are delivered is another important consideration. When programs encompass numerous service provision strategies (as is the case in many JTPA program settings), or change strategies midstream, the evaluation task becomes more challenging. The less uniform the overall treatments provided, the more complicated the task of adequately accounting for program impacts.

Finally, the size of the program may shape the nature and scope of evaluation. In the case of smaller programs or pilot projects, impact findings may be of limited usefulness because sample size may be small or cost inefficiencies may exist.

Organizational Factors Affecting Evaluability

Organizational factors often present the least tangible but most powerful barriers to useful evaluation. Some common organizational factors affecting evaluability are suggested below.

Staffing problems. When a program is plagued with low staff morale or high turnover, something is clearly wrong, but an evaluation may not help. Evaluation activities may create added burdens, which the staff cannot handle. Effective employees are crucial in any social service program. An organization with serious staff problems must focus on rectifying those problems before being able to utilize broad evaluation findings.

Previous evaluation history. Have previous evaluations been conducted? If so, how have they been used? Have evaluation findings been ignored or used to undermine certain factions or personnel within the organization? If so, the credibility and usefulness of the new evaluation may be questioned and staff cooperation lost. Evaluation planners will have to develop initial strategies to build trust and credibility.

Hidden agendas. In some cases, the sponsor of the evaluation is not truly committed to an open inquiry into program operations from which the program can learn or improve. Instead, he or she may want to use evaluation to support a preconceived notion about the program.

Financial difficulties. When a program is struggling to stay afloat financially, the utility of an evaluation is often severely curtailed. Administrative energy is necessarily focused on program survival rather than program improvement. The program may be able to take better advantage of evaluation findings when it is on a more stable financial footing.

Inter- and intra-organizational relations. Turf battles over clients, staff, and other resources can compromise the evaluation effort. If, for example, cooperative support among agencies is lacking, the evaluator may find access to important sources of information blocked or delayed in ways that hurt the evaluation. A comprehensive evaluation planning effort will include strategies to ameliorate or compensate for difficult organizational relations.

An evaluability assessment is not intended to discourage evaluation. Part of the assessment task is to help program operators determine which factors can be manipulated to enhance overall evaluability. Once these are identified, the evaluation planning staff can actively work with program administration and other staff to create a program environment that is more receptive to evaluation.

Examining the Organizational Context of Evaluation

The JTPA organizational context is complex, cross-cutting all levels of government, and embracing numerous agencies and organizational agendas. Because of this complexity, understanding how organizational factors might intervene to help or hinder evaluation is especially critical to the JTPA evaluation planning process. In addition, the evaluation itself may subtly influence program processes and outcomes. Therefore, the *context* in which evaluation occurs and the *manner* in which evaluation is carried out interact to affect evaluation activities. For these reasons, preliminary planning for evaluation must include a focus on how the organizational context will affect evaluation.

The planner's challenge is to identify and work knowledgeably with organizational constraints and supports to evaluation. Since these factors will vary from program to program, the intention here is to provide a general framework for incorporating organizational issues into the evaluation planning process.

Organizational Inertia

To accomplish their specified missions, organizations create mechanisms for promoting stability and efficiency. They develop structures that establish chains of authority and accountability, standardize operations, and routinize and parcel out work in a specific manner. In creating stable structures, organizations also create vested interests; a major goal of the organization becomes self-preservation. Over time, the very structures developed to enhance the organization's efficient functioning have a tendency to become rigid and resistant to change. *Change* means more uncertainty, and as such, constitutes a threat to the organization and its vested interests (Weiss 1983).

The logic of evaluation, on the other hand, is based on *the potential for change*. Ideally, evaluation feedback offers a rational mechanism for planned change in the interest of program improvement. Therefore, as a harbinger of such change, the evaluation planner can expect to encounter some natural organizational resistance to evaluation activities. Sometimes the resistance is not active, but takes the form of passive inability to mobilize for an evaluation effort. Sheer organizational inertia—the urge to follow time-honored structures and patterns that have shaped the organization's identity—inhibits the evaluation undertaking. On the other hand, in an age of shrinking public resources, JTPA and other programs are under constant external pressure to improve their efficiency and effectiveness. Evaluation provides a tool for such improvement, which need not threaten the security and continuity of the organization.

Overcoming organizational inertia or outright resistance to evaluation may present a bigger challenge than the evaluation itself. JTPA's complex administrative structure may demand that not one, but several separate organizational entities be mobilized to cooperate and participate in evaluation activities, if those activities are to be meaningful. A common organizational fear is that the evaluation results will point out only a program's weaknesses and damage program credibility. Program administrators and service providers need to be assured that evaluation results can enhance program credibility in several ways. The fact that a program embraces evaluation as a tool for innovation and improvement, itself, sends a positive message to program sponsors. Moreover, a *balanced* program evaluation will help identify program strengths as well as weaknesses, underscoring program accomplishments that compliance measures alone may not reflect. Finally, evaluation may produce information that compensates for or explains lower compliance with the various performance standards required in JTPA.

Organizational Roles and Relations

In JTPA, numerous distinct state and local level organizations are involved in program activities. Often, at both levels, separate groups set policy, administer programs, and deliver services. In addition, elected officials, business groups, other education or social welfare-related agencies, and economic development agencies may play an active or influential role in JTPA. All these actors have developed an organizational stake within the JTPA system. But will they want to participate in and support an evaluation?

A strategy for developing user participation and support in evaluation must be inextricably tied to an examination and understanding of the broader organizational context in which users are operating. Therefore, before approaching and involving various users, the planner needs to assess the *roles* these various organizational actors play within JTPA. How active or central a role does each organization play?

Program administrative entities, for example, play such a key role in service delivery that in most instances their direct involvement in the evaluation planning will be critical. How receptive to or constrained by evaluation are key actors? What explicit or implicit agency agendas might affect the evaluation effort? For example, if an SDA has not met the federally mandated performance measures, it may be interested in initiating its own evaluation but not interested in participating in an effort initiated by others. Ignoring the interests of a particular JTPA stakeholder in the planning phase may impede the evaluation in later implementation and utilization phases.

It is not sufficient to know who the organizational actors are and what their stakes in JTPA entail; one must also know how these various groups interact with one another. Do the PIC, local program staff, local officials, and involved agencies regularly communicate with each other? Are there unresolved turf battles over JTPA or other program areas? Have personality conflicts marred interagency cooperation in the past? These are the kinds of questions an evaluation planning group will have to pose and answer in order to lay the organizational groundwork to support an evaluation effort.

Sometimes organizational interests are pitted against each other in ways that make coordinated evaluation very difficult. Conflicting interests are most likely to arise where two agencies share the same client base, as is the case with many JTPA and welfare programs. Competition between these two programs can be particularly intense when the fuller funding of JTPA has translated into less funding for welfare. A welfare agency will then perceive that it may not be in its interest to participate in an evaluation that might validate JTPA at welfare's expense.

If agencies have a history of poor communication or struggle over who should administer what programs, or who should set policy, this history can spill over into and stymie evaluation efforts in significant ways. Access to necessary data or information on clients or programs may be denied or delayed, and otherwise useful in-house resources may not be discovered and shared. Moreover, the organizational input necessary for formulating useful evaluation questions may not occur, so that the general utility of evaluation findings may be impaired or simply not recognized by important decisionmakers.

Cooperative Planning for Evaluation

Conversely, identifying potentially positive interagency connections provides a base on which to build the evaluation effort. Evaluation activities that cross agency or divisional boundaries, while providing extra challenges to planning and coordination, may also provide unique opportunities for the exchange of information and ideas within the overall JTPA organization. Since evaluation often requires special coordination among different units, the process can create a supportive context for interaction across territorial lines. Such interaction can itself be valuable in informing people about decisionmaking and work agendas in different agencies, reducing organizational isolation, and improving coordination of resources (Blalock 1988). Whatever the organizational configuration, the planning role cannot remain purely technical. The evaluation planner may need to play information broker and mediator, acting as a conduit to open up or enlarge channels of communication and cooperation.

Each stake-holder needs to gain something from participating in the evaluation effort, whether it is information, public recognition, enhanced support, or credibility. A crucial task for the planner is to elicit from primary actors what it is they are willing to give and need to receive, in return, as participants in the evaluation process. The planner's task is also to help sensitize actors to each other's concerns, bringing covert issues into the bargaining arena (e.g., the perennial problem of data acquisition across agencies) so that necessary agreements can be negotiated upfront before evaluation commences.

Successful cooperative evaluation planning can be supported and sustained through a number of strategies, as summarized below.

1. *Involve key actors.* Preliminary meetings with key actors in the evaluation process will help shape an evaluation approach that accommodates a variety of concerns and does not exacerbate inter- or intra-agency conflict. Staff, as well as administrators, should be included in early planning and/or briefing meetings.

2. *Develop advisory groups.* An advisory group is another way to bring diverse organizational interests together in the evaluation planning process. Group members can include not only agency representatives, but outside professionals or other citizens who can contribute expertise and lend additional support and credibility to the endeavor.

3. *Develop innovative funding and staffing alternatives.* Sources of support for evaluation exist beyond the usual organizational channels. Moving outside an agency for evaluation resources can extend the base of interest and support for such activity.

4. *Put interagency agreements and assurances in writing.* Successful evaluation often depends upon interagency cooperation and resource sharing. Since control of resources is always a sensitive organizational issue, negotiated agreements about access to data, clients, staff, and other resources must be in writing to avoid future misunderstanding.

5. *Use a team planning approach.* A team approach to planning makes sense when a great deal of interagency or intra-agency coordination and communication is necessary to accomplish evaluation tasks. Even if an outside evaluator is brought in to do the work, a team might play a useful advisory role, providing a mechanism for more direct organizational involvement and commitment to the evaluation. In a JTPA evaluation, representatives from a variety of divisions or units within the overall coordinated system might contribute effectively to a team planning effort. Besides a member of the evaluation or research staff involved in conducting the

evaluation, the team might also incorporate representatives from the program staff(s) involved, from relevant policymaking bodies (such as a state or local council), and from the MIS or computer services division.

Choosing Evaluation Staff

The organizational context should also influence who plans, implements, and administers a JTPA evaluation. Should the employment and training staff have primary responsibility for evaluation, or should a policymaking body like the PIC? Or, should an organization more removed from the JTPA system have primary evaluation responsibilities? Should evaluation responsibilities be divided among different entities? Clearly, given the enormous organizational variation across JTPA, no one unit is the "right" place to house an evaluation effort. What works well in one setting may not transfer to another. Some major considerations in choosing an evaluation staff include their position in the organization's authority structure, their objectivity, the degree of trust they engender and their specific research competence.

Authority Structure

The positioning of an evaluation staff within an organizational hierarchy is important. Ideally, evaluation staff will be sufficiently detached from the existing hierarchy to hold no direct power over those being evaluated or, conversely, those in a program being evaluated do not have direct authority or influence over the evaluators. If the evaluator is thought to be too closely aligned with the administrative power structure, his or her credibility may be impaired and with it the ability to carry out evaluation functions. On the other hand, if the evaluator is perceived as lacking sufficient administrative support, he or she may be seen as "marginal" in relation to ongoing program operations. In this instance, the message being sent is that the evaluation is not very important; cooperation in the effort may again be undermined. Greater staff detachment is often achieved by contracting out to a private consultant or establishing an independent evaluation unit.

When the head of an evaluation unit reports directly to major decision-makers in an organization, evaluation activities usually receive better support fiscally and politically, and evaluation information is better utilized by managers and policymakers. Such a direct link to power-holders, however, may have to be offset with extra effort to bring a range of appropriate division administrators and relevant staff into the planning process. Otherwise, there is the danger that those in lower echelons will feel compromised by or excluded from important decisionmaking and become less supportive of the evaluation effort.

The JTPA authority structure at both the state and local level is partially defined by who conducts compliance-related activities. Most JTPA organizations have developed special monitoring and compliance units, which routinely collect and analyze JTPA program data and audit certain aspects of JTPA program operations. Since these units are already collecting information about JTPA, and since evaluation is often viewed as an elegant offshoot of monitoring, the temptation is to add evaluation activities to ongoing monitoring and compliance operations. This tendency is probably reinforced by the CETA legacy of mingling compliance and technical functions under one roof.

From a purely technical standpoint, piggybacking evaluation onto ongoing monitoring operations may make sense: staff is familiar with the data, program operations, and personnel. From an organizational standpoint, however, such an arrangement may be problematic. As mentioned earlier, downplaying the threatening aspects of evaluation and enlisting the cooperation of those being evaluated are important ingredients in planning a successful evaluation. The neutral, nonthreatening posture an evaluation staff seeks is readily compromised in the eyes of those being evaluated, if that same staff is also connected with compliance activities. The inherently threatening aspects of evaluation are heightened by the fact that the evaluating office is also the office that critiques and sanctions. A compromise approach might be to involve monitoring and compliance staffers as special *evaluation consultants,* who can provide unique information and insights into JTPA program operations, while others actually implement the evaluation.

Independence and Objectivity

Since the evaluation mission is to yield the most accurate and objective information possible to decisionmakers, the objectivity of those conducting the evaluation is a key concern. An evaluation staff's actual and perceived neutrality is closely connected to its position in the organization structure and hierarchy. The more involved or invested particular staff is in the ongoing planning, administering, and implementing of a program, the more difficult it is for it to carry out an objective assessment. Its experiences with and preconceived notions about the program may lead to the unconscious filtering of what is observed and how it is then analyzed, interpreted, and reported. If evaluator objectivity is questioned either by decisionmakers or those being evaluated, the whole purpose of the evaluation effort may be called into question, and the potential utility of that effort lost.

The quest for neutrality does not inevitably lead to expensive outside consultants. First, hiring outside consultants does not automatically remove the suspicion of bias—outside evaluators may merely be viewed as an extension of those who hire them. Second, there are alternative approaches to evaluation that sufficiently meet the requirements of independence and neutrality. For example, as mentioned earlier, evaluation can be accomplished through an *independent research unit*, which is under an administrative authority separate from that of the program being evaluated.

If an independent research staff is not feasible and a strictly in-house evaluation effort is contemplated, the evaluation planner must search for other structures or mechanisms to protect the objectivity and credibility of the evaluation. An organization might consider temporarily borrowing outside staff or exchanging staff with other divisions or closely related organizations, in order to achieve some greater detachment from the program on the part of the evaluator.

Trust and Competence

Trust is another important consideration in deciding who is best able to carry out an evaluation effort. Trust enhances the evaluator's ability to gain entry to a program and elicit information and assistance from program administration and staff. An evaluator's neutrality does not necessarily guarantee *trust*; neither does it necessarily engender distrust. In fact, trust may be based on the evaluator's perceived *positive bias* towards a program. In selecting the evaluation staff, tradeoffs may have to be made between the researcher who has greatest rapport and access to program information and the one who exhibits the greatest neutrality and independence.

The technical competence of an evaluation staff is a primary factor in deciding how best to build an evaluation capability. If the technical expertise is inadequate or inappropriate, an evaluation is more likely to waste resources and produce results of questionable validity and usefulness. However, technical competency and efficiency, while of primary importance, should not be the sole criterion for location of an evaluation effort. Familiarity with JTPA programs and the ability to maneuver within that system to accomplish goals are also important attributes for an evaluation staff.

The more comprehensive the evaluation effort, the greater the need to involve different constituencies and coordinate their activities. Who is best able to perform vital coordination efforts, to bring interested parties together in critical planning stages, to establish interagency agreements about data and resource sharing, to bridge communication gaps when necessary? Here again, some argue that these critical nontechnical competencies must be obtained by hiring an outside consultant, whose vision can transcend the narrower perspectives of individual JTPA personnel. On the other hand, in-house staff, by virtue of its superior knowledge of interagency history and personnel, may also be in a good

Preparing and Involving Staff

Even if only temporarily, the evaluator becomes a part of the organizational landscape in which he or she is operating. How those being evaluated *perceive* the evaluator and how the evaluator, in turn, *interacts* with those he or she studies inescapably influences the evaluation process. Therefore, the evaluator must be sensitive to the role as innovator within the organization and anticipate potential difficulties arising from that position (Rodman and Kolodny 1977). The first challenge for the position to perform such support-building and coordination functions. Most evaluators regard themselves as facilitators of positive change. However, it is difficult for those being evaluated to embrace this positive point of view; they assume that the evaluator has come to point a disapproving finger at what *they* are doing wrong. If nothing is done to soften this negative view of the evaluator, that is, if no assurance and protection are given to the evaluated, then an evaluator's presence is likely to induce a defensive posture that is not conducive to the ultimate goals of the evaluation.

If program staffers feel unsure of the *purposes* behind the evaluation, their defensive actions can seriously undermine the process. For example, in one case, JTPA evaluators were investigating the impacts of a special JTPA program through use of a control group of nonpartici-pants. When the evaluation was in progress, the evaluators discovered that program staff members, in their eagerness to prove the program's worth, had become unofficial program gatekeepers, assigning JTPA services only to the most obviously job-ready. As a result, evaluators had difficulty assessing whether positive outcomes were due to the program services or to the select nature of clients receiving those services.

These organizational difficulties can be minimized if the evaluation planner devotes a sufficient amount of preliminary planning time to appropriately involving program staff in the process. As potential *users* of the evaluation, several staffers might participate in the initial evalu-ation planning or advisory group. Later, all affected program staff should have an opportunity to meet with the evaluation staff for a briefing on the planned evaluation activities and purposes.

Unavoidably, the evaluator has an effect not only on the social climate of a program (an intruder on sacred soil), but also on the working conditions within the program. In requiring interviews and meetings, the evaluator distracts staff and administrators from their regular work load. Whether staff members perceive evaluation duties as a burden or an intrusion depends, in part, on the sensitivity of the evaluator and how well staffers are briefed as to the nature of the evaluation and the importance of their role in the process. In a positive context, evaluation interviews and planning meetings can offer program staff a chance to be heard and make a meaningful contribution.

Evaluation planning staff can smooth the way for the evaluator by educating others involved and working out a clear delineation of everyone's role in the evaluation, including the degree of staff participation and staff responsibilities related to the evaluation. Establishing informal channels of communication between the evaluator and others involved in the evaluation process will help reduce inevitable tensions and miscommunication, and protect the ongoing procedure.

Finally, the evaluator must confront the possibility that his or her presence constitutes an additional influence affecting the program in an unknown fashion. If, for example, the evaluator is seen as threatening, staff morale and program effectiveness may decline. On the other hand, because of the evaluator's presence, staff may take extraordinary measures that artificially and temporarily boost program performance.

Even if the evaluator is viewed in a strictly neutral light by staff, the subjects of the evaluation—who may range from JTPA clients to PIC members—may react to the process of being studied (the well-known "Hawthorne effect"). As a result of being observed or interviewed, subjects may consciously or unconsciously alter their behavior, biasing the evaluation results obtained. While such influences cannot be totally eliminated, the planner can help sensitize the evaluator to the organizational setting in an effort to minimize bias in the evaluation process and its results.

Reducing the Threat of Evaluation

The evaluator is not automatically doomed to alien status within a hostile and mistrustful program environment. Although some organizational factors may be beyond his or her control, the evaluation planner can develop strategies to demystify the process and reduce a program staff's initial fears. Such strategies can include the following:

1. Involve program administrators and *program staff* in initial and subsequent evaluation planning activities, in order to enhance user understanding and commitment to the evaluation.
2. Make clear to program personnel the *purposes and anticipated consequences* of the evaluation. Ideally, consequences center around

constructive program change, giving program operators room to experiment, learn from mistakes, and improve programs.

3. Emphasize the *evaluation of programs*, not personnel. The more emphasis placed on evaluating program attributes, as opposed to staff attributes, the less threatening the evaluation process. If staff inadequacies are a predetermined central concern, then other vehicles, such as in-service training, should be considered to address this problem.

4. Establish *clear lines of authority* separating evaluation staff from program administration staff.

5. Introduce an initial evaluation effort into the *least threatening program situation*. For example, focus initial inquiry on overall program structures, processes, or outcomes, rather than on individual service providers.

6. Assure *confidentiality* to clients, staff, and all other participants in evaluation.

7. Select evaluators whose organizational status is perceived as most *neutral* and nonthreatening.

Developing a Specific Evaluation Strategy

The previous section began with a set of key planning questions about evaluation users, program evaluability, and the organizational context in which evaluation occurs. We turn to an additional set of questions associated with developing an *evaluation research plan*, which will lead to a specific *evaluation strategy*.

1. What are the important questions that users wish an evaluation to answer?

2. What general evaluation approach is most feasible for answering such questions?

3. What data will be required, and what demands on the organization will be made in terms of data collection and analysis?

In discussing issues raised by each of these questions, it is important to distinguish between *research tasks* and *evaluation-planning tasks*. Although these may be performed by the same individual(s) in small

JTPA organizations, commonly some or all are performed by various individuals with different expertise and different positions *vis-a-vis* the JTPA organization.

The research steps involved in developing a specific evaluation research strategy, as discussed in chapter 1, require individuals with appropriate research expertise in order to ensure the technical competence of the research design and its implementation. The research tasks performed by these experts, however, are complemented and supported by a series of *organizational* planning tasks, as illustrated in chart 5.2. The evaluation planner works in partnership with the researcher/evaluator to ensure user involvement in and general organizational support for the development of a workable research strategy.

CHART 5.2
Organizational Tasks Associated with the Research Process

Steps in the Research Process	Associated Organizational Planning Tasks
Formulating feasible research questions.	Identifying various users' questions about the program.
	Prioritizing users' questions.
Defining the important factors to study in order to answer the questions.	Making a preliminary assessment of information and resources required.
Developing a Research Design • Sampling • Data Collection • Data Analysis	Determining the organizational supports needed for the research design.
Implementing the Evaluation	Involving users and program staff in the final design and implementation.

Identifying Questions

As stressed in the previous section, an evaluation's usefulness hinges in large measure on providing information that users need in order to make more informed decisions about their programs. The actual design of an evaluation, therefore, develops around a *key set of research questions about JTPA's effectiveness and efficiency*, which flow directly from users' interests. These key questions will, of course, vary at different points in time across different state and local program settings, but in general, useful evaluation will concern one or more of the following generic questions:

1. Was the program implemented as planned?
2. Did the program achieve its stated goals?
3. Did program participants as a whole benefit significantly?
4. Who benefited most/least from the program?
5. Did the program have unintended results (good or bad)?
6. Which program activities were most/least cost-effective?
7. How might implementation be improved?

Defining the most significant questions about JTPA will help set the parameters of an evaluation effort early on in the planning process.

In this question-formulation stage, the evaluation planner plays a key collaborative role with users in shaping the direction of the evaluation effort. As mentioned at the outset, their participation is crucial in the evaluation planning process. User input increases user commitment to the evaluation effort and focuses that effort on relevant issues. During the question-formulation stage, however, evaluation staff do not have to defer exclusively to users.

Identifying specific questions can be a difficult process, and users may have problems developing researchable inquiries about the program. Because JTPA is so tremendously "performance driven," users may have difficulty moving from a compliance and monitoring mode to broader inquiries. In such cases, the evaluation planner plays an important educative role in eliciting or reformulating questions.

Different Users, Different Questions

Bringing different users into the question-formulation stage creates additional challenges for the evaluation planner because different users may be interested in entirely different questions. For example, conflicts may surface between different decisionmaking levels or branches of the program as to what is truly important to know about JTPA. At the service delivery level, program staff may be more interested in the JTPA intervention's impact on clients. Are clients being placed effectively? PIC members may be more concerned with the business community's perceptions and involvement; administrative users may be more intrigued with studying the cost-effectiveness of JTPA. Political leaders may look for information that justifies public expenditures or responds to constituents' needs.

When state and SDA users are jointly involved in evaluation, thorny issues regarding the focus of the evaluation may arise. Since the state can ultimately sanction a poorly performing SDA, that SDA must be more directly and unyieldingly concerned with performance issues. State JTPA policymakers, on the other hand, may feel less compelled to examine immediate performance outcomes, and focus instead on more long-term effectiveness measures of the program.

The question-formulation stage can provide an additional opportunity for information exchange and accommodation between these different factions. Part of the planner's job, then, is to stimulate this exchange and assist in identifying those questions for which there is shared interest or general support.

Determining Priority Questions and Their Feasibility

Once users and planning staff have generated a number of evaluation questions, they must be prioritized and the scope of the evaluation determined, based on allotted time and resources. Though they seem important, some questions may have to be eliminated because pursuing the answers will prove too time-consuming or costly.

Attempting to answer too many questions in one evaluation effort is a common pitfall. When the scope is too grandiose, staff and other resources may be too overextended to produce a quality product. An overly ambitious scope increases the complexity of the evaluation process and the coordination of staff activity, and increases the likelihood that deadlines will be missed and budgets overrun. In addition, some questions simply may not be feasible to study at a particular time, given the existing resources available. Therefore, defining priority questions as early as possible creates an important foundation for later evaluation activity.

Prioritizing a set of evaluation issues can be one of the more frustrating and time-consuming steps in planning a JTPA program evaluation. The planner may have to sustain the process with a generous dose of negotiation among different users. In order to arrive at an ultimate list of shared priorities, the planner may have to sketch several different evaluation scenarios and accompanying contingencies concerning funding, staffing, data collection, and analysis. Users may then be better able to revise their questions and agree upon priorities.

Those engaged in setting priorities must have access to expert research advice as to the feasibility of answering each preliminary question from a research standpoint. If staff research expertise is limited, this is the time to bring in an outside research consultant to help select and refine the questions. This consulting time is well-spent if it yields a manageable set of questions that reflect users' evaluation priorities. These questions will form the heart of the evaluation and inform and direct the research efforts that follow.

Selecting an Evaluation Approach and Methodology

Once key evaluation questions have been selected, they must be translated into the research inquiries to be addressed by the evaluation, i.e., the specific program variables of interest and the critical relationships among these variables to be studied. A subsequent task is to choose a research strategy to use in studying these relationships. The issue at this stage is to select the most appropriate research approach, given the nature of the questions and the status of resources such as time, staff expertise, and data accessibility.

This book illustrates three major kinds of program evaluation: net impact, gross impact, and process evaluation. Each approach has its strengths and weaknesses and is most appropriate to answering particular questions, as described in chapter 1. A *comprehensive* evaluation approach combining both process and impact questions is ideal; it yields useful information on program outcomes and on the *processes* that have contributed to those outcomes.

A number of factors in the real world will influence the kind of evaluation approach selected: evaluation costs, time frame for accomplishing the evaluation, data requirements, staff and other resource capabilities, and organizational demands. The evaluation planner must work in concert with program and research staff to adequately assess these limitations.

Settling on a basic evaluation approach is the beginning step in a series of research and planning decisions regarding implementation of the evaluation. In developing a feasible *research design*, staff must first decide who will be studied and how the necessary data will be collected and analyzed. (The specific tasks involved in developing a design are described in chapter 1 and illustrated in chapters 2 through 4 in this volume.) At this point in the process, the evaluation planner plays an important organizational support role for the technical evaluation designers, ensuring that the technical requirements of the evaluation design mesh with organizational capabilities.

Here again, real world considerations impinge upon the choices evaluation designers would ideally make. The full range of data desired may be too costly or time-consuming to collect. Some information may be difficult to retrieve or merge with other data sets. Staff may lack expertise in specific kinds of statistical analysis required by a research approach. Working closely with research staff, the planner's task is to identify resources and information requirements suggested by a preliminary research plan, and anticipate the various organizational factors that may enhance or constrain particular design options.

Anticipating Data Collection Issues

At this stage, *data collection* may pose special issues for the planner and the researcher to address. Whether data are derived from an MIS or other automated data base systems, access to accurate and valid information is key to designing and implementing any evaluation. Without adequate data, the most careful design may be worthless. Planners should not wait until the evaluation is in progress to study data gathering systems, and *then* discover their inadequacies. Rather, these systems should be explored and their drawbacks uncovered in the early evaluation planning stages. The planner can directly support the researcher in this exploration in a number of ways.

Data Reliability

One of the researcher's primary concerns is the *quality* of the data. In part, data quality is a function of the *reliability* of the data gathering process, that is, how accurately and consistently the data are collected. For example, in an evaluation using MIS information there are several potential sources of unreliable data: (1) the client himself or herself, (2) the staff recording information about the client, (3) the data entry staff transferring that information, and (4) the system classification schemes, which do not clearly or consistently distinguish one data element category from another.

SDAs with highly decentralized intake and service delivery systems, where many different personnel in different agencies input data, have a greater potential for data inconsistencies and inaccuracies. The planner can assist the researcher either by directly reviewing the organization's data collection procedures and safeguards, or by making the organizational contacts necessary for the researcher to undertake this review.

Data Comparability

Comparison of evaluation data across different subunits, such as states, SDAs, or even service providers, may be another concern for the researcher. In order to evaluate program implementation or outcomes, definitions of data elements across systems must be reasonably standardized. Achieving such standardization across different JTPA jurisdictions is often complicated, especially in states that operate a more decentralized MIS system.

Where JTPA services are decentralized among numerous separate contractors, the issue of data comparability extends all the way to the service-provider level. When the SDA or a proxy agency, like the Employment Service, performs centralized intake and service assignment, it can exert more control over the way in which participant information is categorized and codified in the MIS. Where these initial service functions are relinquished to independent contractors, however, standardization of information is more difficult to maintain. Rigorous categorizing and coding guidelines for contractors may not exist; or, if they do exist, they may be hard to enforce at the subcontractor level.

Again, the planner can play a support role by gathering information from the various organizations concerned so that the research staff can better determine whether a data comparability problem exists. If different units within the system are measuring the same variables in an inconsistent manner, the planner will have to assess the organizational feasibility of bringing greater uniformity of measurement systemwide.

Data Availability

In any state or local setting, the Management Information System (MIS), which provides ongoing information on a number of important client and program variables, will be a key factor in the evaluation. Besides data quality and comparability, a primary concern must be the ability of the MIS to meet important data requirements of evaluation. What demands, in fact, will evaluation place on the MIS? If the MIS lacks certain data elements useful to evaluation, how readily can the system be revised? It may be more cost-effective in the long run to hammer out a thorough revision based on multiple evaluation uses, rather than slowly to attack a system piecemeal.

The cost of adding elements to the MIS is an obvious constraint to modifying the system. In the more decentralized state settings, where SDAs operate independent mainframe or software systems, individual modifications may be especially costly because the states are likely to bear less responsibility for locally run information systems.

Computer programming time is not the only cost issue involved in acquiring new data for evaluation. SDAs need to be sensitive to the potential burdens (designing new forms, training intake personnel, etc.) that added reporting requirements will place on themselves and their service providers. Also, there is a limit to the amount of research information an SDA or service provider can collect without compromising its social service mission. Therefore, part of initial evaluation planning must involve the integration of an evaluation's MIS requirements into the SDA's overall information needs.

In the more centralized, state MIS systems, an SDA will have less latitude in independently modifying its MIS. Longer-range planning for evaluation activities likely must entail bringing together state and SDA users to develop an MIS capability oriented toward both parties' evaluation needs. SDAs may have different information priorities from each other and from the state, however, complicating the task of enhancing the

MIS to meet diverse evaluation needs. In some instances, SDAs have collectively negotiated changes in proposed statewide evaluation to include gathering more information of direct concern to the SDAs.

Data Merging

Although MIS information will often be at the core of many JTPA evaluations, additional information may also be critical. For example, merging MIS client data with other kinds of client data on post-JTPA earnings, employment, and welfare dependency permits a more sophisticated analysis of program outcomes and impacts. Frequently these additional data are contained in data base systems completely separate and incompatible with JTPA MIS. The evaluation plan should anticipate the technical difficulties in bringing various data systems together for a unitary analysis.

The task of merging MIS with other data involves organizational considerations as well. The data may be under another agency's authority, and obtaining that data may pose additional problems. Commonly, data requests across agency boundaries are viewed as an imposition, requiring extra staff time or other resources. Moreover, the outside agency may be under a different jurisdiction than the JTPA agency (state rather than local, or vice versa). There may, in this case, be less organizational precedence or support for interaction and cooperation with the JTPA agency.

Such realities underscore the need for strategic organizational planning as part of the overall evaluation planning effort. Representatives of affected agencies should be brought into the planning process early to ensure greater cooperation. Interagency understanding about data sharing and computer use should be put in writing as further insurance against future frustrations or misunderstandings.

Client Confidentiality

Although state agencies and SDAs may routinely share JTPA client information, client confidentiality does not become an issue as long as such information is presented in the aggregate without individual identifiers, such as client name or social security number. However, both the net and gross impact evaluation approaches described in this volume involve merging MIS data with other data sources for which client identifiers are required to accomplish an information match. State statutes on client confidentiality may be restrictive regarding the release of this information to others. Some SDAs have encountered difficulties, for example, in obtaining state-administered UI Wage Records.

When two or more separate agencies agree to share JTPA client data, issues of confidentiality must be understood. Each agency may have its own internal standards regarding access to and use of client data. For example, one agency may strictly limit information containing client identifiers to a small number of special users, while others may allow wide access to such information. Some agencies may permit client data to be used for compliance investigation, and others may not.

Assurances about confidentiality are especially important to service providers because inability to guarantee client confidentiality will impair the client-service-provider relationship and subsequently affect treatment success. For these reasons, interagency discussion and agreement about client confidentiality must be part of the evaluation planning effort.

Planning for the Implementation of an Evaluation

Once staff has developed a feasible evaluation approach, planners can think more specifically about how the evaluation will be implemented, and chart a course for the planning activities that implementation requires. These activities will center on assessing the resources needed, estimating their costs, and developing strategies for acquiring and efficiently allocating them.

Developing an Implementation Plan

A written *implementation plan* is an invaluable tool for conceptualizing and carrying out well-coordinated, timely, and useful evaluation activities. Ideally, such a plan comprehensively documents all planning and management decisions that must precede actual implementation of the evaluation. This plan is, therefore, an indispensable companion piece to the research plan. The *research plan* documents the specific *research tasks* to be undertaken; the *implementation plan* details the *organiza-*

tional resources and activities that support the research.

Committing this plan to writing helps in several ways. First, a written plan creates a *conceptual record* to which one can continually refer for clarification and direction. As a written record, the plan is more subject to outside review, critique, and revision. A written record also allows for a more broadly shared understanding of the evaluation process and the planner's conceptual work that shapes that process. Such an understanding is crucial to the evaluation team for efficient coordination of tasks, particularly between the technical staff and others involved in the evaluation process. Evaluation *users* will also appreciate the opportunity to review the complex organizational considerations that contribute to a sound evaluation plan.

More than a single document, a comprehensive implementation plan consists of a number of interrelated statements, descriptions, charts, and checklists. Informal notes, memos, and interviews serve as supporting or supplemental documents to the main plan. A plan should contain a purpose and goal statement as well as users' questions to be addressed. A purpose and goal statement is the organizing principle behind both the research and the implementation plan. At the end of the evaluation, this statement offers a yardstick for measuring the evaluation's accomplishments. Was the evaluation implemented in a manner consistent with the original goals? How well did it answer the questions originally posed?

Whatever written format is used, the *core* of the plan should provide a detailed blueprint of the sequential activities occurring in each phase of the evaluation. The evaluation process encompasses three major phases: a *planning phase*, an *implementation phase*, and a *reporting and dissemination phase*. The implementation plan sequentially orders all the anticipated evaluation-related activities within each phase, highlighting how organizational planning tasks dovetail with and support research tasks, as illustrated in chart 5.3.

In serving as the evaluation's blueprint, the core of the implementation plan covers *activities* as well as the *timing, management, resources*, and *costs* that these activities entail (Adams and Walker 1979; Fink and Kosecoff 1982). Each of these elements is considered below.

Chart 5.3
An Evaluation Implementation Plan:
Some Sample Activities

Planning Phase:
Research Activities

- Reformulating users' concerns into researchable questions
- Determining evaluability of the program and recommending how to proceed with evaluation
- Developing a basic research strategy
- Refining the research strategy
- Reviewing of strategy by independent consultant, if necessary

Planning Phase:
Organizational Support Activities

- Identifying and involving evaluation users
- Establishing work group and advisory group
- Identifying and prioritizing users' questions
- Identifying organizational supports and constraints
- Assessing preliminary resources required and available
- Reviewing & modifying researchers' required recommendations
- Reviewing (w/research staff) data accessibility, reliability
- Agreeing on a basic research strategy
- Reviewing and approving final research strategy

Implementation Phase:
Research Activities

- Training staff involved in data collection
- Field testing new interview instruments
- Collecting the data
- Preparing data for analysis
- Analyzing data
- Interpreting the results
- Developing recommendations
- Producing draft report

Implementation Phase:
Organizational Support Activities

- Obtaining necessary interagency agreements on data sharing
- Hiring and assigning evaluation staff
- Briefing all program staff and others involved
- Maintaining organizational contacts and support for data collection process
- Providing users and advisory group with interim report(s) on preliminary findings
- Obtaining review and feedback from key users/ advisory group
- Developing a final dissemination strategy

Dissemination Phase:
Research Activities

- Meeting with users for discussion session
- Incorporating feedback into final report

Dissemination Phase:
Organizational Support Activities

- Special packaging and distributing of final report for different users
- Preparing and distributing evaluation summaries to program staff and others

The Time Schedule for Evaluation

As with any project work plan, the evaluation implementation plan should also include a specific schedule for accomplishing tasks. This scheduling dimension is important to the evaluation effort for reasons that extend beyond efficient day-to-day management and resource utilization. If not accomplished within a specified time frame, evaluation results become stale. The organizational momentum behind the effort may die and the results, when finally produced, may no longer be valued or utilized. Over time, the potential users of the evaluation may change substantially, and new users have less commitment to or interest in the evaluation or feel more threatened by the information the evaluation elicits. For these reasons, user input should inform the *scheduling*, as well as the *content* of the evaluation.

Scheduling evaluation activities ideally should mesh with relevant funding, legislative, and planning timetables. For example, evaluation findings with implications for broad policymaking might ideally be coordinated with the policy time frames of the PIC, economic development agencies, or local government. JTPA evaluation planning might also be coordinated with allocation decisions for state set-aside monies or other state and local administrative actions. The important point in overall scheduling is to seize coordination opportunities with other actors within the total JTPA system whenever possible. Such coordination can only enhance the ultimate utility of the evaluation effort.

Monitoring the Plan

In scheduling evaluation activities, planners can build into the evaluation planning process opportunities for review, comment, and revision. Opportunities to monitor each significant evaluation phase can enhance the overall evaluation effort in several ways. Monitoring builds *flexibility* into the implementation plan, allowing for changes and improvements where necessary. Monitoring also encourages the timely discovery and correction of research problems or planning gaps, ultimately *saving time and resources*. Finally, external review by an independent third party can increase users' *confidence* in a predominantly in-house evaluation and its overall credibility. When an evaluation effort crosscuts organizational divisions or agencies, review takes on an added dimension. Whether formal or informal, the ongoing review process, by inviting feedback, can be an effective mechanism for sustaining interest and involvement by initial supporters and participants.

Resources Required

As evaluation needs, interests, and capabilities vary across local setting, so will the required implementation resources. As part of the overall plan, a written strategy, or *resource plan*, for acquiring appropriate capital is essential to planning and managing the evaluation effort. It may begin as a tentative document for debate and revision in the initial stages. Before the actual evaluation focus (which questions are to be answered?) and approach (what evaluation design is appropriate?) are delineated, the plan will be sketchy, but as early decision points are reached, the plan will take on greater detail and form.

A resource plan can be devised according to a number of formats. Whatever format is chosen, the basic elements of the plan include the following:

1. A sequential listing of evaluation tasks to be performed and products to be produced.
2. A time allotment for each task.
3. The staff and other resources needed for each task.
4. An estimate of the quantity or amount of resources required (number of staff hours, computation or word processing time, etc.).

These elements must be *identified in writing* and combined in an easily readable form. Chart 5.4 contains a sample format of an evaluation resource plan. As this design suggests, program evaluation will often require special staff or consultant input at key junctures.

Determining Costs

Estimating evaluation costs is a critical step in the planning process. Funders must have preliminary cost parameters before authorizing an evaluation effort, and evaluation planners will want to anchor evaluation options to financial realities as early as possible. The thorough costing-out of the major evaluation components, as listed in a preliminary resource plan, provides a practical basis for comparing evaluation alternatives and assessing the relative merits of different data collection and staffing strategies. An estimate encourages planners to rethink alternative resource and staffing strategies more creatively, or consider one or more scaled-down versions of the preliminary evaluation design.

Costs will vary tremendously depending on the purpose and scale of the evaluation effort, the kinds of resources an organization can marshal to undertake the task, and the existing market cost for external resources,

Chart 5.4
A Sample Format for a Resource Plan

Phase of Evaluation	Personnel Resources Needed							Other Resources Needed					
	In-House Resources			Outside Resources (Contracted for or Contributed)				In-House			Outside		
	Staff Responsible	Tasks	Estimated Time Commitment and Cost	Consultant	Tasks	Estimated Time Commitment and Cost		Type of Resource	Estimated Cost Value		Type of Resource	Estimated Cost Value	
Preliminary Planning	Staff A			Consultant A				Supplies			Supplies		
	Staff B			Consultant B				Equipment			Equipment		
	Etc.			Etc.				Computer Time			Computer Time		
Planning for Implementation													
Implementation													
Dissemination													

such as consultants. For example, consultant fees for an evaluation specialist may range from $100 to $600 a day, or more. Personal interviews with participants or others can cost between $100 and $500 per interview, depending on consultant fees and the ease with which the interviewee is located and the information collected.

Sometimes reduced fees or in-kind contributions are available, substantially altering the cost framework for evaluation. A comprehensive assessment should include *all costs borne by all organizations* supporting the evaluation, not just the direct monetary expenses to the main sponsor. (For a different perspective on evaluation costs, see Alkin and Solmon 1983.) Such an approach ensures that various projected contributions of different funders and sponsors are recognized. When in-kind resources, such as internal staff time, computer time, administrative overhead, and materials, are shifted to an evaluation project, they should also be fully costed out. In some cases, it may be more convenient and meaningful to cost out some costs in other than dollar terms, e.g., staff hours to be donated to the evaluation. Examples of various evaluation expenses are shown in chart 5.5.

Quantifiable costs, such as labor and materials, are only part of the total equation; these must be considered in concert with other, less definable expenses. Examples of this more elusive spending category might include the level of anticipated program disruption caused by the evaluation or resource losses associated with an inexperienced staff.

Some of these nonquantifiable outlays can best be assessed in terms of comparisons across different evaluation strategies being weighed. Consider the strategy of using in-house staff vs. outside consultants. In some cases, the former may be much cheaper, but the results less credible to important funders or decisionmakers. Although not measurable, the potential price of reduced credibility and utilization is nonetheless important to the overall calculation.

The costs of various evaluation strategies are most meaningfully interpreted in terms of comparative benefits to be derived from each strategy. However, evaluation benefits are far more resistant to comparative calculation than are expenditures. First, most potential evaluation benefits are intangible or difficult to measure. The primary benefit

Chart 5.5
The Costs of Evaluation

Quantifiable Costs	
Direct Costs	• Travel
	• Evaluation staff salaries/benefits
	• Consultant fee
	• Per diem expenses
	• Telephone and mail
	• Computer time for data processing
	• Printing/duplication
	• Published materials
	• Supplies
Indirect Costs	Overhead
	• Facilities and space
	• Equipment rental, use and repair
	• Utilities
	• Administrative time
	Support Services
	• Secretarial/office
	• Accounting
	• Legal (e.g., contracting, client confidentiality issues, data use issues, etc.)
	• Public relations
	• Publishing
Non-quantifiable Costs	
Potential Costs to Staff and Client	• Interagency coordination costs
	• Program disruptions
	• Service inefficiencies
	• Interview time
General Program-related Costs	• Credibility problems and costs
	• Mistakes, inefficiencies of inexperienced staff
	• Time delays
	• Staff resistance to evaluation
	• Inadequate or inappropriate utilization of evaluation results
	• Political costs

of evaluation is to gain better information about JTPA; whether that information is well-utilized and leads to program improvements will not be known for certain.

In addition, the evaluation process may lead to certain organizational enhancements, or *indirect benefits,* which are often not considered because they are not explicitly connected to JTPA goal achievement. For example, effective evaluation planning with many users may result in improved inter- and intra-agency communication and/or coordination in the future. Evaluation implementation may result in enhanced MIS or other data collection improvements. Although these kinds of benefits are generally not quantifiable, a thorough checklist of potential direct and indirect advantages provides a richer context for decisionmakers to use in weighing the cost of evaluation alternatives.

Acquiring Resources

While JTPA legislation supports various evaluation activities, no specific funds are allocated to this purpose. As long as administrative funds remain so limited, finding financial support for JTPA evaluation will be a fundamental concern for most states and SDAs. Decisionmakers and planners must think broadly and creatively about funding possibilities.

Several general planning assumptions underlie the various funding possibilities discussed below. First, it is assumed that JTPA's orientation toward interagency coordination and public-private collaboration sets the stage for exploring new funding partnerships for evaluation as well as for other program activities. A corollary to this assumption suggests that others outside the JTPA system are interested in evaluation specifically linked to program improvement and may be open to requests for assistance.

Second, whatever funding strategy is ultimately considered, those who will use the evaluation, if they are truly committed to the process, represent the logical source to approach for funds. While key users themselves may not have direct access to funding, they may help in other ways to contact sources, provide staff for the fund search, or deliver other valuable in-kind services.

No funding strategy should overlook potential sources of *in-kind* contributions for the evaluation effort; a far broader range of supporters will be able to give noncash contributions to the effort. The strategy may include approaching multiple contributors for different kinds of support. Furthermore, funders will often be more interested in supporting a project if they see that others are contributing as well.

Finally, the fund-search process is a capacity-building undertaking for the organization. It requires creative program marketing to potential supporters and provides opportunities for strengthening networks of important contacts in and out of the program.

Internal Funding and Assistance

State JTPA agencies will probably have a more centralized and developed research capability than their local counterparts. As states and SDAs better define their respective roles and interrelationships, increasing opportunity for cooperative state-local evaluation activities will arise. Many states are in a good position to offer valuable technical assistance and special services to SDAs contemplating JTPA program evaluation.

In addition to state-local cooperative efforts, both administrative levels might want to explore funding leveraged from other agencies or governmental units participating in JTPA (e.g., local welfare offices, economic development agencies, city community development offices, etc.). Evaluation supported *across* agencies can focus more on issues of administration and service coordination of shared importance to constituent funders. With joint funding for a particular or ongoing evaluation, an independent evaluation unit may be acceptable to all parties. Whatever the arrangement, evaluation activities will have to answer varying needs and provide recognized benefits to all participants.

External Funding and Assistance

Evaluation funding possibilities exist beyond government funding sources connected directly or indirectly to JTPA. State and local agencies, however, have historically been reluctant to tap outside resources. Finding and approaching these other funders requires staffing and time investment for busy administrators, which initially discourages organizational risk-taking.

Ultimately, however, casting a broader net into funding realms beyond the familiar pays off in many ways. Even if adventureous searchers are not rewarded directly with the cash support they seek, their efforts will prove valuable in a number of ways: nonmonetary contributions, increased contact and interaction within the business, academic, and professional communities, increased program visibility and credibility, and expanded possibilities for future funding. The remainder of this section outlines some of these alternative funding possibilities.

Academic institutions often offer unique evaluation resources at reduced costs. Faculty are a major resource; they frequently have the specialized research expertise needed, and are often available at a lower salary than private consultants with similar expertise. Through their institutional ties, faculty are better able to leverage related resources, such as research materials, computer expertise, or other faculty and students. If the consultant time required of a faculty member is below a certain amount, academic institutions will often reduce or waive the indirect costs they normally charge.

State-supported educational institutions, including community colleges, are part of the state agency network. Their public-sector status provides an opportunity and rationale for developing closer ties that can be mutually beneficial to both parties. In terms of hiring a JTPA evaluation consultant, contracting with state-supported colleges or universities may be simpler, less formal, and involve lower indirect costs than would other contracting arrangements.

Students are another potential source of support for evaluation. Frequently, graduate students are willing to devote research time to an outside evaluation project in order to gain practical work experience or develop material for a thesis or doctoral project. Many professional graduate schools encourage or require their students to engage in such research. Sometimes students, as well as faculty, can partially or fully support their evaluation research activities through research assistantships, postdoctoral fellowships, or individual research grants. Although limited, federal work-study funds do exist at the graduate level. These funds pay a portion of the wages going to a work-study student. An added benefit is that students bring the advice, interest, and support of supervising faculty, who can act as an additional quality control on student's work, and who themselves may be willing to play an active role in the evaluation effort, contributing specialized expertise.

In some cases, graduate departments or professional schools may partially or fully fund studies of evaluation issues of special relevance to their faculty and students. One local JTPA evaluation, for instance, was largely sponsored by a nearby university's graduate business school. Faculty and SDA staff planned the evaluation; students collected and analyzed data under faculty supervision.

A number of nonprofit business, labor, professional, social service, and public interest organizations are interested in improving employment and training programs. A JTPA evaluation can capitalize on this interest in a number of ways. Members of such groups can serve as formal or informal advisors to the evaluation planning process and offer reduced fee services or provide certain resources in exchange for public recognition of their contributions.

Private foundation support used to be almost entirely the preserve of educational institutions and nonprofit organizations. Increasingly, however, public agencies have broadened their funding strategies to include soliciting foundations for support. Foundation backing, as with other support, is not limited to direct services. Many foundations are concerned with developing innovative approaches to service delivery and are willing to fund applied research activities in a number of service areas, including employment and training.

Most major metropolitan libraries carry standard directories profiling the larger national and regional foundations and their contribution patterns. Regional directories of state and local funders are also usually available. These references provide initial information needed to identify funders who are most likely to be interested in enhancing social programs.

The major directories include fairly detailed profiles on foundation activities (previous funding patterns, kinds of costs covered, special requirements, current recipients of support), which help the researcher quickly narrow the search effort. Financial reports of foundations, charities, and trusts within a state also provide useful information on the kinds of individuals and organizations they fund and their funding philosophies and agendas. These reports are generally available through a state attorney general's office or the state agency that oversees the financial reporting of charitable organizations.

Such funders may be more attracted to programs that are innovative or can serve as *demonstration models* for other programs. Evaluation of programs geared to *special populations* (e.g., youths, ex-offenders, welfare recipients, older workers) may also interest certain funders who otherwise would not want to become involved with JTPA evaluation activities.

Foundation size and location are often important considerations. Smaller and more local foundations may be unpredictable in their outlook, but they will be more geared to local actors and interests. They may support an especially appealing local project outside of their usual framework.

In contrast, larger, national foundations are more bureaucratic, engage in a very formalized selection of issues to be funded, have more specifically defined application procedures and fixed funding parameters, and apply more rigid criteria in making funding decisions. Larger foundations tend to have lengthy time frames for review and final decisionmaking. The tradeoff is that major foundation support, while more competitively sought and more difficult and time-consuming to achieve, offers larger pots of money, greater prestige, and increased likelihood of supplemental funding in the future. Therefore, while an SDA's best chances for funding may be at the local level, the fund seeker should not automatically preclude national and state sources.

JTPA envisions a close working relation between government and the private sector to better connect those who are being trained with those who can offer jobs. In the interest of learning more about and improving current JTPA operations, the public-private partnership might arguably be extended to include joint support for evaluation activities.

Large companies utilizing JTPA services such as OJT may be particularly receptive to requests for assistance in evaluating and improving those services. More support may be available if the company also views its participation in terms of public relations returns. Although local service agencies may be unaccustomed to approaching the private sector directly for help, a mechanism for making such contacts is built into JTPA through the PICs and state councils. Council members often have extensive business and community ties, and are in a good position to help planning staff identify not only who should be approached, but how they should be approached as well.

In addition to approaching business contacts through JTPA channels, other sources of information on private sector companies are available to help in the fund search. State employment agencies, economic development organizations, and private research companies often publish information on the largest employers in the state. Also, major university and public libraries in each state usually carry reference guides on corporations and their endowment programs.

Local companies can be contacted directly for information about their funding interests and requirements. Funding proposals usually are not required to be as long or complex as those of other funders, and decision time is much shorter. With major national corporations, the scenario can be quite different. They may have special (usually nonlocal) corporate contribution units that handle all funding requests, often requiring more sophisticated and detailed proposals. Although these special units may make the final selections, local corporate branches may also wish to be involved in the review process, and may have influence over the ultimate corporate funding decision.

Examining Staffing Options

Concommitant with efforts to obtain adequate evaluation resources, the planner must develop strategies for the optimum use of these means. A key source will be the evaluation staff. Because each organization will have its own evaluation interests and needs, every evaluation effort will be unique; no single staffing pattern suffices for all. In some settings, an in-house team of specialists is most feasible; in other contexts, an outside consultant may make more sense. An important consideration is whether available in-house staff has the technical skills to accomplish the required evaluation tasks. In addressing this consideration, the planner must first consider specialized staffing requirements the evaluation might entail.

Comprehensive evaluations will probably require evaluation specialists in areas such as research design and statistical analysis; more scaled-down efforts might manage with fewer expert sources, acting in a more limited consultant fashion. Whatever the scale, most evaluations will require some special staffing, as suggested by charts 5.6 and 5.7.

Chart 5.6
Core Evaluation Staff

Type of Specialist	Examples of Specialist Activities
Program Evaluator (specializing in employment and training programs)	Develops and implements a feasible conceptual evaluation *approach* (the questions to be investigated) and research *methodology* to meet the information needs of users.
Evaluation Planner/Coordinator	Coordinates organizational activities *in support of* evaluation. Assesses the supports and constraints for conducting evaluation; develops strategies for increasing the utility and utilization of evaluation. Coordinates activities across agency and division boundaries. Plans and/or coordinates resource utilization, staffing, and other implementation components of the evaluation.
MIS Programme/Analyst	Develops software programs needed for merging categorical data from different sources. Creates customized data sets for analysis purposes and does data analysis under the supervision of the program evaluator.
Data Collections Staff	Carries out the actual collection of information required by the research approach and methodology.

Chart 5.7
Additional Evaluation Specialists

Type of Specialist	Examples of Specialist Activities
Evaluation Researcher specializing in evaluability assessment	Determines the feasibility of carrying out different kinds of program evaluations, given users' evaluation needs.
Research design specialist	Advises a program evaluator on the most appropriate and efficient strategies for data collection and analysis.
Sampling specialist	Advises program evaluator on sampling strategies to ensure maximum validity and reliability of information collected.
Survey research specialist	Advises on the construction of interviews and questionnaires. Assists in implementation of phone, mail, or in-person surveys of participants, employers and others. Trains and supervises interviewers.
Applied social statistician	Advises on appropriate and efficient methods for statistical analysis of data in order to obtain valid information.
Public information staffer	Assists in promotion of evaluation effort, developing informational materials and/or funding solicitations. Assists in packaging and dissemination of final reports.

At first glance, the specialized staffing needs listed in charts 5.6 and 5.7 may seem formidable. The list is offered, however, to suggest the kinds of special advice that may be needed to sustain the technical competency and ultimate utility of an evaluation. The experts listed in the second chart are necessary only if the evaluation questions present special research challenges to which the core staff cannot adequately respond. Alternatively, a small core research staff can be constructed to include people with such specialized skills, reducing the cost of contracting out for such expertise.

There are two major staffing configurations for carrying out evaluation: in-house staffing and outside consultant staffing. Each has its benefits and drawbacks, which will be more or less pronounced depending on the particular evaluation context.

In-House Staffing and the Use of Consultants

Some states and SDAs can meet the JTPA evaluation challenge through creative in-house approaches. Although many SDAs or their CETA predecessors have not conducted comprehensive evaluations of their employment and training programs, they often have access to untapped resources sufficient for such an undertaking. In larger organizations, although requisite staff are scattered throughout JTPA or local government systems, these resources can be drawn together as a special interagency evaluation team, or loosely coordinated as an in-house consultant panel.

Certainly, cost is one of the most compelling arguments for seeking in-house expertise. However, in certain settings such an approach may involve many *hidden* outlays that must be entered in the overall calculation in deciding which staffing strategy to pursue. To locate and involve special evaluation staff may require significant organizational effort. Division or agency heads are likely to be skeptical and resistant to loaning personnel, underscoring what has been said earlier about the importance of building broad organizational support for evaluation. Moreover, pooling in-house staff resources requires extra management staff to bridge the communication and coordination gaps that arise.Finally, inefficiencies associated with less experienced and less specialized evaluation staff attempting to negotiate a learning curve are time-consuming and expensive.

Cutting corners on evaluation specialists may cost the organization more than the fee that would have originally been spent on consultants. Where in-house evaluation staff lacks requisite technical expertise, the great risk is that the information obtained will lack sufficient reliability or validity, and the findings will be of diminished value. Another danger in using in-house evaluators may be lower credibility for evaluation results.

On the other hand, the in-house approach to evaluation carries with it some potentially important benefits:

1. Staff familiarity with the organizational setting, data collection systems, staff capabilities, time schedules, program procedures, etc.
2. Fewer entry problems for evaluation staff, more rapport with program staff, greater receptivity to programmatic needs of staff.
3. Potential cost savings through closer monitoring and control of the work in progress.
4. Opportunities to foster inter- and intra-agency communication.
5. Capacity-building for further evaluation efforts.
6. Flexibility in reassigning noncontract evaluation staff to evolving tasks.

In-house staffers also help maintain the momentum of a user-centered evaluation. If they become involved and invested in evaluation in the early planning stage, they may be more committed to facilitating or encouraging the active use of the results. Critics of the in-house approach argue that even if these resources are available, some important *potential* benefits offered by outside consultants should not be overlooked. These potential benefits include:

1. Greater credibility with evaluation users, particularly funders.
2. Separation from the organization, which allows for greater objectivity and fairness (actual or perceived).
3. More acceptance from program staff who feel less threatened.
4. Greater assurances of a quality product produced by an experienced specialist.
5. Ability to allow staffing levels to fluctuate in response to varying resource needs.

Outside evaluations may be most appropriate where organizational tensions or mistrust call for an evaluation with maximum separation from the JTPA system. For example, outside consultants may provide greater credibility when the evaluation calls for a more subjective assessment of process or implementation factors. In such a case, service providers, SDA staff, and other stake-holders may more easily trust and accept the interpretive evaluation results of an outsider.

Compromise Staffing Strategies

A compromise staffing strategy involves the judicious use of consultants at critical planning and implementation junctures of the evaluation, where expertise is most needed. For example, a consultant might be brought in solely to assess the *evaluability* of a program or to develop the *evaluation design*, which others may carry out. A consultant can contribute by performing those tasks most associated with objective judgment: the research design, the data analysis, and the evaluation report. Alternatively, a consultant's role might be strictly advisory, limited to reviewing and commenting on the in-house evaluation work in progress. In this manner, quality control can be assured, while consultants' fees are contained. When a formal review is conducted by a completely independent party, the process is considered an *evaluation audit*.

An evaluation audit by an independent third party serves several functions. An auditor can formally review and critique the evaluation plan as well as the implementation procedures and the final evaluation report. By reviewing the plan before evaluation commences, the auditor can spot problems, gaps, and weaknesses in the plan and suggest changes to improve the scientific soundness, the organizational effectiveness, or the efficiency of the evaluation.

Using an outside evaluation auditor improves the utility and appropriateness of the evaluation, and enhances the credibility of an effort planned and executed by in-house staff. Because the use of an auditor offers many of the protections of contracting-out, at reduced cost, it is an attractive staffing alternative.

Conclusion

Technical concerns about planning and implementing an evaluation often overshadow organizational issues, but organizational factors can

tremendously influence the evaluation process and the ultimate usefulness of the evaluation results. In a user-centered approach to this
planning, the organizational context is the primary focus for all evaluation planning activities. This context defines who the key users of the
evaluation will be and how the evaluation must be generally molded to
meet their information and other program-related needs. Users and their
needs drive the evaluation from preliminary planning to ultimate dissemination of results.

Organizational planning to support evaluation also places importance
on defining and engaging additional key actors, such as program staff,
research staff, computer and data technicians, and evaluation funders, to
work with one another in a coordinated fashion. The collaborative
involvement of all participants in the planning process is important on
many levels. Collaboration on evaluation creates new communication
pathways across traditional organizational divisions and helps overcome
organizational isolation. It fosters cross-fertilization of ideas regarding
what is important to study in a program and how best to undertake this
effort. Collaboration encourages greater organizational support for
researchers so they can better protect and enhance the technical competence and reliability of the evaluation results. By the same token, this
approach sensitizes researchers to user perspectives at all levels, ensuring that the research approach selected truly reflects users' needs.

The evaluation planning process requires the planner to play a particularly strong, proactive role in creating organizational support. In addition to identifying potential users and other key actors, the planner
develops strategies for maintaining their involvement and interest. He or
she may have to market the evaluation actively both inside and outside
of the immediate organization and help potential users create new and
mutually beneficial partnerships in support of evaluation. The planner
may be an organizational ground-breaker in developing new communication and coordination links to facilitate evaluation implementation and
dissemination. And finally, the planner may have to assist in or direct a
creative search for new evaluation resources.

Proactive planning translates into a special challenge for those involved in the process. Bringing together people from different perspec-

tives and experiences to play new roles and perform new tasks entails a degree of uncertainty and risk-taking for everyone. In openly recognizing this challenge, the evaluation planner takes the first step in incorporating the organizational context into the evaluation planning process.

REFERENCES

Adams, Kay A. and Jerry P. Walker. *Improving the Accountability of Career Education Programs: Evaluation Guidelines and Checklists.* Columbus, OH: The National Center for Research in Vocational Education, Ohio State University, 1979.

Alkin, Marvin C. and Lewis C. Solmon. *The Costs of Evaluation.* Beverly Hills: Sage, 1983.

Alkin, Marvin C. and Associates. *A Guide for Evaluation Decision Makers.* Beverly Hills: Sage, 1985.

Austin, Michael J. and Associates. *Evaluating Your Agency's Programs.* Beverly Hills: Sage, 1982.

Blalock, Ann B. "Bureaucracy, Politics, and the Evaluation of JTPA." Paper presented at the annual conference of the American Evaluation Association, 1988.

Bricknell, Henry M. *The Influence of External Political Factors on the Role and Methodology of Evaluation.* Portland, OR: Northwest Educational Laboratory, 1975.

Davis, Howard R. and Susan E. Salasin. "The Utilization of Evaluation." In *Handbook of Evaluation Research,* edited by Elmer L. Struening and Marcia Guttentag. Beverly Hills: Sage, 1975.

Fink, Arlene and Jacqueline Kosecoff. *Evaluation Basics: A Practitioner's Manual.* Beverly Hills: Sage, 1982.

Patton, Michael Quinn. *Utilization-Focused Evaluation.* Beverly Hills: Sage, 1978.

Rodman, Hyman and Ralph Kolodny. "Organizational Strains in the Research-Practitioner Relationship." In *Readings in Evaluation Research,* edited by Francis G. Caro. New York: Russel Sage Foundation, 1977.

Rutman, Leonard. *Planning Useful Evaluations.* Beverly Hills:Sage, 1980.

Schmidt, Richard E., John Scanlon, and James Bell. *Evaluability Assessment: Making Public Programs Work Better.* Washington, D.C.: The Urban Institute, 1978.

Weiss, Carol H. and Allen H. Barton. *Making Bureaucracies Work.* Beverly Hills: Sage, 1983.

6
Strategies for Supporting Comprehensive Evaluations

Ann Bonar Blalock
Washington Employment Security Department

The active-reactive-adaptive evaluator works with decision makers to design an evaluation that includes any and all data that will help shed light on evaluation questions, given constraints of resources and time. Such an evaluator is committed to research designs that are relevant, rigorous, understandable, and able to produce useful results that are valid, reliable, and believable.

Michael Q. Patton
Qualitative Evaluation Methods

In the last chapter, the author discussed important aspects of initiating, planning, and implementing state and local evaluations from an organizational and political viewpoint. In the chronology of user-oriented planning activities associated with program evaluation, information dissemination and utilization represent the final set of related planning and research responsibilities. Communicating evaluation information that is usable by decisionmakers, and at those points in the decisionmaking process where receptivity to such information is likely to be the greatest, requires a conscious effort on the part of evaluators and agency planners working in partnership with them. The author made it clear that dissemination and utilization must be anticipated and dealt with throughout an evaluation effort. Doing so increases the relevance of the *conclusions* based on research findings and the *recommendations for action* that flow from these conclusions.

Information Dissemination and Use

The political process tends to resist research as a source of information, unless it can be used to support a position already formulated

353

(Lindblom 1968). Bureaucracies are the foundation of modern societies, but one of their enduring traits is resistance to change, which is a potential outcome of program evaluation (Perrow 1979). The academic training and professional norms of evaluators predispose them to use technical language in explaining evaluation plans and results. These realities have affected the ability of evaluation sponsors, planners, and researchers to influence the policy process.

Even though well-understood by program practitioners, the "organizational politics" of evaluation has only recently been given serious attention by those involved in evaluation research (Cronbach 1980; Chelimsky 1987a; Palumbo 1987). And most of what has been written about this phenomenon has been applied to national-level evaluation. State and local environments differ regarding the specific political and organization influences operating, but common issues surface at all levels of government regarding the most effective context for disseminating and using evaluation information.

For example, a 1987 exploratory survey of state and local program directors and oversight staff in JTPA yielded insights similar to those reflected in the new national literature on evaluation politics (Blalock 1989). There was a consensus among respondents that the following conditions were essential to the successful communication and use of evaluation information:

1. Evaluation questions must be framed in such a way that their answers will be policy relevant.
2. Policymakers, planners, and managers must be invested in these evaluation questions and the use of evaluation results *from* the beginning of the evaluation planning process, i.e., evaluation must be perceived as meeting their decisionmaking needs and interests if they are to commit needed evaluation resources.
3. Determining how the new information from an evaluation is to be used is a prerequisite to deciding how feasible it is to conduct the evaluation, i.e., determining whether this information will be used for ongoing operational management, short-term policy decisions, or major long-term policy shifts.
4. Decisionmakers must be involved at some level with the *develop-*

ment of evaluation plans and strategies for using the results for future planning and program operation, i.e., they must be kept in the review and approval loop.

5. Top management must be involved to some degree in the *evolution* of evaluation plans and activities.

6. To be considered credible, research designs must be as unbiased as possible, and the sources of data as accurate and reliably collected as can be accomplished within existing resources.

7. Evaluation activities must be presented to program staff in a positive, nonpunitive, nonthreatening way to assure their acceptance and co-operation, i.e., presented honestly as a way to make practical improvements in policies and programs.

8. Program oversight staffs must have more support for and access to intensive training in the specialized skills required for both evaluation planning and program evaluation.

9. Evaluation findings must be timely, directly applicable to programs, and presented to users in nontechnical language.

Although this survey reported a surprisingly high level of evaluation activity on the part of most states and a large number of local service organizations, it also revealed a candid litany of barriers to bringing program evaluation into the JTPA system. The following were the issues of greatest concern:

1. Lack of commitment to evaluation as an organizational goal, paucity of management directives supporting evaluation, hesitance of managers to raise evaluative questions, and difficulty in gaining acceptance of evaluation as an integral oversight function and practical management tool.

2. Difficulty in interesting state and local policy councils in evaluation and in generating questions of potential use in carrying out their policy development, coordination, and oversight responsibilities.

3. Insufficient funding, staff time, and research expertise.

4. Unclear differentiation between monitoring and evaluation in designing and implementing evaluations, and difficulty in discarding a "monitoring mind-set" that associates evaluation results with program sanctions.

5. Intra-organizational bureaucratic territoriality, competition over turf, fear of losing control over programs, and displacement of evaluation goals by organizational agendas.
6. Problems with data reliability, access, and confidentiality, and a lack of imaginativeness in merging data from multiple data bases across programs.
7. Concern about building the necessary collaborative relationships with other agencies, and assuring that important constituencies have a sufficient sense of ownership in evaluation efforts to support an appropriate use of evaluation findings.

In general, the most disturbing issues were evaluation funding, the research sophistication of evaluation efforts, and their neutrality. Implied was an understandable resistance to moving beyond traditional program perimeters and their organizational contexts to seek funds, acquire expertise, and develop new ways to make evaluation relevant to the policymaking process.

This viewpoint on the evaluation challenge reveals themes common to other social programs concerning the organizational status of evaluation, evaluation commitment and capability, evaluation resources, and the utilization of new objective information. Such themes are not new. Those involved in knowledge production have always faced fundamental problems of this kind. While recognizing that such problems exist, we are entering a particularly exciting period in terms of the application of scientific tools to the study of state and local programs.

The scientific and technological base for program evaluation was never stronger. There is a new legislative oversight mandate in many programs, which supports evaluation. States and local areas have greater control over the resources that reinforce such a commitment, and there is growing acceptance, interest, and activity at the state and local level in establishing an evaluation capability. State and local program evaluation is a rapidly evolving phenomenon of considerable significance and potential utility. Therefore, it is important to give attention to some changes that might enhance the ability of states and local program organizations to meet the evaluation challenge.

Strategies for Meeting the Challenge

Unflattering myths persist in the practitioner community about research, but the assumptions that keep these myths alive are weakening. The increased emphasis on cost-efficiency now supports the analysis of routinely collected program information to answer more complex and useful questions than are posed or can be answered by program monitoring activities. The more visible influence of the private sector in program decisionmaking has brought with it the rhetoric of industrial quality control and product research, which has indirectly supported the objective study of social program processes and their outcomes.

Congressional pressure on states to assume new oversight responsibilities as a tradeoff for increased power has led states and local areas to consider how to accommodate the evaluation function. The risks in having only subjective information to offer to decisionmakers now frequently outweighs resistance to mounting scientific studies. The tedious withering away of myths, however, is not enough. Changes must be made in how we view the *role of evaluation,* the way we *acquire resources* to support and use it, where we *locate it organizationally*, what *range of methods* we need to consider in studying evaluation issues, and the *kinds of expertise* we must acquire to conduct comprehensive evaluations.

Redefining Expectations about the Role of Program Evaluation

In this book we have repeatedly emphasized that the major role of evaluation is to improve programs as strategies for resolving social problems. But we must guard against overstating the ends that evaluations can accomplish in terms of affecting the conclusions of key decisionmakers in the policy process. Exaggerating the role research can play merely sets up evaluation sponsors and participants for a chronic sense of failure regarding the impact of research efforts. Furthermore, it can distract research advocates from identifying and utilizing more realistic opportunities for affecting program decisions.

An overly dogmatic and inflexible view of what can be accomplished with evaluative information can also deflect policymaker's attention from the complexity of social problems—the multiple causes that must be addressed, and the myriad interrelated program alternatives that must be marshaled to resolve them. We need to develop a less territorial, more pragmatic, and shrewder view of evaluation's role.

An adjusted definition of the role of evaluation might more wisely view decisions as the result of debate among many actors, the outcome of negotiation and sometimes conflict. As Lee Cronbach comments, "Action is determined by a pluralistic community" (1980). No one evaluation or series of evaluations readily supports one right decision. Too many important questions for making an ideal decision have to be left unanswered, or are unanswerable even by scientific means. As Carol Weiss suggests, there are only "best compromises" (1988). Also, decisions frequently bypass formal decisionmaking processes. They are often the by-product of a progressive, largely nonrational narrowing of existing alternatives—a "nonlinear process," according to Gary Henry (1987). In this context, we must appreciate the significant and more subtle indirect effects as well as the more immediate and tangible direct effects of evaluation activities on the nature and content of social programs. These quite different *kinds* of influence may be equally pervasive.

There is little question that certain evaluation contexts and situations produce *immediate* policy or program effects. In cases where decision-makers have requested a specific evaluation for the purpose of making immediate changes within a particular time frame, for instance, or where the underlying agenda for conducting an evaluation is a clear demand for and commitment to change, there is often a visible, easily describable influence for evaluation. There are situations in which the policy question is of fundamental interest to the intended user, and the evaluation findings clearly answer that question.

Findings can lead directly to legislative action, i.e., program reauthorization and new program rules and regulations. Synthesizing findings from past evaluations and applying this analysis to a high-priority subject area can sway decisions. Over a particular year, the U.S. General Accounting Office produced 290 evaluation reports with 1,135 recommendations. A study of what happened to these recommendations revealed that 80 percent were accepted by the federal agencies to which they were directed (Chelimsky 1987b).

Other contexts and situations—conceivably the majority—involve indirect influences. Evaluation information may shape *assumptions* subsequently taken for granted by political and organizational decision-makers in the process of negotiating decisions, such as assumptions about the nature of the problems to be resolved, the characteristics of those to be changed, the change strategies considered most effective. This information may influence the *design of new programs* through the accumulation of evidence from past research. It may influence the *language* of the policy debate—reporting empirical evidence to support positions lends credibility and power to those positions. It may have an effect as a *rationale for change*, circumventing more obvious barriers to the utilization of evaluation information. It may *expand the policy debate* by including a broader range of alternatives to consider. It may *set parameters around the debate*, such as which issues are to be given attention, and how they are to be defined and prioritized. It may *reorient policy agendas* by suggesting which program implementation theories may be flawed and which reasonably effective in producing the desired results (Cronbach 1980; Chelimsky 1987a).

Evaluations can also alert decisionmakers to an immediate social *crisis* or to troublesome long-term *trends* requiring a policy response. They can help provide a new *framework* within which issues are considered, supporting innovation in policy development and program design. They can contribute information that supports the formation of *coalitions* that do wield direct persuasive power over the policy process. In rethinking the role of evaluation in the policy process, we may have to relinquish the naive expectation that evaluation must always have a prominent, direct, measurable, and immediate impact on policy and program decisions.

Developing New Approaches for Securing
Evaluation Support, Resources, and Utilization

The impressive evaluation efforts now occurring at state and local levels have, nevertheless, been constrained by dependence on scarce resources *within* the programs being evaluated. The JTPA survey, for instance, indicated that nearly all state and local organizations paid for evaluation activities exclusively with JTPA administrative funds, a small pot of money. Only two states had ever leveraged funds across the programs to be coordinated with JTPA. Only one had acquired funding outside the JTPA system. Most agencies used in-house JTPA staff in program monitoring or management information system (MIS) units to design and implement evaluations. Remarkably few engaged in joint cross-program evaluations, relied on research consultants, or used a combination of in-house and outside research expertise.

One would suppose that concern about a lack of general support for evaluation within JTPA and the recognized need for new in-depth information would have led to more imaginative efforts to combine resources from multiple sources. Yet, it was clear that in most cases states and local areas had not fully exploited chances to expand their resource bases. Although survey respondents were concerned about evaluation utilization, it was obvious that minimal energy had been invested in systematically anticipating utilization issues throughout an evaluation, or in advocacy and marketing activities once an evaluation was completed. In a period of reduced resources in the 1980s, this revealed a confining bureaucratic mind-set about resource opportunities.

This suggests the need for a new sense of empowerment at the state and local level that resists the tendency to rely on limited, traditional sources of support. There is risk in leaving the apparent safety of familiar organizational territory—a sense of loss of control in reaching out to other people and other programs. Collaboration involves an inevitable renegotiation of authority and ownership. Nevertheless, new attitudes are liberating in terms of expanding the scope of evaluation efforts and increasing evaluation resources.

Empowerment, however, will require the purposeful creation of new *collaborative relationships*—from the beginning to the end of the evaluation process, and beyond. States and local organizations will need to construct *support networks* that bring together representatives of constituencies that are significant sources of support in considering evaluation issues, provide a base for evaluation activities, and ensure the appropriate use of new information.

Rather than focusing on a lack of access to resources needed for evaluation, it will be important to concentrate on identifying potential resources, bringing them into the social service system, investing contributors as partners in efforts to make that system more accountable, and offering something of value to these new partners in return. New partners can be offered public recognition, increased organizational credibility, and information required to pursue their own goals. New linkages can be established, giving them greater access to the resources they need. In building support networks, ways to offer opportunities for a mutually profitable exchange with these constituencies will have to be developed.

Experimentation with leveraging funds and other kinds of assistance should also be encouraged across different pools of funds within programs, across different service providers who are expected to function cooperatively, and within a larger system of integrated services. Developing *funding consortia* to jointly fund evaluations, and *collaborative bodies* to receive and allocate jointly contributed resources is important.

Crafting general strategies for approaching funding sources at the national level and developing specific strategies tailored to carefully selected private corporate and foundation sources should be part of this innovative resource acquisition effort. To be successful, these strategies must be responsive to the kinds of social exchanges required to interest and invest potential contributors. (See Feldman, chapter 5 in this volume.)

These suggestions should not imply the creation of a large, *amorphous* network of people; acquiring resource partners should be a highly selective process. The core of a support network needs to be organized as a formal *advisory body,* which consolidates the network's influences and helps maintain it over time. The size and purpose of such a group can be limited, so that its mission is not easily displaced. Composition can be confined to representatives of constituencies that wield the most power in obtaining evaluation resources and securing the use of the information produced. Assigning a specialized planner to act as a liaison between this advisory body and ongoing evaluation activities can develop important bonds among program practitioners, evaluators, contributors, and users, and can help them to coordinate their agendas.

Building effective organizational linkages secures mutual investment over time, so that future evaluations will have an immediate base of support. Formalizing a support network increases opportunities to generate otherwise inaccessible funds and nonmonetary contributions outside the program. It protects evaluation activities from being co-opted by special interests, including those invested in the program, and provides a buffer when evaluation results are controversial. More important, it can influence a program's status in its environment by increasing public perception that a program is genuinely accountable, and by giving evaluation special legitimacy as an accepted part of decisionmaking.

Increasing the Autonomy of Evaluation Activities and Their Influence on Policies and Programs

The JTPA survey referred to earlier identified a problem faced in most social programs—the organizational location and autonomy of program evaluation activities. Most JTPA evaluation activities had reportedly been carried out by staff *within* programs being evaluated, in particular by monitoring and reporting staff. Only a few of the larger state agencies and urban program organizations had used evaluation units *separate from program divisions* to carry out JTPA evaluations.

This is understandable; funding for oversight activities has traditionally emphasized monitoring programs for compliance with rules and regulations. The new interest in meeting formal performance standards has increased the priority given to monitoring the allocation of scarce program dollars. Expectations for monitoring staff have encouraged a strong investment in the program being reviewed, and the location of monitoring activities within program divisions has legitimized this interest. This lack of neutrality, however, can seriously reduce the objectivity of evaluation activities.

One practical resolution of this problem is to relocate evaluation activities where they can be given greater organizational priority, funding, and autonomy. One of the most useful ways to accomplish this is to develop *evaluation units* that are semi-autonomous from program divisions and serve an evaluation function for multiple programs within a state agency, or are given responsibility for a singular and separate oversight function within a local program organization. The directors of such units would be required to report to the decisionmaking level of the organization. This concept of state or local level "general accounting offices" has been applied successfully by several states and large program organizations.

This kind of unit could be the focus of network building for evaluation activities, and assume responsibility for working with an evaluation advisory body. It could become the focal point for assessing resource needs for evaluation and contracting with state universities, local community colleges, and private research firms for additional expertise. Its basic funding within state agencies could be collaborative, drawing from multiple sources of administrative and technical assistance monies as well as outside sources. At the state and local level, separate evaluation units could more easily attract contributions specifically targeted to program evaluation activities, and legitimize the acquisition of staff sufficiently trained to participate in designing and implementing comprehensive evaluations.

There is always the danger that autonomous evaluation units will become isolated from programs, exercise too much professional discretion, develop their own language and agenda, and become threatening to program management. However, such units could be mandated to maintain close connections with program divisions through liaison personnel with evaluation planning expertise, who are outstationed with evaluation units, or through staff working within a program division and in close partnership with the evaluation unit's research staff.

A significant advantage of such units is their potential for concentrating evaluation fund search, networking, research contracting, research, and evaluation marketing activities in one place. Their position on the organizational chart permits them to be direct recipients of high-level decisions and to exert an influence on the organization's overall oversight commitment and direction. Perhaps most important, this kind of organizational niche for program evaluation assures maximum objectivity, encourages research competence, adds stature to the role of evaluation in the organization, and offers the best opportunity to actively advocate the use of evaluation information.

Expanding the Evaluation Repertoire

As discussed in chapter 1, there has been a tendency to oversimplify programs in order to study them more quantitatively, and to focus on highly selected aspects of programs without considering how they fit together. There has been little systematic interest in testing the accuracy of the assumptions underlying program design, or in viewing the components of programs as part of a larger organizational system.

As perverse as it may sound, increasing interest in the social sciences over the last three decades is in part responsible for these limited perspectives. This interest led to specialization within social science research and the professionalization of *evaluation research*. It has had an unintended divisive effect on the research community, regarding which approaches and methods are "best"—experimental vs. nonexperimental, quantitative vs. qualitative, outcome-oriented vs. implementation-oriented. The strong traditional emphasis on net impact studies and, more recently, on experimental field studies has assigned a higher status to research in the policymaking community, but a price has been paid for greater rigor in the narrow sets of issues that can be addressed.

Even as the significance of implementation studies has gained deserved recognition, most process evaluations are being carried out independently of outcomes studies. This limits their usefulness in offering explanations for the results of outcome evaluations. This "either-or" attribute of evaluation research has restricted the evaluation repertoire unnecessarily. It is a particularly restrictive perspective in evaluating state and local programs.

As Chelimsky suggests, when the context of an evaluation involves a heated policy debate, a rigorous generalizable net impact study may offer protection to the evaluator, but be neither feasible nor appropriate in answering the question of greatest interest (1987a). Even when such a research design is the appropriate choice, timeliness may take precedence over the power of scientific rigor. Under different circumstances, a net impact study would be imperative in answering the policy question. The increased flexibility sought in wider choices should not be viewed as compromising scientific principles and methods. It simply allows us to fully utilize them.

At state and local levels, the repertoire should offer the full range of theoretical and methodological choices and encourage the use of combinations of choices in undertaking comprehensive program evaluations. We may want to combine a rigorous net impact study using econometric methods with an exploratory study of particular aspects of implementation, or combine a survey to determine the attitudes of program personnel with a study of the gross outcomes of program participants. We may want to combine a survey of employers with a survey of clients who have been trained or employed by them. Opening up the evaluation process to more diverse opportunities that cut across different approaches and methods can free us to study issues of more direct interest to those making decisions about program change.

In expanding the evaluation repertoire we can benefit from a consideration of a broader set of research choices. We should also be concerned about the manner in which information yielded by these choices is communicated to users. We must be more responsive to decisionmakers' requests to translate evaluation findings into meaningful form from *their* points of view. The scientific interpretation of results must be converted into a *political* and *organizational interpretation*.

Clearly, the evaluator is obligated to make the appropriate distinction for the user among *findings*, *conclusions*, and *recommendations*. The evaluator's primary responsibility is to report findings as honestly as possible, with all of the necessary qualifications. There is, however, an important secondary obligation for those working in applied research. They must draw pragmatic conclusions from those findings, if possible, and suggest effective action that can be taken to improve policies and programs.

In some cases the findings will not warrant this leap. Even in this instance, the evaluator can recommend issues to study in future evaluations. In most cases, however, something will have been learned from an evaluation that supports making these progressive leaps from the research itself. These conclusions and recommendations will not be heard by the decisionmaker unless the evaluator—with advice from practitioners—presents these ideas attractively and in nontechnical user-oriented language, trims what is irrelevant, condenses, and decides which findings are the more important ones and which can actually be addressed by those making decisions (Chelimsky 1987a; Cronbach 1980). If evaluation information from a more varied set of research opportunities is to be effective, the presentation and marketing of this information must also become an accepted part of the evaluation repertoire.

Using a New Approach in Staffing Evaluations

If a broader research repertoire is used, staffing evaluations differently at state and local levels is essential. Although some state agencies and local program organizations have evaluation units whose staff is well-trained in research, many more depend on staff with considerable managerial, planning, or computer science expertise, but minimal research training. It is frequently assumed that these staff members can be formally or experientially retrained to conduct evaluations, and that assigning staff members dual oversight roles is an efficient way to meet accountability responsibilities.

It is extremely difficult for those monitoring program compliance to maintain objectivity about the program being evaluated, and it is unrealistic to expect that even an intensive series of courses can substitute for graduate research training. A less-than-thorough grounding in research principles and methods constrains staff in judging the feasibility of evaluation questions, identifying the resources needed for sound evaluations, and developing viable research designs.

A separation of talent is, therefore, not only necessary but efficient. Researchers are best equipped to carry out program evaluations. Monitoring and MIS staffs have key roles to play in reviewing evaluation issues and plans, and in opening access to program information in the process of implementing evaluations. Basic evaluation training can be extremely useful in increasing their sophistication as they contribute to the evaluation process in that role.

There are several changes that can be explored, including hiring an interdisciplinary research team as the core of a central evaluation unit, having this unit selectively use outside research consultants, and redefining the evaluator's role. The benefits gained in undertaking these activities, include the following:

1. A core in-house research staff with exposure to the knowledge base of more than one social science discipline can draw from alternative theories about social *problems* and how they can be resolved, and from a range of methodologies for studying social *programs*.

2. Job descriptions for such a staff benefit from consultation with experienced researchers willing to contribute their reviews and comments. The choice of consultants should reflect the nature and extent of education, specialized training, and experience needed to construct an interdisciplinary team. Personnel selection should focus on a knowledge of social theory, research design, advanced research methods, social statistics, and computer analysis. The applicant's level of experience and success in working collaboratively with program practitioners throughout the evaluation process, including securing the use of the information produced, is also important. The *political*, *organizational*, and *interpersonal* skills needed to work cooperatively in pragmatic program settings requires the research team to be familiar with concepts in political and organizational theory and behavior, and interpersonal negotiation.

3. As effective as an evaluation unit may become, its integrity and objectivity will need to be maintained by supplementing this in-kind research expertise with assistance from outside researchers. An effective strategy is to contract selectively for time-limited, specialized expertise required by a *particular* evaluation, i.e., expertise needed but not available in-house, or expertise that needs to be obtained from a source clearly seen as politically neutral.

4. The cost of hiring researchers and contracting for specialized research expertise are important considerations. This expertise, however, is not as expensive as most states and local organizations may suppose. Many applied researchers are accessible to states and local areas through state community college and university systems, other

state higher education institutions and related research institutes, and private research organizations. These evaluators are often eager to utilize opportunities to work in applied settings and to make such experiences available to graduate students. A social exchange, as well as an exchange of fiscal benefits, is involved. Also, in servicing more than one program, an evaluation unit can be partially supported by pooling administrative and technical assistance funds. An evaluation support network can be a critical asset, and an advisory group an important source of contributed expertise.

5. Thinking more creatively about constructing a competent interdisciplinary evaluation team and maintaining useful linkages with program divisions should not distract us from expanding the role of the program evaluator. A perennial complaint is that this role is too intellectual and removed from organizational realities. Evaluators must be willing to learn to play roles beyond their primary technical responsibilities in the evaluation process, including the following:

    (a) Students of organizations, the policymaking process and how the political system works.

    (b) Research advocates with information users.

    (c) Catalysts for listening to users' concerns and helping them raise useful, researchable questions about programs.

    (d) Organizational team players within an evaluation unit, and members of a working partnership with evaluation planners operating within program divisions.

    (e) Political and organizational interpreters of evaluation findings, conclusions, and recommendations to users and the media.

    (f) Evaluators of the *impact* of evaluations, i.e., the effectiveness of evaluation efforts in influencing the direction programs take.

    (g) Consummate agents of change.

Unquestionably, the suggested changes will require more effective *educational efforts* to explain the benefits of applied science, *increased funding* for evaluation, *bureaucratic commitment* to evaluative activities, *inventive collaboration* among those responsible for programs, *more sophisticated research and planning expertise*, and *greater appreciation* of the value of accumulating a usable body of knowledge about social programs.

Concluding Thoughts

The authors of the preceding chapters have offered distinctly different, but complementary, perspectives on program evaluation at state and local levels. In the three research-oriented chapters, each author has drawn from his or her own area of social science research to design a practical, scientific approach to studying a number of important aspects of programs: the array of program outcomes experienced by clients and others to be affected by a program, a program's net effects, and the organizational policies and practices that shape a program's influence in creating the intended changes. Nevertheless, a commitment to comprehensive program evaluation remains the central theme. There is continuing emphasis on the informational benefits of evaluation efforts that inform decisionmakers about the multiple facets of programs and how they function in pragmatic environments.

In this respect, the authors of chapters 2, 3, and 4 encourage the reader to move toward evaluations that take into account the complexity of relationships between program outcomes and program organization. Studying high-priority implementation and outcome issues within the *same* historical period—a given planning cycle—permits an evaluator to explore important interrelationships among organizational factors, social interventions, and outcomes for a particular *historical cohort* of individuals exposed to a program, and with the group of program actors who have developed and applied program policies within that same period. This approach provides the opportunity to acquire considerably more useful information than can be obtained from isolated process and outcome studies conducted in different periods under varying program conditions.

A better understanding of the intricate relationships between program implementation and impact is directly responsive to the needs of policymakers, administrators, planners, and managers who must routinely identify problems, develop new policies, and modify programs. Part of their mission is to determine which program changes are most appropriate in resolving problems and develop strategies for making those changes. In order to carry out this mission successfully they must rely on a broad, accurate information base.

The author of chapter 5 shifts our attention from the technical aspects of this expanded view of evaluation to the organizational and political *context* and *environment* of state and local evaluation activities. This chapter defines significant partnership roles for the evaluator and program planner in the evaluation process. It also explores some of the organizational and political barriers to evaluating, and suggests ways to reduce or work around them. Most important, it dramatizes the importance of assigning sufficient resources to the evaluation process, since the nature of those resources subtly direct and shape information production.

Viewed as a whole, the interrelated chapters of the book express the concept of evaluation introduced in chapter 1, which defines evaluation as an undertaking demanding a conscious, purposeful use of scientific and organizational knowledge, skills, and sensitivities.

REFERENCES

Blalock, Ann B. "Are We Evaluating What We Do? An Exploratory Survey of JTPA Professionals." *Evaluation Forum,* Issue 5/6 (1989).

_____. "Politics, Bureaucracies and JTPA Evaluation." Paper presented at the annual meeting of the American Evaluation Association, 1988.

_____. *Strategies for Funding and Staffing State and Local Evaluations.* Monograph prepared for the Washington Employment Security Department, 1987.

Chelimsky, Eleanor. "The Organizational Politics of Evaluation," *Society* 25:1 (1987a).

_____. "The Politics of Program Evaluation." In *Sage Yearbook of Politics and Public Policy.* Beverly Hills, CA: Sage, 1987b.

_____. "Linking Program Evaluation with User Needs." In *The Politics of Program Evaluation,* edited by Dennis Palumbo. Newbury Park, CA: Sage, 1987.

Cronbach, Lee J. et al. *Toward Reform of Program Evaluation: Aims, Methods and Institutional Arrangements.* San Francisco: Jossey-Bass, 1980.

Freeman, Howard E., and Clarence C. Sherwood. *Social Research and Social Policy.* Englewood Cliffs, NJ: Prentice-Hall, 1970.

Guba, E. G., and Yvonne S. Lincoln. *Effective Evaluation: Improving the Usefulness of Evaluation Results Through Responsive and Naturalistic Approaches.* San Francisco: Jossey-Bass, 1981.

Henry, Gary. "Interview with an Evaluator," *Evaluation Practice* 8:4 (November 1987).

Lincoln, Yvonne S., ed. *Organizational Theory and Inquiry.* Newbury Park, CA: Sage, 1985.

Lindblom, Charles E. *The Policy-Making Process.* Englewood Cliffs, NJ: Prentice-Hall, 1968.

Louviere, Jordan J. *Analyzing Decision-Making.* Newbury Park, CA: Sage, 1988.

McLaughlin, John A. et al. *Evaluation Utilization.* Newbury Park, CA: Sage, 1988.

Palumbo, Dennis. *The Politics of Program Evaluation.* Newbury Park, CA: Sage, 1987.

Patton, Michael Q. *Utilization-Focused Evaluation.* Beverly Hills, CA: Sage, 1986.

Perrow, Charles. *Complex Organizations,* 2d ed. Glenview, IL: Scott, Foresman and Company, 1979.

Rivlin, Alice. *Systematic Thinking for Social Action.* Washington, D.C.: The Brookings Institution, 1971.

Sieber, Samuel. *Fatal Remedies: The Ironies of Social Intervention.* New York: Plenum Press, 1981.

Weiss, Carol. "Where Politics and Evaluation Meet." *Evaluation Practice* 1 (1973).

_____, ed. *Using Social Research in Public Policymaking.* Lexington, MA: Lexington Books, 1982.

_____. "Evaluation Decisions: Is Anybody There? Does Anybody Care?" *Evaluation Practice* 9 (February 1988).

_____, and Mark Bucuvalas. *Social Science Research and Decisionmaking.* New York: Columbia University Press, 1980.

Appendix

This appendix is designed to provide additional information of interest and use to the reader.

Appendix A affords an overview of the distinctive features of JTPA, the case example used throughout the book as an illustration to which general evaluation concepts are applied.

Appendix B addresses an issue referred to in all chapters but not fully developed—the capacity of program MISs to support program evaluation.

Appendix C outlines the series of evaluation guides produced by the JTPA Evaluation Design Project, on which the book is based.

Appendix D provides background information about the book's authors.

Appendix A
The Case Example:
Characteristics of Title II Programs
Under the Job Training Partnership Act

Ann Bonar Blalock

The application of general program evaluation concepts to a case example requires that the reader have an understanding of the major characteristics of the illustrative program. In this section the key attributes of JTPA are described, consistent with the classification scheme used in discussing social programs in chapter 1.

Appendix Chart A.1
Target Groups Expected to Receive the Program's Interventions

Participants	Other Entities
Those who can benefit from, and are most in need of employment and training opportunities.	**Participating Employers**
	Those providing work experience or occupational training to participants
Economically disadvantaged youth age 16-21 and unskilled economically disadvantaged adults 22 and over: 90% of the total target population.	Those hiring participants at the end of program participation
Definition: Those who have, or are members of families who have received a total income at or below the official poverty level or 70% of the lower living standard income level (excluding unemployment compensation, child support payments, and welfare grants).	**Participating Educational Agencies/Institutions**
	Those providing classroom training to participants
Non-economically disadvantaged adults and youth facing serious barriers to employment in special need of training to obtain productive employment: 10% of total target group.	**Related Programs**
	Other educational and vocational education agencies/institutions
	Public assistance agencies
Examples:	Employment Service
• those with language deficiency	Economic development agencies
• displaced homemakers	Vocational rehabilitation agencies
• school dropouts	Other community social service agencies
• teenage parents	
• handicapped	**The JTPA Organizational System**
	State and local personnel
Note: forty percent of Title IIA funds are to be spent on youth (adjustable for differing state circumstances).	Members of state and local job training councils
	The JTPA fiscal/programmatic system as a whole

Appendix Chart A.2
Desired Outcomes

For Adult Participants		For Other Entities
Short Term	**Long Term**	**For Educational System**
Increased employment placement: placement in unsubsidized employment	Increased employment	Partial subsidization of tuition/fees
Increased earnings: higher hourly wages	Increased earnings	**For Employers**
Reduced welfare dependency: fewer individuals and families receiving cash welfare payments/ reduced payment amounts	Reduced welfare dependency	Partial subsidization of wages
	Additional outcomes desired by the states and/or SDAs, such as:	Partial subsidization or training costs
Additional outcomes desired by the state and/or SDA, such as:	• increased job quality	Tax credits
• increased job quality	• increased job retention	**For Cash Transfer Programs**
• increased occupational skills	• increased occupational skills	Reduction in welfare costs
• increased job satisfaction	• increased job satisfaction	Reduction in Unemployment Insurance costs
For Youth Participants		**For JTPA System**
Short Term	**Long Term**	Compliance with performance standards
Attainment of employment competencies recognized by the Private Industry Council	Increased employment, earnings, and reduced welfare dependency	Reduced costs per placement
Completion of an educational program: elementary, secondary, postsecondary	Additional outcomes desired by states and/or SDAs, such as those listed for adults above	Increased funding
Enrollment in other training programs or apprenticeships, or enlistment in Armed Forces		
• increased employment		
• increased earnings		
• reduced welfare dependency		

Appendix Chart A.3
Range of Interventions Expected to Produce the Desired Outcomes

Targeted to Program Participants	Targeted to Other Entities
Outreach	**Targeted to Employers**
Education:	Employment/Training Services
• Literacy training	• Case management of participants
• Bilingual education	while in work or training
• Basic skills/remedial education	
• Assistance with attaining GED	Employment/Training Subsidies/Discounts
• Institutional classroom training	• Wage subsidies
• Education-to-work transition services	• Tax credits
• Educational programs that coordinate education with work	
	Targeted to Educational Organizations
Preparation for Employment	• Tuition
• Programs to develop good work habits, obtain/retain employment	• Fees
• Vocational exploration	
• Job counseling	**Targeted to JTPA Environment**
• Work experience	• Job creation efforts
• Education-for-employment: for youth without high school education or with educational deficiencies	• Collection, analysis and dissemination of labor market information
• Try-out employment for youth	• Marketing of program to employers
	• Coordination efforts re: integrating JTPA with related social programs

Appendix Chart A.3 *(Continued)*
Range of Interventions Expected to Produce the Desired Outcomes

Targeted to Program Participants

Occupational Training

- Institutional classroom training
- On-the-job training
- Pre-apprenticeship programs
- Upgrading and retraining services
- Advanced career training combining on-the-job training and classroom training + internships
- On-site industry-specific training programs supportive of industrial/economic development
- Customized training associated with an employer commitment to hire participant upon successful completion of training
- Training programs operated by private sector, consortia of private sector employers, labor unions
- School-to-work assistance for youth 14-15
- Pre-employment skills training for youth 14-21 (those who do not meet established levels of academic achievement and plan to enter full-time labor market after leaving school)
- Exemplary youth programs
- Full-time/part-time summer employment with educational/training activities

Job Search Assistance

Job Placement

Follow-Up Services

Services in Support of Employment and Training

- Services necessary to enable individuals to participate in the program and assist them in retraining and employment (up to six months following completion of the program)

Subsidies Associated with Employment and Training

- Needs-based payments necessary to participants

Appendix Chart A.4
Characteristics of JTPA Program Implementation Expected to Foster the Desired Outcomes

A. Characteristics of the JTPA Organizational System

Structural Characteristics	Functional Characteristics
The Authority Hierarchy	
Public Partnership at the Federal Level:	
U.S. Congress	Design and legal authorization of the program, program oversight, and subsequent program modification
U.S. Department of Labor	Allocation of funds to states
	Development of legal rules and regulations interpreting the legislation authorizing the program, including measures and methods to be used in judging compliance with performance standards
Public/Private Partnership at the State and Local Level:	
State Job Training Coordinating Council (SJTCC) and Governor	State policymaking, coordination[1] and oversight [2]
	Note: Council oversight includes recommending adjustments to federal performance standards to fit specific state conditions if justified, allocating incentive awards to local SDAs for exceeding standards or recommending technical assistance for those failing to meet standards
Private Industry Councils (PICs) and Local Elected Officials	Local goal setting, planning, coordination and oversight
State and Local Administrative Organizations/Fund Recipients:	
State Liaisons/State Administrative Agencies	Distribution of funds to SDAs
	State program administration, planning, management, service delivery (for certain programs), coordination, program oversight
Local SDA Administrative Organizations (separate from or under PICs)	Local program administration, planning, management, service delivery, coordination, program oversight

Appendix Chart A.4 *(Continued)*

Characteristics of JTPA Program Implementation Expected to Foster the Desired Outcomes

A. Characteristics of the JTPA Organizational System

Structural Characteristics	Functional Characteristics
Local Subcontracting Organizations:	
Private/public organizations with whom state agencies and/or Private Industry Councils or local JTPA organizations subcontract, to perform certain service delivery functions or to deliver services to clients	Receipt and allocation of resources
	Organization and operation of the service delivery system
Other Structural Characteristics	
Limitations on costs: administration, training and technical assistance	
Limitations on target groups: adults vs. youth; economically disadvantaged vs. otherwise disadvantaged	
Limitations on services: the percent of participants in OJT in the public vs. private sector	
Provision of funding setasides for (1) particular purposes or target groups within JTPA: older workers and educational programs (2) and the Employment Service: performance incentives, and programs for groups with special needs	

[1] Coordination refers to linkages between JTPA and related organizations, programs, or services: the Employment Service, the WIN Program, the Unemployment Insurance system, education and training organizations/institutions, Public Assistance, rehabilitation agencies, energy conservation programs, economic development agencies and labor unions.

[2] Oversight is defined as plan/budget review and approval, program monitoring and program evaluation, oriented to a two-year planning cycle.

Appendix Chart A.4 *(Continued)*
Characteristics of JTPA Program Implementation Expected to Foster the Desired Outcomes

B. Generic Characteristics of the JTPA Delivery System

Outreach

Intake

Eligibility Determination

Client appraisal of employability and attributes related to employability.

Development of individual service plans for clients, which fit program resources to client needs.

Assignment to a particular mix and sequence of employment and training and supportive services and subsidies related to employment and training.

Case management

Training or worksite supervision

Referral to other programs, services, or organizations if useful:
    Related programs/services
    Armed Forces
    Job Corps

Individual job development

Placement into employment:
    public/private

Follow-up beyond program completion or drop-out

Appendix B
General Requirements of a JTPA
MIS Supporting Evaluation

David Grembowski

Evaluation of social programs requires management information systems (MISs) containing the necessary data for performing net impact, gross impact, and process evaluations. In the first section of this supplement the general requirements of an MIS supporting evaluation are described. In the second section alternative MIS structures are discussed. Because the structure and content of an MIS may vary by program, the Job Training Partnership Act (JTPA) is used to illustrate these issues. The design of the system is perhaps more complex than for other social programs because it must satisfy the information needs of three organizations: states, service delivery areas (SDAs), and subcontractors.

General Requirements

Six general requirements of a computerized JTPA MIS must be satisfied if states, SDAs, and subcontractors are to perform impact and process evaluations of their respective programs: (1) satisfaction of data needs, (2) incorporation of an appropriate MIS structure, (3) attention to data communication, (4) data processing flexibility, (5) statistical software capability, and (6) skilled staff. Each requirement is discussed below.

Data Needs

Impact models have specific information requirements. Net impact evaluation requires data from the JTPA MIS as well as other sources. The gross impact evaluation requires mainly JTPA MIS data, supplemented as needed by information collected through participant and employer surveys. Process evaluation uses a mixture of quantitative data from the MIS and both qualitative and quantitative data from other sources. The

JTPA MIS must contain, or have access to, data elements that satisfy these requirements.

Table B.1 contains a list of the data elements, or variables, required to perform net and gross impact evaluations of JTPA. Unemployment insurance (UI) data limitations will likely prevent most states from expanding the variable list for the state net impact evaluation. Local administrators, however, may wish to include other variables from the MIS in their gross impact evaluations.

Table B.1 provides *minimum* data requirements. State and local officials may add variables to the list as needed. In either case, the computer must contain sufficient storage capacity to record the variables over relevant periods for all participants included in the evaluation. In general, as the number of participants and variables and their length of storage increase, so will the costs of maintaining the MIS. However, these costs can be offset by the benefits of new information, which these additional variables can produce in an evaluation. In constructing an MIS suitable for evaluation, state and local officials must seek a balance between the information needs of the evaluation and the various costs associated with satisfying those needs.

The variables in table B.1 must be generated from data elements in the JTPA MIS. Each variable must be defined in the same manner across all SDAs and subcontractors in a state. This is particularly important for the net impact evaluation, where data from several SDAs are combined for analysis. If variables are defined differently across SDAs and subcontractors, the evaluation may produce erroneous conclusions.

For example, one variable in the MIS might be "classroom training." In SDA I the classroom training variable contains a "1" for every participant who receives this service. In SDA II, however, the service is defined as classroom training plus job search assistance, and the classroom training variable contains a "1" for every participant who receives both services. The definitions of classroom training in the two SDAs differ, which can lead to misleading results and conclusions in a net impact evaluation. For similar reasons, variables should also be defined in the same manner whenever gross impact results of several SDAs are compared.

Table B.1
Crosswalk Between the JTPA Impact Models

Variable	Local/State Gross Impact Model	Net Impact Model
Outcome		
Whether employed	X	X
Earnings	X	X
Hourly wage	X	
Whether receiving welfare grants	X	X
Amount of welfare	X	X
Skill transfer	X	
Job quality	X	
Noneconomic benefits	X	
Treatment		
Training vector (0,1) variables	X	X
Classroom training — remedial education	X	X
Classroom training — institutional skills	X	X
On-the-job training	X	X
Job search assistance	X	X
Work experience	X	X
Multiple activity variable	X	X
Other activity variable	X	X
Training intensity:		
1-digit DOT code of training	X	X
Length of program participation in weeks	X	X
Number of hours of training per day	X	X
Whether complete treatment	X	X
Screening selection and intake services:		
Whether client received testing	X	X
Support services (0,1) variables:		
Whether received transportation	X	X
Whether received child care	X	X
Whether received handicapped services	X	X
Whether received health care	X	X
Whether received meals/food	X	X
Whether received temporary shelter	X	X
Whether received financial counseling	X	X
Whether received clothes	X	X
Whether received other services	X	X
Control		
Age	X	X
Sex	X	X
Race/ethnicity	X	X
Handicapped	X	
Veteran status	X	
Displaced homemaker	X	
Education	X	X
English-speaking ability	X	
Pre-JTPA earnings	X	X
Pre-JTPA wage rate	X	X
Pre-JTPA employment	X	X
Pre-JTPA unemployment	X	X
Welfare status	X	X
Marital status	X	X
Economically disadvantaged	X	X
Local unemployment rate	X	X
Average wage rate in area	X	X
Whether resides in an urban or rural SDA	X	
Labor market variables:		X
a string of (0,1) variables indicating the market where the participant resides		

MIS Structure

The structure, or configuration, of the MIS must support the evaluation models. Two basic MIS structures exist: centralized and decentralized. Centralized structures usually consist of participant data for all SDAs stored on a mainframe computer located at the state level (though some states have developed minicomputer systems). SDAs are usually connected to the mainframe through terminals, personal computers, or minicomputers. In some states SDAs have no access to the state computer but receive reports on a periodic basis. Few subcontractors have access to state systems unless the subcontractor is a state agency.

In decentralized structures, each SDA has one or more personal computer or minicomputer containing its participant data. The state's computer may or may not be linked to each SDA's computer. The system's design and data definitions may be established by the state, and both may become standard across SDAs. Thus, the state and SDAs share control of the MIS; the state controls through system design, while the SDA controls through system operation.

Participant and financial systems are usually separate in both centralized and decentralized structures. In fact, the two systems sometimes exist on different computers. For example, some SDAs with a decentralized participant system have financial data maintained by the state. While existing JTPA MIS structures are not barriers to evaluation, their structures must be taken into account in designing a prototype MIS to support the evaluation.

Communications

Because implementation of JTPA is dispersed among state, SDA, and subcontractor organizations, information about "what goes on" in the program is also dispersed. In the JTPA MIS, agencies must have mechanisms for communicating or transmitting data from one agency to another. In SDAs that subcontract intake, mechanisms must exist for transmitting application and enrollment data from the subcontractor to the SDA, regardless of whether the MIS has a centralized or decentralized structure. Different forms of data communication are possible:

The subcontractor enters the applicant data into its own computer and transmits it to the SDA by telephone;
The subcontractor is linked to the JTPA MIS and can enter applicant data directly into the MIS; or
The subcontractor sends the applicant forms to the SDA or state, which enters the data into the MIS.

Each subcontractor must also be able to access its data in the MIS. This is essential if subcontractors are to conduct gross impact and process evaluations of their own programs. Again, different MIS-to-subcontractor communication modes are possible, such as a direct communication line with the MIS or monthly extracts written on a floppy disk and mailed to the subcontractor for analysis on its personal computer.

Mechanisms must also exist for data communication between the SDA and the state. In centralized MIS structures each SDA must have the capability to enter and extract its data from the state data base. In decentralized MIS structures the state must be able to extract data from the SDA computer systems. Ideally, this is performed using telephone lines or other communication channels that link the SDA with the state MIS. However, other forms of data communication are possible, such as monthly extractions of requested data on floppy disks that are mailed between the state and SDA. In short, in decentralized structures states need data from SDAs to perform state net impact evaluations; in centralized structures SDAs and subcontractors need data from the state to perform gross impact and process evaluations of their own programs.

These communication requirements apply to both impact and process evaluations. Net impact evaluation, however, has additional requirements; it also requires data from UI and welfare information systems. Assuming the net impact evaluation is performed at the state level, the state computer system must be capable of accessing data from these other systems. If the JTPA, UI, and welfare data are all on the same computer, access to the appropriate data can usually be readily achieved. If the data reside on different computers, the UI and welfare data must be transmitted to the JTPA MIS, using computer tapes or data communication channels.

Two issues usually determine whether interagency data communication occurs. The first issue is *control*. That is, the agency that controls the data may be reluctant to release them to other agencies, reducing the agencies' ability to conduct evaluations of their own programs. The second issue is *technical*. In order for two computers to communicate, data must have standard formats, such as ASCII. Proper system design and use of the same brand of computer equipment across agencies can overcome this potential problem.

Data Processing Flexibility

All forms of evaluation require the freedom to manipulate and analyze data in a variety of ways. To satisfy this requirement the JTPA MIS must employ software known as a *data base management system* (DBMS). In most computer systems in JTPA, data are distributed across several files. A DBMS can access data across files through relatively simple data retrieval commands that can be applied in a wide variety of data processing environments. The commands selectively pool information from the DBMS files into a form that satisfies the analyst's information needs. Further, a DBMS is adept at modifying files after they are created. Variables and records may be freely entered and deleted from previously developed files. In short, a DBMS provides a flexible mode of data processing capable of addressing the information requirements of the evaluation.

DBMS software commonly used on mainframes includes ADABAS, DATACOM, IDMA, IMS, SYSTEM 2000, TOTAL, and several others. Personal computer DBMS software includes RBASE 5000, REVELA-TION, DATAFLEX, DBASE, HELIX, ORACLE, and many others. Each software package has its own strengths and weaknesses; they are by no means equal. However, a JTPA MIS using DBMS software should provide the data processing flexibility required by the evaluation.

Some agencies may not have DBMS software in their MIS, and the costs of adding the software to their information systems may be prohibitive. When a DBMS is not possible, a satisfactory alternative is to develop user-friendly, general purpose computer programs for ex-tracting data from the data base. The user, who may be a computer programmer or a JTPA administrator, supplies the program with a list of desired data items and other parameters, and the program retrieves the requested items from the data base and writes them onto an output file for subsequent analysis.

Statistical Software

Although DBMS software is adept at manipulating data and generating report lists, it does not have the capability of performing the statistical analyses required by the impact models. Therefore, the JTPA MIS should also include statistical software, such as SPSS, SAS, SYSTAT, or other major brand. SPSS, for example, has developed a statistical package that runs on most mainframes and personal computers.

Skilled Staff

Satisfying the above requirements will be of little value if skilled staff is not available to perform data processing. This does not necessarily mean that staff members with computer science degrees are needed for data processing to support evaluation. In gross impact and process evaluations, for example, the chief skill requirement is experience with DBMS and statistical software packages. States may wish to offer technical assistance to SDAs and subcontractors in the area of software use. The state net impact evaluation, however, will probably require data processing personnel to combine the UI, welfare, and JTPA data sets into a form required for performing the evaluation.

Types of MIS Structures

In this guide "structure" refers to the components of the information system and how data are organized into files. The former may be one of two basic types, centralized or decentralized.

Centralized MIS Structure

A centralized structure is presented in exhibit 1. The centralized MIS features a mainframe (or mini-) computer containing the JTPA MIS, located at the state level. The MIS uses DBMS and statistical software. The MIS contains the participant system as well as data required for the benefit-cost analysis. The latter data are transmitted to the state by each SDA, which operates its own financial system. However, in some states (such as those with no SDAs) the financial system is either a part of the

Exhibit B.1
Centralized JTPA MIS

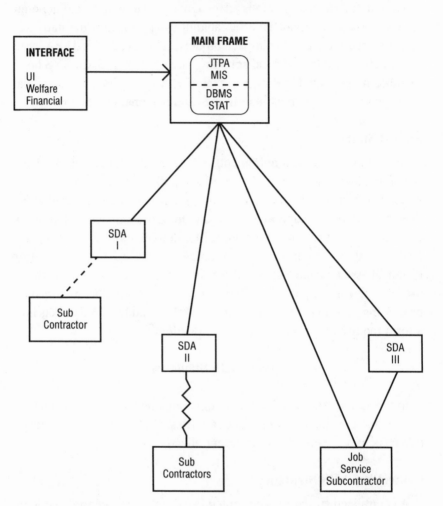

centralized JTPA MIS or located on a separate computer at the state level. In the latter case a communication interface links the JTPA MIS with the financial system (if needed) as well as the UI and welfare systems. As mentioned earlier, this interface may be either a direct communication channel or tape transfer.

Evaluation can occur at each level—state, SDA, and subcontractor. States can use the JTPA MIS to perform state process, gross, and net impact evaluations. SDAs and subcontractors can perform process and gross impact evaluations of their respective programs. In this case, communication links connect the state JTPA MIS with all SDAs and, in some cases selected contractors, such as a local Job Service office. Different links may exist, such as follows:

Local offices use terminals or PCs to access the data base, and all analyses are performed on the mainframe computer. Communication occurs through telephone lines (or other electronic medium). Security controls in the DBMS permit each SDA to access only its data. The DBMS does not allow SDAs either to delete data from the data base or to modify existing records. Thus, while SDAs and subcontractors can add new records to the data base, they can only "read" data after they are entered.

Telephone lines (or other electronic medium) are used to transfer data from the state MIS to the SDAs or subcontractor's PC or minicomputer.

Each month the state provides each SDA with a floppy disk(s) containing all data entered into the MIS during the period. SDAs analyze the data on their own PCs or minicomputers.

Periodic reports, one method of state-to-local data transfer, are not included because they do not satisfy the information requirements of the local evaluation.

Different types of SDA-subcontractor communication channels exist as shown in exhibit B.1. SDA I provides its subcontractors only with paper reports; subcontractors can only perform crude evaluations of their programs. After receiving its data from the state, SDA II relays appropriate data to each subcontractor using floppy disks. Subcontractors perform their own evaluations using their own PCs. In SDA III the job service subcontractor has a direct communication line to the SDA's computer for accessing its data. In short, if subcontractors are to gain access to MIS data in most states, the data must first be transferred to the local level (usually the SDA), and the SDA must then grant its subcontractors access to the data through one mechanism or another. Thus, although data redundancy is inevitable under this arrangement, it gives service providers the information they need to evaluate their programs.

Decentralized MIS Structure

The distinguishing features of the decentralized MIS structure are that (1) each SDA operates its own MIS, and (2) communication channels link SDA computer systems with the state (see exhibit B.2)). SDA data are transmitted to the state either over telephone lines or through mail

Exhibit B.2
Decentralized JTPA MIS

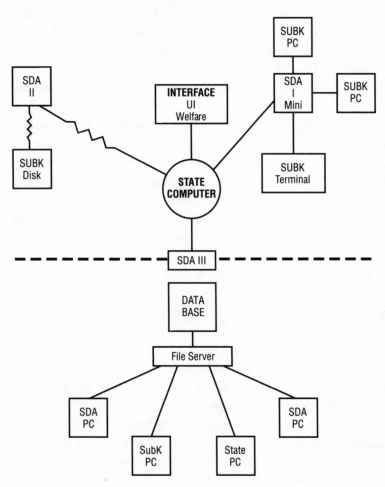

delivery of floppy disks. The state computer has interfaces with the UI and welfare data bases for performing net impact evaluations.

A decentralized MIS can be created in several ways, as shown in exhibit B.2. In SDA I a minicomputer holds its JTPA MIS, which includes the DBMS for the participant and financial systems as well as statistical software. The minicomputer has "multi-user software" that allows subcontractors and the state to access the data base simultaneously through terminals or PCs. These agencies communicate with the minicomputer using a telephone and a modem.

SDA II also operates a minicomputer, but it does not permit outside access to the data base. However, the state and subcontractors regularly request data from the MIS, which the SDA provides on floppy disks.

The bottom half of exhibit B.2 presents an SDA MIS using personal computers and a local area network. Although participant and financial systems are separate, both data sets are stored on a single hard disk. (The financial system could be located on a different computer.) The size of the disk varies with the size of the SDA, but disks with 50 to 80 megabytes of storage should be adequate for most SDAs.

Personal computers located at the SDA, subcontractor, and state levels form a "local area network"; each PC in the network gains access to the data base through the network's "file server." The file server, which is actually a PC with local area network software, acts as the gatekeeper. It regulates access to the data base throughout the network. Using a telephone modem, state officials and subcontractors with PCs can enter the network and access the data base. Each PC must use common DBMS and financial software to gain entry.

File Structure

Different file structures are possible in the JTPA MIS data base. Only one file structure is described in this section; it can be used in both centralized and decentralized systems. JTPA data bases in most states have more complex file structures than the one described here. Our intent is not to describe the ideal JTPA MIS, but rather to identify elements that are essential to performing evaluation. For evaluation purposes the JTPA MIS contains the following six files:

1. Participant Master File (containing application and termination information).
2. Participant Service File (containing training and support service information).
3. Participant Follow-Up File (containing information on each follow-up).
4. Employer Master File (containing information on local employers).
5. Staff Master File (containing information on SDA and subcontractor staff who serve participants).
6. Subcontractor Master File (containing information on SDA subcontractors).

The DBMS uses common identifiers to interrelate data in one file with data in another file. For example, if the Participant Master File and the Participant Service File both contain the participant's ID, the DBMS can interrelate master file data with service file data. This is essential to performing gross impact evaluation, where we are interested in correlating the services participants receive (Service File) with their outcomes (Participant Master File).

Program administrators sometimes wish to supplement program data with additional information collected through special surveys of clients or other sources. These data can usually be added to the data base as a separate file physically, but linked with other files through common identifiers.

Appendix C
Evaluation Guides Produced by
the JTPA Evaluation Design Project

The comprehensive concept of evaluation demonstrated in the JTPA Evaluation Design Project and expressed in the Project's series of evaluation guides and regional evaluation workshops required an interdisciplinary team committed to a high level of intellectual interaction and the production of research tools that were both competent and useful. The team that was brought together to prepare the series of volumes below combined expertise from economics, sociology, planning and social work.

Title of Volume	Author
I. OVERVIEW	Ann Bonar Blalock and Deborah Feldman
II. A GENERAL PLANNING GUIDE	Deborah Feldman
III. A GUIDE FOR NET IMPACT EVALUATIONS	Terry R. Johnson
IV. AN IMPLEMENTATION MANUAL FOR NET IMPACT EVALUATIONS	Terry R. Johnson
V. A GUIDE FOR GROSS IMPACT EVALUATIONS	Carl Simpson
VI. A GUIDE FOR PROCESS EVALUATIONS	David Grembowski
VII. ISSUES IN EVALUATING COSTS AND BENEFITS	Ernst W. Stromsdorfer
VII. MIS ISSUES IN EVALUATING JTPA	David Grembowski
VIII. THE DEBATE OVER QUASI-EXPERIMENTAL VS. EXPERIMENTAL DESIGNS	Ann Bonar Blalock

Note: These volumes are accessible through the ERIC Clearinghouse microfiche series in public libraries.

Appendix D
Information About the
Book's Authors

Ann Bonar Blalock is Special Assistant to the Deputy Commissioner, Washington State Employment Security Department. Her assignments have involved policy analysis, evaluation research, and the design of demonstration projects in employment and training, work/welfare, and human services integration. She was responsible for developing the concept for *The JTPA Evaluation Design Project*, acquiring funds to support it, and initially directing the Project. She subsequently served as the Project's senior consultant, participated in the initial evaluation workshops, and is currently editing the Project's national evaluation journal. Her publications focus on basic social science research methods, particularly in policy research. Her graduate academic training is in sociology and social welfare research.

Terry Johnson, senior economist at the Human Affairs Center, Battelle Institute, is an expert on net impact studies. He has combined in chapter 2 the major ideas in his two volumes for the series of guides. His experience in evaluating the net impact and cost effectiveness of national employment and training programs and demonstration projects is extensive, including studies of the Comprehensive Employment and Training Act programs, the Employment Service, the Unemployment Insurance Program, the Job Corps, and programs under JTPA. He has specialized in the development of techniques for constructing comparison groups and statistically adjusting estimates of net program effects to increase their precision. His graduate academic training is in labor economics.

Ernst Stromsdorfer is a member of the economics faculty at Washington State University. He has integrated in chapter 2 the ideas in his separate volume for the Project on cost/benefit analysis, which usefully expands the study of net impact. He was also the major reviewer of the Project's series of volumes. His evaluation background is the most extensive of any of the members of the Project team, having participated in the evaluation of a wide range of national employment and training programs and demonstration projects as an academic, a research administrator in the U.S. Department of Labor, and vice president of a major national research firm, Abt, Inc. His numerous publications have focused on evaluation research in employment and training. His graduate academic background is in labor economics

Director of Western Washington University's Office of Survey Research and member of the sociology faculty, Carl Simpson has taught, conducted research and published in the areas of education, occupational training and employment. He has designed, directed and implemented major research in higher education and was responsible for a series of substantial implementation and outcome studies of Washington's CETA programs which contributed significantly to state employment and training policies. He has also carried out extensive evaluations of local programs under JTPA, focusing on integrating information from studies of both implementation and outcomes. His publications span the fields of education, employment and training, and community development. His graduate academic training is in sociology.

David Grembowski is on the faculty of the Department of Health Services, University of Washington. He has based chapter 4 on his volume for the series of evaluation guides, adding considerable information on measurement and methodological issues. He has broad experience and a number of publications in the area of human services planning and evaluation, and the design and use of management information systems for evaluation. He was a member of the research staff of the Seattle/Denver Income Maintenance Experiments which focused on work and welfare, and was the primary planner and information system specialist for Washington State's participation in the national Flexible Intergovernmental Grant Project, an experiment in integrating welfare, employment and training programs. He is currently part of the research team for a major national health planning project and evaluation. His graduate training is in planning and evaluation research.

In chapter 5, Deborah Feldman shifts the reader's attention to the development of a capability to evaluate programs, and to organizational and political issues surrounding the initiation, planning, implementation and use of evaluations at the state and local level. Working on special planning, technical training and evaluation projects for the Deputy Commissioner's Office, Washington State Employment Security Department, she organized and directed the Project's regional evaluation training workshops, and contributed extensively to *Evaluation Forum*. She has broad experience in organizational development, planning and project development in the areas of worker dislocation, economic development and women's issues, and has published in the area of plant closures and worker readjustment. Her graduate academic training is in planning.

INDEX

Accountability: effect of new technology and research methods on, 3-4; under JPTA opposed
to CETA, 48; oversight functions to assure, 11-14; social program need to demonstrate, 43

Adams, Kay A., 332

Adult groups, male and female: estimates of JTPA net impact,100-105; preprogram analysis files for, 83-85; sample design frame for JTPA net evaluation model, 64-65, 67-68, 72-74; separation of noncomparable segments in JTPA evaluation model, 57-58, 73

AFDC. *See* Aid for Families with Dependent Children (AFDC) Grant Records

Age groups: JTPA net impact evaluation, 58, 65-66, 71

Agency characteristics, aggregated; 174-75

Aid for Families with Dependent Children (AFDC) Grant Records, 54-57

Alkin, Marvin C., 337

Anderson, Andy B., 142, 154, 161

Astin, Alexander, 164

Auditor for evaluation processs, 348

Babbie, Earl R., 142

Bangsor, Michael, 245

Barnow, Burt, 17, 37n1

Bassi, Laurie J., 125n4

Benefit-cost analysis: for employers, 208-15; for JTPA net impact evaluation, 107-10; for net impact evaluation, 47

Benefits, postprogram: measurement for JTPA net impact evaluation, 111

Benefits and costs: of evaluation plan, 335-39

Bias: control of, 141; potential for severe, 170-71; in selection, 17-19, 91, 139-41, 165-69; *See also* Selection bias

Bivariate analysis, 191, 193

Bjornstadt, George W., 192

Blalock, Ann B., 14, 18, 31, 133, 163, 196, 314, 354

Blau, Peter M., 261

Bloom, Howard S., 184

Borus, Michael, 162, 184

Bradburn, Norman, 207

Burstein, Leigh, 278

Burstein, Paul, 133

Campbell, Donald T., 33, 43, 162

Caporaso, James A., 162

Causal analysis, 166

Causal relationships, 162-64

CETA. *See* Comprehensive Employment and Training Act (CETA)

Characteristics. *See* Comparability characteristics; Individual background characteristics; Trainer characteristics

Chelimsky, Eleanor, 301, 354, 359, 364, 366

Classroom training (CT), 58, 60

Communication of data. *See* Data communication

Comparability characteristics: JTPA evaluation model, 72-73

Differential impact analysis: definition and use of, 136, 137-39, 168-69, 222-23; effect on bias of, 165; with employer data, 216-19; estimating change in, 197-99; estimation of influence on program outcomes, 162-65; including employer participation information, 216-19; measurement of influences on postprogram outcome, 171-91; research design for, 154-62; statistical methods for, 191-203; threats to reliability of, 138-39; value of, 221-23; See also Control variables; Program implementation; Program variants; Service providers
Dillman, Don A., 142, 154, 161, 207, 264
Doeringer, Peter B., 146
DOT. See Dictionary of Occupational Titles (DOT)

Educational level, 58
Edwards, A. L., 284
Employer participation measurement, 203-16
Employment Service (ES) data, 69, 106
Employment Service (ES) registrants: as comparison group in JTPA evaluation model, 69-73; exclusions from group of, 71-72, 106; See also Comparison groups; Selection bias
Environment: for JTPA Title II program process evaluation, 254-56; for organizational system, 234-35, 261; relevance in net impact evaluation of JTPA, 61-62; role of inputs in, 235
ES. See Employment Service (ES)
Estimation of change, 197-99
Ethnic groups, 58
Evaluability assessment, 308-11
Evaluation: as distinct from monitoring, 13-14; as management tool and information source, 4-6; of national and state programs, 19; as policy and management tool, 5; research design alternatives for, 28, 31-33; use of information in MISs for, 14-17
Evaluation, program. See Program evaluation
Evaluation activities proposal, 362-66
Evaluation concept, 7-9
Evaluation guides, 6, 395
Evaluation implementation plan. See Implementation plan
Evaluation information. See Information
Evaluation planner: assessment of organizational roles within JTPA, 313-14; role in data collection of, 327-31; role in identifying evaluation staffing requirements, 344-48; role in preliminary evaluation plan, 311-22; role of, 301-8, 349-50; support role for evaluation designers, 327; work with researcher/evaluator of, 322-23, 326
Evaluation planning: effect of organizational inertia on, 311-12; feasibility of analyzing programs, 307-8; in JTPA program, 311-22; preliminary issues in, 305-22; strategies for cooperation in, 315-16; user approach to, 302-5; See also Evaluation planner; Evaluation staff; Evaluator; Implementation plan
Evaluation plan users, 8, 9, 306-7
Evaluation process: groups active in, 303; lack of state experience in, 4-5; phases of, 332
Evaluation research: for program and organization analysis, 133-35; role in public policy of, 3-4
Evaluation researcher: role in data collection of, 327-31